BIO
RATHER

Rather, Dan.

The camera never
blinks twice.

DATE		

The Camera
Never Blinks Twice

Also by Dan Rather

The Camera

RATHER

WITH MICKEY HERSKOWITZ

Never Blinks Twice

THE FURTHER ADVENTURES OF A TELEVISION JOURNALIST

WILLIAM MORROW AND COMPANY, INC. NEW YORK

Library of Congress Cataloging-in-Publication Data

Rather, Dan.
    The camera never blinks twice : the further adventures of a television journalist / Dan Rather.
        p. cm.
    Includes index.
    ISBN 0-688-09748-0
    1. Rather, Dan. 2. Journalists—United States—Biography.
3. Television broadcasting of news—United States. I. Title.
PN4874.R28A34 1994
070.4'092-dc20   94-12836
  [B]   CIP

Printed in the United States of America

First Edition

1 2 3 4 5 6 7 8 9 10

BOOK DESIGN BY CAROLINE CUNNINGHAM

dedication

THIS BOOK RELATES A NUMBER OF CLOSE SCRAPES, SOME OF WHICH may seem skin-of-the-teeth and others of which may seem funny. All are written with an awareness that the adventures of many American journalists have not always had happy endings.

Every year in New York, the Committee to Protect Journalists publishes a roster of those killed. Every year we find the names of men and women who worked beside us, on assignment at home or abroad. Every year we find recorded the names of outstanding journalists who still had much to report.

Their commitment to the idea and the ideal of an informed American citizenry was so great that they placed their lives at risk, and they made the ultimate sacrifice.

The names and final datelines of only a few whose lives and work have touched mine: George Polk, CBS, Greece; George Syvertsen, CBS, Cambodia; Karin Wimberger, CBS, Afghanistan; David Jayne, ABC, Jordan; David Kaplan, ABC, Bosnia; Ted Yates, NBC, Israel; Wells Hangen, NBC, Cambodia; Dan Eldon, Reuters, Somalia.

It is to their sense of duty, to their spirit of service, and to their memory that this book is dedicated.

acknowledgments

When this book's predecessor, *The Camera Never Blinks: Adventures of a TV Journalist,* was first published in 1976, it was both a surprise and a joy.

A surprise because I had no idea it would wind up being read by so many people; a joy because I got as much satisfaction from it as from any work I've ever done.

Many people helped with that book. Many more have helped with this one. First among them are my wife, Jean Grace Goebel Rather, and my family, especially my children, Robin and Dan, along with my brother and sister, Don Rather and Patricia Rather Thompson.

Second, William Madison, my all-around right hand at CBS News, and on outside projects such as this book. What he has given in support, friendship, talent, and hard work is more than can ever be repaid. Bill is on his way to becoming a great novelist. For setting aside his own writing to pour himself into helping with mine, I shall be forever grateful.

Then there is, of course, Mickey Herskowitz, who helped mightily the first time around, and did again this time.

For their assistance preparing this manuscript for publication, I am grateful to Toby Wertheim, Janis Kinzie Culhane, Deborah Morgulis Rubin, James Moore. Their wisdom, their scholarship, and their friendship have been an enormous help to me, as they are every day. Suzanne Nederlander and Terri Belli were, as always, unstinting in their support.

Richard and Carole Leibner, David and Susan Buksbaum, Tom and Claire Bettag, Herb and Pat George Rowland, Joel and Toby Bernstein, Bill and Carolyn Johnston, Sam and Mary Ann Quisenberry, Perry and Betsy Smith, and Eunice Martin are people who have made my personal and professional lives more meaningful than I have words to say.

Andy Lack, although he has since jumped to the command of another ship, will always have my gratitude for the adventures we shared.

The people I work with today, especially Connie Chung, Howard Stringer, Eric Ober, Erik Sorenson, Catherine Lasiewicz, Andrew Heyward, Linda Mason, Joel Bernstein, Joe Peyronnin, Lane Venardos, Larry Cooper, Al Berman, Kathy Sciere, Kathy Moore, Michael Fountain, George Osterkamp, Wayne Nelson, Al Ortiz, and Tom Flynn. My friends Donna Dees and Kim Akhtar helped me place some of the material in this book which originally appeared in other publications.

Of the many radio essays cited in this book, most were prepared during the tenure of producer Virginia Pittman-Waller. My gratitude to her is enormous, but also extends to her successors, Kevin Rochford and Kathleen Biggins.

I am forever grateful to the Radio-Television News Directors Association, who gave me the opportunity to deliver the remarks which form the basis of the last chapter of this book.

William Schwalbe, my editor at William Morrow, revived and saved this book when it was in intensive care and dying of neglect. His predecessors, Lisa Drew and Hillel Black, had kept it alive for many years. So did my book agent, Bill Adler.

Among others noteworthy for their special help are Marty Eisenstein, Ethel Goldstein, Renée Itzkowitz, Nancy Kay, Allen Zelon, Stuart Witt, Hugh Cunningham, Eve Bartlett, Joan Amico, and the valiant members of my staff, Susan Martins Cipollaro and Allison Zarinko.

contents

OUTTAKE: *Closing the Gap*   *15*

ONE: IF YOU CAN KEEP YOUR HEAD . . .   17

OUTTAKE: *Wreck of the Old 97*   *26*

TWO: AFGHANISTAN'S PLAINS   29

OUTTAKE: *Kids, Don't Try This at Home*   *62*

THREE: AFGHANISTAN: A BRIDGE TOO FAR   64

OUTTAKE: *Miami Blues*   *89*

FOUR: WHOSE AMBUSH WAS IT?   96

OUTTAKE: *When Bad Things Happen to Good Towns*   *125*

FIVE: CHINA: REVOLT OF THE STUDENTS   131

OUTTAKE: *Franny*   *155*

SIX: THE PARTY'S OVER: GORBACHEV AND THE FALL OF THE WALL   157

OUTTAKE: *Dialogue with the Dictator*   *177*

SEVEN: IRAQ: SLEEPING WITH THE ENEMY   180

OUTTAKE: *Winged Victory*   *197*

EIGHT: THE SEARCH FOR SADDAM HUSSEIN   200

    OUTTAKE: *Reporting Desert Storm*   223

NINE: SOMALIA: THE POLITICS OF HUNGER   229

    OUTTAKE: *Heroes*   251

TEN: VIETNAM REVISITED   256

    OUTTAKE: *Sevareid*   285

ELEVEN: AND A CATFISH RUNS THROUGH IT   289

    OUTTAKE: *Hurricanes Then and Now*   304

TWELVE: THE ACCIDENTAL TOURIST   308

    OUTTAKE: *Malik*   324

THIRTEEN: THE WEAPON IN THE BOX   326

    OUTTAKE: *Happily Ever After*   344

APPENDIX: THE MEN AND WOMEN OF CBS NEWS   347

INDEX   361

The Camera
Never Blinks Twice

outtake

Closing the Gap

IT IS MORNING IN A LARGE FLORIDA CITY. I HAVE FLOWN IN LATE during the night, after midnight, have not slept well, and am now up early to go downstairs in the hotel to make a speech before several thousand people.

I am not in a good mood and am silently asking myself unjustifiably self-pitying questions such as "Why am I doing this?" I dress hurriedly, shun the breakfast tray, gulp down black coffee that tastes like day-old drained transmission fluid, and go to the elevator.

It is crowded. I nod glumly as I get on. Not a word is spoken as we go down ten floors to the lobby, but I feel all eyes on me. In the egocentric way of anchors generally, I am thinking, *Okay, I'm on television. But didn't any of these people's mothers teach them that it's rude to stare?* Besides, I have the uncomfortable feeling these people aren't just staring, they're looking me over, top to bottom. And why do I have the feeling some of them are smirking?

The elevator reaches the lobby. As it empties, a woman of about forty, crisply and immaculately groomed, gently takes hold of my sleeve. "Mr. Rather," she says quietly, "I don't mean to intrude." *Then why are you?* I think. She continues, "But I have admired you for years." *Well, of course; now I understand,* your anchorman is thinking. "And this will only take a moment." *It had better, madam; I'm already late to this big important speech I must deliver.*

She looks first to one side, then to the other, making sure no one else is listening.

"I don't want this to be awkward or embarrassing in any way." Pause. "But your fly is unzipped and a piece of your shirttail is sticking out through it."

She smiles and strides away.

Thank you, ma'am, wherever you are.

ONE

If You Can Keep
Your Head . . .

ERIK SORENSON WAS TICKING OFF THE DAY'S NEWS TO ME, GIVING ME
a sense of the way the *Evening News* would probably shape up that
day. The last item on his list was, to his mind, potentially the most
important: "The cardinal in Chicago has been accused of sexually
abusing a boy. The boy is grown now, in his twenties, and he's
pressing charges. There was a big press conference this morning,
and Chicago is reeling."

Erik Sorenson, executive producer of the *CBS Evening News,* is a
laid-back, amiable guy, given to blue jeans and loud ties. The
younger set around CBS describe him as "boppy," although I don't
know what that word means; the less discreet point out that he's
only a little older than my children, although I would prefer they
keep their math to themselves.

Most mornings I'm on the phone early, checking in with Erik and the senior producers in the "Fishbowl" (a glassed-in office within the *Evening News* studio) to find out what news has broken and what stories we're working on.

That doesn't mean that what we discuss is exactly what will appear on the broadcast. At any minute, something could happen—a plane crash, a terrorist attack, a surprise announcement from the White House—that could require us to overhaul our plans. But the staff of the *Evening News* sometimes change our minds for another reason: We debate, we argue, we bicker, we cajole, we plead, and sometimes we persuade.

This was going to be one of the times we'd debate. All day long and right up until the last minutes before the broadcast.

"There is some sentiment among our senior producers that we may want to lead with the cardinal sex abuse story," Erik said.

I respect Erik's judgment, and that of all the *Evening News* people with whom I closely work, but I disagreed. I said, "Erik, that's not a story, that's an accusation. If we gave our best slots to every accusation that comes along the pike, we'd never have time for anything else."

He came back with a broader view, far from sensationalized. "Child sex abuse is an important story, and every part of the Church's attitude toward sex has been coming in for close scrutiny." He explained that it isn't just that people are titillated by the Church's relation to sexuality. There may be the beginning of a philosophical change of course for the Church, seen also in the heated debates over birth control, abortion, women priests, and the celibate clergy. The increasing number of accusations of sex abuse by priests had already colored the debate on celibacy.

This was all well and good, I thought, but the accusations against the cardinal seemed like a slim peg on which to hang the story. In practical terms, what Erik described sounded like a long, thoughtful piece, something for our regular "Eye on America" feature, and something that couldn't be ready by airtime this day. There were a lot of ideas to be thought through, and to complicate matters, in television you need pictures: Eric Sevareid used to say, "You can't take a picture of an idea." The scramble for pictures would cut down on the time for thought. And you don't have to be in the business for very long before you realize that your probing, deliberate think-piece can start hemorrhaging substance the closer you get to deadline. (This is why we try to allot as much time as possible to the production of "Eye on America" segments—and a few of those segments have in fact focused on issues of the Church and sexuality.)

Erik and I agreed we would continue to monitor the story, and that a lead slot was a possibility, although I remained unconvinced it was advisable.

When I got into the office a short time later, the debate had expanded from a dialogue between Erik and me to include all the senior producers in the Fishbowl: Kathy Moore, Kathy Sciere, Al Berman, Mike Fountain. These are bright, intelligent people, and I love kicking back and talking the issues with them. They're all hardy veterans of fierce campaigns, but none of them old enough to have worked in the trenches back in the days when almost any mention of sexuality in a national news program was unthinkable.

A lot of the press, print and electronic, comes in for some justifiable criticism for keeping the sex life of President John Kennedy hushed up: Most White House correspondents knew plenty, but none said a word. The most frequent accusation is that the press's silence revealed a pro-Kennedy, pro-Democrat, pro-Liberal bias. What people seem to have forgotten is that, in those days, before the Sexual Revolution, sex wasn't discussed or seen on television. On CBS, even a hip, sexy young couple like Rob and Laura Petrie slept in separate beds. Not only was there no equivalent of Madonna to grab her crotch and bare her breasts, or Marky Mark to grab and bare himself, but Ed Sullivan (again on CBS) would permit Elvis Presley to be photographed only from the neck up—to spare our children the unseemly view of his gyrating pelvis. You might have discussed sexual matters with your very closest friends, but many people still couldn't talk about sex with their own doctors.

In many ways, we're a lot better off today. We *need* to be able to discuss sexual problems with qualified care-givers, and we *need* to be able to discuss sexual matters with our partners. If we've relaxed a little about the body, if we're less squeamish and can discuss like sensible, mature adults a few details of President Ronald Reagan's rectal surgery, or First Lady Nancy Reagan's breast cancer, then we're probably helping many, many Americans to cope with the realities of their lives. I think the Reagans probably don't get enough credit for being so open about their health, and in the process removing a lot of the embarrassment felt by other Americans who had similar difficulties.

But I am not one of those reporters who believe that every sex story is another brick in the foundation of wisdom. I know that sex sells, and I knew that our competitors were going to run with the story of the accusations against the cardinal—and they would run hard and fast. But I believe that if we do not treat sex stories responsibly—and, more to the point, if we do not treat sex stories exactly as responsibly as we would treat a story on any other subject—then we're not helping anybody, least of all ourselves. Our credibility will go, and we won't be able to get it back.

These are more or less the arguments I made in discussions with the senior producers of the *Evening News,* over the course of a long afternoon. Due to a family emergency, Erik Sorenson had left the command of the broadcast to Kathy Moore, a Carolina-bred wonder woman who now had to wrestle with a thorny professional dilemma: how much coverage to allot to a potentially explosive story.

I was pushing for minimal coverage—at most a "tell" (so called because it's not a videotaped report; the anchor simply tells it). But there were other factors.

One producer, seizing on the probability that ABC and NBC would give significant coverage to the accusations, asked what would happen to our credibility if we didn't match their coverage. "Won't we be seen as soft on the Church, or blind to issues of sex abuse, or just lagging behind in our reporting?" she asked.

This was a genuine concern, and the kind of concern that does determine our coverage sometimes—probably more than it should. We sometimes run with a story because we don't want it to appear we don't have the story, not when the other guys have it. If you don't carry the story, you will run the risk of looking like the gang that couldn't shoot straight—or the official party newsletter for whatever group you're "protecting." And the competitive side of me is always pushing, as if whispering in my ear, "Don't let 'em scoop you."

But I continued to feel, and tried this day to explain, that an accusation is not a story. We hear all kinds of accusations, some credible and some not: One viewer has written a couple of times with the theory that President George Bush *died* at the state dinner in Japan where he became so ill; she believed that the real, dead President Bush was replaced by an impostor. This, she explained, is why Bill Clinton *had* to win the 1992 election. The impostor couldn't keep up the deception any longer, despite all the help he was getting from Peter Jennings, Tom Brokaw, and myself.

We haven't broadcast *those* accusations, or plenty like them. But back on Planet Earth, the accusations against the cardinal, although pronounced by a seemingly earnest, credible young man, could not be independently substantiated, nor could they be corroborated by anyone else. They were, for the moment, just "one man's opinion."

In the late afternoon, just as I was working on my daily radio broadcast, Kathy called me: "The cardinal is holding a press conference to deny the accusations," she said. "That makes the story—if we choose to look at it that way."

"Kathy," I said gently, "that's not a story, that's a denial." True, the denial meant the story was no longer one man's word, but it didn't yet add up to *two* words: just "Yes, you did" and "No, I didn't."

Now Kathy was leaning against big play for the story, but was still worried. I knew she'd instructed a solid correspondent, Frank Currier, to get working on a piece as sober and unsensational as possible. But she was clearly concerned by the prospect of dropping or burying a story that might be big, and that would certainly play high on rival broadcasts. She was torn. And now, given the cardinal's news conference, plus heavy emphasis from the wire services and radio newscasts throughout the day, I was torn, too.

The debate kept up all day, one side pushing for heavy coverage, the other side pushing for little coverage. But a newsroom is not a philosophers' retreat. As the day winds down, the preparations for the broadcast gear up.

There are a couple of scenes in James Brooks's movie *Broadcast News* in which the wonderful actress Joan Cusack has to dash pell-mell across a network's Washington bureau in the final seconds before airtime, scooting past bystanders, slamming through doors, sliding under file cabinet drawers, to get the videotape to the studio and meet her deadline.

For those of us who work in the real broadcast news, such scenes are not comedy. They are reality. All of us, including your narrator, have had to run that race many times.

By the time those races had begun on this evening, the correspondent's report on the accusations was ready. Our writers had drawn up six different lead-ins to the correspondent's piece, plus a couple of scripts in which we wouldn't use the correspondent's piece at all. Graphics had been prepared, spelling double-checked in all the captions. Tape was ready to roll. Six or seven Joan Cusack imitators were already starting to dash through the building. But Kathy and I were still talking it out. Nobody felt good about running hard with the story. Nobody felt good about running light with the story. Nobody thought we could afford to drop it altogether.

Finally, with the clock ticking to airtime, stage manager Scott Berger ready to count down to the broadcast, I said, with as much anchor authority as I could muster, "Kathy, this is not our lead."

And she agreed. We used Currier's piece, but within the body of the newscast, alerting our audience to a story of interest and possible importance, yet by no means the most significant event of the day.

We thought we were striking a blow for responsible coverage in the war of sensationalism that is always raging at the borders of good journalism.

What we were really doing, it turned out, was not just the right thing but the prudent thing. Months later, it turned out that the young man withdrew his accusations, said he wasn't sure his memories were accurate, how much was imagination and how much was reality. The cardinal and his congregation had weathered the storm—no easy task, possibly even the kind of miracle required to qualify for sainthood. But the "story" had turned out to be . . . nothing more than an accusation. Unsubstantiated and uncorroborated. And, in our coverage on the *CBS Evening News,* unexploited.

There will always be more judgment calls like this, but we may not always feel as good about the judgments we make.

This is just one example of the ways in which I've been called upon to act as managing editor of the *CBS Evening News.* That's a title and a part of my job that are not well understood outside our newsroom, and not the kind of thing you can tell adventure stories about, but being a managing editor has turned out to be one of the great adventures of my life.

I have been at CBS News since 1962, have worked with the greatest legends and seen them pass, have tried to preserve their memories even as I have tried to move forward. Besides *The CBS Evening News,* I spend a good deal of my time working on *CBS Reports* documentaries, live special event coverage, and the weekly documentary series *48 Hours.* I have also worked in radio ever since I came to CBS News: I take great satisfaction in that. I do spot pieces when I'm covering a breaking story, and I have a daily radio essay called "Dan Rather Reporting."

What I have sought, over a lifetime in news, is to earn a reputation as a "pull no punches, play no favorites" experienced reporter of integrity. My intent has been to try to uphold the highest standards of American journalism, even when there is reason to believe this will cost me something.

I certainly have made mistakes—may have made more than my share of them.

But I have tried hard to be as accurate, fair, and unafraid as is humanly possible. And along the way, I have also tried to lead an interesting professional life, including some adventures.

I grew up on adventure stories. I thrived on them. Cowboy movies at the picture show. At home, I read Rudyard Kipling and plenty of his less distinguished imitators. Kipling is out of fashion now, perhaps rightly so. His adventure stories depend on some racism and a lot of imperialism, as well as a willingness to violence that won't help you get along very well in the modern, multicultural world.

But I wouldn't trade anything for the color and excitement of Kipling's stories—and, most of all, the idea that your integrity, your sense of honor, of justice, of duty to others and to country, counted for something. Life would very often present you with situations in which your core values would be tested. Those with faulty values would be led astray, like the English soldiers in *The Man Who Would Be King.* Those with strong values would prevail, like (to pick one of the less controversial examples) the valiant mongoose Rikki-Tikki-Tavi, who saves a household from a vicious cobra.

I can tell you without apology that Kipling and his colleagues fired my imagination when I was a little boy, in a way that no one else did.

Well, almost no one. The exception, of course, is Edward R. Murrow. To this little boy listening to the radio during World War II, Murrow was a hero right out of the adventure books. Risking his life for the *truth.* His work heightened my sense, even then, that being a reporter was a kind of vocation: demanding sacrifice, needing courage, requiring honor. Only with those qualities could a reporter endure one adventure and go on to the next.

If I'm reckoning up the adventures of my life, I've got to put first on my list the adventure of getting to know, over four decades (so far), Fighting-Heart Jean Grace Goebel Rather. A gifted artist, a wise mother, a loving partner, whose intelligence has gotten me out of countless scrapes and whose natural beauty and style turn heads and win hearts to this day. I'm blessed just to know her. Actually to be married to her, to share my life with her, is some kind of miracle. Every time I think she's come to the end of her surprises, she finds some new way to amaze me.

The way she decided, not too long ago, to learn French. Her husband, of course, has barely learned to speak English, and looks on foreign languages as something only slightly less difficult than quantum physics. But Jeanie put her mind to it—so *voilà,* now she speaks French. Recently she joined us in Normandy for the shooting of a documentary on the fiftieth anniversary of D-Day with General Norman Schwarzkopf. At the hotel and everywhere we went, everybody complimented her facility with the language. I couldn't have been prouder if I'd understood what she was saying.

Because most of the adventures in this book are adventures that took place away from the anchor desk, away from New York, I think it's important to reemphasize that I think every day is an adventure. Some of those adventures may not make gripping yarns, but for me they're exciting, demanding, and rewarding.

I knew I was in for another such adventure when Connie Chung was named the first co-anchor in the history of the *Evening News.* Some skeptics shook their heads and said, "Dan'll never make it: you can't teach an old dog new tricks."

Maybe. But I think they're wrong, and have been trying to prove it.

The adventure of working with and as a co-anchor has made it possible for me to undertake more adventures, from Shanghai to Moscow to Des Moines. And learning to share has been a rewarding challenge, not unlike the personal growth that comes when the only child becomes the oldest child and acquires brothers and sisters.

Maybe my experience with my brother, Don, and sister, Pat, gave me the confidence that made me one of the people who came up with this plan. Others have said they'd have thrown a fit and refused to go along with it. Maybe they lack my willingness to try something new.

Co-anchoring is our combined effort to be more flexible, more relevant, more ready. It's a service to our viewers, which is why we're here in the first place. But it's also a service to ourselves. Cooperation builds character. And Connie's professional attitude and winning personality make her a grand partner.

We broadcast the *Evening News* in two feeds, one at 6:30 and one at 7:00 P.M. In the second feed, we update with any new information, and correct any production errors. Often we update again for broadcasts to the West Coast and Pacific.

Throughout the day, I'll have been in conversation with correspondents and producers in the field and in New York, still trying to find out what's going on, but also offering advice when it's solicited. The reporter may be working on a story that has something to do with a story I once covered, or may want my ideas on how to treat a sensitive issue. But sometimes the reporter may want nothing more complicated than the name of a good restaurant.

I may prescreen a report or read the script well in advance to make sure it's fair, reflects what I'm hearing from my own sources, and adheres to the standards of the News Division. By the time I'm reviewing final copy, around six o'clock and half an hour to airtime, I have a clear idea of how the broadcast should look and sound. I usually don't need to make many changes: The News Division took some heavy hits in the eighties and lost some outstanding journalists, but we've weathered the storms and still have some of the finest writers and reporters in the business. I believe it still to be a fact that CBS News has more top-rank reporters and writers, with more experience, than any other electronic news organization in the world.

All of the staying in touch with the news and with news sources, the cross-checking, the copyediting, keeping myself available to our news team for consultation on matters large and small—this is what it means to be managing editor, and it is important to me.

I believe it is also important to viewers to know that the person on-screen presenting the news to them is directly involved in gathering the news and putting the newscast together. A managing editor should help direct coverage, help to set standards, and keep morale up. Say what you will, this is part of my work, and I'm responsible for it. I would not want to be anchor without also being managing editor.

On most nights around 7:45, once all the updates are finished and the broadcast is put to bed, and if we're not on standby for any breaking story, I can head for home, a hot meal, and the company of my wife.

But those are typical days—or as near to a typical day as I ever get. The standout adventures, of course, don't much resemble typical days: that's why they stand out. What follows is an account of a few of my standouts, a few adventures I've had lately.

outtake

Wreck of the Old 97

I HAVE DODGED BULLETS ON THREE CONTINENTS, I'VE BEEN MACED, mugged, and arrested by the KGB, and I've flown on planes so flimsy that the length of the flight depended on the size of the bugs that hit the windshield.

And I've been frightened every time. Fear is useful to a journalist. Fear sharpens the senses, gives you an edge. Nervousness just makes you smile harder. One of the only times I get nervous anymore is just before I appear with David Letterman.

Appearing on *The Late Show* is a joy, but also a terror. Anyone who has ever watched Letterman knows he is spontaneous. You have a rough idea of what is planned, but at any moment David can throw out his producers' hard work and jump the tracks. I consulted a friend who had been on the show, and he advised me, "If you're prepared to be yourself, and to laugh at yourself, you'll do fine. If you bring any pretense along, you are asking for it. David is a master at puncturing pretense."

Letterman is thorough, with a humor that is effortless, and, contrary to an impression some may have, a gracious host. His entire show hums with excellence. His producers in particular are so good that I study them, trying to figure out how to apply their brand of skill and efficiency to our news broadcasts.

It didn't take long for David's team to worm out of me the fact that I enjoy, and know the lyrics to, a few old railroad songs. Once, as a gag, I pulled out the cover of a compact disc, showing me in a conductor's uniform and standing next to an engine, with the title lettered in red: "Dan Rather Sings His Favorite Train Songs." (This was the handicraft of Letterman's brilliant art department.)

For good measure, I belted out a chorus of "The Runaway Train," a cappella, and the bit came off better than I had any reason to expect. I joked that the CDs were on sale at the Oklahoma Railroad Museum, and Dave added that you could find them in the CBS gift shop.

And to my amazement, my office received around 250 orders for this product, which didn't exist. Ah, show business.

David is wound tightly, a judgment I don't think he would argue with. One reason we do get along is the fact that for all the quips and ad-libs, he pays strict attention to business. The first time I appeared on the show, I was struck by how alert he is. He's taking in the audience, the band, the director, and still hearing every word you say. He almost vibrates with energy.

David enjoys hearing about anyone's early days. He listened raptly when I told him that as a combination disc jockey and news reader on a Houston radio station in the early 1950s, I was introduced to a teenaged Elvis Presley. Our expert on hillbilly music at the station told me, "Dan, this young man can be big in the business someday."

I mentioned that my wife had heard that story once too often. Finally Jean smiled sweetly as wives do. Not only would butter not melt on this smile, it's a no-stick smile, too. She broke in: "Hoss, I can beat that two pair."

Before I could continue, Letterman almost came off his chair. "Your wife calls you 'Hoss'?" he yelped. "It must be like the Ponderosa around your household."

I explained that she sometimes does, when she's about to top me. And the punch line was that she had dated Elvis when she was sixteen and he passed near the little central Texas town of Winchester.

I said, "Well, Jean, if things had gone differently . . ."

And she said, "Yes, Elvis would be alive today and anchoring the *CBS Evening News.*"

Well, if we must have singing anchormen, better they should be Elvis Presley than I. I'm more than relieved to say that appearing on *The Late Show with David Letterman* is only an occasional adventure for me.

TWO

Afghanistan's Plains

When you're wounded and left on Afghanistan's plains,
And the women come out to cut up your remains
Jest roll to your rifle and blow out your brains
An' go to your Gawd like a soldier.
— RUDYARD KIPLING,
"The Young British Soldier"

WHEN I FIRST WALKED THROUGH THE HINDU KUSH INTO AFGHANI-
stan in 1980, just after the Soviet invasion, I had no idea what I was
getting into.

I came out knowing that Afghanistan had become one of the
most dangerous places in the world and believing that it could develop into one of the most important battles of the Cold War. It did
that and more.

Afghanistan became one of the least understood but most decisive battles of the twentieth century. The Soviet defeat in Afghanistan was and is an underestimated factor in the sweep of people and
events that led to the fall of the Soviet Empire.

This is the story of how I came to Afghanistan and what happened when I got there.

* * *

Just after Christmas, 1979, the Soviets invaded Afghanistan. I was shocked and surprised—and very interested from the beginning.

It was front-page news when it first happened but began to fade as a story almost from the first day. For one thing, Afghanistan was a long way off and long out of the news. For another, the United States was absorbed by the hostage crisis in Iran. For another, America's intelligence community, military, and diplomatic corps all had been caught by surprise. They didn't seem to know what to make of it. And besides, they were all in a kind of hiatus—partly because of the holidays.

As for the press, well, the Indian subcontinent and Middle Asia never have been very well covered by anybody and weren't then. A few U.S. newspapers had regulars posted in India and other nearby places such as Thailand. And there were a few, only a few, electronic news regulars in the general vicinity. But almost no major Western news outfit moved into Afghanistan to cover the story.

As soon as I heard about the invasion, I said, "This is a big story. This can be a really big story, a very important development." It was mostly just hunch, a feeling, a gut instinct. No reporter can explain these things. You just begin to get a vibration in your reportorial bones.

It doesn't always happen that way. And sometimes, ofttimes, when it does happen—when you do get a hunch, a feel—it doesn't pan out. That's why a good reporter never reports his hunches. But a good reporter does develop his sensitivity to his instincts. And while he or she doesn't report them, an experienced reporter learns to follow them, check them out, follow them through.

I had covered the India-Pakistan war in 1965, and because of that knew a bit about the subcontinent. But not a lot and I certainly wasn't an expert on the area. While there I had crammed in a crash course on the history of the region, both modern and ancient. And I had tried to keep up over the years, going back a few times, including one fairly long trip through that general part of the world for *60 Minutes.*

But mostly it was just something inside me that shouted "Big Story. Jump on it."

The Soviets invaded on December 27. On December 29, 1979, I went into executive producer Don Hewitt's office to tell him I wanted to go to Afghanistan. It was late. Don and I were the only two people left in the shop. Christmas lights were blinking outside the windows of his corner office. He was smoking a cigar.

I told him I had a feeling about Afghanistan and that I wanted to go. He looked surprised, then took the cigar from his mouth and looked me over, for a long time.

By this time in our careers Don and I had developed a close, good relationship. In 1961, when I first walked into CBS News, Don was executive producer of *The CBS Evening News with Douglas Edwards.* I worked with and for him, first under Edwards, later under Walter Cronkite on the *Evening News.* He and Mike Wallace were responsible for bringing me into *60 Minutes.* We had been through a lot of situations and many tight corners well before we wound up working together on the news magazine. In *60 Minutes* we worked together more closely than ever, choosing stories, editing stories, fighting over stories. We both considered it to be a special environment and a special relationship and both felt lucky to be there.

Don was fifty-seven when I walked into his office that night. I was forty-eight. He stared at me with his blue eyes, shifted his medium-framed body and his cigar, and said, "Forget it."

He looked at me hard again. He recognized, he knew, by body language, facial mien, tone of voice, and from years working with me that he couldn't just brush off the idea, not this one. The next instant his expression changed, to one that said, in effect, "Hey, he's serious." And he smiled.

"Come on," he said. "It's New Year's. Go home. Enjoy the holidays. Just kick back and coast through them. And then you come back and think about it. Then, if you still feel the same way, well, maybe we'll see."

I said, "Okay, but what do you think? Why did you say so quickly, 'Forget it'?"

"Well, for one thing," he answered, "it's a long way from Broadway." And he winked.

I telephoned him once during the holidays and said, "Are you reading the papers? Do you see what's happening in Afghanistan?" He said no, other than he had noticed that the story seemed to be fast going to the inside pages. And he added with a smile in his voice, "I told you to enjoy the holiday."

After the first of the year when we came back I told him again that I really wanted to go, that my feeling about the story had grown, not faded. He still was far from enthusiastic. But he responded along the lines of "If you're hell-bent to go, then we'll see what we can do."

This demonstrates one of the keys to why Hewitt became the preeminent producer in television news. He listens to his correspondents. He believes and practices the creed he has long stated: "When I hire reporters, I want only the best. And then I listen to them. My job, my role is to help them get the best out of themselves and get it on the air in the best possible way."

It is fundamental, it is elemental, but it is absolutely key to what makes Don Hewitt what he is and what has made *60 Minutes* the phenomenal success that it is.

Don didn't care about Afghanistan in 1979 and early 1980. He didn't know much about it. That is not said in any patronizing way. He couldn't, can't know everything about everything. He wasn't convinced that Afghanistan would make a good story for *60 Minutes*. And he knew it would be expensive and time consuming just to try for the story, with no assurance of success.

But his attitude was "Okay, you feel it, you want to go after it, you're convinced it can be something good; let's at least scout it out. Who do you want to work with you?" Another of the keys to Hewitt's success is the care he takes in trying to match the right correspondent with the right producer, and to carrying that care right on down the line.

On the average *60 Minutes* story, the team consists of a correspondent, field producer, researcher, cameraman and soundman, and videotape editor. No one in television pays as much attention to mixing and matching members of the team as does Hewitt. I told him I wanted Andy Lack to produce it and that we could talk about the rest of the team later.

When it came to Afghanistan, he requested and I agreed that we shouldn't just plunge into it and rush over there. "Let's don't make this one of your trademark operations where you just sort of go head down, ass up crashing into some Gawdforsaken place. Let's find out a few things first, get a little more to go on than just your gut feel."

Fair enough. Lack and I began making telephone calls, contacting people. Fortunately for purposes of this story, we were closer to the Vietnam era then. I still knew a lot of people in government and in the military from my experience as a correspondent in Vietnam. We asked a lot of questions and quickly confirmed a problem. I had anticipated it but hoped I would be proved wrong. It was the dead of winter. All the mountain passes in Afghanistan were blocked with snow. It was frustrating but obvious that just then, January, wasn't a smart time to go. Too far to go with too much risk that we wouldn't even be able to get into Afghanistan, much less find out and get pictures of what was going on inside the country.

So I turned to other things but kept monitoring the situation. *Sixty Minutes* is a factory of sorts. A correspondent has to keep turning out the goods. The program is on every week. To meet the constant demand for on-air product, a *60 Minutes* correspondent shuttles from one producer to another, one story to another. There are many more producers than correspondents, so while correspondents must keep moving, a producer can linger on a story and is never working as many stories at the same time as a correspondent.

Lack began working on other projects, too, but he remained my point man on Afghanistan. After a few weeks we decided that Lack should go to the Afghan rebels' main staging area in Pakistan, get to know people and check out the situation, take a good look around. By that time we had some knowledge of who was who and what was what. Everybody we talked to said it was next to impossible to get in, that there just was no getting in. And if by any chance you did get in you probably would not get out alive. This, to say the least, gave us pause. And all the more reason for Lack to go to Pakistan, across the border from Afghanistan, to check it out.

He went and we were soon talking regularly by telephone and telex. He reported that it was an extremely complex situation, that the rebels were split into a number of different camps and were at each other's throats—loosely, very loosely united only in their absolute determination to expel the Soviet invaders. They didn't know what they were doing and couldn't even agree on what to do, he reported. But he said he was impressed, nonetheless. He said they would never give up. And he said to me, "You are right about one thing—the Soviets may have bitten off much more than they realize. These Afghans are fanatic in their zeal to do whatever it takes, however long it takes. There are signs of a potentially effective guerrilla army in the making."

As to whether we could get into Afghanistan, Lack said it was odds against, but he wanted to keep working on it.

Don, in the meantime, began saying, "Andy Lack has been over there quite awhile. Time and money are wasting. Is this thing going to be or not be?"

Don was hoping it wouldn't be. And in fairness to Don, I don't believe that was only because, or even mostly because, it was a long way away and so far not a story our audience or anybody else's was indicating much interest about. Nor because it figured to cost more than most *60 Minutes* pieces. Don was concerned about those things, but increasingly his biggest worry, I thought, was that the operation looked very dangerous. He didn't say that. He didn't have to. It just came through, in all of those ways such things do when friends and fellow pros have been a lot of miles and worked a lot of stories together. It also came through in the kinds of indirect questions he asked. And God and everyone who has ever worked with him knows Don asks a lot of questions.

Don would worry about the danger, but costs and cost control were worries, too—bigger worries in the *60 Minutes* of 1979–80 than they would be later. Through the late 1980s and on into the '90s, *60 Minutes* had become such a reliable cash cow, it had become such a separate fiefdom within CBS and CBS News, and Don Hewitt had created such a cult of personality (his) and climate of fear among those above him—including the network owners and board of directors—that Hewitt and *60 Minutes* pretty much did what they damn well pleased and spent what they pleased.

But in the 1979–80 period, costs and cost control were monitored closely. Bill Leonard was CBS News president at the time, having succeeded Richard S. Salant. Leonard was coming under cost-control pressures the likes of which Salant had never known. It was just the beginning, but a definite beginning, of what was to come later in the 1980s—a "cut costs wherever the costs" corporate dictum to the news.

Leonard was a shrewd, dedicated executive who had come up through the ranks as a correspondent and producer. He was committed to the idea that the best way to protect the integrity and flexible worldwide reach of CBS News was constantly to demonstrate to the corporation that it was getting good value for every dollar spent. Cost was not his first priority; coverage and quality were. But he *was* cost-conscious, as well he should have been.

Leonard's vice president for "longer form news" was Robert Chandler. Chandler's portfolio included practically everything except daily news broadcasts and the overall CBS News world news-gathering operation. His main responsibilities were *60 Minutes* and documentaries.

Chandler was as good on accuracy, fairness, and ethics as anybody CBS News ever had. He also was a crisp decision maker, budget master and editor. He is one of the few executives ever to maintain any real measure of control over Don Hewitt, partly because Hewitt respected him so much. He and Hewitt often had their versions of the Great Tong Wars, but they were a superb combination.

As *60 Minutes* left the 1970s and went into the 1980s, Chandler had a rough budget for the program that included "approximately" $45,000 per field-produced piece. Three pieces from the field in each program, total budget per week for those pieces about $135,000.

An expedition into Afghanistan could not be mounted for anything close to $45,000. It might easily cost twice that, or more, in 1979–80 dollars.

We fairly often were over budget on pieces, sometimes far over. Nobody raised much if any fuss. There was simply a very loose understanding that if you did an overbudget piece, it would be good if you could bring one in under budget to balance it off—for example, do a big-name interview in New York or Washington. These cost comparatively little and were great to offset a big-ticket piece.

In its early years, 1968 to 1977 or so, *60 Minutes* worried not at all about budgets. In fact, for some of those years it didn't really have a budget. The "budgets" were just guesstimates. But by the late 1970s the network brass realized what a gold mine *60 Minutes* had become. There was real money in the program and corporate executives began yearning to make the most of it. This started happening shortly after I had joined the program in 1975, when *60 Minutes* began moving up rapidly on the ratings charts. It soon was in the top-twenty rated programs, then began being number one.

(My joining the program probably had little if any connection with this. It has been opined from time to time that my joining Mike Wallace and Morley Safer just as *60 Minutes* moved to a new time period—the one where it is now—helped boost the broadcast to the top in the ratings. I would love to believe that but, in all candor, discount it. Adding a third experienced reporter did, however, give the program a wider, deeper reach and more variety. That couldn't have hurt.)

All of that just by way of background. Budgets, boards of directors, and bureaucrats never have been what *60 Minutes* is about, not for the men and women who work on the program. Stories, a commitment to journalism that matters, and a sense of adventure are what it is and always has been.

And while it may be self-serving to say so, these are what our persistence with the Afghanistan story exemplified.

We had been up and down and all around with discussions about whether to do the story, and if so when, for more than two months. Then Andy Lack telephoned from Peshawar, Pakistan, in late February 1980. The Soviet invasion was two months old. Winter and the war had been brutal to all parties involved in the fighting—just how brutal the world was not to know until later because there was virtually no independent reporting coming out of Afghanistan. The story had not, as we sometimes say in news, "taken traction."

Lack said, "If it's going to happen, if we are to do a story, you, Dan, need to come here and you must come now." He went on to say that he believed it was odds-against that we could get into Afghanistan, and that he was in no position to guarantee that we would get a *60 Minutes* piece if I did come. His point was that it was now or never for trying.

Don Hewitt, with reservations, agreed. Neither he nor I was convinced that those above us at CBS News would agree, so we made a secret plan. We would not tell them that I was going. I had just signed a new contract in the middle of February to become the successor to Walter Cronkite on the *CBS Evening News.* Walter would continue in his position for another year (and beyond if he chose to do so, his choice), and I was to continue in *60 Minutes* until he was ready to leave.

My belief, shared by Don, was that if we informed top management—if we, in effect, asked for permission to go—they might very well say no. Better, we thought, not to place them in the position of having to approve or disapprove—not before I went anyway.

Few people even in *60 Minutes* knew I was going. My friend David Buksbaum, Susan Shackman, my personal right hand in the office, and Mike Wallace knew. I think Bob Chandler had an inkling, but he was wise enough not to let on—to us or to those above him.

Jean Rather, my daughter, Robin, and my son, Danjack, had a last family council before I took off. We talked about the danger. Both children had been old enough during my assignments in Vietnam to have clear memories of the fears and realities of their father's reporting from a war zone. But Afghanistan would be different, not least because there would be no U.S. military, no representatives of the U.S. government, not even any other press around to protect or to help in case of emergency. And the lack of other reporters meant a lack of reporting—which only contributed to my family's uncertainty and concern. They couldn't be sure what I was getting into.

Jean and Robin both said frankly that they had "bad feelings about this one." Danjack said he was worried but did not share their worst fears. His opinion was: "Since you survived Vietnam I prefer to believe that you can somehow survive this, too."

Jean and Robin wept as I kissed them good-bye. They told me

later that once I was gone, they hugged each other and said, "We'll probably never see him alive again." About this trip into the unknown they didn't like the portents and were worried as they had never been before.

This may all sound and read a bit overdramatic now, years later. And perhaps it was. But that's the way it felt, and the way it sometimes goes in the families of journalists. The craft has its dangers, and flying into hellholes is one of them.

The flight to the Afghan freedom fighters' base camp in Pakistan was long and lonely. From New York to Karachi, Pakistan's largest city, then on to Islamabad and finally a small plane hop to Peshawar.

The minute I stepped off the last leg of flying, into the dingy grime of Peshawar, I could sense war, desperation, and death. One could feel it, see it, hear it, smell it. It permeated the air and your consciousness.

Peshawar was dusty. The bazaar was filled with bazaar sounds: men, always men, hawking wares often made locally and just as often stolen or traded from afar. The original middlemen, moving products from one part of the world to another the same way their ancestors did when Marco Polo rode through this outpost at the foot of the Khyber Pass. Soon the goods would be sent by a number of nations trying to help the Afghan freedom fighters. The sounds of the bazaar are sounds of intrigue: men trading goods but also trading news and rumor, truth and lies, without any sure way of knowing which is which.

Peshawar was filled with refugees from Afghanistan, mostly living in tents on the sandy plain outside of town. The city turns to mud in the rainy season. And the refugees would be there for many years of changing seasons.

Peshawar was the rear guard for those fighting the Soviets, but the frontline of the war of information and misinformation. It's the traditional way of fighting in this still-ancient world that is part Persian trader and part mountain herdsman. Warriors who are both trusting and faithful and at the same time cunning and deceitful. Half of what is said is true, and you'd better believe it. Half is false. Follow the falsehood, and it will be your undoing. The survivors are those who can tell the difference—or, if they can't, they can at least be more devious. The twin coins of this realm are treachery and trust.

On this dusty plain and in these rugged mountains truth is told with a glimmer of mischief and lies are told with direct-eyed honesty. Here the two superpowers came to fight. Both would lose. And the survivor, the Afghan, would live to fight another day—this time with his ancient enemy, his neighboring tribe.

Even now, few realize how sure of his ground the Afghan fighter was. He did not need to know about modern warfare. After all, the battle was fought on his turf. It wasn't hard to make the combatants fight on his terms, too: trust and treachery.

Andy Lack and I immediately began working around the clock.

Intrigue and betrayal among the various Afghan resistance forces abounded. The tribal leaders were understandably suspicious of one another and everyone else. We went around and saw the leaders of every major faction, at least seven. This one eyed us and listened as he smoked opium. That one did so with his knife drawn. Still another circled us continuously, looking us up and down menacingly. None gave us much encouragement. We were increasingly tired, frustrated, and frazzled.

After almost two days and nights, it became clear that there were two people who might agree to take us inside Afghanistan, each representing a different group. We eventually made a decision on the one that we distrusted least. And with that one person and his group, we pleaded. We begged, just short of groveling. The leader of the faction finally agreed and turned us over to the man who had "volunteered" to try to get us in. His name was Mirwaz. He was twenty years old. A small, wiry man-child with intense dark eyes and broken English.

Over the years since I have asked myself many times why and how we came to place our lives in the hands of such a stranger so far from home in such a dangerous place.

Instinct, intuition, just a kind of sixth sense, and wanting badly—perhaps too badly—to get to the heart of a big story are the only answers I've ever been able to come up with. Crazy thing to do? Well, to be a journalist is to be a little bit crazy. It's a crazy business. Why Mirwaz would do it is simpler to explain. First, he was a patriot and a true believer in Islam and in the cause of expelling the invaders, the Soviets. Second, his leader, the leader of his clan, the patriarch of his tribe, an old man who was a distant relative, had ordered him to do it. He was a volunteer in the same way U.S. Marines volunteer for hard-duty assignments; he was told that he had volunteered.

It was impossible not to like Mirwaz, right from the start and right the whole way through. For one thing he was so energetic and

enthusiastic. For another, he never stopped smiling. The more difficult things got—and things soon were to get very difficult indeed—
the more he smiled. He was tough, smart—mountain
smart—quick-witted, and a born leader. As time and events unfolded, he eventually made us true believers in his own, apparently
private, unstated code: When the going gets tough, the tough start
smiling.

With God's grace, luck, and Mirwaz's leadership, we walked into
Afghanistan and we walked out.

It began with a fast trip to Peshawar's open-air market. Under
Mirwaz's direction we bought secondhand Afghan clothes: loose-
fitting, wide-legged, baggy cotton trousers with drawstring waists,
equally loose long-sleeved pullover shirts that resembled pajama
tops, and the worst-looking hats in all the world. These were wool
"cap-hats," knit but with a little bit of a brim, the kind Afghans
have been wearing at least since the last century when they an-
nihilated British invaders in the Khyber Pass. To all of this was
added a large combination blanket and wrap. The whole outfit was
brownish gray and olive drab in color.

Shoes? Mirwaz said it didn't matter, so long as whatever we
chose would be comfortable for us to walk in for long, very long
distances, and so long as they weren't new and were dirty. He wore
sandals. "Jesus boots," our cameraman Mike Edwards called them.
I had a pair of Clarke's Desert Boots, fifteen years old, my lucky
boots that I had worn all through the Vietnam War. Jean had
bought them for me in London just before I first went to Saigon in
1965. Now dirty, beat, and torn, but comfortable as well, comfortable as an old shoe, they were my own footwear of choice.

Funny, but the moment I knew I'd be wearing the old Desert
Boots into Afghanistan, a certain sort of peace and confidence
surged. And I knew, just knew, we'd get in and out all right. Somehow just knew. I began to understand for the first time, a little, why
some women attach so much significance to shoes, and why they
often become so attached to certain pairs of footwear.

Andy, Allah bless him, decided on a stylish pair of crepe-soled
brown lace-up brogans. They looked like something a yuppie might
wear for antiquing weekends in the Hamptons. (How Andy loves
the Hamptons!) He and Mirwaz scuffed them up and muddied them
up appropriately for this trip, and we all had a good laugh over
them.

We worried, though, about the choice made by our interpreter-
historian, Eden Naby. She chose what looked like a pair of light

ballet slippers. Mirwaz smiled, but it was a tight little smile when she showed them to him. They didn't strike him as built for long hauls. But Eden made an argument about maximum comfort and he eventually, reluctantly, said okay. Eden was leaning toward being the fifth member of our CBS team that would be going inside Afghanistan but had not finally, completely, agreed yet.

She was thirtyish, a short, solid, and stolid woman of about 130 pounds, five feet four, a dark-haired, dark-eyed American of Middle Eastern heritage. We had found her at Harvard in the early stages of our research. She and her husband were professors at Harvard's School of Near Eastern studies. Both were experts on Iranian-Pakistanian and Afghan history, culture, and archaeology. She was fluent in Farsi and Pushto, the languages of Afghanistan. (Better-educated Afghans speak Farsi; peasants speak the Pushto dialect.) Mr. and Mrs. Naby had agreed to accompany us to Peshawar to help with translations and setting up the trip (plus tutoring us in a crash course about local history and culture) but had originally made it clear that neither wanted to risk going to the war. But as our plans took shape and the time for going in drew near, two things became clear. One, Eden was increasingly tempted by the prospect of adventure and of being able to learn firsthand what was going on in the area of her most intense academic interest. And two, we desperately needed her translating skills.

Near the end she and her husband debated (and even argued some) over the pros and cons. And in the end, she waveringly decided to chance going with us. When she told us, Andy, who is Jewish, crossed himself, I breathed a silent prayer of thanks, and Mirwaz went to his carpet for a conversation with Allah.

So going in we would be six: Andy Lack, producer. Cameraman Mike Edwards and soundman Peter O'Connor, both out of the CBS News *60 Minutes* London operation, myself as correspondent, Mrs. Naby as translator and general resource, Mirwaz as our faithful (we hoped) Afghan guide. Mr. Naby declined to go, mostly because of his age (he was probably in his fifties) and fragile health. We were relieved, partly because we wanted to keep our team small and mobile, partly because Mr. Naby, while unquestionably brilliant, unfortunately was very nervous (with good reason) and was obviously not in the best of health. I liked the man, and admired him tremendously, but was mightily relieved when he announced that he would not be going—noway, nohow.

We had another camera crew with us in Peshawar, Jan Morgan, and his soundman. They, too, had volunteered to "go inside." But to keep our numbers for the trip to a minimum, I had to tell them they would not be going—not initially, anyway. Perhaps if we actually got into Afghanistan and found that we could stay, I thought, then we might be able to send for them. Or send them in when and if we got back.

We could also use them as decoys. They would keep themselves obvious around the best of the bad lot of local hotels and possibly draw the eyes and ears of potential competitors and any other nosy folk, such as intelligence operatives, away from our tracks.

But their main role was this: To be a kind of communications and logistics operation for us back at what now amounted to our base camp, Peshawar.

They would keep abreast of any news filtering back about our movement, or lack of movement. And if we were not back in twelve days, they would begin checking as best they could on our safety. They were not to tell even CBS in New York anything, if they could keep from it, for twelve days. And anything they might be forced to communicate to New York or anybody else would be kept to a minimum.

Our plan was to steal away after bedtime on a moonless Tuesday night.

That evening we made a point of being seen in our hotel restaurant for dinner. Later, in our quarters upstairs, we toasted the mission with shots from my flask of Wild Turkey bourbon, in a spirit of comradeship—for luck. And then we were gone. We left the hotel singly, using three separate exits, and made our rendezvous with Mirwaz at a prearranged spot.

By the last hour before dawn, we had made it to the Pakistan border with The Territories. The Territories are Pakistani protectorates, buffers between Pakistan and Afghanistan. To call them a no-man's-land would not be entirely accurate, not legally. But as a practical matter that's pretty much what they are.

There is a regional headman in charge of each individual territory. And various headmen in charge of various villages and encampments within each territory.

To cross a territory, travelers—especially foreigners—are supposed to have permission from the territorial headman. That permission, in turn, mostly depends on whether you pass muster from at least one and usually several of his village "precinct captains." This, we had been told, could take hours or it could take days or weeks. And then again, it might never happen.

Once we had crossed into one of the territories, we halted. Mirwaz herded us into a large mud and straw hut, complete with animals and people who spoke no known language. We were to eat, then sleep while Mirwaz did the following: check to see if we were being followed, scout out what lay ahead, make contact with the local authority, and try to win permission for us to proceed.

The food did not look appetizing, to put it mildly. The camera crew and I ate a little from the inside of bread rolls. Andy took a complete pass. (Rather's Rules for Survival in strange, distant places—taken from the tutoring of old CBS News correspondents—are: Don't drink the water, don't eat the meat, and don't even look at the women. Eat the bread, but never the outside of it. Many different hands from various food handlers often touch the bread. Eating the crust can cause you more trouble than you can possibly imagine. Trust me. I learned this the hard way. It is as true in The Territories as it is in Somalia or Sarajevo. Come to think of it, it is even true some places in the States.)

Then we slept. Some of us. A little.

We all slept in one room, with the resident family and with the animals. As we were to do throughout the trip, we took scheduled turns on watch. In one-hour shifts, one of us would be up, alert, and scanning for possible trouble at all times while the others slept.

Several hours after dawn, Mirwaz returned. There were no signs we had been followed; the straightest, shortest route ahead into Afghanistan was reportedly clear, and we had an appointment with the local main man.

On the way to see him, trouble developed. Some of the locals suspected we might be Russians. They stopped us, crowded us, and pushed and shoved us. Knives and guns were brandished—theirs, not ours. Mirwaz was the only one among us who had a gun. He and our passports and something about buying a round of tea finally eased the situation and we moved on. We looked at one another and rolled our eyes. Nobody had said this was going to be easy. And they were right.

When we got to the man in charge of this particular zone, more trouble. He was watching a cricket match on Pakistani television and refused to meet with us until it was over. I had been CBS News bureau chief in London years before and I knew cricket.

"This could take days," I told Andy. We all groaned. A fine rain began to fall, what the English call "mizzle." Damn. We stood outside in the mizzle, listening to the damn cricket match from inside for more than an hour.

Fortunately the match ended then and we were allowed inside.

The local authority was a small, thin man dressed in a dark suit, white shirt, and a tie. He apparently had not only the only television set for miles, he had the only Western-cut business suit. Turned out he was British-educated and trained as a British-style bureaucrat. Was he ever. He was officious and efficient. He made reasonably quick work of giving us notes, complete with an official stamp of sorts, that were supposed to give us safe passage to his boss, the territorial chief, at his headquarters miles ahead.

The papers worked. By late afternoon we were in front of the territorial chief. He was a direct opposite. A tall, portly man dressed in local garb, including colorful headgear, he received us warmly and immediately. Speaking through an interpreter, he wanted to know all about us, and he studied each of us with eyes that had the intensity of an owl's.

After the niceties and after studying us, he spoke directly and to the point. The rough translation was: "You lie, you die." And with that he proceeded to interrogate us for about an hour. He needn't have said it. Everything about him fueled the judgment that you would not want to lie to this man. Not even a tiny white lie. Don't even think about it. And we didn't.

Near the end, he took me alone into another room, pierced my eyes with his, and, in effect, made me swear to God and Allah and on my mother's grave that we were who we said we were and wanted to do what we said: specifically, report accurately and fairly back to the American people the reality of the war.

Then he gave us his approval and, with a smile and a wave, sent us on our way.

We walked a long way that late afternoon, into the twilight and on into the night.

For a long while, we walked along sorry roads clogged with refugees. The tide of humanity was staggering, every road choked with them, and it was against this tide that we walked. Women, children, the elderly and the crippled. The cries of the children never seemed to stop.

We would try to sleep a couple of hours, on the ground, on the roadside, then walk on.

Later, we left the roads and started up into the mountains, headed into a pass. The refugee lines thinned out, the cries of the children grew less frequent, and then more distant.

The mountains loomed, dark and foreboding. Soon the refugees were far behind us and we were alone, walking with the silence and discipline our guide commanded.

Night turned to day, then to night again, and on we walked. We tried to rest ten minutes out of every hour, and every six hours we stopped and tried to sleep for four—minus the one hour each of us stood watch.

Eventually we were out of The Territories and clearly into Afghanistan. No customs house, no signs, no one announced it. Some jet fighter-bombers flew low overhead, followed by helicopters. We took cover and froze. When the choppers passed, I quietly asked Mirwaz if we were now inside and he nodded yes. The aircraft were from Jalalabad, Afghanistan's fifth-largest city and a Soviet stronghold fifty miles from the border. Our first day in, we reached the mountains that surround Jalalabad and a place just three miles from where the Afghan resistance forces had been launching attacks on the Soviets. There we hooked up with a small guerrilla band, fourteen men led by a white-bearded man named Yassini.

Yassini was of medium height and weight, with bulging forearms and calf muscles. His physique was that of a halfback. His age was mid- to late forties. He lived on the run, moving from mountain hideouts through tiny villages of straw and mud huts to the opium fields that often provided him and his men cover from the Soviet aircraft that patrolled continuously.

Yassini had what military people and combat correspondents the world over would immediately categorize as "strong command presence." I recognized it and, frankly, was more relieved than I can describe. This man was no amateur. He knew what he was doing and he had tight control over his unit. What he did not have was very much in the way of weapons or ammunition. And he had no communications equipment, no medical supplies. The latter fact was quickly noted and was sobering. Their weapons consisted of two Russian-model AK-47s, one antitank contraption carried in a sort of backpack, plus assorted old (very old) semi-automatic and bolt-action rifles, plus grenades, a few mines, and many knives. The word "ragtag" came to mind. But then I thought of Vietnam. Numbers and types of manufactured weapons can be misleading. Hearts and minds and feet can be more important weapons, as can the advantage of fighting on home ground.

We filled our canteens from a spring and dropped in our water purification tablets as the guerrilla band watched in amusement, and soon we were on the move again, now part of a larger group.

Yassini made us walk spread out, with one man far out front, scanning constantly for mines, signs of possible ambush or enemy

We walked a long way again. Only two mines were found along the road. The point man far out front found both of them, one on top of the ground, as though it might have fallen out of someone's pack or off some mule. The other one was barely concealed under freshly and hastily scraped dirt. Neither exploded.

But ever since the child had died in the village and all along this move, my mind kept going back to another long "walk in the sun," long ago and far away. It was in Vietnam, just before Thanksgiving, 1965. A company of U.S. Army soldiers were being marched in from the field for Thanksgiving dinner. The commander would not let them walk on the road for fear of mines. He had them walking double-file on both sides of the road, where the going was wet and sticky from adjacent rice paddies. Four soldiers in front of me was a teenage private from Tennessee. Suddenly, there was a muffled *bar-RROOM,* and the kid's legs were gone. He had been blown completely in the air as we, gape-mouthed, watched in shock and horror. When his lieutenant came running up, the young soldier was, miraculously and unfortunately, still conscious. He was, of course, crying as excruciating pain enveloped him. Before he passed out, he looked his officer in the eye and asked him to call his parents: "And tell 'em, Lieutenant, please tell 'em—I gave it all I had."

It was a moment of heroism like something out of a book or movie, but the blood and the pain were real. I had nightmares about that day for years, long after I had been to Vietnam for the last time. But by the time I went to Afghanistan the nightmares had long since passed. The memory had not. And I thought about it repeatedly, almost constantly, in the mountains near Jalalabad this day.

Night came again. And again we walked on, well into the night. When we finally bedded down on the dirt floor of the main mud hut of a compound belonging to a huge extended family, there was trouble.

The trouble was women. And our historian-translator Eden Naby. She had been sleeping with us, so to speak, everywhere. That is, she slept in the same crowded huts and bombed-out covered places where we did. When we had slept in the open air, she had slept close by, right in the same area. The reasons—obvious, I think—were her safety and ours. Of course we were too dirty, too smelly, too weak, and too scared to be anything but perfect gentlemen. Eden had never been safer from unwanted advances in her life.

But Afghanistan then and now was oblivious to the modern

women's movement, most definitely oblivious in the countryside. This was and is a male-dominated Muslim society, with all that this entails for good and bad. These were an eighteenth- , in some ways even a seventeenth-century peasant people of ancient Islamic faith and teaching, fighting a late-twentieth-century war. The combination of all this made matters especially hellish for women.

For one, women were considered to be, in effect, chattel. In this environment, a Western woman had two marks against her: She was both an "infidel" and chattel.

Eden Naby was not afraid. She is among the bravest persons I have ever been around. But we were afraid for her. And, truth to tell, we were even more afraid for ourselves. In case of attack, in the confusion and chaos of a sudden fight (and, hopefully, flight) for our lives, especially in the dark, without Ms. Naby and her language skills and her immense knowledge of the place, our chances would plummet. And we knew it. We worried, too, because we were not traveling with choir boys, and neither did we encounter many as we traveled. In war zones, thugs, highwaymen, con men, and renegade soldiers abound. Dangerous for us, as Western men, but even more dangerous for Eden Naby.

There had been rumbles and mumbles before, among various Afghans with whom we came in contact, even some of those with whom we were traveling. But a combination of Ms. Naby's tact, diplomacy, and knowledge, plus the intercessions of our faithful Afghan guide, Mirwaz, and the formidable Commander Yassini, had put down previous grousing and potential trouble over "the American woman with the men."

Not this time. The extended family with whom we stayed was larger than any family who'd offered us their hospitality before. This family had a fairly large compound, with a half dozen or so mud huts around a common, outdoor cooking center.

In this place, as in so many others in this devoutly Islamic, rural world, the women had separate quarters. In this world, not only do women remain covered, top of head to toes, but even when fully covered they are seldom if ever seen by anyone, *any*one, other than their husbands and very close family. And no one, *no* one, save husbands and children, is supposed to see them even slightly uncovered.

The women in the compound numbered about twenty (there were many girls, too). They were uncomfortable about our being among them at all. But they had been ordered to accept that these were highly unusual times requiring, among other things, that they help to hide us. So they accepted our presence.

But when it came to Eden Naby's sleeping in the same room with the men, including their men, they revolted. Eden translated for us later, but one didn't have to speak the language. The volume and the tenor of their voices coming over a mud and straw wall made their meaning unmistakable: No way, nohow, was the American woman going to sleep anywhere but the women's quarters. Period. No, not even for three or four hours. (Bear in mind that our rule was never to remain in any one place for more than four hours. Keep moving. Word travels fast.)

We were mighty nervous about parting company with Eden Naby, but we finally had to give in. That is, Ms. Naby gave in. Then she insisted we go along with it.

This was the deal: She would sleep with the women. But we would rig between us, between the men's quarters and the women's, a very crude makeshift "telephone" system. A collection of tin cans hanging closely together at each end of a rope. Quick jerks on the rope, either end, would set off a clanging noise. This would sound an instant alarm in case of trouble, real or imagined, and bring help running from the other end. Or such was the plan, anyway.

It wasn't much, but it was the best we could do. Ms. Naby was sanguine about it. The men in our team were not.

After a fitful period of what passed for sleep, we awakened just at daybreak to the unmistakable smell of fresh bread. Two things flashed through my mind. One, the humid, joyous afternoons at Buffalo Stadium in Houston, watching baseball double-headers with my father when I was a child. The Houston Buffs minor league team played in an old wooden stadium with railroad tracks on one side and the Holsum Bread bakery on the other. The cracks of the bats, the roar of the crowd, the smells of beer, popcorn, tobacco juice, and fresh-mown grass, mixed with sights and sounds of passing freight trains and the smell of bread from the bakery. And two, the nights early in our marriage when Jean and I slept over with her Grandmother Goebel, out in the country along Pin Oak Creek near tiny Winchester, Texas. Granny Goebel arose at 3:30 A.M. most of the mornings of her adult life to bake bread, there in the house where she was born and had lived ninety-plus years, and the smell of her bread from scratch permeated the old wooden farmhouse.

This was all a long time and distance from that early morning in Afghanistan, and the flashes of it disappeared as I saw Andy Lack peeking outside through a crack in our hut's door.

A woman was baking the bread in a low earthen oven outdoors.

She was covered from head to toe, even wearing a kind of cloth mask. She was taking the wonderful smelling bread out with a long wooden spatula several feet long.

"I'm going to ask her for some of that bread," said Andy as he started to move out the door. I sprang and tackled him, and pinned him with my body, covering his head with my chest. He was amazed—astonished might be the better word.

I was scared. "Good God, Andy, if you even look at that woman, much less go near her, we will all be buzzard bait," I managed to whisper. "And before that we will die slow, painful deaths." He knew instantly that I was right. His hunger and the near-hypnotic effect of the smell of the bread had just momentarily scrambled his brain.

We were all tired, edgy, hungry, and constantly trying to suppress the psychological background drone of fear. We untangled ourselves and got up, careful to keep our backs to the woman baking outside.

In a few minutes, Afghan men, who had been tending their animals, came back and brought us some bread. We ate it (from the *inside*) eagerly.

The night had passed uneventfully. There had been no cause to use our makeshift alarm and communications system. We were full of questions for Eden Naby about her time in the women's quarters. She declined to reveal much, except that one of the younger women had some interesting tattoos.

The plan for the day turned out to be that we would be taken even closer to Jalalabad. How close we did not know, but we were soon to find out.

I had mentioned to Yassini that the Russians seemed to have an extraordinary amount of aircraft. He answered, through Eden Naby's translation, something to the effect of "You don't know the half of it."

His plan for this day was that we would find out, firsthand. We moved to a tiny village within sight of the end of some runways at Jalalabad's airport. It took my breath away when I realized how close to the Soviets we had gotten. And it gave our entire CBS team a new attack of nerves.

But we were to get closer still. Following the lead of Yassini and four of his best men, we quietly dropped down into some four-foot-high grass and began crawling toward the nearest runway. Mike Edwards had a hard time crawling with his camera strapped to his chest. Amazingly, almost unbelievably to us, we crawled to within about three hundred yards of the runway. It was loaded with helicopters, fighter-bombers, and larger planes. They were parked practically on top of one another. We were awed and—there's no nice way to put this—scared sheetless. We were almost literally afraid to breathe.

There were no guards in sight, no airport security observation posts—none that we could see, anyway. If the Soviets had any perimeter defense around this end of the runway, it wasn't apparent.

In hurried, low whispers we tried to decide whether to risk trying to film anything. As you would expect of one of the world's great TV news photographers, Mike virtually refused to leave before at least trying to get the picture.

It was decided that he and Yassini would inch even farther forward, partly to get a better shot, partly to separate them from the group in case they drew fire. They moved up. Mike carefully got his camera in position to shoot. The rest of us held our breaths. Some couldn't bear to watch, looked at the ground instead. And some, including your narrator, silently repeated several Our Fathers.

Nothing untoward happened. Mike slipped the camera down, we slipped away on our bellies through the grass.

When we got back to the dirt of the half-road, half-trail from which we had started crawling, we were breathing hard and drenched with perspiration, most of it not from physical exertion.

Besides silent prayers of thanks for deliverance, I was thinking anew: The Soviets and their cause are in deeper trouble here than even they may know, and certainly more than most of the world realizes. Here we had just been within a few hundred yards of the runways at what couldn't have been less than their second-most-important air base for the war. If the Afghan resistance fighters had mortars (they didn't at that time) they could cause great damage anytime they chose. No patrols out from the base (or none that were evident). No perimeter defense or warning systems. What in the hell could they be thinking? What kind of military force was this? Experiences and lessons learned in Vietnam raced through my head, and so did the thought (thought many times before, under other circumstances and in other places) that the United States might overestimate the Soviet military.

As we were collecting ourselves, a kid on a bicycle came riding by. Nobody had to say anything. Most of us were experienced enough to know that a kid on a bicycle can be dangerous, even fatal, in circumstances such as ours.

Scouting for somebody? Definite possibility. But even if he

wasn't, all he had to do was mention that he had seen some strangers with funny-looking equipment down the trail, and if he mentioned it to the wrong people, we could be in a heap of trouble.

We went scat like a cat, pronto, on the run, and not the way we had come. After a long sprint, we hid in some bushes, to catch our breath and asses—to watch and listen. Then we stole away.

By late afternoon we reached another "safe camp" (as in "safe house"—but without the house). Yassini's raiders had used it before, many times, I think. Other armed men were there, only a few women. It was a tiny staging area, base camp for guerrilla hit-and-run operations.

Yassini said we would rest a bit and then he would show us something "very interesting." We had already experienced enough interesting things and seen enough interesting sights for one day, in my opinion, but he insisted. Afterward, he promised with a twinkle in his eye, we would have "a full, good hot meal."

It was the first and last twinkle we had seen from him. Commander Yassini was not the twinkling type, generally speaking. This promise, though, brightened everyone. We had eaten little since we came into the country, nearly all of it on the run, none of it hot, nearly all of it bad. Some cold poor man's oatmeal here, the inside of some bread there, one of the trail bars we had brought with us, a couple of mouthfuls of peanut butter from our packs—that kind of thing. "A full, good hot meal"? Lead on!

We began a long, slow climb up the mountainside. Part of the low part of the mountain was a combination of gravel and hard, crusty soil. Rough going, hard walking.

Suddenly there was the unmistakable *whomp-whomp* of helicopter blades. Far off, but they struck terror in all of our crew. Not in our escorts. They calmly but instantly froze. So did we. We were in the open, wide open. There was no cover. The choppers came closer. They were going to fly right over us.

"No way they don't see us," I thought to myself. And every man in our team was thinking the same thing. Again, we were almost literally afraid to breathe. Closer and closer they came. Then they were directly above us. Decisive moment. Nobody looked up. Nobody moved.

The sound of the blades and motors crescendoed. Then the sound seemed to be moving away from us. Can it be? Yes. They moved away and on. But wait—they're circling. Circle they did. Big, wide circle. We froze hard as stone again. Again they passed.

Did they see us? We'll never know. My impression was then and is now that they never knew we were there.

But we couldn't be sure. The Afghans decided to abort our trek up the mountainside. Instead, we turned back and, following a different route, returned to the "safe camp." We got back just past sunset.

"Sleep now," we were told. "When you wake up, we will have a good meal." Big smile. We dropped our gear, collapsed, and slept like children. I had the watch for the last hour of the three-hour sleep time. Events of the day—what a day!—were playing like reels of videotape in my head. Reels would play, then rerack and play again. Over and over. About all I could think about was how lucky we were to have survived this day. And I thought of Jean, Robin, and Danjack, and the green, green grass of home.

With me I had brought a very special cigar, a big obscene Cuban cigar given to me by Fidel Castro during a trip to the island a long while before. I found it in my pack, took it out of the canister in which it had been lovingly preserved (one doesn't have to love Castro to love his cigars), and fumbled around looking for my waterproof matchbox.

My Afghan companions were intrigued with the cigar. They giggled and smirked while looking it over. But "light discipline" was in effect, nary a spark so that we wouldn't be seen in the dark, so I had to put it away without lighting up.

I went to my pouch of Red Man chewing tobacco instead. This interested and amused my Afghan compadres even more. But not enough for them to try it. They declined offers to indulge and share a chaw.

(Tobacco is a foul and unhealthy habit. I was never addicted, fortunately, and have since mostly given up even occasional uses of it, except for every once in a while when I am fishing. No cigarettes, but a cigar or chew now and again, yes. I know better, but must admit I do still backslide just a bit.)

Soon all of our crew were awakened and we were walked to a small cave about a half mile away. A piece of tarp was stretched tightly over the entrance. Inside, by very low candlelight, food had been spread. Two or three dozen Afghans sat around the food in a circle three deep.

Places had been saved for us front and center, first row. There was rice, and bread, and two covered dishes. Andy Lack was smiling, salivating audibly, and looking poised to pounce.

Andy weighed more then than he does now. He wasn't fat, but he wasn't far from it. He was carrying about two hundred pounds, I'd say, on a five-foot-ten-inch medium frame. He admittedly was in the worst physical shape of anyone on our team.

For one thing, Andy loved the good life, especially good food and drink. I kiddingly and good-naturedly had dubbed him "Champagne Andy" long ago. Back in Peshawar, where champagne worthy of the name was scarce, Andy and I had taken to consuming large quantities of the most popular and readily available soft drink, bottled orange Fanta. The local grapevine had it that Fanta had the best quality control and health standards of any bottler in the region. Besides, Coke and Pepsi were for some reason hard to find. So we washed down Fanta.

Once inside Afghanistan, anytime the going was especially tough, hot, and dusty, I would kid Andy that a big champagne glass filled with ice-cold bubbly would sure hit the spot just now, and he would wink back along the lines of "Hell, I'm reduced to fantasizing about Fanta."

Now, around the dinner circle in the cave, he was saying quietly, "Just give me a Fanta and a little time and I will dine as if in Paris or Rome."

This did not last long. They took the tops off the covered dishes. What was revealed looked and smelled suspicious right from the get-go. Most of what we saw and smelled was a kind of slightly greenish-brown gravy-looking mess. There *was* meat barely visible in it. It was not immediately recognizable as anything we had seen anywhere before.

Andy gulped and began moving, easing his way back from the front row. "What do you suppose it is?" he whispered.

"Dunno," came the reply.

Some small animal, maybe a rabbit or a squirrel—maybe. Whatever it was, it did not smell tasty.

Andy moved even farther back. Those of us still in the honored seats on the front row were served the mystery meat. Once it was on our plates, we had to face the increasing possibility, yea, probability, that the mystery meat came from some form of small rodent.

The word "rat" was never spoken, but it was surely thought. By this time Andy was way back in the third row, gulping repeatedly and turning olive green as he inched toward the entrance to the cave.

Those of us who had been served looked at one another, smiled at our hosts, who by now were watching intently, and finally proceeded to eat. But not before I pulled from my pocket a small bottle of Louisiana Tabasco sauce that I always carry. I applied it liberally and passed it to my colleagues. They eagerly accepted. Mike and Peter, being British, didn't know exactly what Tabasco was. They simply operated under the correct assumption that whatever it was, it could not possibly make what we had any worse.

Andy was out of there. And he didn't return. We later brought him some bread. He ate some of the inside of it—not, as they say, a happy camper.

To this day, I know not what it was we ate. A version of the "Don't ask, don't tell" policy prevailed in all discussions even remotely associated with that dinner.

Around midnight, we were on the move again. As had become our routine, we walked awhile, slept awhile, then walked again. Eden Naby's shoes had begun to come apart. We bound them up with twine and gaffer's tape, and she walked on. All of us had trouble keeping up with the long-striding, seemingly indefatigable Afghans. Given Eden's short legs and sorry shoes, how she managed to keep pace was mystifying and inspiring. The lady had guts, and a heart as big as a locomotive.

By midmorning we arrived at another safe camp. This one had at its center an actual house. Made of stone and concrete, it had what was left of an old opium poppy field on one side and on the other side a rice paddy that showed signs of being recently worked.

Inside the house we lay down for what was supposed to be three or four hours' sleep. It didn't last nearly that long. Mike Edwards, who was our first-hour watchman, shook us awake, saying, "Helicopters!" We could hear them. They were close.

Only four Afghans, besides the headman, Yassini, and our guide, Mirwaz, had made the trek from the cave with us. Why, we had not known, and would not find out for a while yet.

Now the Afghans came from the room in which they had been sleeping, next to ours. They were checking their weapons and putting on their bandoliers of ammunition. We got together in the middle of the room, away from the windows. Using hand signals, the Afghans posted themselves hard against the doors.

These helicopters were low and sounded as if they were coming straight toward us. We could tell by the sound that there were at least two of them, and that they were large. These weren't the small, two- or three-person "scout" helicopters. The noise level and heaviness of the blades as they chopped the air told us they were most likely of troop-carrying size.

Our quick supposition—our fear—was that this was a raid. Had we been followed, or spotted coming in? Had someone seen us and squealed?

They passed just to the side of the house. As the noise began to fade away slightly, Yassini risked a careful peek out a well-positioned window. He held up two fingers, then signaled for his men to scan the ground approaches carefully in every direction.

We were told that the Soviets had been using helicopter assault troops for raids and as shock troops throughout the Kunar Valley, where we were. And as the noise from the choppers indicated they were coming back, or that perhaps some more were coming our way, we began bracing even harder for the worst.

We waited what seemed an eternity. Helicopters, again at least two, swooped right over us this time, even lower than before. I would have sworn they were landing. Mike Edwards had his camera on his shoulder, his finger on the button to start rolling the film. Our Afghan companions had their guns cocked, at the ready.

Nothing happened. The helicopter noises faded into the distance, then disappeared. We waited a long time more, as the Afghans eyed the ground approaches in all directions. After about half an hour, two Afghans were sent out to position themselves in clumps of bushes and trees about twenty-five yards from each long side of the house. They were to act as combination lookouts and forward observers, and to provide covering fire for the house if necessary. The tension held for another hour. Then, and only then, did we begin to breathe even a little bit easier.

We decided to move out. With ears cocked and eyes alternating between sky and ground, we stole away. A walk of a mile and a half took us to a partially concealed, dilapidated lean-to near a small, abandoned house. This was on somewhat elevated ground, giving us a good view of the flatland from which we had come.

Seemingly out of nowhere, a dozen new Afghans materialized, each well equipped with small arms.

There was a council, a group meeting in which, through translation, it was explained to us that the Afghans had decided to go on a dangerous reconnaissance patrol. Fourteen Afghans, including the quiet one with the backpack rocket-launcher rig, would be going. Yassini would lead, and a stocky younger man with the new additions would be second-in-command. The plan was what amounted to a forced march into the nearby mountains. The goal was a ridge that, according to the guerrilla grapevine, looked down on a Soviet emplacement.

We were told straight out that it would be a difficult march, partly because they wanted to arrive at a precise time. And we were told that it would be "extremely dangerous." Some might make it back, or none might. What about *all* making it back? the leaders were asked. A shrug of the shoulders, followed by the answer "Could happen."

They wanted to leave immediately. They left us to mull and decide whether we would join them. Some of us could go or all of us could go, but anybody joining from our group had to get ready to leave now. The second-in-command said quietly, in what he intended to be an aside, that they would prefer the woman not go. When they went away to form up, Eden Naby spoke up.

She did not have a good feeling about this operation and would not recommend anybody going. If any of us did decide to go, she felt obliged to underscore that she believed our chances of coming back alive were less than fifty-fifty. There was a little instinct operating, but her judgment wasn't based only on a sixth sense: Remember that Eden Naby knew the area and the conflict stone-cold; we depended on her informed analysis.

Andy and I took her warning seriously. We started cogitating. Mike Edwards spoke up and said he would go. There was no way we were going to let our cameraman go alone. I told him that if anybody was going, I was, and that I was prepared to go alone with the Afghans. I would take the camera and the sound gear, both of which I knew how to operate (not well, but I did know how). Mike said he couldn't and wouldn't let me go alone. Andy offered to go but said frankly that he wasn't enthusiastic about it. He, too, had bad vibes about the whole thing and, besides, he did not know how much use he could be. Peter O'Connor, the soundman, also said he would go, that he was willing to do whatever we wanted him to do, but he would not be disappointed to stay behind.

This was not a contest of pride or bravery. It was a conversation among experienced pros about what was best, what made sense, and honest expressions about how each of us felt.

If it made sense for any of us to go—and I couldn't be certain that it did—then what made the most sense was for Mike Edwards and me to do it. This meant risking the fewest people for the potential maximum gain. The problem was that we had to have a translator. No way could we go without someone, and someone at least fairly good, to translate. This is what I was thinking.

Although I hadn't said anything about translation, I didn't have to. Mirwaz had already gone over among the other Afghans, obviously readying himself for the march. I went over and offered him a chance to stay behind. He smiled his infectious wide smile and said what amounted to "Forget it. You go, I go."

So we went: Mike, myself, Mirwaz, and fourteen other Afghans.

The march was as advertised. Steady, fast pace. At first, through the rice paddies and opium poppy fields, through trees and over rocks, but most of the climb was nearly straight up. The ridge we wanted was at ten thousand feet. We stopped seldom, rested little. The Afghans expected us to keep up, no matter how hard we panted, no matter how loudly we grunted. It was keep up or be left behind. Somehow, we managed to keep up.

Our unit arrived at the top just as the sun set behind the far mountain. The objective was to scout a possible location of tanks on the perimeter of Jalalabad. We crawled on our stomachs the final few yards to the edge of the ridge. There was the sound of helicopters in the medium distance. Below, on both sides of a small bridge, we could clearly see two tanks. Was that two more behind them a ways? Or were those armored personnel carriers? Couldn't be sure. There definitely were two tanks, some tents, and big guns.

As Mike and I took in the scene with awe, we were startled by a sudden flare. First one, then another. The Afghans with us opened up with automatic weapons from the top of the ridge toward the encampment below. Another flare, then another. The whole area, the ridge where we were and the tanks with their support below, was bathed in an eerie light. The Afghans fired off one of their antitank rockets. Then another. Silence. Followed by a tremendous explosion near us. Artillery shell. Then another blast near us. Mortar. Dirt flew over and onto us. The Afghans shot another antitank round. Impossible to know where it hit or if it struck home. There was another earsplitting sound almost on top of us. Another artillery round had struck very close. They were beginning to get our range.

The Afghans began scurrying slightly down and off to the side of the mountain. They didn't want to go back exactly the same way we had come up, partly because of their concern that a blocking force might be coming around back from down below. As they retreated to the side, the Afghans took turns raking the forward base of the ridge. This was in hopes of discouraging any effort by the enemy to scale the ridge from the front, from down where the Soviet encampment was. After scrambling somewhat down but mostly sideways for a bit, we began heading straight down the mountain. An explosion rang below us and off to the side in the direction from which we had come. That round blasted a smaller ridge just below the one where we had been. If we had scurried immediately straight down from our original position, that latest shot might have hit us. The Soviets were trying to walk arching mortar fire down what they figured might be our escape path. Once again, the Afghan resistance fighters had demonstrated their guerrilla combat savvy, correctly predicting the Soviets' thinking.

The last light from the last flare went. I don't know when or if anybody has been as glad to see stars as we were at that moment.

The Afghans were moving surefootedly and swiftly down the mountainside. Mike and I were half stumbling, half tumbling. We were now having a hell of a time keeping up. Mirwaz breathlessly explained that we were now in a desperate race against time and a probable Soviet reaction force circling around the mountain. Such a force would be hoping to catch us coming off the mountainside.

Mike and I fumbled, stumbled, and tumbled more quickly. We resembled human pinballs, bouncing off first one big rock and then another, headed down. As we all reached the base of the mountain, we could hear the roar and rumble of vehicles coming fast along the dirt road we were crossing. We sped across the road, then sprinted harder into the darkness beyond and wound up diving into a deep ditch at the edge of a rice paddy.

The lead vehicles of the reaction force came racing along the road, spraying the base of the mountain with heavy machine gun and 20-millimeter cannon fire.

"They'll never leave their vehicles," our leader said. That was the book on the Soviets and their Afghan allies, the few they had left willing to fight anymore in the countryside. They were reluctant to leave their forts, base camps, and other ground encampments. When they did, they generally refused to get out of their fighting machines (such as tanks, personnel carriers, and jeeps). The Soviet troops from purely airborne divisions were said to be an exception, and Afghan rebels were most wary of them. But Yassini and his second were willing to gamble that these were not Soviet paratroop units with which we'd been engaged.

As soon as the lead vehicles passed ahead of us, we were out of the ditch and fleeing farther into the darkness.

We waded a short ways through rice paddy muck. Then we were

up on the slick, narrow dikes that crisscross such paddies. The Afghans, who had climbed up and down the mountain like goats, were now speeding along these dikes like cats. How they could run that hard, that fast, on such thin, slippery, rounded surfaces was a marvel. Mike and I couldn't. We were slipping and sliding, falling and crawling between dashes. We jettisoned some of our equipment but were still farther behind than our fears wanted us to be. We finally began to get the hang of it, this running over and across the dikes, and were beginning to catch up a little when, wham, I slipped at top speed. Among other things, I busted my balls, hard, against the dike. That doubled me over in pain and I thought I might faint. Mirwaz half picked me up, half made me get up. "Must keep running," he said with heavy breath. "Must keep running."

I wanted to throw up, but forced myself not to, forced myself to block out the pain and kept silently repeating to myself, "Get up, stay up, don't quit, keep moving, keep running, don't give up." I had a bad case of the staggers and a worse case of the stone-aches.

But fear can be an amazing motivator. If it disintegrates into panic, fear can be debilitating, and in cases such as this, even a killer. But up to a point somewhere before panic, fear can motivate as few, if any, other things can. This lesson I had learned other times, other places along life's way. This scary night, and especially the run through the rice paddy, was a potent refresher course.

Run until you drop—then walk. That was the Afghans' way. We came out of the rice paddy into an opium field, where the running and walking was easier, to say the least. We got to a fairly good dirt road and soon came upon a house. There was an old school bus in the side yard. Yassini and two of his men bounded up to the front door of the house as if they owned the place, pounded on it a couple of times, then kicked it in. A couple of small screams and some hollering followed. Our second-in-command came out of the door holding the man of the house by the nape of the neck and the seat of the pants, pushing him ahead. With Yassini right behind, they went to the school bus. The man tried to resist getting in, but they popped him a couple of punches to the head and he got in. They were in no mood to argue or to tarry. This was not a pretty picture, this little vignette, a reminder that war is not fair. It is indeed hell, in ways large and small, and the weakest—those least able to defend themselves—usually suffer most. And so it was here.

We were all motioned aboard the bus, as the terrified driver's women, children, and what appeared to be grandparents looked on in even more terror from the porch.

The driver was told to move the bus rapidly but not pell-mell out of the yard and down the road, and to keep his lights off. After those commands, there was silence. Except for the low clanking and grinding sounds of the worn-out bus, and the sound of a small caged bird. Little birds in little cages are a favorite of Afghans. I was told later they are especially popular with bus and truck drivers of all kinds in the country. This one was up, off to one side of our bus's steering wheel. He chirped and sang as if to say, "What's happening?"

Our sentiments exactly. Neither Mike nor I had any idea what was going on or where we were going. We were relieved to be riding. We felt awful about what had just happened, but I can't lie and say we were anything but happy to be off our feet, for however long it might be. For one thing, my nuts still ached. For another, this was the first chance we'd had in a long while to swig some water.

Yassini obviously wanted to put as much distance as possible as quickly as possible between us and any efforts by the Soviets to follow us from the mountain or to find us at all.

He wanted the bus to go fast, but not too fast, because he didn't want to send up any telltale cloud of dust from the dirt road.

The Afghans were all alert and peering into the night through the bus windows for any signs of potential trouble from any direction. They also scanned the sky for any helicopter or fixed-wing aircraft lights. Luckily for us, all they saw was stars.

The bus driver was told to stop just short of where the small dirt road T-junctioned into a larger one. We were told to get off quickly and take cover in a ditch. As we were disembarking, our second-in-command put the cold steel of the muzzle of his AK-47 flush against the bus driver's chin. His finger was on the trigger. The driver was told that if he, or any member of his family, ever said a word about what they had seen and heard, they would all die. The driver gulped and said the equivalent of "Yes, sir." There was a long silence as the man with the gun stared hard into the driver's eyes. Then there was the sound of the gun being uncocked. And we heard the caged bird sing.

There was a large culvert under the main road. We squirmed through it to the other side of the road, and began sloshing through the rice field beyond.

outtake

Kids, Don't Try This at Home

MAKE NO MISTAKE. CHEWING TOBACCO IS AN ART.

There is always an art to doing anything your wife and your mother would sooner shoot you than let you do.

Chewing tobacco has its disadvantages. It is linked to some particularly nasty and disfiguring cancers. No woman with any sense will kiss you—afterward. No woman, period, will kiss you *during*. Chewing makes a mess, and it can louse up your professional life. I know of a U.S. Army field-grade officer who didn't get an important command because his superiors didn't approve of his chewing.

Network anchors are not allowed to chew. And, for the record, I don't. Never have. For one thing, I can only barely stand the taste or the way it makes my cheek puff out like one half of Dizzy Gillespie. But I base that remark purely on indirect experience, mind you. I wouldn't know personally.

But (I'm told) chewing has its advantages, too. One advantage is that it is easy to do. Just open a package (Red Man and Beechnut are what real cowboys and oil-field hands chew). Dip into the pack with your thumb and two lead fingers, pull out a glomp (that's the terminology for a precise measure, something between a fifth and a sixth of the whole pack), open your mouth wide, stuff it in, and close your lips *fast*. Chomp down on it and then begin shifting it all to one side of your mouth. *DO NOT SWALLOW*. Swallowing this stuff can be injurious to your health. Like instantly. *DO NOT SWALLOW* the chewing tobacco now or ever. Chewing tobacco is made to spit, not swallow.

One exception is when you have a tapeworm. If you have a tapeworm, and after you are an experienced tobacco chewer, you may want to swallow once—just a little. I'm told it will kill that sucker within half a day.

But otherwise, forget swallowing, unless you are suicidal or want to learn firsthand how a stomach pump works.

Anyway, once you get the tobacco in your mouth, have it all worked over to one side, and are chewing nice and easy: Spit. Spit early and often. Small missiles, no spraying. Practice can prevent tiny dribbles from edging down one corner of your mouth or another. Sometimes you may actually want to dribble for effect, but it is not recommended in the presence of clergy.

Among other advantages are these:

- You can blind a snake by squirting a jet of tobacco juice between his eyes.
- Tobacco juice makes all knots, especially those tied with fishing line, cinch up tighter.
- Spitting keeps the pitcher's mound from getting uncomfortably dry and dusty.
- It's great for punctuating colorful speech (watch Strother Martin in *Butch Cassidy*).
- Unlike smoking, chewing runs little risk of setting the barn on fire.
- And when you're trying to outpace the bad guys, and your horse is running fast as she can but the bad guys are still gaining on you, if you lean forward and spit a little tobacco juice in her ear . . . she'll run a *little* bit faster.

THREE

Afghanistan: A Bridge Too Far

OUR DESTINATION TURNED OUT TO BE A SMALL ANCIENT MOSQUE AT the farthest corner of the rice paddy. We crouched just across from it while Yassini whistled some signals. There were signal whistles back. We stood up and went into an animal shed at the rear of the mosque. A man came out of the shadows. Whether or not this man was clergy, a mullah or some other Muslim cleric, was unclear, but I thought he worked in an official capacity at the mosque. Mirwaz wouldn't give a straight answer when asked. Which alerted me that I shouldn't ask any more. The man of the mosque took us through a door into a fair-sized room. Inside, in the dark, he and our leaders had a whispered conference.

Mike and I were near collapse from a combination of exhaustion, tension, and fear, a kind of combined delayed reaction to events of the past couple of days and especially this night.

But even the Afghans were showing some signs of being tired and, besides, they had to be ready to fight and run again, perhaps for a long time, if anything untoward happened.

They began bedding down on the straw-covered dirt floor. So did we. The straw was old, damp, and musty with the odor of animals. But we wouldn't have any trouble sleeping. Or so we thought. No sooner had we settled into fetal positions and dozed off than there were commotions and harsh words among the Afghans. You didn't have to know the language to know they were cursing. Mike clicked on his tiny camera flashlight with the low light intensity red lens. The Afghans were all standing, dusting themselves off vigorously. And then we felt them, Mike and I: creepy-crawly things on our clothing. As we beat them off and away, Mirwaz tried to tell us what they were. But he couldn't find the English word. He said something in Pushto and held a thumb and forefinger about an inch and a half apart, to indicate size.

Suddenly, Mike exclaimed, "Scorpions! Gawddam scorpions!" You talk about shouting fire in a crowded theater. We nearly trampled two Afghans getting out the door.

As the group reassembled out under the shed, Yassini and his second shushed everybody as we all continued running our hands over ourselves to make sure all scorpions were off, and stomping on the few that had been carried out with us. But make no mistake, Yassini was not pleased. His second went for the Man of the Mosque. And I thought for a moment, "Uh-oh—we're about to see a replay of the boogie he did with the bus driver at the farmhouse." But it didn't happen. There were urgent whispers between the two, with Yassini joining at the end, indicating that the Man of the Mosque was being told off, but there was no rough stuff.

Finally, everybody just began smiling and chuckling, Afghans and Westerners alike.

We all began to lie down again in the dark, this time outside under the shed. About the scorpions, the consensus seemed to be: to hell with them.

After all we had been through, we were beginning to feel lucky enough to be invincible, and tired enough not to give a scorpion's arse.

I dropped into a deep and dreamless sleep. (There were no more scorpion attacks. Apparently the mosque scorpions slept only indoors in the straw.) I was awakened once by the widespread, rhythmic snoring of the Afghans. They were honking like a flight of geese. The thought crossed my mind, "Now wouldn't it be something if, after all this, we were discovered and overrun by enemy soldiers because they heard our snoring!" The thought faded quickly as I dozed back off.

The sleep was short. Just past sunup we were urged to prepare to move out. Mike and I had a lovely breakfast of the last squeeze from my tube of peanut butter and my last can of little Vienna sausages. We chugalugged some water to wash it down, all the way down, and were gone.

Mirwaz explained that we were headed for yet another group of distant mountains. Our one unit of Afghans would be splitting into three, each headed in different directions, to make it more difficult to trace or trail us.

Mirwaz, Yassini, two other Afghans, Mike, and I were grouped together and headed off for the mountains.

The trek took a day. The last of it was a steep climb through a narrow pass, with armed Afghan lookouts posted on the heights. We arrived at what turned out to be a major command post, the main camp of a large, spread-out guerrilla force, of which Yassini was a part.

The heart of the command post was a large cave that ran deep into the side of the mountain. We were given some tea, bread, and rice, and warm water in which to soak our feet.

The post commander then produced a pipe, an elaborate hookah. He looked at me, smiled, and with translation said, "I understand you like to smoke." He was offering a friendly opium smoke on his water pipe.

I quickly stammered something like, "Thank you profusely, kind sir, but I only smoke cigars these days, and then only occasionally, every other war-moon or so. But I sure appreciate your offering. No offense, I hope."

Whether our Afghan hosts ever smoked opium themselves, or offered it only because they knew Westerners bought so much of the stuff, I don't know. And will never.

I changed the subject, the pipe disappeared, and we began looking over the Afghans' store of weapons around the command post. The collection was pitiful. They had a few true relics, candidates for museums. A Gatling gun. Some old Enfield rifles. They also had some more modern, Rube Goldberg–style pieces: a 72-millimeter Pakistani-made field cannon, for example, for which they had only twenty rounds. And one Chinese mortar. For this, there was no ammunition. (Which explained why they hadn't mortared the Jalalabad airfield to which we had crawled so close.)

Mostly what they had were Kalashnikovs, Russian-made rapid-fire hand weapons that are the small gun of choice for guerrilla armies the world over. It's the choice because it is a combination of dependability and simplicity.

America's M-16, standard for all U.S. troops, may be better—when it works and when you know how to work it. But the M-16 tends to jam in sand or mud, and if it is not cleaned regularly. It also is comparatively complicated to assemble and disassemble. Another consideration is that Kalashnikov ammunition tends to be more widely available in the Third World. Naturally, in Afghanistan Kalashnikovs themselves were in great supply, since they were the Soviet army's standard issue.

But to the Afghans, their Kalashnikovs were second in importance as weapons. The best weapon of those opposing the Russian invasion was a belief in a cause. The resistance fighters were consumed with expelling the Soviets, as their forebears in the nineteenth and early twentieth centuries had been consumed with repulsing the British. For them, this was both a deeply patriotic fight to the death for home and hearth—and a holy war, a jihad. Their faith in Islam was complete, and so was their confidence in themselves and the rightness of their struggle.

Belief in "Right makes might" may have been fading in other parts of the world. In Afghanistan, it was alive and well, and beating the Soviets. That was the Afghans' view, at least.

They were pleading for American weapons. At this time, in 1980, they were getting none. And it would be a long time before they got any to speak of. This was because first President Carter, then President Reagan, were convinced by the CIA, plus the State and Defense Departments, that:

- the Afghans were destined to lose, the "mighty" Soviet army sure to make quick work of them;
- relations with the Soviet Union were of prime consideration, and must not be risked by our getting involved in their war; and
- there was little to be gained and perhaps much to be lost in helping deeply religious Islamic forces defeat the secular regime installed by Soviet Communists. There was a belief among American so-called experts that Iran might take over all or some of Afghanistan if resistance forces prevailed over the Soviets. Their view was that it was better to have all of Af-

ghanistan controlled by the Soviets than to have any of it run
by Iran.

I thought that was a questionable view—overly simplistic, for
starters. There were other possibilities, including an independent
Afghanistan. But it was a key view in high levels of the U.S. government for a short while at the end of President Carter's term and for
a long while at the beginning of the Reagan years.

Even more important, however, was the view that our diplomatic
business with Moscow was paramount—the idea that nothing else
much mattered in what some called "the geopolitical context." This
theory was brought to dominance during the presidency of Richard
Nixon. Under this theory, for example, Vietnam didn't matter
much. Oh, certainly better to win there than to lose, but winning
there was not all-important. Some subscribers to this theory in the
upper reaches of the Nixon administration even referred to Vietnam privately as a "dustbin," a sideshow to the main arena: U.S.-
Soviet relations. Of course the young Americans fighting and dying
in the hell that was Vietnam were not told that. They and the American public were repeatedly told that the war in Vietnam remained
absolutely necessary "to stop communism." But behind the scenes,
secret at the time, cynicism and what were too glibly called
"geopolitical realities" ruled. John Kennedy and Lyndon Johnson
may have been wrong, but they really believed in the importance of
the Vietnam War. Kennedy, I think the record demonstrates, believed at least as strongly as Johnson. This, despite what some
Kennedy-inclined historical revisionists now seek to have us think.
Many Republicans, such as Barry Goldwater, believed victory in
Vietnam was important. Richard Nixon never believed, not in the
late 1960s and early '70s. Whatever one thinks of that, it was wrong
of Nixon not to level with the American people about what he truly
thought. If, as I am convinced, he did not really believe Vietnam
worth the cost—in prestige, world strategy, U.S. treasure and
lives—he should have said so, and acted accordingly, before so
many more lives were lost. Compared with his grand plans for dealing with the Soviet Union, he cared much less about a victory in
Vietnam. (And the U.S. Congress, as Nixon later argued, cared
even less than he did.) Nixon's "Moscow First, and Just About
Only" strategy would permeate top echelons of the U.S. government for years to come. Partly this was because so many of his pro-
tégés became so influential in later presidential administrations,
especially Reagan's. And so it was that President Reagan stuck with

an "Afghanistan doesn't matter" policy for so long.

Yassini, that wily mountain cat of a real combat leader, had a wholly different idea of "geopolitical context." He hadn't been to Duke or Harvard, and nobody called him "Mr. President" or "Mr. Secretary" but he, too, knew his history and thought a lot about strategy.

Outside that big cave, in the late winter and early spring of 1980, he told me that if America helped defeat the Soviets and communism on the battlefields of Afghanistan, then America would win the Cold War. If the United States did not aid the Afghans, he theorized, then the Cold War would continue indefinitely, and the Soviets might eventually win it.

"Your hands were burned in Vietnam," he said, "but if you don't agree to help us, if you don't ally with us, then all of you, your whole body, will be burned eventually. Because there is no one in the world who can and will really fight and resist as ferociously and well as we Afghans."

I told him that even if that was true, no American mother wanted to send her son or daughter to Afghanistan. Yassini shot back: "We don't need anybody's soldiers here to help us. What we need, all we need, are American weapons. We can do all the fighting ourselves." His eyes fairly burned with passion now.

Some of the historical and political references of my Afghan companions are polished and clarified here for the reader's benefit, and some of what they said at the time reflected my input as I tried to identify any vague reference. But I haven't altered an iota of the breadth or sophistication of their knowledge of the world scene.

"If we don't survive, if we don't win, if you allow this situation to continue, if you allow the Russians to hammer us down, then there is no place in the world that the Russians will not have the courage to go," Yassini said. He believed a Soviet victory in Afghanistan would mean a second wind for the Soviet Union and communism. They would take control of vast new territories and new resources, and they would take on new confidence. The Soviet military and Communist party rule would both be enormously strengthened by victory in Afghanistan, he said; increasing difficulties with the 70 million Soviets of Islamic heritage inside the southern rim of the Soviet Union and ruled by Moscow would diminish. Spurred on by a victory in Afghanistan, Moscow could contain and perhaps even put down Islamic dissatisfaction.

But Yassini's "geopolitics" reached even farther. He said that Soviet influence, already strong in India, would spread rapidly throughout the Indian subcontinent. Pakistan, a U.S. ally, might fold. Russians would achieve the warm-water ports their empire-driven plans had historically sought, all the way back to the days of the tsars. Soviet victory in Afghanistan, Yassini said, would also put new pressure on Iran, with new opportunities for Russians to get the Iranian oil they coveted. And there would be new pressure on China to reverse course again and return to an alliance with Soviet communism, as in the early days of Stalin and Mao. China, it was pointed out, remained volatile under its Communist dictatorship, and could still go in any of a number of directions. What happened in Afghanistan might be more important in influencing the future course of China than we could know, Yassini said.

"Look at the map," he urged. "See how Afghanistan opens possibilities for warm-water ports. See how part of eastern Afghanistan juts into western China, and know that the Russians want to put big new air and other military bases in there. And see how Afghanistan would help the Russians develop a wider 'pincer,' a territorial half-circle around China."

One of the other command-post leaders came back to the subject of dissent and dissatisfaction welling up against hard-line, old-style communism within the Soviet Union itself. "Give a victory here to Moscow's ruling Communist party and bureaucracy, and to the Russian military, and their hold over their own people will be mightily strengthened."

Another Afghan chimed in. What he said was along the lines of this: "America after Vietnam and after the Iranian hostage debacle is seen by much of the world now, and perhaps even sees itself, as having gone soft and being in retreat. And throughout Islam, because of the Iranian hostage trouble, America-haters are exploiting all kinds of doubts, questions, and fears, including the most infectious propaganda that says America hates Islam and Islamic people. You help us win, you become allies with us here in our triumph—and we will triumph—then you can go a long way toward reversing the Vietnam syndrome and the worst vestiges of the hostage experience."

This is the gist of what these Afghans were saying. Others throughout history had been undone because they underestimated the Afghans as fighters. It now seemed to me an equally bad risk to underestimate their political savvy.

Sure, some of this at least was spinning their own propaganda for their own purposes. And yes, some or all of it may have been, may be, wrong. Some of it even half-baked and vastly oversimplified.

But it did not strike me then and does not now as any less reasonable than what the Nixons, Kissingers, Carters, Reagans, Caseys, and Bushes of the elite and pretentious U.S. foreign policy establishment had been and were talking. These Afghans were at least dealing on the basis of firsthand, on-the-ground information and thought. They were outside a big cave, not inside any ivory tower.

Hindsight shows them to have been more right than wrong in what they thought, and their strategic understanding of the "geopolitical context" equaled that of the big boys in Foggy Bottom, with all of their educational pedigrees and pretensions. For my money, the Afghans' understanding was better. At the time, however, without the benefit of hindsight, I wasn't totally convinced.

But I *was* convinced that I didn't want to spend any more time around the Big Cave. It and the compound outside of it, where most of the Afghan weapons were kept, were too inviting a bombing target. While the Afghans hoped the site was secret and concealed well enough to avoid discovery and attack, they were worried, too. Shifts of special lookouts concentrated on nothing but the sky, while regular guards watched the ground passes and other approaches. Also, before we had gone to the mountain firefight, Yassini and company had worked out some prearranged rendezvous times and places with other Afghans who had set out as escorts for Eden Naby and Andy Lack. We needed to move and hook up again with them.

Before leaving, we went to a high vantage point from which we could see the confluence of the Kabul and Kunar rivers. The two rivers stretched below us, and beyond was the Kunar Valley. While we stood there, a squad of Russian bombers pounded a village in the far distance. We caught glimpses of the bombers and heard the low rumble of the bombs. And my mind went back to a time in Vietnam when, on patrol with a U.S. unit, we were on a mountainside as B-52s attacked the valley just below. Nobody in our unit had any idea it was coming.

B-52s flew only long distances, from bases in Okinawa and in Thailand. They were dispatched only by the highest of combined political and military brass. U.S. ground combat units, and especially small local sector patrols such as the one we were with, often never knew when or if B-52 raids were coming.

It was cloudy that day in Vietnam. Our patrol saw nothing, heard nothing, until suddenly the ground under our feet began to shake and sway. We were startled and confused and scared. Was it an earthquake? What in the hell was this? There was this sound like thunder rolling, and the ground of the valley began to look like an erupting volcano. Then and only then did we realize what we were experiencing. Carpet bombing! We and the troops with us were awestruck—and terrified. All of the B-52 bombs hit in the valley, none on the nearby mountainside where we were. Soon there was only a moonscape of craters in the section of the valley hit. We were left shaken and wondering. We could only imagine what it might have been like to have been down in the valley itself.

The Russians had no B-52s. Their strategic air command, their long-range bombing corps, and the big bombers they had inside the Soviet Union, designed to be in the B-52 class, paled by comparison.

In Afghanistan, the Soviets did try some carpet bombing in the long course of the war. But it was not the same. Not because they didn't want it to be the same, but rather because their equipment, training, and know-how for strategic high-altitude fixed-wing aircraft bombardment were nowhere near that of the U.S. Strategic Air Command.

The bombing of that village in the far distance of the Kunar Valley this day was on a far smaller scale. But it rained down death and destruction, and the echoes of my memory.

As we walked back to the Big Cave and prepared to leave, our Afghan hosts were asked about a leader we had heard might be the most effective, most ferocious of all the Afghan large-command leaders currently involved in the fighting. We had heard his name bandied about back in Peshawar, and heard it again in our travels around Afghanistan, around the campfires, and back in the ranks.

The name was Eunice Hollis. An unusual name, to put it mildly, for an Afghan. His *real* name was more authentically Afghan: Younas Khalis. But it took me a long time to think of him as anything but Eunice Hollis.

He was becoming a hard-fighting legend among the Afghans we had been moving with. And some knowledgeable diplomats and defense experts (in Washington, London, and other places we had checked in researching our trip) mentioned him in passing as an Afghan leader they had heard was actually fighting inside his country—rather than just talking and bickering outside in Peshawar—and that he might even be fighting the Russians effectively over a wide area.

I was, of course, intrigued and interested. But we had been reluctant to bring up his name earlier with any of our lead hosts, fearing that we might offend, given all of the rivalries and jealousies among the many, varied Afghan resistance factions. Lack of unity has been a historic weakness of the Afghans. Mostly they have long been able to achieve even a semblance of unity only on matters of religion and when repelling invaders. And so it was now.

But we had heard Younas Khalis's name mentioned in the Big Cave complex, so I gambled and brought it up.

Judging the response was difficult. Our hosts confirmed that Khalis was fighting to the north of where we were, and that, to hear them tell it, he was having many victories. Our hosts agreed to send a runner to contact Khalis's outfit while we rejoined the rest of our reporting team. (Recall what communications conditions they and we were operating under. No radios, no telephone, no telegraph. Nothing. Word of mouth and runners. That was it.)

Yassini stayed at the Big Cave. One of his lieutenants, a couple of gunmen, and Mirwaz took us on a journey to the river's edge, right down near where the Kabul and the Kunar met.

It was a slow, circuitous trip, walking, sleeping, and walking again. We took the long way with several diversions, apparently out of concern that we Westerners might be beginning to attract attention, with plenty of potential for word to be spread. Word spreading could be injurious to our health.

When we reached our destination by the riverside, we had our rendezvous with Eden Naby and Andy Lack. Our spot was back in the trees a short distance from the rivers. The water's rushing took me back to a place in western New York where I often fly-fish for trout. And the sound reminded me, too, of a spot close to where Jeannie was born, where Pin Oak Creek meets the Colorado River in Texas—a place where I taught Danjack to cast live bait for catfish, and where Robin and I sometimes walked and talked.

I admit I was a little homesick. We were eight days into Afghanistan by now, the days and nights were dragging, and this trip was getting long. I gave myself a pep talk. "What were you expecting? Disney World, maybe? Suck it up, you're doing what you came to do—and this *is* one helluva story."

That night a runner returned from Younas Khalis. (The runners went in relays, carrying messages as the Pony Express carried mail.) Khalis would see us.

We made our plans: We were to cross the Kabul River this night. At the confluence of the Kunar and the Kabul, the Kabul was the wider, and especially deep and swift at our designated crossing. That's one reason we chose it. It was considered an unlikely point for anyone to try to cross, so no one would be looking for us, although the opposite banks of both rivers were patrolled regularly by the enemy. We must cross at the roughest, least suspect, and least watched place.

We and our equipment would be ferried across with flotation aids. Very original and imaginative flotation aids. We would cling to the inflated bellies of dead animals—cows and water buffalo. These would not only help to get us and our equipment across, they would hide us. Dead animals were common in the river now, and floated by from time to time—not constantly, because even living animals were not plentiful, but from time to time. We could float behind these carcasses and even dive under them if we were seen or fired on. The Afghan gunners would go first; they would scout the far bank and establish a kind of beachhead.

At the first mention of the flotation aids, Andy Lack looked at me as if to say, "Oh, great, I don't believe what I'm hearing." Eden Naby immediately started frowning. I wasn't exactly breaking out in smiles myself.

"If, *if* we make it to the other side," I asked, "realistically, how long in and how long out?"

Another week or ten days, minimum, came the answer. Danger factor?

"More dangerous than anything you have done so far" was the answer, with a reminder that we were very near Jalalabad, which now had one of the country's largest concentrations of Soviet troops, including an exceptionally large concentration of planes and helicopters. Given our recent tour of runway endings, up close and personal, nobody had to elaborate on that last point.

Plus, the area through which we would be traveling was more populous—still rural, generally, but with many more people than we'd seen so far. The control of this area and these people by the guerrilla forces figured to be somewhat less, and the loyalty to the cause of the resistance on the part of all or most of the inhabitants also figured to be less than in the areas where we'd been.

That was what lay between us and Younas Khalis.

A snap decision would be easy: Eunice Hollis, baby, we love you, but no thanks. Maybe next time.

But we didn't want to make a snap judgment, Andy and I. We consulted awhile with Eden Naby. Too dangerous, she opined, way too dangerous. She did not take this assignment to get killed or to get us killed. She was thoughtful about it, good-hearted and understanding. She understood why we were tempted. But clear thinker and straight talker that she was, she wanted us to understand. She had told her husband she would be back in Peshawar within thirteen days. We were now entering our ninth day inside Afghanistan. It would take two, possibly three days to make our way out now—if we were lucky and God continued to smile on us. We should make our own decision, and should not be overly influenced by her, and she would understand if we went on. But she was going back to Peshawar.

It was not a question of courage. She had already displayed more courage in a few days than most people exhibit in a lifetime. She had nothing to prove to us or to herself.

Each of us in our small band from CBS News could say the same about ourselves. And did.

Still, there was the mighty pull of the story, of the opportunity and challenge for adventure, and of the unknown.

Younas Khalis was up there, out there, a great character, a major player, in a big story at a decisive time. We were already convinced that if the Soviets didn't finish off the Afghan resistance by the following winter, it was going to be a long, long war. And we were already convinced that the Soviets couldn't make short work of the resistance. Indeed, from what we had seen and felt, we already figured that Moscow and Washington and all the other capitals would be wrong about the Soviets' winning. This is not hindsight; this is exactly what we thought and said to one another at the time.

I have been wrong on judgments about many stories, many times. This would not be one of those times, and everything in me that night on the riverbank shouted it.

And everything in me said to keep going, to go to Younas Khalis. Hell, I had smelled dead cows before. You can't grow up in Texas and not become accustomed to the stench of dead cows. And we had come this far without a scratch, hadn't we? Well, almost: true, my testicles still hurt some and we had our odd scratches and bruises, but nothing serious. We were on a roll. We were hot. We were out front, exclusive on what might be one of the best stories of our time. This is what a reporter dreams of, works for. This is why you paid the price all those years, standing in the rain with a microphone in your hand, covering dull city hall zoning hearings and the cop shop overnight. This is why you sold radio time, "a dollar a holler," to stay on the staff in Huntsville. This is why you took all that bull from newspaper city editors, nightshift wire-service supervisors, station managers and sales directors. This is why you left a young wife home with your babies when you knew what a wrench it was. It was all to get to a place such as this, at a moment such as this. Frontline, cutting edge, in the right place at the right time on a world-class story.

I'd had such times and places before. Enough to recognize the moment—the opportunity and the challenge—when it came again, here and now.

But there were other people involved, other people for whom I was responsible. And there were other thoughts.

I did not want it on my conscience that I had gotten anyone else killed or seriously wounded. Never had and didn't want to start now. Andy and Mike and Peter had been brave and wonderful. They would follow me till hell froze over and then try to help cut through the ice. They would go, any and all of them. And they would not let me go beyond the rivers alone. And because of that I had a responsibility to them, and to those who loved them, waiting back home. I also had my own very special responsibilities to Jeannie and to Robin and to Danjack; to my brother, Don, and sister, Patricia. My mother and father were long in their graves, but I often heard my mother's voice gently saying, "Now don't be foolish, Danny. Be brave, do good, have fun—but don't be foolish." I was also acutely aware that I had no desire to die on Afghanistan's plains. Like everyone else, I wanted to live a long, full life. This, too, weighed heavily in my thinking.

We were out of food—no more peanut butter, no more Vienna sausages. We were low on water-purification tablets. We also had only a limited amount of film and audiotape left. Two of us had dysentery, one of us bad and getting worse. Nobody was complaining, and there was no doubt we could go on. But there also was no doubt that if we went on, deeper into the unknown, things could get worse. And hairier and dicier. And the chances of our coming back, chancier.

In addition, there was this to consider: Journalistically, I had lived by the dictum "No story is worth a damn unless you can get it out." Experience also had taught me that when you have a story, a good story, and you know you have it, it's usually best not to try to hold it, not to try to push it an extra day or week hoping to improve it. Experience is knowing when you have it, knowing when you have enough, and going on and filing the story. Usually the upside potential for what you may gain is not worth the downside risk of what you may lose.

Experience had also taught that most times when journalists were killed or maimed, it was by pushing just a tad too far. All of this is a kind of journalistic version of an old card player's adage,

"You got to know when to hold 'em, know when to fold 'em; know when to run 'em and when to walk away." (And, yes, the words of Houstonian Kenny Rogers's song based on that adage flipped through my mind as Andy and I walked and talked.)

This was the proverbial tough call and we were torn.

"Ever read Cornelius Ryan?" I asked. No, he said. "Well, I was thinking, he wrote a book about World War Two, about just after D-Day, entitled *A Bridge Too Far.*"

"And?" said he.

"Nothing," I replied. "Except the thought nags at me that *this,* this whole idea, just may be 'a bridge too far.' "

"Not sure I know exactly what that means," Andy smiled. "But if it means that maybe the better part of wisdom and valor is to take a pass, I can say amen to that."

We went back and put it to a vote, just among our CBS team. The vote was four to one against. Nobody felt especially good about it. But we had decided. And we had decided the right way, under the special circumstances. We had decided thoughtfully and democratically.

After the decision, we quietly began moving about. The way back out of Afghanistan, back across The Territories and back to Peshawar, didn't figure to be any cakewalk. We had to get ourselves up for it, steel ourselves, and remind ourselves not to let our guard down, to remain watchful and alert. We did so in silence. For a long time second thoughts about whether we were doing the right thing, whether we had made the right decision about not going in deeper, were at the front of all of our minds.

Mirwaz finally broke the silence. He had no doubt that we had made the right decision, and said the other Afghans thought so, too. He would have gone, but he wouldn't have been happy about it, he said.

I believed he was saying what he really thought. Whether he was or not, he made me feel better.

We were not leaving the country via the same route we came in. As we neared the border with The Territories, Mirwaz bought me a large blue and white turban cloth. We had fun winding it around and fitting it over my head. It wound up being one of those high, heavy turban-hats favored in the paintings by colonials of Afghans and other natives of the Near and Middle East.

We had a couple of last stand ups to do on camera for later use in our televised reports, and I suggested to Andy that it might be fun, might be interesting and different for me to do one of them in the turban. Fortunately, he nixed it. Wouldn't hear of it, and suggested that I get the damned thing off pretty quickly. He was afraid I would draw too much attention to us there, and afraid I would make an ass of myself, a laughingstock if I appeared on camera in such a rig.

He was right, of course. It was yet another of my damfool ideas. Part of any producer's job is to save his or her correspondent from the correspondent's own self. Being a correspondent—never mind an anchor—just being a television correspondent is an incredibly vain, self-centered, and egocentric line of work. (I know those three words all mean about the same thing, but I'm trying to make a point here.) This holds true even, sometimes especially, with the best among us. Even with those who have proven they are least susceptible to egocentricity—Bob Schieffer, Linda Ellerbee, John Cochran, and Tom Jarrell, to name four—even among them, the pull is strong and they sometimes succumb. That's why God made producers.

I saw Andy's point immediately, was embarrassed (TV correspondents do not embarrass easily), and sheepishly took the thing off. Mirwaz was disappointed. Andy was grumpy.

We wrote and shot the last of our "in-Afghanistan" stand ups, a variety of on-camera opens, closes, and bridges to provide for any need we might have when we got back and were piecing together our stories in the edit room.

As we began crossing out of Afghanistan back into The Territories, we again found ourselves caught up in the great, unending tide of refugees. Only this time, we were going with the flow rather than against it.

Ten thousand refugees a day were streaming out of Afghanistan at this time, in March of 1980, just three months after the Soviets had invaded. A half million refugees were already registered with the Pakistani government. There would be a million before that summer was over. Before the war ended, possibly as many as ten million. It was part of the Soviets' strategy to create as large a refugee population as possible, as quickly as possible, as a way of winning the war. Displaced persons, split families, and all of the other havoc, chaos, and misery created by large numbers of refugees sap morale and effectiveness from an enemy's fighting forces, and create pressures for surrender from the allies of the enemy—especially those such as Pakistan, who were forced to take in and directly aid the refugees. Many years later, Serbs trained by and allied with the Russians would use the same strategy in their war of aggression in Bosnia.

Six miles inside the Pakistani border, we came upon two refugee camps adjacent to one another. The first was filled with widows and orphans whose husbands and fathers had been massacred in the Afghan village of Kerala. Kerala was the My Lai of the Afghanistan War. That probably should read *"a* My Lai"; although proof is not absolute, there is evidence and testimony that what happened in Kerala happened a number of times over the length of this still underreported war.

Eleven hundred Afghan men reportedly were slaughtered in Kerala just before the Soviets' full, official military invasion. We were told they were massacred for not complying with Russian "reforms." The story was repeated to us over and over by eyewitnesses now in the refugee camp in The Territories. A government information officer confirmed their accounts, and told us the story was well known and had been confirmed by many governments. But, he said, there had been a conspiracy of silence about it.

This, he said, is what he and others had confirmed: Soviet cadres with officials from the Moscow-installed puppet regime in Kabul came into the village with soldiers. They had come to install their own village chief and what they called "discipline and reforms." The village people replied that they believed in their own local Islamic society and government, and that they would not accept the Soviets' communistic, socialistic, atheistic regime. When the villagers refused to accept, the soldiers systematically fired on all of the men, killing well over a thousand on the spot. And then went house to house, killing more.

We moved on to the neighboring camp, where three thousand new refugees had just been settled. New camps were being established throughout the border area daily.

The new camp, too, filled our ears with stories of atrocities. Villages put to the torch. The men rounded up and shot, often before the eyes of their women and children. Villages and towns bombed out. "Bombs on our villages, tanks and mines on the land" was how more than one put it.

Paratrooper and helicopter-borne–troop assaults had begun before the full invasion was announced, and the assaults had intensified since. Airborne attacks were usually by Soviet troops, nearly all Russian, with follow-up occupation and mop-up operations using Russian-led soldiers of the Kabul regime's Afghan army, nearly all of those young conscripts.

This was the picture painted repeatedly to us by refugees and local officials who had interviewed refugees by the thousands. And it matched what we had seen and heard inside Afghanistan, from those still inside, fighting and living the combat.

What we had seen small snatches of while we were inside was a new Russian offensive in the Kunar Valley. The refugee and other interviews now were giving us a more complete picture, helping to piece together the facts of the offensive.

We moved out and began traveling south again, with images of the Kerala massacre dancing nightmarishly through our heads.

Wherever there is war, there are profiteers. In The Territories, where we were now walking, some of them profited from tractors. "Tractor Vultures" roamed the edges of the refugee hordes, offering rides at extortion prices. We hired one. Our way back was a two-day walk through a no-man's-land of ancient tribal territories adjacent to the northwest frontier province of Bajaur in Pakistan. The high Himalayas were to our left and rear, the Hindu Kush to our right rear. The sights and sounds of the refugee thousands streaming day and night out of the mountains like so many rivers of destitute humans were reminiscent of the biblical exodus.

Riding the tractor might save us a day, and it took us off our feet. It was worth any price.

As we scrambled aboard the John Deere machine and it began to pull away, we nearly ran over a man and his wife. She had one small child by the hand and a baby in her arms. They all were emaciated and stumbling from hunger and fatigue. The young father was shaking, holding his head skyward as if in prayer. The young mother was also trembling, and had just fallen to one knee. She got up but appeared on the verge of falling to the other knee. The older child had tears cascading down her cheeks; the baby was screaming.

"Stop!" Andy and I shouted almost in unison. "Stop, dammit!" Our Mad Max of an extortionist-tractor driver paid no attention and put the accelerator down. Andy and Mike jumped on his back and shoulders and made him stop. Mirwaz and I jumped off and hustled back to the family. We offered to let them ride with us. The father hesitated. The mother's head and face were completely covered; she wore the most severe-looking kind of Muslim cloth helmet-mask, with only eye, nose, and mouth holes—resembling a knight's helmet from the Crusades, and similar to the one worn by the woman who was baking bread at the "safe camp" back in Afghanistan. We couldn't see this young woman's expression. But we sensed it. She began trembling even more. She was scared. Until recently she probably had never seen any male outside her blood and married families. Until now, she probably had never seen anyone of European heritage. Mirwaz repeated the offer, softly, gently. I motioned again toward the tractor and put my hands together, as if praying she would accept.

She whispered something to her husband, barely audible against the background of moving masses of refugees and through the cloth of her helmet-mask. Mirwaz told me she said no, she wouldn't go. Said their religion would not allow it, and besides that she was afraid of me, the pale man, and the machine. The thought occurred that she might never have seen a tractor before the day she'd fled her home, or might never have seen any kind of gasoline-powered vehicle before.

The husband told Mirwaz no, they wouldn't go.

The tractor driver was giving Andy and Mike a piece of his mind about being jumped on and stopped. An angry group of men began to encircle the tractor, shouting denunciations and threats. The driver began shouting back and telling Andy and Mike that he wanted all of us and our gear off, *now*—that he was going on without us. Of course he had half of the agreed-upon holdup price of the trip; the other half of the money was to be paid after he took us as far as promised.

I asked Mirwaz to tell the woman that I was Muslim, that there were American Muslims and I was one of them. Mirwaz smiled, said he couldn't talk to the woman—against the mores of her culture—but told the man. The husband told the wife. She looked down. I couldn't see her eyes. But I felt that, though her head had turned down and away, her eyes were toward me. She was looking me over and considering, back there behind her mask.

She whispered one word to her husband, maybe two. Like "Let's go," or "Okay." They came. We hustled them aboard the tractor, taking care not to touch, not even to look at the woman. Everything they owned now, all they had was in a farm tow sack. We boosted that and the older child onto the rear of the tractor. And we told the driver to hit it.

He balked. "More passengers, more money." That son of a bitch. I scurried forward and gave him a crisp hundred green. He glanced at Ben Franklin's likeness on the bill, then turned his attention to the barrel of Mirwaz's Kalashnikov that was now pointed at his chest. He hit the accelerator and we were off.

After about an hour we were delivered to the prearranged place, a staging area for a collection of dilapidated jeeps, vans, and beasts of burden, including camels, all for hire. Once we were all off the tractor, Andy paid the driver the rest of what we owed him. I told Mirwaz to give this despicable wheelman a proper cursing, which Mirwaz gladly did.

The Afghan family who had ridden with us started back for the refugee trail—a little stronger now, perhaps, but we were still worried about them. I asked Mirwaz to offer them another ride if they were continuing in our direction, but they refused. They thanked us profusely, but I could tell the tractor ride had made them nervous— they wanted to be on their way. We gave them a little money. They gathered up their tow sack and were gone.

We immediately struck another deal with one of the jeep owners. None of the vans looked dependable enough to us. So we rode crowded into the ancient jeep like so many clowns in a circus car. We laughed with joy and relief at speeding to freedom and safety with a refreshing wind in our faces.

When we got to the crossroads, a trading village and watering hole, the jeep jitney would go no farther. Mirwaz did some business with one of the locals and we were soon ushered through a beaded curtain into an indoor oasis. In there, sitting cross-legged on cushions, we were served tea and biscuits, served by barefooted women with smiles behind their half-veiled faces, thin bracelets on their ankles, and tiny rings on their toes. The bracelets and rings had little bells. The bells made soft sounds as the women went to and fro with the refreshments.

I reminded Andy, "Don't look." He obeyed, but did look askance at me. We both were thinking that maybe, when we were young men, we had been in this kind of place before, except the other places usually were done in red and had rooms upstairs. We probably were wrong, but that's what we were thinking.

Mirwaz disappeared, then returned to tell us that we soon would be boarding a bus. It was still a long distance to the border between Pakistan and The Territories. There was sometimes a bus that ran to the border, and one would be running today.

When we left the indoor oasis and went to the bus, it was a sight. It was a 1950s-era converted school or tourist bus. Bald tires, no hood, slightly steaming radiator. The inside was already jammed past capacity with women, children, old people, and a couple of goats. The makeshift upper deck was rapidly filling to the railings, too. We climbed the back ladder and muscled our way onto the upper deck.

A man suddenly roared out of an alleyway, firing wildly with Kalashnikovs in both hands. Most of the shots were into the air; a few hit buildings across the street. We ducked down as best we could. The man acted as if he were hopped up on something or crazed, or both.

"So," I thought, *"this* is how it ends." Shot to death by a crazed hophead on top of a lousy bus on a dusty street in a no-name crossroads town in a "Territory" whose name I didn't know and couldn't even pronounce if I did.

Champagne Andy dove down just before I did, and was now underneath me, cursing in every language he knew, including French. Among his other troubles, I must have smelled lovely, not having bathed in well over a week. You get to know each other pretty well on trips such as this. Andy was getting to know me better than he would have liked. On the other hand, I might have smelled somewhat better than some of the other people who were on top of him at that moment.

Fortunately, some Afghan men pounced on the gunman from behind, wrestled him to the ground, and took his weapons. They stabbed him to death on the spot.

"Lovely beginning to our bus trip," mused the laconic Mike Edwards.

Still more people got aboard the bus. The driver refused to leave until the goats were put on the upper deck with us. Just what we needed.

Eventually the bus lumbered on its way. The afternoon was clear and hot. The bus stank like a septic tank and was enveloping us in gasoline and oil fumes while still belching steam from the faulty radiator. The women chattered, the babies squalled, the goats bleated, and Andy bitched. Well, we all did, silently or otherwise. We were headed for the finish line, the worst part of our adventure: the Pakistan border. But we weren't there yet, and given the condition of the bus, there was considerable doubt we would make it—this day, anyway. Mentally, we were rapidly reaching the last-straw stage.

The bus chugged up an ever-narrowing, winding mountain road. It shuddered and swayed around the most dangerous curves, hairpin numbers with scant room for driver error. It was like being on some old rickety amusement-park ride. We could not help but gasp when the top of the bus seemed literally to hang over the high mountain ledges. In those moments all we could see was blue sky and rocks thousands of feet below with an occasional glimpse of the inches between the bus tires and the edge. This was a thrill a minute, and as terrifying as anything we had been through.

As we began the downhill part of the ride, it got worse. Worse because the bus picked up speed, careening even more as the driver negotiated the twists and turns. It was better not to think about the brakes. The bus had some, we knew, because otherwise we already would be dead. But they weren't much and they seemed to be getting worse. Either that, or the driver wasn't using them much. Probably both.

The air was thin and we were getting dizzy. A baby chose this moment to vomit on Andy. We're talking major upchuck here, full and big time. Champagne Andy was covered in baby puke. He took one look and began turning the same olive green he had been the night inside Afghanistan when he fled the Mystery Meat.

"Steady," said Peter O'Connor, "steady, Andy." *Steady,* a very British thing to say. Ed Murrow admiringly quoted Brits as saying it during the London Blitz in World War II.

But Andy shot back a look that could kill. "Steady, my ass," his eyes said—"and another thing, you Brits are starting to get on my nerves; I've had about enough of you and this whole frigging story." Tempers and nerves were fraying fast, nearing the breaking point.

I tried to mop Andy off with the red bandanna from my pocket and the turban cloth, my recent gift, from my pack. Just then the baby crapped all over his mother, who was still cheek by jowl with Andy. I feared the worst. Here's where he blows, I thought. He didn't. Instead, he broke out in that wide, warm smile that is his trademark. The baby obviously was ill, perhaps very ill, losing it from both ends. Clearly much worse off than we were.

After all, we were alive and healthy, would soon be in a hotel shower, and not long after that we would be home. That is, if the damned bus didn't plunge off the mountainside. I asked Mirwaz to hand the mother some antibiotics from my pack, the erythromycin I usually carry.

The bus made it down to a place near Darra, inside Pakistan. We were let off at another refugee camp just outside of town. But this one was different. It was a combined refugee and training camp, populated by Afghans who had settled their families in Pakistan and were now ready to go back home and fight. The spirit was there, but organization and discipline were seriously lacking.

Many in the West believed Afghan resistance fighters had been generally overromanticized. Historically, they had fought among themselves as much as they had fought outside interference. They were thought in Western capitals to lack enough leadership to last long in the face of what was viewed as overwhelming Soviet might.

But the training commander in this camp, a prominent Afghan who had fled his country several years earlier and who called himself Mujahadee, saw it differently.

He told me: "I think no power can stop the general rise-up of the public. Now, when Afghanistan's seventeen million or nineteen million people—children, women, and old people, young people, and all people—they have decided that they will fight until the last moment of life. They will contribute to the struggle. And no power, I think, will be able to stop it. Either the Russian power will destroy all the people of Afghanistan—nobody will be left here—or, by help of God, we shall kick them out."

If I needed any further convincing of the determination of the popular uprising against the Soviets, Mujahadee had just provided it. Not to mention a powerful on-camera interview for our reports. There are sound bites and there are sound bites; this was more of a sound chunk. And we would use it as such. Not just because it was riveting and powerful but even more because it was thoughtful and substantive: meaty, real meat, not just a nibble or an hors d'oeuvre. And mostly because it represented what I was convinced was an emerging truth about this little-reported war: The Afghans would win or die. No other option would be possible.

We walked into Darra, a town we had been to before when we had been making our rounds, trying to find a way into Afghanistan. It was a town of perhaps two or three thousand, a town as old and as famous in this part of Pakistan as Dodge City was in the American West. There was no law west of Darra, no law in any of the area around it, and no law in it. In Darra, the gun and the fastest draw ruled. It was a one-industry town, and guns were that industry. Guns were bought, sold, traded, and fired around the clock. Imported guns and guns manufactured right there. Local craftsmen could rip off copies of practically any small- to medium-sized weapons that weren't technologically advanced. Knockoffs of the Russian Kalashnikov were their specialty. Afghans had turned Darra into a boomtown, selling their homegrown opium for the best available weapons, then going back into Afghanistan to fight.

We hired a car and driver in Darra, plus a marksman to ride shotgun, and we headed for Peshawar. I told the driver we would double the price for him and the gunman if we got to Peshawar safely in half the usual time. We did.

As we burst back into our hotel, we were stared at by the Western journalists and their camp followers who were gathered around the bar. When we got to our rooms upstairs, we were greeted with hoots and hugs by the CBS News crew who had stayed behind.

"Man, are we glad to see *you!*" exclaimed Jan Morgan. "We were about to give up on you. You're on the agreed timeline, but just barely. We've been plenty worried—heard rumors that you had been killed inside—New York has been all over us—Mrs. Naby's husband has been worried sick. He's already gone to the U.S. Consulate to ask for help—may be there now." With that, Eden Naby rushed out to find him.

"See if you can get through to New York by telephone," I said. "I want to let Jean know we're back and okay, and I want to talk to Hewitt. Also, let's check when the next plane's out."

"Already know," said Jan. CBS News to the core. "One leaves for Islamabad in twenty minutes. If we hurry and are lucky, you can make it."

"Let's go," I said. We hauled for the airstrip.

When we got there, it was a zoo. Many more people wanted on the plane than it could carry. We paid off every airport worker we could collar. One finally got us two boarding passes, thanks to our paying the price of the ticket plus two hundred dollars each to two people already on board. Andy and I barely made it aboard before the door closed for takeoff. Just before we stepped on the ramp, Jan handed me a note with scheduled times for connecting flights from Islamabad to Karachi, and from Karachi to London. From London, we might make a Concorde flight for the final leg to New York. He'd try to have CBS News staffers or stringers meet us at each stop to help. Everything would have to break lucky for us, but we might be back in New York this same day, given that the time zones were favorably aligned.

Jan Morgan winked as he handed me the note, gave me a big firm handshake and said, "Hell of a job, mate. Hell of a job." I bounded aboard with Andy and a yellow grapefruit bag marked CBS NEWS—URGENT in big letters, filled with cans of film.

Inside the plane, we were a sight to behold, with smells to match. But we were aboard, we had made it, and the plane was taxiing for takeoff. Soon we were up and away, headed for home.

No hard drinks were served on domestic Pakistani flights. Andy and I helped ourselves to the last of the Wild Turkey from my flask. But for these last shots, we had ice. Ah, ice. We breathed deeply and relaxed for the first time in two weeks.

Everything worked. Word spread quickly through New York headquarters and then to every CBS News bureau worldwide about what we had tried, that we had gotten in and gotten out, had the goods and were headed for the barn—the huge old milk barn that was now the CBS News Broadcast Center on West Fifty-seventh Street in New York.

The appropriate CBS News bureaus, sub-bureaus, and stringers along the route home were given their instructions and told they must not fail. Whatever it took, however it took, do it. And they did. This was CBS News at or near its best, the CBS of yore and lore, the CBS that had invented modern electronic journalism, the CBS News of history, tradition, and big story can-do. It was a thrill and a joy to see it working like a well-oiled machine. It didn't always work this way. Journalism and journalistic organizations tend to be messy. But when it all works well, as it was doing now, it was wonderful. And when CBS News was right, when it was hitting on all cylinders, nobody could do it better.

Andy and I rode the crest back to New York. It was a precious moment and we knew it. How sweet it was.

We made the final connection to the Concorde in London by the thinnest of margins, and only through the smarts and serendipity of Patricia Bernie. Pat was one of CBS's old-school, quiet, behind-the-scenes leaders. In her youth she had worked with all of the great ones, including Murrow, Sevareid, Collingwood, and Cronkite. Later she had tutored me when I was London bureau chief in the 1960s. She was older now and near the twilight of her career. But she was on point this day in London, a city she knew like the back of her hand and in which she had fabulous connections. Our Concorde flight had to be delayed if we were to make it. Delaying a Concorde is not easy. Lots of people said it was impossible. Not for Pat. Somehow, someway, she made it happen.

When our flight arrived in London from Karachi, we were whisked into a Mercedes pulled up alongside the plane, and sped directly to the New York Concorde door. Although it had taken something over twenty-four hours, because we had been flying against the clock, we arrived in New York the same day we had left Peshawar. From the base of the Hindu Kush to the core of the Big Apple, all in the same day. Even the blasé were impressed. We could barely believe it ourselves.

Jeannie was waiting for me at New York's Kennedy Airport when we arrived. She greeted me with a smile as wide as Texas and a great hug and a long, long kiss. She kidded me about my beard and quipped that Andy and I looked "like homeless people."

I wanted to go home to our apartment, of course, but we were hard against deadlines now. Another battle against the clock was just beginning. News deadlines are called that because, like death, they wait for no one and cannot be pushed back, especially not in television. The clock strikes, the camera's red light goes on, and you're on, ready or not.

Jeannie dropped us off at the CBS News complex on Fifty-seventh Street. As we entered the *60 Minutes* area, Don Hewitt and Mike Wallace were waiting with warm congratulations. So was CBS News president Bill Leonard.

We all plunged into planning our work and working our plan. The news never stops. We needed to file for radio immediately and get a television report ready for the next *CBS Evening News,* plus the *CBS Morning News* and the worldwide news syndication feed (now known as Newsnet) for CBS-affiliated stations and other clients. At the same time, we had to be writing and editing for our main piece, the long story that would air Sunday on *60 Minutes.*

Andy and I had changed clothes during one of the longer flights, getting out of the Afghan gear and into bush jackets and jeans. But we still looked ragged and worn, and smelled like garbage. The straggly beards didn't help.

As I walked into my office, my assistant, Susie Shackman, looked this desperate character up and down, smiled, and said, "Welcome back. Now, for you and you alone, today and today only, I'm going to light you a cigar." And she did. Probably just trying to relieve the smell.

Within hours after our first stories aired, there were reports out of Pakistan and Moscow that Soviet radio was broadcasting into Afghanistan and the subcontinent offers of rewards leading to the death or capture of CBS News correspondent Dan Rather. This reportedly was part of an all-out effort by Moscow to deny flatly that the Russians were using gas in Afghanistan. These reports also said the Soviets were mounting a big disinformation campaign, accusing me and our crew of all sorts of ghastly deeds inside the country.

At first I didn't believe the stuff about a reward. But it proved to be true. For a long time after we returned, some Soviet radio broadcasts offered rewards of many thousands of dollars (the exact amounts varied) for my death or capture.

I wasn't angry. I was honored. It was the best compliment they could have given me. And having a price on my head was a small price to pay for the truths we told about Afghanistan.

outtake

Miami Blues

W<small>E SELDOM KNOW THE PRECISE INSTANT WHEN EVERYTHING GOES</small> wrong. A blunder can be weeks, months, even years in the making. What we can pinpoint is the moment we became aware of it, in this case at 6:12 P.M., on Friday, September 11, 1987.

Six minutes of my life disappeared forever that night in Miami, and several years later there is no agreement on what actually happened to them.

For those six minutes, an infinity in television, CBS was off the air, while Pope John Paul II was in Miami on his second trip to the United States, and Steffi Graf and Lori McNeil met in the women's semifinals of the U.S. Open tennis tournament. And there a dilemma was born, of many things, among them the unusual circumstance that CBS had two remote broadcasts under way at the same time—one for sports and one for news. Between the broadcasts, there was no direct contact, no direct phone line, and, at our end, no picture of the tennis match as it unfolded. No one was in command of both broadcasts; they were being produced by two separate divisions under two separate leaderships.

But let me say, right from the start: CBS has been and continues to be staffed at every level by some of the smartest, toughest, most dedicated people I've ever known. That was true on September 11, 1987, and it's true today. At corporate headquarters downtown and in the management offices of the News and the Sports divisions, CBS has always been able to boast of men and women who are quite rightly the envy of the industry: in this case, Howard Stringer, Gene Jankowski, Mark Harrington, and Neal Pilson. I like, respect, and in many cases feel I owe something to each of these people. The trouble is, on September 11, 1987, and the days that followed, none of us had one of our best days.

What may not be clear to the viewer is the chaos that so often takes place behind the scenes under the best of conditions. It is a combination of a frantic Lucy Ricardo trying to keep up with the chocolates as they roll off the assembly line, and a hard night in the control tower at Kennedy Airport. You remind yourself that midair collisions are rare, but based on the number of near-misses you wonder why there aren't more.

To report on this rare papal visit to these shores, CBS News had leased the eleventh floor of the building on Biscayne Boulevard where our CBS bureau was located in Miami. Our local affiliate, WTVJ, had not picked up the match, preferring to provide coverage of the pope's visit. On the eleventh floor, the local broadcast was the only one we could see.

Through the entire day, we believed and had been given every reason to believe CBS would be on the air at 6:30, eastern time, with our first of two broadcasts, as we were scheduled to do. Our second feed would be at 7:00 P.M. At about 6:12, for the first time, we received word from the main facility in New York that the tennis match was tied and might run over, followed by a wrap-up.

I thought the idea was outrageous, given the importance of the timing of this papal visit: "the Cold War pope," the first Polish pope, arriving directly from Rome, landing in Miami with its large Catholic community and its very large Cuban exile community, with the abortion issue growing more and more divisive across the United States.

And CBS was giving its priority to tennis? I couldn't believe it.

And there was one more factor to make us even edgier.

The ratings. Since I had succeeded Cronkite, the *Evening News* had had its share of victories, including over two hundred consecutive weeks ranked at Number One, despite a decline in the network's overall ratings. Finally we were overtaken, but mostly we ran second while the network was more often in and out of third.

By midsummer and all through August, we were coming back. Our ratings began improving. I believe this was mostly because we were producing a stronger newscast, but there were other factors, including the Nielsen Company's new method of measuring the audience. So, in September, for the first time in many months, we were expected to win the week. All we needed was to have a reasonably good Friday. We could not afford to be preempted, or to have a delayed telecast, while viewers flipped to other channels.

I understand that this emphasis on the ratings may seem about as important as toy boats and rubber ducks in the bath. But the News Division had been under heavy pressure about not being first. And more pressure means less money. Less money means fewer bureaus, fewer resources for reporting, and fewer people working for the News Division. We'd just weathered a devastating series of personnel cutbacks, like *Alien* or one of those horror movies where the monster strikes widely, indiscriminately, and fatally; you didn't know who'd be next. Many of us were unsure that the News Division could continue to produce the high-quality programming we were known for. I wrote an article for *The New York Times,* "From Murrow to Mediocrity," warning of the jeopardy that such cuts presented. We wanted no more cuts, and we thought good ratings would provide us with armor.

Now we were in Miami, on the verge of breaking through and winning the week with an important story, and the network was going to let tennis take precedence over the Pope's coming to America?

Even before he'd told me, Tom Bettag, our executive producer, had already called Howard Stringer, the president of CBS News, in New York. Howard said this was the first he'd heard of it. Tom told him that if what we were hearing was true, we were in big trouble. At the least, we needed more time to rearrange the newscast and decide which stories could be cut, and by how much.

When Tom told me, I reviewed the arguments with him: Surely nobody really thought that a semifinal tennis match was the more significant story. Surely no one could justify coming to us eighteen minutes before airtime to tell us to prepare for a shorter newscast, when no one could say how *much* shorter. I didn't think CBS would allow a tennis match that had been dragging on since 3:00 P.M. to blow out the pope's visit. I asked Tom to call Howard again, and I got on the phone with him, too. Howard called Gene Jankowski, the president of the CBS Broadcast Group, at home that Friday evening, then called us again.

I'm sure other conversations buzzed across the network with executives at other levels. In our makeshift studio in Miami, it was unclear where the match was, unclear whether they were going to throw the feed to us, or how much time we'd have—five minutes, ten, fifteen—to do the broadcast. To make matters even more complicated, Tom and I had to conduct these conversations *away* from the anchor site: The nearest telephone with a private outside line was in an office down the hall. It is safe to say that confusion reigned.

But about these points, there could have been no confusion: That is, Sports had said they intended to run tennis to the end of the match and then do a wrap-up. What I intended was clearly stated, over and over: "If tennis isn't off and you don't come to us at six-thirty, don't come to us. I'll be in place, ready at six-thirty, but not immediately after that if our newscast doesn't start. Give us a chance to regroup and to get ourselves together; have Sports hold it until we can know what we're doing."

Tom repeated this to New York with fewer than three minutes to go and stayed on the phone. There was no phone at the anchor site where I had to be. I was in place when 6:30 came and went. Tennis still on. I took off my microphone and walked slowly out of the room. I was described in some printed accounts as doing "a slow burn." Maybe so. What I remember was an overwhelming feeling of disappointment. I thought the incident set an incredibly bad precedent. The message we sent to our audience was that CBS thought sports was more important than news.

I suppose the crew covering the Open must have felt as ours did: that nothing was more important at that moment than what they had on the screen. Their pride was involved, as ours was, but their thumb was on the button. They had control.

I headed back down the corridor, where I could have a private phone conversation with Howard Stringer. Tom had followed me into the hall, saying, "We need to talk about this." I asked him to return to the control room and monitor the situation. He had just stepped back inside when the director of the *Evening News,* Richie

Mutschler, said with numbness in his voice, "The network is in black."

"You mean," said Tom, "they're taking a commercial break."

"No, the network is in black. Sports went off the air."

Tom almost tore the door off its hinges getting to the corridor and running me down. He told me what little he knew, and the only thing that mattered: There was a blank screen on TV sets tuned to CBS across America.

There were several options that might have been used, but in the confusion none was. The network—meaning New York—could have put up a commercial or a series of them to borrow time; we had no commercials in Miami. We could have rolled a four-minute tape we'd prepared to introduce the pope's visit. New York could have flashed a "Please Stand By" message. New York could have thrown the signal back to Sports, but Sports wouldn't take it. At 6:33 P.M., they were gone.

All I could think was, we can't let the network go black. In television, that is unpardonable, the kind of extraordinary glitch that makes people wish they had been snatched out of the cradle by wolves. I hurried back to the studio, thinking, "What is this? This can't be happening." But we were definitely in black. The whole network was off the air and no one knew why.

I understood this much. As soon as we turned on the camera, the responsibility for what happened was going to be ours. But I knew we had no choice. Tom suggested that we take a minute to get adjusted, and I could hardly have agreed more. The place was in a shambles. Six minutes elapsed from the time Sports put us into black until Tom and I could return to the anchor chair, get me hooked up, organize the opening, and get back on the air. I thought it was a wonder, thanks to a masterful job by Tom Bettag and Richie Mutschler, that we got through the broadcast.

Even to those who believe they know a good deal about television, much of this must seem like hair splitting: three minutes over, six minutes off. But this is the world we exist in; our stories are timed to the tenth of a second. We use stopwatches, not sundials.

While I was still on the air, an executive in New York called and told Tom Bettag that CBS had a disaster on its hands and we would need a cover story. Tom and I opposed a cover story on both moral and practical grounds. You don't have to keep revising the truth. And it hasn't been legal for many decades for employers to cut out the tongues of their employees to stop them from talking.

So Tom and I consistently told those who suggested it that there would be no phony cover story. We would tell the truth: A lot of well-intentioned people, working for both Sports and News, were in separate orbits. They had no clear channel of communication. A bad thing happened. Mistakes were made, some by me and some by others. I was prepared to shoulder the blame for mine.

The argument had been made that any public debate on the six-minute gap would only lead to bad blood between the Sports and News divisions, so I was encouraged to leave the talking to CBS management. That suited me fine, except that I overlooked a couple of important details. Number one, in such a crunch, the corporate agenda, the corporate priority, the corporate needs dominate. And bureaucrats high and low, up and down the chain of command, suddenly have their egos and careers in danger, so they act first out of self-protection—not out of loyalty to you or to the company.

Those who spoke to the press laid the guilt squarely on me. The prevailing attitude became: "Dan is out front, he gets paid a lot of money, his job is secure, and instead of having five or ten guys taking arrows, let Dan get hit with one big spear. He'll survive." It certainly made a clearer, neater tale than a complicated story of woeful confusion—and that was how *The New York Times* and some others wrote it over the decisive next few days. Their stories effectively blamed me for the whole incident.

Maybe I deserved it, but I certainly didn't believe I deserved all that I was getting. My silence, keeping my word about not talking, hadn't helped. I was in trouble now, deep trouble, and hurting. Nothing hurt more than the constant reminders that some people I had trusted were talking, and were saying a lot of damaging, untrue things on a "don't use my name" basis.

Relief came when the chief executive officer of CBS, Inc., Larry Tisch, who had the final say, dealt with this clumsy situation calmly. He didn't believe everything he had read. He took the position that it was counterproductive to wallow in the exercise of who said what to whom and why. He refused to believe that it was all my fault. Let's face it: I could have been fired. Much, much later, when I suggested that to Tisch, he indicated he didn't think that would have been fair, nor good business.

I took a lot of criticism for those six minutes. Perhaps the worst: During my interview with Vice President Bush, he referred to it as *seven* minutes.

I still fault myself a great deal about that night in Miami and its aftermath. Most of all I fault myself for failing to make the point that a matter of principle was involved. It was perhaps not something worthy of a talmudic scholar, but worth exploring. Within the company, there was a growing argument that Sports should take primacy over News. I don't think, and never will think, that this should be the case. (I say this as a lifelong sports fan and a fellow who got his start broadcasting games of the Houston Buffs in the Texas League.)

In 1992, CBS was the only network to preempt one of the presidential debates. We were committed to the baseball playoffs.

The trend is worrisome. And looking back on that September night in 1987, I fault myself not because I didn't make the case effectively. I didn't make it at all.

It's some consolation that, in Miami on another September night six years later, I tried to stick up for my professional standards. And I got a much different reaction.

FOUR

Whose Ambush Was It?

OTHER COUNTRIES DO IT DIFFERENTLY: YOU TAKE WHAT THE GOVernment spokesperson gives you, you don't ask questions, you run with it. The official line, all the way. Never a deviation, never a government mistake or misdeed, never a scandal. Very tidy.

But not the American way. For the American journalist, independence is everything; you tap all kinds of sources, you *do* ask questions—and nothing is tidy. Sure, you take what the government spokesperson gives you, but that's not your only source. If you're any good, you're working the phones and the pavement, crisscrossing the corridors of power, talking to anybody who'll talk back. Sometimes you learn that things really are as rosy as the government invariably says they are. But most times, there's more to the story. And your reporting attitude must be that there are no bad questions—only bad answers.

When things are going wrong, seriously wrong, a long line of epic and illegal wrongs, nobody wants to take blame, and only a few will want to answer questions. That makes interviewing sources more difficult. An interview isn't an exact science or a fine art. Sometimes the messiest, least decorous questioning yields the most information. But the public usually doesn't see most of these interviews. For print or for the airwaves, interviews are usually edited. The reader or listener gets the most important quotes from the interview, and the story proceeds. But in a *live* interview, almost every hairy wart of interviewer and interviewee is on display. (However, even in a live, unedited interview, there's a lot of hello and good-bye the public never sees, days and weeks before and after the interview itself.)

And this is important, too: A serious journalist can't run with a story without confirmation. *Two* sources at the absolute minimum. It doesn't matter if you're covering the garden club and one person tells you that Mr. Smith's ranunculus beat Mrs. Jones's hydrangeas. Rarely if ever do you run the item until a second person confirms it.

This is how your narrator made it through Watergate. If I'd gone off half-cocked, if I'd gotten my facts scrambled, if I'd run with unconfirmed leads, I'd be selling insurance right now. The public and my bosses at CBS would have demanded that, and they'd have been justified. There were nights in the last two years of the Nixon administration that I'd come home late and face Jean across the supper table and say, "If I'm wrong on this Watergate story, I'll be destroyed in journalism. We'll have to start over in something else." When the sky cleared, I stuck with the methods that got me through the storm.

But with a lead from one credible source, a good reporter will dig harder, trying to find that confirmation.

In January 1988, I interviewed the sitting vice president of the United States, George Herbert Walker Bush, who was running for the Republican presidential nomination. That nomination, to say nothing of his election, was by no means certain.

Despite having more money and other resources, plus all the advantages of being vice president, Bush was in trouble in the first full voting test for the nomination, the Iowa Republican caucuses. He was an early favorite to win, but his lackluster campaign had begun to show signs of faltering.

Also, you have to remember what was happening in America in 1988. Some of the glamour had worn off of Ronald and Nancy Reagan as they counted down the final months of his second term. The Iran-contra scandal had called unwanted attention to the inner workings of the Reagan presidency. The Reagans were the target of painful personal attacks, not by their political opponents but by two of their children. The economy was heading into recession. Reagan seemed less than coherent in his rare unscripted appearances.

Beginning in 1986, and for the next eighteen months, the *CBS Evening News* investigated the Iran-contra debacle. Considering the magnitude of the constitutional questions raised, I believe this has been one of the most underestimated, poorly reported, and misunderstood political scandals in all American history. Our staff sorted through court records, congressional testimony, intelligence files that had been declassified under the Freedom of Information Act, and conducted dozens of interviews around the world.

The reason for the investigation, and for spending so much time and effort on it, was the mounting evidence indicating that a secret cabal of ideologically motivated operatives inside the White House, Defense Department, and Central Intelligence Agency was carrying out its own agenda. It appeared this was done outside of the American system of constitutionally mandated checks and balances—a system that includes accountability to the law and to the people's elected representatives in Congress. The operatives' agenda appeared to include secretly sending some of America's best high-technology weapons to this country's sworn enemies, such as Iran, and waging undeclared wars, such as the one in Nicaragua. Appearances also suggested private profiteering by these operatives with large sums of the American people's money.

If such things were truly going on, then the American people needed to know. We were attempting to find out what was true and what was not, whether appearances matched reality.

Our findings led us to the possibility not only that George Bush knew from the start, and was kept informed, but that the diversion actually ran through the office of the vice president. These findings were, in fact, confirmed to me by a source who saw Ronald Reagan virtually every day for four years.

A highly credible source. A source I trusted, then and now. But only *one* source. I'd have to ask questions, seek further confirmation.

My source described a vivid scene in which Bush eagerly volunteered to take on more responsibility while an uncomfortable Reagan, unable to look him in the eye, kept glancing out the window of the Oval Office. Two other people were in the room, including a high government official who was a close friend of Bush.

According to my source, the Iran-contra network had been constructed in such a way, Reagan believed, that if the secret operation became known, George Bush would ultimately be pulled down by it. This prospect was not necessarily viewed with foreboding by those closest to the president. One of these was Nancy Reagan, who confided to a friend that Ronnie would prefer Jim Baker as his successor.

Whether Mrs. Reagan reflected her husband's feelings or her own, I can't say. Of this much I am certain. Reagan, who had no taste for backroom political combat, and who glorified loyalty when he recognized it, would never withdraw his support from Bush as long as the scandal didn't ensnare him.

For the moment, I was concerned with our source at the White House. This person was highly placed and had proven to be reliable on other stories. He was our only source for some of the hottest new inside revelations, some of which contained damaging information about George Bush.

Could this source be pursuing a personal vendetta against Bush? Could he be hooked in with the arch-conservative crowd that had never trusted Bush and wanted to bring him down? I had to keep these questions in mind.

Also in mind were questions about some recent, uncharacteristic behavior by Bush. In recent weeks, he had exploded the few times he had been asked about Iran-contra by print reporters and others. This was at such variance with the George Bush I thought I knew, and so contrary to the image of New England calm and Connecticut cool he usually tried to convey, that I had to ask myself what prompted it.

All the while, more questions kept piling up about his involvement in the secret and possibly illegal wheelings and dealings with money and weapons. These were some of the currents at play as CBS persisted in seeking an interview with the vice president.

I honestly believed at the time that George Bush would be eager to answer the questions, as fully and as often as it took to get them over with, set aside, and, if possible, out of the way of his campaign. Otherwise, I thought, he risked having the questions hound him at every debate, press conference, and speech on the campaign trail.

I was wrong, about that and much else.

I thought I knew George Bush pretty well. I'd certainly known him a long time. Our relationship had always been mutually respectful.

But now, unbeknownst to me—unplanned and unwanted by me—that long history of mutual respect was about to change.

The *CBS Evening News* was in the midst of trying to conduct individual interviews with all the Republican and Democratic candidates for the presidential nomination. Bush had ducked, but now, after long negotiations with his staff setting numerous conditions for the interview, we had a commitment.

Our intention, my intention, was to ask him questions concerning the most substantive issues—*plural*—in the campaign. These were to include but not be confined to questions about Iran-contra.

Questions about the secret dealings were inevitable, I believed, for any major, sit-down interview on network television. I did not view them as optional: I thought I had no choice but to ask him about serious allegations concerning the conduct of his official duties.

We had heard allegations of many unethical if not outright illegal acts. There were discrepancies between what he said he had done and what others had said, and discrepancies between what he said and the documented record.

We had a lot of information indicating he had done wrong and spoken untruths. But did we *know?* No. We suspected, but we did not know whether we had the truth, any part of the truth, or not. One reason was that we had not been afforded an opportunity to ask George Bush himself.

Under such circumstances, journalists of integrity ask questions. We don't come to conclusions before getting what can be considered reasonably honest answers.

Especially when an interview subject is involved with allegations of serious wrongdoing in public office, it is the responsibility of an ethical journalist to ask direct questions—and keep on asking them until the subject answers, or until it is clear he refuses to answer.

All of this was in the background on January 25, 1988, a Monday night, as I prepared to interview George Bush, vice president and candidate for president. I was to question him in what the CBS News staff believed was an interview that might yield some news, perhaps even make a headline. We always hope that when we allocate time for a comparatively lengthy interview with an important person.

Well before the interview, we called around to various people to help refine our thinking and to hone our questions. This included telephone conversations with one Republican and one Democratic paid consultant, outsiders brought in by CBS News to advise us on our campaign coverage. Consulting of this nature is routine, standard procedure during election campaigns, at CBS and at other networks.

Late afternoon the day of the interview, we held a small meeting of about a dozen CBS staffers involved in campaign coverage, to go over possible lines of questioning—about Iran-contra and other issues. But that was as heavy as the brainstorming got. Whatever anyone else wants to believe, the interview was not intended by me to be an interview only about Iran-contra. There was an intention to try to get him on the record about discrepancies in his story about that case, because the case was one with serious constitutional ramifications. But we also wanted to ask about the economy and education, and changing relations with the Soviet Union.

I felt confident going into the interview. We didn't know yet who the Democratic contender would be, but I thought to myself, "We have the man who may be the next president, and we have him live." And there was a question I really hoped I could get answered: Why did we send over two thousand of our best missiles to the Ayatollah, after 241 of our best servicemen had been blown up on his orders? I thought a majority of Americans were troubled in the same way I was. And as a journalist, you want answers more than you want to question.

I believe it would be difficult to understand the depth of the furor that developed without reading what was actually said that night. (Take careful notes; there will be a quiz.)

Also, you may want to consider that I was then and am now complying with a demand made by the Bush campaign: They'd refused to do any interview except a live, unedited interview on the *Evening News*. The formerly live, still unedited transcript, then, follows:

"And still to come on tonight's CBS Evening News, we'll ask Vice President George Bush the questions that keep coming up in his presidential campaign—a live interview with Mr. Bush on arms to Iran and money to the contras."

My introduction included a public opinion poll, a package of film clips, and prerecorded statements by other Iran-contra figures:

RATHER: One of the most striking results of today's poll is that many people felt, rightly or wrongly, that Vice President Bush is hiding information that the public ought to know. Despite the fact, and it is a fact, that the Tower Commission and the Iran-Contra Committee did not implicate Mr. Bush, almost one-third of all Republicans and a quarter of the Bush supporters interviewed say he is hiding something. CBS News has spent more than a month preparing tonight's report on the Vice President and the Iran-Contra affair. During that period, the Vice President has asked reporters, all reporters to submit substantive questions, if they want to ask questions, in writing, and he has issued one written response. He declined to be interviewed in advance for our report, but he watches with us tonight from his Capitol Hill office, and he agreed to respond this evening on the condition that he speak live and unedited.

Our report traced the broad strokes of the secret diversions of weapons and money, and listed the dates of the fifteen meetings in the Oval Office attended by the vice president at which the arms sales were known to have been discussed. He said he could not recall hearing any strong objections. The record showed that he was there when Secretary of State George Shultz argued against the sales, in his words, "as forcefully as I could . . . I was intense." (The stand taken by Shultz would be documented again, under questioning by Special Prosecutor Lawrence Walsh in the midst of the 1992 election, raising again questions of credibility. Bear in mind, this broadcast was airing in January of 1988.) The vice president contended that he would have opposed the plan, and would have "weighed in heavily with the President to that effect," if only he had known the real terms. My narration continued:

> But the record shows he did know. Mr. Bush was told it was an arms-for-hostages swap by this man, Amiram Nir (*pictured on screen*), the Israeli who coordinated the trade. At a briefing arranged by Oliver North, Nir told Bush directly the deal was "an effort to get the hostages out . . . the whole package for a fixed price . . . they fear that, if they give us all the hostages, they won't get anything from us."
>
> So Mr. Bush was told in July 1986 (*Vice President Bush and entourage seen in Israeli hotel, July 30, 1986*) that we were trading arms for hostages with "the most radical elements" in Iran. But the record shows he never objected.
>
> For all the questions about the Iran arms deal, there are even more about the Vice President's link to secret contra aid.

The Vice President's office says he and his aides were "never involved in directing, coordinating, or approving military aid to the contras." But the record is riddled with inconsistencies. Questions center on this man, Donald Gregg, Bush's national security adviser and a veteran CIA agent.

When the Sandinistas shot down the plane carrying Eugene Hasenfuss (October 7, 1986), the first U.S. official alerted was Gregg's assistant, yet Gregg denied it in this brief film clip:

Q: He contacted someone who worked for you?
GREGG: No.
Q: I think he—he contacted you indirectly—
GREGG: (overtalking): No, no.
Q: —in some way?
GREGG: No.

Gregg later admitted that [statement] wasn't true; but then, just three days ago, Gregg again denied any involvement with the contras.

Q: Mr. Gregg, do you still insist that you played no role in—in aiding the contras between 1982 and 1987?
GREGG (pause):   Yes, I do.

But the record shows Gregg pushed for more secret aid to the contras early in 1982, when he was responsible for covert operations at the NSC (from 1979 to 1982). After he joined Bush's staff, Gregg promoted a plan to launch air strikes against leftist guerrillas in Central America. Targets included Nicaragua. The plan was found in Oliver North's safe. Its author? Felix Rodriguez. A Bay of Pigs veteran, Rodriguez had worked for Gregg on secret CIA operations in Vietnam. Just after U.S. aid to the contras was made illegal, Gregg met Rodriguez again (December 21, 1984). That same day, Rodriguez met North for the first time. A month later (January 22, 1985), Rodriguez joined the Vice President and Gregg to discuss a job in El Salvador. All three men say they talked about fighting Communist insurgents. All three claim the contras never came up.

BUSH (*on tape*):   I have never, ever had a discussion with him about the contras and contra support of any kind.

The record shows Rodriguez was in Central America just two weeks later. General Paul Gorman, the U.S. military commander in the region, reported Rodriguez was sent by "Ollie North" (*on screen: "Subject has been put into play by Ollie North"*) and his primary commitment was to "assist the F.D.N., the contras" (*on screen: "He wants to assist the . . . contras."*) We asked Gregg about that last Friday.

GREGG: I've heard about that memorandum, and I have no explanation for it.

By fall, Rodriguez was managing North's contra supply flights from El Salvador, but North grew uneasy about Rodriguez. He wrote in his notebook (*handwritten excerpt shown on screen: "Felix talking too much about Vice President connection."*) Rodriguez stayed in touch with Bush's office. By April, he was threatening to quit. Rodriguez came to Washington for a series of meetings, including one with Mr. Bush and Donald Gregg. A briefing memo prepared for the Vice President (April 30, 1986) listed the topic as "resupply of the contras." (*highlighted phrase appears on screen: "Participants: The Vice President; Craig Fuller; Don Gregg; Sam Watson."*) Bush and his aides claim the subject never came up. By summer, relations between North and Rodriguez grew tense. North asked Gregg for help, telling him: "You're the only one who can control Felix." Gregg and Rodriguez met in the Vice President's office that August. Rodriguez told him North was supplying the contras with arms. But Gregg claims he never told Bush, because the information was "not vice presidential." Today, Donald Gregg still works inside the White House as Vice President Bush's trusted adviser.

All of this audiovisual foreplay, the recital of dates, the reference to diaries and memoranda, putting faces with the names, was to set the stage for questions that George Bush had never fully answered, and in several instances had avoided altogether. In the previous two weeks or so, he'd even lost his temper with the people who'd questioned him—blown up at rival Republican candidate Bob Dole, at Jim Gannon, editor of the *Des Moines Register,* and at a reporter for *The New York Times.* None of those Q & A sessions had been conducted on live national television, of course.

And so the live interview began:

RATHER: Mister Vice President, thank you for being with us tonight. Donald Gregg still serves as your trusted adviser. He
was deeply involved in running arms to the contras, and he
didn't inform you. Now, when President Reagan's trusted adviser, Admiral Poindexter, failed to inform him, the President
fired him. Why is Mr. Gregg still inside the White House and
still a trusted adviser?

BUSH: Because I have confidence in him and because this matter,
Dan, as you well know and your editors know, has been looked
at by the ten-million-dollar study by the Senate and the House.
It's been looked at by the Tower Commission. The Rodriguez
testimony that you put on here, I just think it's outrageous, because he was totally vindicated, swore under oath that he never
talked to me about the contras; and yet, this report you're
making, which you told me, or your people did—you have a
Mr. Cohen that works for you—was going to be a political
profile. Now, if this is a political profile for an election, I have a
very different opinion as to what one should be. But Don
Gregg wor—works for me because I don't think he—he's done
anything wrong. And I think if he had, this exhaustive exami-
nation that went into—was gone into by the Senate and by the
House would have shown it, and you've impugned the—my integrity by suggesting, with one of your little boards here, that I
didn't tell the truth about what—what Felix Rodriguez—you
didn't accuse me of it, but you made that suggestion, and other
people were in the meeting, including Mr. Nick Brady, and he
has said that my version is correct. And so, I find this to be a
rehash and a little bit—if you'll excuse me—a misrepresented
. . . tation on the part of CBS, who said you're doing political
profiles on all the candidates, and then you come up with
something that has been exhaustively looked into.

DR: Mister Vice President, what we agreed or didn't agree to, I
think you will agree for the moment, can be dealt with in another way. Let's talk about the record. You say that we've misrepresented your . . .

GB: Let's talk about the full record.

DR: . . . record. Let's talk about the record.

GB: Yeah.

DR: If we've misrepresented your record in any way, here's a
chance to set it straight. Now, for ex . . .

GB: Right. Can I just set it straight on one count because you
implied from that little thing, I, I have a little monitor sitting

on the side here . . . that I didn't tell the truth. Now, this has all been looked into. This is a rehash.

DR: Where . . . where did we imply that, Mr. Vice President?

GB: Well, just here, on this board, where you had the idea that Bush says that he didn't tell, didn't tell, contra . . . didn't hear about the contras' supply from Felix Rodriguez.

DR: Mr. Vice Pres . . .

GB: Felix Rodriguez testified under oath. He has been public, and you could have at least run a little picture of him saying that, "I never told the Vice President about the contras." I'm asking for fair play, and I thought I was here to talk about my views on education or on getting this deficit down . . .

DR: Well, Mr. Vice President . . .

GB: Yes?

DR: We want to talk about the record on this . . .

GB: Well, let's . . .

DR: . . . because it . . .

GB: Well, let's talk about the full record. That's what I want to talk about, Dan.

DR: The . . . the framework here is that one-third . . . one-third of the Republicans in this poll . . .

GB: Yeah.

DR: One-third of the Republicans and . . . and one-fourth of the people who say that, you know, they rather like you, believe you're hiding something. Now, if you are, here's a . . .

GB: I am hiding something.

DR: Here's a chance to get it out.

GB: You know what I'm hiding? What I told the President. That's the only thing. And I've answered every question put to me. Now, if you have a question, what is it?

DR: I do have one.

GB: Please fire away.

DR: You have said that if you had known . . . you said that if you had known this was an arms-for-hostages swap . . .

GB: Yes.

DR: . . . that you would have opposed it. You also said that . . .

GB: Exactly. Now, let me . . . let me ask . . .

DR: . . . that you did not know that you . . .

GB: May I answer that . . . directly?

DR: That wasn't a question. It was a statement.

GB: Yes, it was a statement, and I'll answer it.

DR: Let me ask the question, if I may, first.

GB: The President created this program, has testified . . . or stated publicly that he did not think it was arms for hostages, and it was only later that . . .

DR: That's the President, Mr. Vice President.

GB: . . . and that's me . . .

DR: But . . .

GB: . . . 'Cause I went along with it, because . . . you know why, Dan? Because I . . .

DR: That wasn't a question, Mr. Vice President.

GB: . . . worried when I saw Mr., Mr. Buckley, heard about Mr. Buckley being tortured to death, later admitted is the CIA chief. So, if I erred, I erred on the side of trying to get those hostages out of there. And the whole story has been told to the Congress.

DR: Mr. Vice President, you set the . . . you set the rules for this . . . this talk here. I didn't mean to step on your line there, but you insisted that this be live, and you know that we have a limited amount of time.

GB: Exactly, and that's why I . . . that's why I want to get my share in here on something other than what you want to talk about.

DR: The President . . . the President has . . . has spoken for himself. I'm asking you . . .

GB: Please.

DR: To speak for yourself, which you have not been willing to do in the past. And, if I . . . if I may suggest, that this is what leads people to say, quote, "Either George Bush was irrelevant or he was ineffective. He said himself he was out of the loop." Now, let me give you an example . . .

GB: Uh, may I explain "out of the loop"?

DR: You said, "Ask a question."

GB: May I explain "out of the loop"? No operational role. Go ahead.

DR: Now, you've said that, if you'd known it was an arms-for-hostages swap, you would have opposed it. You said the first you knew it was an arms-for-hostages swap was in December of 1986, correct?

GB: When the whole thing became briefed to me by Senator Durenberger . . .

DR: Exactly.

GB: . . . and the proximity of arms to hostages much closer than we had thought on these hearings that were . . .

DR: But Mr. Vice President, you went to Israel in July of 1986 . . .

GB: Yes.

DR: . . . and a member of your own staff, Craig Fuller, has verified, and so did the only other man there, Mr. Nir, Mr. Amiram Nir, who's the Israelis' top anti-terrorist man . . .

GB: Yes.

DR: . . . those two men were in a meeting with you and Mr. Nir not once, but three times, three times underscored with you that this was a straight-out, arms-for-hostages swap.

GB: What they were doing . . .

DR: Now how do you . . .

GB: Read the memo, read the memo.

DR: I have, sir.

GB: What they were doing . . .

DR: How can you reconcile that you were there, Mr. Nir underscored three separate occasions that it was an arms-for-hostages swap and told you [that] you were dealing with the most radical elements in Iran. You were dealing straight away with the Ayatollah Khomeini.

GB: I was told what they were doing and not what we were doing, and that's the big difference; and, Dan, I expressed my concerns and reservations about that. That has been testified to under oath by Mr. Poindexter. And it's been confirmed that I had reservations and spoke up by Don Regan. In fact, he said the other day that I expressed them to the President.

DR: That's correct.

GB: I don't discuss what I talked to the President 'cause there's a principle involv . . . It has nothing to do with Iran-contra. It's the principle of confidentiality . . .

DR: But Mis . . .

GB: . . . between the President and the Vice President.

DR: . . . Mr. Vice President. Mr. Vice President . . .

GB: Yes.

DR: . . . the President has said he wants all the facts out. He gave up such things as even his own diary. Every principle, including . . .

GB: He did not give up his own diary.

DR: . . . Secretary Shultz. He gave up some of it.

GB: His diary, his brief. Well, Dan, let's be careful here because you're explaining a political profile.

DR: Yes, sir. I want you to be careful, Mr. Vice President . . .

GB: I will be careful.

DR: . . . because the problem here . . .

GB: But I want to get my side of this out.

DR: . . . is that you repeatedly sat in the meetings. You sat in a meeting in which Secretary Shultz, in the most forceful way, rais . . . registered his objections, and then you said you never heard anybody register objection . . .

GB: I wasn't there, if it was the most forceful way. If it was the most forceful way . . . I've heard George Shultz be . . . be very forceful; and, if I were there and he was very, very forceful at that meeting, I would have remembered that. I don't remember that. And that is what I'm saying.

DR: Then how do you explain that you can't remember it and the other people at the meeting say that he was apoplectic?

GB: Well, then, maybe I wasn't there at that point.

DR: You weren't . . . you weren't in the meeting?

GB: I'm not suggesting. I'm just saying I don't remember it.

DR: I don't want to be argumentative, Mr. Vice President.

GB: You do, Dan.

DR: No . . . no, sir, I don't.

GB: This is not a great night, 'cause I want to talk about why I want to be President, why those 41 percent of the people are supporting me. And I don't think it's fair . . .

DR: And Mr. Vice President, these questions are designed . . .

GB: . . . to judge a whole career, it's not fair to judge my whole career by a rehash on Iran. How would you like it if I judged your career by those seven minutes when you walked off the set in New York?

DR: Well, Mister . . .

GB: Would you like that?

DR: Mr. Vice President . . .

GB: I have respect for you, but I don't have respect for what you're doing here tonight.

DR: Mr. Vice President, I think you'll agree that your qualification for President and what kind of leadership you'd bring the country, what kind of government you'd have, what kind of people you'd have around you . . .

GB: Exactly.

DR: . . . is much more important than what you just referred to. I'd be happy to . . .

GB: Well, I want to be judged on the whole record . . . and you're not giving an opportunity.

DR: And I'm trying to set the record straight, Mr. Vice President.

GB: You invited me to come here to talk about, I thought, the whole record.

DR: I . . . I want you to talk about the record. You sat in a meeting with George Shultz . . .

GB: Yes, and I've given you an answer.

DR: He got apoplectic when he found out that you were . . .

GB: He didn't get apoplectic. You have to ask **Don Regan.** Ask . . .

DR: . . . you and the President were being party to sending missiles to the Ayatollah . . .

GB: Ask . . .

DR: . . . the Ayatollah of Iran. Can you explain how . . . you were supposed to be the . . . you are, you're an anti-terrorist expert. We . . . Iran was officially a terrorist state.

GB: I've already explained that, Dan.

DR: You went around telling . . . you . . . you . . .

GB: I wanted those hostages . . . I wanted Mr. Buckley out of there . . .

DR: But Mr. Vice President, the question is . . . but you . . . you made us hypocrites in the face of the world.

GB: . . . before he was killed, which he has been killed.

DR: How could you . . . how could you . . .

GB: That was bad.

DR: . . . sign on to such a policy? And the question is . . .

GB: Well, had the same reason the President signed on to it.

DR: . . . what does that tell us about your record?

GB: The same reason the President signed on to it. When a CIA agent is being tortured to death, maybe you err on the side of a human life. But everybody's admitted mistakes. I've admitted mistakes. And you want to dwell on 'em, and I want to talk about the values we believe in and the experience and the integrity that goes with all of this, and what's . . . I'm going to do about education, and you're . . . there's nothing new here. I thought this was a news program. What is new?

DR: Well, I had hoped, Mr. Vice President, you would tell us to whom you expressed your reservations . . .

GB: Yes, I did.

DR: . . . when you expressed them and what were the reservations?

GB: Poindexter testified under oath.

DR: What were the reservations?

GB: His testi . . . reservations about getting the control of an operation in the hands of a foreign power. Don Regan stated the
other day, and I never heard a word of it on CBS, that the Vice
President, in the presence of the President, spoke up about his
concern about the whole cover of an operation being blown
and secret—and people that you're dealing with putting their
lives in jeopardy.

DR: And you weren't concerned about sending missiles to the
Ayatollah Khomeini?

GB: And I felt that always on every covert . . . every covert action.

DR: You weren't . . .

GB: The President has explained that. The committee looked at
that, and so there's nothing new on this.

DR: Mr. Vice President, I appreciate your joining us tonight. I
appreciate the straightforward way in which you engaged in
this exchange. Clearly, some unanswered questions remain.

GB: Fire on another one.

DR: Are you willing . . . are you willing to go to a news conference before the Iowa caucuses, answer questions from all . . . all
comers?

GB: I've been to 86 news conferences since March—86 of 'em
since . . .

DR: I gather that the answer is "No."

GB: . . . March . . .

DR: Thank you very much for being with us, Mr. Vice President.
We'll be back with more news in a moment.

The interview alone had consumed nine minutes of a twenty-two-
minute broadcast, an unprecedented length for a live interview on
the *Evening News.* My executive producer, Tom Bettag, was pleading with me in my earpiece to "wrap it up." I was acutely aware that
it had ended too abruptly; it was like a door slamming in someone's
face. The phrase I would keep hearing over the next few days was
"It could have been done more gracefully."

Under the circumstances, I'm not so sure. I had no way of know-
ing then how much Bush relished the circumstances, and that he, in
Washington, with the microphone still open, had turned to his cam-
paign people and gloated, "The bastard didn't lay a glove on me."
He also said, and tried frantically to backtrack from it: "He
[Rather] makes Lesley Stahl look like a pussy." Only his good luck

in choosing a word that most papers won't print and most broad-casts wouldn't say kept the quote from haunting him.

I had no way of knowing how well the interview had fit the Bush campaign's strategy: Bush's explosions with other questioners hadn't been a fluke, more like a trial run for that night's interview.

Moments before airtime, there had been a brief flash of what was to come. As Bush sat in his office in Washington, Bettag heard him say over an open microphone, "They aren't going to talk about Iran-contra, are they? If he talks to me about the Iran-contra affair, they're gonna see a seven-minute walkout here." (A not-too-casual reference to my absence from the *Evening News* set for *six* minutes in Miami a few months before.)

From the control room to the anchor desk is a distance of only a few feet, but the desk might as well be an island. Bettag could only blurt into my earpiece: "Dan, Bush is saying he didn't know the subject. He's threatening to walk. I don't know what to do. Just be aware of it."

Still, I was not prepared for the degree to which the viewers would be both upset and fascinated by what they had seen—one TV critic said it was like watching two scorpions in a bottle.

I have to admit, I feel a grudging admiration for the vice president's performance, before, during, and after the newscast. He was like a veteran character actor preparing his audience for a surprise. It wasn't simply the fact that his representatives had been told the interview would be "issue-oriented and tough," although that is an important fact. We had also run promos throughout the weekend, even during *60 Minutes* (the network's top-rated program), clearly stating that Iran-contra questions would be asked. If we'd meant to stage an ambush, we'd let an awful lot of people know ahead of time. This was not an ambush, not on our part, and Bush and his people knew that.

The indignation of Bush was as sincere as that of Captain Louis Renault, when he orders the closing of Rick's Café in *Casablanca:* "I am shocked, *shocked* to find that gambling is going on here," the captain protests, as he slips into his pockets the winnings handed him by a waiter.

I made mistakes that night, but this is no *mea culpa.* I was wrong in believing that Bush would want to confront the questions. I'd even thought he'd answer the questions so promptly that we'd be able to move on to a number of other issues. My biggest mistake was not anticipating the pitfalls and that the interview might evoke such a powerful national reaction. I'm not naive; some of it I know was orchestrated by the Bush election campaign. But long after they gave the wheel a spin, the ball kept bouncing.

I guessed right in one respect and gained nothing. In one of our staff planning sessions, I said I thought if I pressed him hard he might give me a jab on the Miami episode. One staffer said, "Forget it. You said yourself he doesn't hit below the belt."

I said, "If he does, I think the best thing is to pause and then politely get back to the questions." (This may be part of some cowboy code instilled in me when I was young: You pause so you let them know you're thinking it over, and then continue with your most polished manners to show that you have decided you must've misheard, that they couldn't possibly have said what they just said. I think of it as a Gary Cooper thing, but Gregory Peck does it brilliantly in *To Kill a Mockingbird.* Most of the time, it works pretty well for the rest of us mortals, too.)

A newscast is not an out-of-body experience. I was aware that we had made the needles on the sound meter jump, that we were talking at the same time, and my questions were hanging in the air like big round bubbles. Then it was over; I didn't know if the interview had been good or bad; I only knew that it had been different.

No one said anything when I walked off the set, but they seldom do. I am usually out there alone, surrounded by the technicians. Head writer Lee Townsend's desk was welded to the anchor desk, and he called out, "Great interview." Lee doesn't kiss ass, so I was happy to get his vote. Then I did what I do every night. I started walking up the stairs to my office. There I would take a minute to unwind, then go back to the studio to meet with the staff and critique the broadcast. How did it go? How did we compare to the competition? What do we have for tomorrow?

Halfway up the stairs, I bumped into Suzanne Meirowitz. Nowadays she goes by Suzanne Nederlander, her married name, and she is one of the most valuable producers of the *CBS Evening News.* But at the time she was my senior assistant, a Bryn Mawr grad who kept my office humming. I learned early that her opinions were solid, principled, and well considered, and I wanted her opinion now. I said, "What did you think?"

When she took a deep breath, I sensed the first sign of trouble. She said, "I think you're an interesting person who does interesting interviews."

I was brought up short by that answer. Suzanne is smart and loyal and she was ducking me.

When I reached the second floor I saw Donna Dees, who was at that time the press rep for the *Evening News* and another person whose opinions I did and do value. I said to Donna, "Look, are we in trouble with this, and if so, what can we do?"

She burst into tears. Let me be honest, that told me more than I wanted to know. Then she managed to get out one word: "Apologize."

I turned steel cold right there. I made sure my eyes locked onto hers. "Wait a minute," I said. "I haven't done anything to apologize for, and I'm not apologizing."

On a normal night, I would have called home by now and talked to Jean Rather. This was not going to be a normal night. Everywhere I looked I could see that the phone lines were lit up. The production assistants were answering two calls at a time. The switchboard was swamped. Someone said, "I think they must be rotary calls."

Executive Producer Tom Bettag was still in the control room. I walked into the Fishbowl, and senior producer Bill Crawford was waiting for me. I had met him the first day I walked into CBS News in 1961. He stuck out his hand and said, "Good interview. Really tough. Now you start to pay the price."

I didn't quite grasp what he meant. But I could see that in general the building was emptying out as though there had been a bomb scare. Every phone line was ringing; we were starting to get calls from other media. A fellow from our press relations office had invited a *New York Times* reporter, one I did not count among my closest friends, to watch the broadcast.

No one answered on Mahogany Row, where the top executives had their offices. Bettag walked into the Fishbowl and I said, "Tom, we need help on the phones."

He nodded and said, "Sorry I jumped in your ear. We were in danger of not getting out." I was starting to think it would have been better to let them cut us off.

Now Tom Donilon, our paid CBS News consultant from the Democratic party, joined us. He had been consulted only by telephone, about several matters, before the interview, as had his various Republican counterparts. It had been my decision, and I'd wanted only CBS people for the real planning session. Another second guess, probably another mistake. Late on Monday, Donilon did fly into New York and watched the interview.

Now Donilon, an old political pro, tried to get my attention. "Listen," he said, "you're alone here. You have got to get busy with the spin. These phone calls, some of them are coming from sophisticated phone banks, from party operatives well organized in advance to make exactly this kind of telephone call to newspapers and to radio and television stations anytime of the night or day. You have to realize that they are already calling to press rooms around the country, and that's going to influence tomorrow's press coverage."

Sometimes a little paranoia is a healthy thing. But this was not the mysterious, faceless "they." Donilon was referring to the Bush campaign and its operatives in key cities. Of course, he knew that they would be scoring points with newspaper editors, and Donilon had a more than humanitarian interest in whether or not CBS (and Dan Rather) got clobbered.

We had no contingency plan for what might happen during or after the interview. I don't think it was even discussed. Why would we discuss it? We report the news, not make it, or so we want to believe. It may have been that way once, but will never be so again. The roles are not so clear, the lines not so clean, in an age when television can act as a broker for diplomatic initiatives (Sadat and Begin), launch presidential candidacies (Ross Perot), observe criminal misconduct as it occurs (in the Los Angeles riots), and baby-sit our children.

Some future young anchorperson might learn a lesson right there. If you are going on the air with a newscast that has the potential for an explosion, a major controversy, you need to be organized. I was trying to muster some help. Within seconds, I knew there was none coming. Donilon's words rang in my ears. *You're alone here.*

The Republican party has operated a slick public opinion task force since 1972, geared to bombarding radio or TV call-in shows and letters-to-the-editor columns. My reaction is close to awe for how successful they are both in bashing the media and in making the media their accomplices.

The early mechanisms are referred to in memoranda written in 1972 by Charles Colson to Jeb Magruder ("We have programmed telephone calls throughout the day to Rather's Washington office") and to President Nixon from his speechwriter Pat Buchanan ("I have a dozen friends around the country, who will call on their dozens of friends, and so on, to put [sic] the letters we draft and carry out our line of attack"). These memoranda became available when the courts upheld a law that made presidential papers and other material public property. The documents dealing with the media machinery generated no great outcry, nor did any of the authors feel compelled to defend them or even to blush.

None of this is to imply that the Democrats do not engage in such tactics because they are more pure of heart. In truth, the Democrats were simply not very good at organizing such a massive effort; if they had tried it, they would not have been able to do so on such a scale and keep it a virtual secret. Not until the Clinton campaign of 1992, when the Democrats cried *"En garde!"* and dashed off to their fax machines, did they concede that the new technology offered an advantage over dropping your message in a mailbox.

One other distinction in techniques: The Republicans tended to get up close and personal ("Rather is a liberal," or somesuch ad hominem attack). The Democrats always seemed to be mailing out long letters warning against a revival of the Ku Klux Klan.

I am not trying to cast myself in the role of Little David. I would prefer that this story not take on a partisan coloring. In my first years as a White House correspondent, I went more than a few rough rounds with Lyndon Johnson, and did not always hold my own. *That* Democrat used to haul me into his office to say, "Ah'm disappointed in yew as a Texan, boh," words which no Texan offers lightly to any other Texan. But my profile was lower then and TV reporting was less combustible. Things changed in the 1970s and '80s, and for all but four of those years, the Republicans occupied the White House.

There was never a scene with Jimmy Carter, unpleasant or otherwise. We sort of looked around and he was gone. But I don't think anyone with at least a one-volt memory cell would claim that the media were soft on Carter. And I know Carter wouldn't make that claim.

It wasn't a question of Republican or Democratic ideology: I've crossed the highest-ranking officials of every major political party since the day I started as a reporter, and I'm proud to say I've never been anybody's lapdog or anybody's attack dog. On my best days, I'm a watchdog, calling out when there's something going on.

At the moment, on that night in late January 1988, this watchdog couldn't call out—the telephone lines were jammed. The production assistants were already starting to look like punch-drunk fighters—they'd hear the bells and start slapping at the telephones. I knew we'd need some central, reasonably efficient way to answer the callers' questions. My impression was that most of the callers were upset by what they perceived as my rudeness, that I had cut off the vice president. I wanted to explain that the end of the interview was not by design, that we had given Mr. Bush as much time as we could. But these are not things you can say to a caller in the heat of the moment. And it hadn't fully dawned on me yet that many of the callers didn't care about the appearance of rudeness. They wanted to score political points.

I had this sense of being in a submarine, and the depth charges were going off all around us.

I instructed the production secretaries who were grabbing the phones to ask the callers to write letters stating their question or complaint. We would answer them.

I wanted to get in touch with some of our key affiliate stations. If we were getting calls, so were they. I didn't have the whole picture then, but I suspected, and Donilon pressed the point, that the Bush campaign had its phone banks humming. Whatever this apparatus was, it was rolling our way like a huge street sweeper.

I called Howard Stringer, the president of the News Division, and his secretary said he had just left. He had theater tickets. I said I thought we needed to beep him. She said, "Oh, dear, Howard left his beeper here."

He wouldn't be home until midnight. I began to get that sinking feeling. Outside of our own staff, everywhere I turned there was no answer, no one to tell us if we had gone wrong, and how far. My attitude was that I had done my job. I felt I had asked at least some of the right questions. For better or worse, I take satisfaction in saying that I have not lost touch with what I believe are the fundamentals of journalism.

That thought was going to have to carry me awhile. I believed that others in the media would follow up on the questions I had tried to ask; I was dead wrong. As the wire services moved their stories, the focus was not on the missiles and the Ayatollah, the evasions of Iran-contra. They were getting into the ins and outs of network television; whether George Bush had been badgered and treated with disrespect.

I heard that the Bush people had called *The New York Times* and told them that complaints were pouring in from our affiliates; a manager in the Midwest was said to be outraged and demanding that I be fired. I recognized that one as an old technique: Catch them on deadline when there's no time to check it out. And nobody bothered to check whether the manager in question might be a big wheel in the state Republican party.

After the building had emptied, I stayed at the office much later than I usually did. I got through to Jean, talked to her twice. She said she thought I was in for a shelling. I told her someone suggested that I apologize. She said, "Don't you dare." She never hesitated to tell me when she thought I should apologize; she wasn't hesitating now, either.

It was Tom Bettag who finally tapped me on the shoulder at around 10:30 and said, "Let's go home." When I walked in my front door, Jean fixed me a drink, we talked a little, then had a light dinner. I barely ate. She tried to steer the conversation in other ways, and it didn't work.

I said I had to think about what I would say in the morning. It was going to be one of the critical times of my career, and I don't think I was being dramatic. Whatever happened, I had to deal with it. Nobody was going to deal with it for me, and it was beginning to look as if precious few people were going to deal with it anywhere near me.

I watched the eleven o'clock news and my worst fears were realized. The sound bites and the wire copy that provided much of the coverage disregarded the questions and dwelt on the theatrics. I didn't come off well. The perception was that there had been a contest and I had lost.

Without fail, what every newscast played was a clip of Bush saying: "How would you like it if I judged your career by those seven minutes when you walked off the set in New York?"

There was an almost eerie silence coming from our home phone. I started sketching out in my notepad the questions I might have to answer the next morning. Then, well after midnight, a nice thing happened. Jay Kriegel, Larry Tisch's executive right hand, called. "I'm just now realizing what happened, and what is happening. Beginning now, you're going to get my help and a lot of it. By the time you walk out of your apartment in the morning, the press will be there. Here's what I think: You need to face them by yourself. Don't have anyone there, no manager, no PR people. Answer every question. You won't like it, but you're going to be fingerprinted, mug-shot, and indicted. You're on trial."

I said, lamely, "What about the missiles to Iran?"

Jay said, "This isn't the time to talk about that. You have to be focused. You have to get some sleep." His next words startled me: "How do you feel about apologizing?"

I said, "About what?"

He said, "Some of the affiliates said you were rude to him, especially at the end. The guy in the Midwest is all over us."

I knew then he hadn't seen the interview. I said, "Jay, the guy in the Midwest is practically the Republican campaign chairman for the state. What do you expect him to say? The affiliates will do what they did when I had a run-in with Nixon. Some of the affiliates are politically partisan. Some are better than you think they are."

Jay's moved on now, left CBS for other endeavors. He and I had our difficulties over the years, but I shall never forget his help that night.

I wanted to sleep that night, couldn't, and finally dressed, tossed down a cup of coffee, and walked out of my apartment an hour or so after daybreak. There were camera crews waiting. I had thought out what I wanted to say.

"This is my home," I said. "Other people live in this building. If you don't mind, most of what I have to say I will say at 524 West Fifty-seventh Street. If you will go there, or have someone there, I'll answer every question for as long as you ask them."

And that was how it was done. I stood on the sidewalk outside the headquarters of CBS News, surrounded by camera crews and reporters. They shouted their questions, and I assured them I had all the time they needed.

One of the first questions was whether the vice president and his staff had been deceived, even tricked.

"We don't mislead people," I said. "We come straight at them. There are situations—they happen every day on the campaign trail—in which there are spirited questions and spirited answers.

"My job as a reporter is to ask honest questions and try to get honest answers. That's what I tried to do last night."

The rest of the day, I felt at least a sense of relief. I had had my say. As the hours passed before airtime, I was getting strong hints, if not outright pressure, from various sources to issue an apology. It was put to me that "this would be the smart thing to do." I made it clear that I would apologize if I thought an apology was justified, but I didn't and I wouldn't.

One of the arguments was: "Dan, you may not understand it, but the Bush campaign has been unrelenting. They are painting you as a person who was not only rude, but ill-tempered and out of control." My response was: "Anyone who knows me, knows that isn't true."

"Well, that's how they're portraying you. And unless you give them the apology, you're going to be stuck with it."

I tried not to bristle. "Won't anybody point out," I asked, "that he didn't answer the question?"

My remark drew laughter. I already knew the refrain: It doesn't work that way.

The story made the front page of both New York tabloids. The *Daily News* ran a photograph taken from behind me, with Bush facing the camera, and a headline that read: IN LIVID COLOR. The entire front page of the *Post* was devoted to the clash, under the headline: RATHER BUSHWHACKS VEEP.

On that morning after, the calls were running about five to one against me, my supposed politics, and my manners. By midday, the CBS switchboard had logged in six thousand calls. Several executives offered to draft a statement for me. I declined. I said, "If there's going to be anything on the *Evening News,* I'll write it." I spent most of the day resisting people who wanted to put words in my mouth.

I decided right then I would live with what was in the transcript, and I'd live with the footnote I planned to write for that night's broadcast. In what was probably a television first, both NBC and ABC led off their own broadcasts Tuesday night with stories about CBS, with footage from the interview and long stories on the fallout. It would also be the primary topic on ABC's *Nightline* and Public Broadcasting's *MacNeil/Lehrer Report.*

On the *Evening News,* I went right to the controversy, with sound bites from Iowa, where the Republican candidates, including Bush, were campaigning:

A caller to KCCI in Des Moines: "Well, I think Dan Rather is a jerk."

And another: "I think that question needs answering, and I think Bush was the one that was very rude."

At radio station WHO, Lee Martin, host of a call-in show, said the reaction was "about fifty-fifty, with a small but mighty lunatic fringe in the middle that said, 'Who really cares'?"

Then we cut to one of Bush's rivals for the nomination, Congressman Jack Kemp: "I don't think it should dominate the rest of the campaign, but it certainly was an electric moment."

To General Alexander Haig, another Republican candidate: "The issue's still hanging out there, and he's going to have to face it, going to continue to face it."

To David Garth, the longtime political consultant: "I think he [Bush] handled it well."

To Robert Squier, the Democratic political consultant: "I think that George Bush has decided that press bashing is a blood sport, and since he needs to pick up the manliness in his profile, he picked out Dan Rather last night and had a shot at him."

Bush offered an assessment that struck some as overkill. He described the interview as "Tension City," and said, "It's kind of like combat."

And then it was my turn. I looked into the camera and read the words I had written only an hour or two earlier:

"There are a couple of points to clear up about our live interview with Vice President Bush. Opinion polls, including the CBS News/ *New York Times* poll of yesterday, point out that a sizable number of voters believe there are questions Vice President Bush has not yet answered about the arms-for-hostages deal.

"The point of our interview was to get those answers. To that end, we pressed hard. I know of no other qualified reporter who knows another way to do it. We introduced the interview with a report on those unanswered questions.

"He was interested in discussing his presidential candidacy in general terms. That continues to be part of our continuing coverage of the 1988 campaign—to report on Vice President Bush along with all the other candidates.

"So the interview was heated, two people on something like a collision course. There certainly was no disrespect intended here for the office of the vice presidency—and on the basis of what the vice president is saying today, no hard feelings on his part, either.

"Finally, we just ran out of time. There was other news to report on a busy news day, and if the end of that interview seemed abrupt, it was dictated by the terrible hands of the clock. The interview certainly generated heat. I hope it also shed some light."

By the end of the second night, things had begun to stabilize. Once the Bush campaign's calls tapered off the calls turned around and wound up split down the middle. In a *Newsweek* poll, 37 percent of those questioned thought I did a "good, tough job" and 37 percent thought I was "too aggressive." I'm not a great believer in polls, as a rule, but those results were interesting.

None more interesting, at least to my mind, than the finding in the CBS News/*New York Times* poll that 79 percent thought the vice president knew more about the Iran-contra affair than he had told the public.

Some of the station owners and managers among our affiliates were distressed. Some were not just Republicans but diehard Bush partisans. One of these said I had been unprofessional. But the attitude of most was: "We don't think you handled it the absolute best it could have been handled, but we respect the fact that you tried to ask the tough questions."

Nor did every columnist heave a brick at me. In *Newsday,* Murray Kempton wrote: "Their encounter seems already to have been assigned its place in the realms of epic myth. The *New York Post* even had the luck to find a citizen outraged enough to cry out that Rather 'had insulted the vice president of the United States.'

"That is an utterance pregnant with patriotic fire and, like many such, it clouds a deal of American history with smoke. The endurance of degrees of insult is every vice president's incessant responsibility; a man inured through seven years of having to bear up uncomplainingly with the condescension and even the disdain of ineffables like Donald Regan and Mike Deaver could be, if anything, relieved for company as ungentle but never ungentlemanly as Dan Rather's."

The word soon reached us that both *Time* and *Newsweek* might run cover stories sympathetic to the vice president. *Time*'s was a cover story, but the pieces in both magazines were long and thorough. While I don't feel I got the better of it, I can't say they were openly one-sided.

Time's subtitle had a slight tilt: "Dan Rather sets sparks flying in a showdown with the Vice President." Calling the interview a "defining moment," the story went on to say:

". . . It came upon the viewer unawares. Unlike others, it was staged, self-generated, almost ceremonial: a media event. Dan Rather was interviewing George Bush on the *CBS Evening News*— live. Unusual, but not unprecedented. But what could have been just another conversation between two familiar talking heads turned into a collision with a resonance far out of proportion to the intense nine minutes of airtime. Their contretemps was not just a conflict between two men, but between two institutions, two symbols: the Vice President and the anchorman, the loyal emissary of the Reagan establishment taking on the embodiment of the East Coast liberal press."

There was an interesting sidelight to the coverage. A contributing writer to the *Time* magazine story was David Beckwith, who traveled with Bush and treated him kindly. After the election, Beckwith wound up as Dan Quayle's press secretary.

Newsweek had tried harder to be fair, I thought, in its reporting of the broadcast, noting how the tide of public opinion changed in the days that followed, and even pouncing on what most of the press had missed: "In the days that followed, something peculiar happened. An older value slipped in: substance. There was no getting around it: Bush had simply not answered Rather's questions about the Iran-contra affair. . . . Rather made a graceful explanation the next night, and the media began assailing the vice president for ducking the issues."

I am not positive about how much assailing Bush had to endure. Not until much later, when Bush's campaign operatives Roger Ailes and Lee Atwater boasted about it, did I realize how carefully their side of the interview had been staged. CBS News producer Mary Martin first revealed and Bob Schieffer later reported (in his book *The Acting President,* written with Gary Paul Gates) that Ailes stood beside the camera, holding up a yellow pad with cues for Bush. One cue read: "not fair to judge career . . . yours." (Maybe if Ailes had remembered to write the number, the vice president wouldn't have accused me inaccurately of being off the set for "seven" minutes.)

In the end, Bush was haunted by Iran-contra, although very few people in the press did much of the haunting. It's entirely possible that the treatment I received at the hands of the Bush campaign discouraged other reporters from asking Bush any more questions about sending missiles to Iran. The troublesome Donald Gregg, who said first one thing, then another, was shipped off to Seoul as U.S. ambassador to South Korea, but other voices kept piping up with new information that must have embarrassed the president.

And the special prosecutor, Lawrence Walsh, kept digging tirelessly, seeking convictions and, when convictions weren't to be had, seeking justice. He had the proof that wrongs had been committed—but by the time the trials began, the whole country had heard some of the confessions of the guilty parties, which helped to tangle up the judicial process. If crimes are committed in the government, then someone ought to be held accountable—that's the American way. So Walsh kept pressing. All the final months of the Bush presidency were marked by new revelations. Most striking were Bush's diaries, with admission of much greater knowledge of the Iran-contra affair than he'd ever publicly avowed. The fact is, he lied. It is an unpleasant fact, but a fact nevertheless. And just before he left office, George Bush handed out pardons right and left to the Reagan and Bush administration officials under indictment in Walsh's prosecutions. Had those officials been forced to face trial, they figured to tell much more about Bush than he wanted known.

Lawrence Walsh released his final report in 1993. Although

Walsh didn't find grounds to press criminal charges against George Bush, he did find that the vice president knew plenty about the Iran-contra operation. George Bush admitted as much—just once, under oath, in sealed testimony to Walsh's prosecution team. But to make such an admission to this reporter, or directly to the American people, letting them make an informed judgment about the leadership of their country, George Bush was not willing.

Not a great day for American politics—but not a great day for American journalism, either.

outtake

When Bad Things Happen to Good Towns

THERE'S A SAYING AROUND CBS NEWS, SO OFTEN PREACHED AND SO often practiced that it seems to have become our unofficial corporate policy: "No good deed goes unpunished."

But in the spring of 1993, some fellow Texans did their darnedest to prove otherwise. Thanks to them, I have a new perspective—not to mention a host of new friends and a treasure trove of happy memories—all stemming from one of the most unfortunate stories I've ever covered: the armed confrontation between law enforcement officers and members of David Koresh's Branch Davidian cult at their compound outside Waco, Texas.

That *outside* is a key word, and one not enough reporters paid attention to in the first days of the standoff. Most of these reporters had never been to Waco, didn't know their Brazos from a barn door, had never even sampled the town's native elixir, Dr Pepper. To these folks, ten miles outside of Waco was the same thing as ten steps from the McLennan County Courthouse. When they finally did get around to background research on the area, they continued to blur boundaries. And they thought Waco was *wacko.*

The proof was in their reporting, and many of them were guilty of sweeping generalizations and selective fact checking. One week into the standoff, *The Washington Post* ran a long, front-page article that set out to relate every weird thing that ever happened in Waco. This turned out to be a surprisingly short list for such an old town, and the two reporters had to stretch to make some events seem weird enough. My favorite example of this was the attempt to make something weird out of the fact that Bonnie and Clyde, Texas's most famous bank robbers, once had lunch at Leslie's Chicken Shack, a popular local restaurant that's still doing big business.

Well, for pete's sake, I thought as I read the article, every Texas schoolkid knows that Bonnie and Clyde had lunch *all over* Texas. This is one of the reasons Bonnie and Clyde were folk heroes: They helped the economy. Tough on banks—but they did great things for lunch counters. So why not the Chicken Shack?

And as far as calling Waco "wacko," that's a pretty old joke. Even Sam Houston himself, the Father of Texas, used that joke, and it wasn't very fresh then. Did you ever notice that people never find jokes on their names very funny? It works the same for jokes on the name of their hometown.

But my amusement and bewilderment evaporated as I read on. The article (and please understand, there were several others just like it) went on to say that because Waco is in the middle of the Bible Belt, and in the middle of the gun culture, it was only natural and inevitable for local citizens to "get a message from God" as Koresh claimed to have done, and then haul off, shooting at people. They even quoted an expert from Baylor University, the jewel in the crown of the area's intellectual riches who talked about Waco's "frontier mentality" and other such theoretical concepts.

The whole thing struck me as pretty unfair—and it would have even if the Koresh compound were in downtown Waco. First off, it looked as if all of these reporters from around the world were piling on Waco during a crisis. Second, my father and I used to go fishing on the Brazos River, long before anybody ever heard of David Koresh. I thought I knew Waco fairly well, and I wasn't seeing the town in most of the press coverage I'd come across.

I sat down and hammered out a radio piece. I fired off one draft, broadcast it, and kept going. I had in mind pitching an essay to the *Waco Tribune-Herald,* right where the out-of-town journalists would see it first thing in the morning. Here is some of what I wrote:

> There's nothing like a weeklong armed standoff between the law and a religious sect to damage a town's good name: Waco, Texas, is finding that out in the continuing confrontation between law enforcement officials and David Koresh.
>
> From Waco's point of view, the hitch is that all this is happening about ten miles out of town, and nobody *in* town ever asked for credit for David Koresh's activities. But Waco is getting the credit anyway—and the blame.
>
> Now, in a relatively quiet moment during the standoff, I'd like to defend a perfectly decent city—Waco. Unlike some of the reporters swarming around Waco the past week, I'd actually been to Waco many times before the standoff started. I expect I'll be visiting again. And I speak with confidence when I say that, ten miles *inside* or ten miles *outside* the city limits, Waco has about the same chance of rearing a gun-toting cultist as any other city in America.
>
> You're going to find persons of extreme religious beliefs in any town in America, and you'll find some in Waco, too. But Waco is mainly a town of churchgoers—not cultists.
>
> Waco is a town smack in the middle of Gun Culture—but so is the whole country. America's gun culture is ancient, widespread, and deep. Honorable people may debate whether that's as it should be. But that *is* how it *is.*
>
> Waco may not be the prettiest town in America, but there are bends of the Brazos River as pretty as any place you can name. I've seen spots where an old oak will reach over the river like an old uncle reaching for biscuits across the supper table, nice enough that I'd gladly spend a whole afternoon fishing even if the fish weren't biting. Some of those spots are a way out from town—but some are within the city limits.
>
> Waco is a town of good schools and sturdy homes and interesting museums. Mostly, folks there just try to do right—about like folks in any town in America.
>
> There's nothing very out of the ordinary about Waco. Even Waco's wackos are about like wackos anywhere else in this country.
>
> Which is something to remember. Bad things can and do

happen in good places. But how can anyone say bad things are more likely to happen in some places than in others? Anybody who does try to say things like that ought to be more careful—especially if they're reporters from New York or Washington. As if those "normal" towns never set eyes on a gun or a cult or a nut case!

And I added this byline: "Dan Rather is a Native Texan, born in Wharton, raised in Houston, and schooled in Huntsville." I grew up believing that you never have to ask a man where he's from: If he's from Texas, he'll tell you, and if he isn't, you don't want to embarrass him. And like most Texans, I'm proud of my *whole* state, including Waco. Some might call that bias, and say it slanted my essay, but I wanted it on the record.

Rowland Nethaway at the *Waco Tribune-Herald* liked the essay and ran it as a guest column on the op-ed page on March 10. I was pleased, and figured that was the end of it.

It was not.

Almost immediately, I started getting wonderful letters and phone calls from the good people of Waco. Some had heard my radio broadcast, others had read the essay in the newspaper, but most of them told me how much they appreciated my speaking up for the city. A few thought I'd left out some of the town's principal attractions, and two or three wondered why anybody was supposed to give a cuss what Dan Rather thought about anything: Waco, they said, could do perfectly well without any help from me. Hard to argue with that, actually.

All of them told me how much *they* loved Waco, whether they were born there or only recently arrived. I knew that their kind of civic pride is hard to earn and hard to beat. These people would make it through the unpleasantness of the Koresh confrontation, and be stronger for it. I couldn't remember a community that had things in better perspective.

I knew that the staff at KWTX, our CBS affiliate station, was representative of the community: Buddy Bostick, the owner of the station, is a local legend and justifiably so; his news director Virgil Teeter has turned the station's news programming into a standard of excellence that most larger cities can't rival. Bostick and Teeter, along with station president Tom Pears and station manager Ray Deaver, consistently kept their heads, turning out first-rate journalism and truly serving their community throughout the crisis.

The standoff between David Koresh and the law lasted almost

two months more. Keeping the vigil became pretty dull. CBS News correspondent Vicki Mabrey spent fifty-five days in "Satellite City," the pasture near the Koresh compound where most news organizations had set up tents and trailers to cover the story. Vicki never complained, God bless her, although many other reporters did. I'm not sure I blame them. Hard to muster much enthusiasm for the umpteenth FBI briefing.

But nobody covering the story could have been happy with the outcome: On April 19, the compound turned into a fireball, dozens of lives were lost, and you could hardly see straight for all the finger-pointing, as most officials tried to pass the blame for the tragedy.

I stayed on the air late that night and flew to Dallas before sunrise the next morning. I had agreed to deliver a speech in Dallas that morning for an old friend of mine, Perry Smith. Somehow, I made it through my remarks without falling asleep (more than I can say for many in my audience), and then hopped into a car and drove to Waco to cover the aftermath of the shootout and fire. Understandably, Waco was fed to the teeth with reporters. For weeks, it had been extremely difficult to get phone lines out, every hotel was booked, and the beams from reporters' strange communications devices from satellites to cellular phones were causing all kinds of havoc with each other. Waco was still one of the most hospitable places in America, but that welcoming civic smile was getting just a *little* tight around the corners. As one Wacoan said to me, "If there's any good to come out of the tragedy at the compound, it's this: The reporters will go home."

But Waco was unfailingly friendly to this reporter, who appreciated every kind word. Being ridden out of town on a rail is the kind of reception most reporters expect under most circumstances—we're grateful for anything friendlier. Waco was full of big hellos and extra cups of coffee, firm handshakes and Sunday manners.

I learned that the Greater Waco Chamber of Commerce had scheduled its annual fund-raising dinner on, you guessed it, April 19, the fateful day the Koresh compound burned to the ground. Of course they postponed the dinner. Now, having rescheduled for June 3, they wanted to invite me as a keynote speaker. I was pleased to accept.

I prepared some remarks about neighborliness, showing consideration and compassion for the people whose lives touch ours, which I did and do believe is a quality we all need to consider and preserve. I'm sure my Waco audience hears better sermons every Sunday. My point was only that although we hadn't told David Koresh to do the things he did, and did not approve of them, he was our neighbor and we should have had a neighborly concern for him and for *all* of those involved in the tragedy at the compound. But nothing could rival the neighborliness Waco showed me.

I was made an honorary citizen of Waco. That's a wonderful gift: People saying, "Consider yourself one of us." I was also given the key to the city, a crystal eagle, a proclamation declaring this "Dan Rather Day" in Waco, and more goodwill than you can imagine. This was better than Christmas.

The best moment came when Mayor Robert Sheehy, Sr., spoke of reading the *Washington Post* article about the weird history of Waco. He'd heard about the article, and someone had sent him a copy the day it appeared. His voice grew thick as he described the anger, disappointment, and sorrow he felt when he read these descriptions of his city, and others like them, and the bewilderment he felt as he wondered what, if anything, Waco had done to deserve such treatment. I looked out across the audience and saw many others nodding. They'd heard about the article and felt the same way.

It took only one lesson to teach me to avoid overgeneralizing about entire communities. I remember the pain that Dallas suffered after 1963, when too many people in the rest of the world assumed that Lee Harvey Oswald was representative of the entire city, and that all of Dallas had wanted President John Kennedy dead. That reputation was undeserved, and Dallas struggled with it for many years. Since then, I've tried especially hard to remember that bad things can and do happen in good towns.

If that's a good deed, so be it. At least in this case I wasn't punished. In Waco, they seem to be making an effort to reward good deeds. Here's hoping the philosophy catches on.

FIVE

China: Revolt of the Students

T HE TRIP OF TEN THOUSAND MILES BEGINS WITH A SINGLE STEP, AC-
cording to an old Chinese proverb. For CBS News, the trip to our
coverage of the historic drive for democracy in Tiananmen Square
in 1989 began with a step in a different direction: not toward China,
but toward Japan.

Tom Bettag is a serious student of Japan. As a Fulbright scholar,
he'd lived in Japan for a time, learned some of the language, and
never lost his scholar's passion for the place. Under his guidance,
I've developed a better understanding of Japan as a military and
economic superpower and its continuing importance to the United
States as an ally. Indeed, I am convinced that the security of the
United States, now and well into the twenty-first century, could de-

pend more on whether we are allies with Japan than whether we are allied to any other single nation on earth.

But how to tell the story—or, more precisely, the many stories—of modern Japan? Some news organizations don't even try. Tom and I were constantly on the lookout for an opportunity, and in the winter of 1989, we saw it. Emperor Hirohito died, and Tom turned to me with the gleam in his eye that said this was our window.

The emperor's funeral, which the Japanese called "the final farewell," gave us the hook we needed to take the *CBS Evening News* overseas. I mean a fully staffed road operation, not for a day but for a period of time before and after the Japanese paid their final respects. I realized it was a reach, and we might need not only a hook but a ladder to sell this idea.

Keeping a promise to ourselves to think big, Tom and I wanted to lead every broadcast with a focus on Japan, across-the-board CBS News coverage. We would involve *60 Minutes, CBS This Morning,* and the *Weekend News;* every show would have at least a segment. Tom thought of an umbrella title for our coverage: "The Dawn of a New Era."

All that remained was to get the decision makers to fall in behind this strategy. We knew it would be a hard sell. Such a massive project would require coordination and expense, and in the stormy, increasingly competitive environment at all three networks, the trend was away from putting so many hands and so many dollars into a story, especially an international story.

I called the office of David Burke, the third president of CBS News in three years, and asked for an appointment. Normally, I would just walk in or call up and say that I wanted to see him. But I didn't always have a proposal of this magnitude (although I may have made it seem so). This was one of those times when you asked, respectfully, to see the captain in his quarters.

Even Tom spruced up for the occasion. His usual attire was what I would call slightly upgraded L. L. Bean. It was not uncommon for him to come to work in jogging shoes; loafers were for "formal" occasions. Now, as we neared Burke's outer office, I noted that Tom was wearing a necktie and lace-up dress shoes. We were off to a good start. Burke's secretary, Yvonne Connors, welcomed us while looking over the tops of her glasses, without raising her head. This is a habit of many good secretaries, enabling them to do at least two things at once. Yvonne usually did five. Extremely well, I might add.

I was pleasantly surprised by Burke's reaction to our request.

The first surprise was that he didn't throw us out. David Burke is a tall, lean, broad-shouldered, long-armed, slightly hunched Boston Irishman, the son of an Irish cop, and a very tough man. He listened and he listened intently. He had his fingers in the church-steeple position, with the fingertips touching. Dammit, I wished I had read one of those books on body language. He didn't say yes, didn't say much of anything beyond an occasional word. One was "risky" and another "expensive." The only complete sentence I remember his saying was, "I'll think about it."

I thought that David had shown a genuine interest, and that turned out to be the case. He had been for most of his life the quintessential Number Two, second-in-command to Roone Arledge at ABC, to New York Governor Hugh Carey, to Senator Ted Kennedy, and with the Dreyfus Corporation. Finally, he had emerged as Number One, and I was willing to bet he would want to make a splash.

"The Dawn of a New Era" would be that splash. He called Tom and me back to his office a few days later and, pacing in front of a map of Boston Common, gave us approval to move ahead. He still thought the idea was risky, but he was taking a chance. Tom and I left in a hurry, taking the prudent approach: Let's get out of here before he changes his mind.

And so we began "The Dawn of a New Era." For eight consecutive telecasts over a period of ten days, we transmitted the *Evening News* from Japan. No American network had ever done a remote broadcast of this scope from Japan, and few times from anywhere else. We achieved our goal of wall-to-wall coverage, and with outstanding contributions from two of our best correspondents, Bob Simon and Susan Spencer, we provided analysis of the rise of Japanese militarism today, a profile of the Japanese middle class, a look at the rigorous Japanese educational system, and a clear view of the decline of agriculture in Japan's new urban society. We also showed how the Japanese handled the teaching of their defeat in World War II: sort of a Japanese history of World War II as told by Hans Christian Andersen. On *48 Hours,* we carried live coverage of the emperor's funeral.

It was Bettag's idea to keep our cameras on the move: If you are in a foreign country, what's the point of broadcasting from a studio or your hotel balcony? We filmed little postcards from around Tokyo, anchoring from a Buddhist temple, Tokyo University, and a busy downtown street. We created special graphics and used original music to give our coverage as consistent a feel as possible.

At almost the last moment, President Bush decided to schedule a state visit to Japan and attend the funeral. I understood the trip almost didn't happen. The president tended to lean toward the Chinese, having served there briefly as a special envoy to Beijing in for part of 1974–75. Now, in 1989, his top advisers discouraged him from going to Tokyo, thinking it would send the wrong signal to the Chinese, who were brutalized by Japan in World War II. Chinese resentment and suspicion of Japan have never diminished much. So as a gesture to Beijing, when he confirmed his visit to Japan, President Bush expanded the itinerary to include stops in China (and in South Korea, as well) after the funeral. Although not everyone at our or other networks thought the effort was worthwhile, CBS News then decided to make a stop in China, too.

And that was a stroke of unbelievable luck. We had been in Beijing only a short while when I began to feel that something had changed since my last visit. Something was happening. A whiff of discontent was in the air.

"Something is boiling up from below," I said to Tom. "You can hear it, see it, feel it everywhere." We had checked into the elegant but eccentric Hotel Mandarin, where Chinese musicians in tuxedos played Mozart in the lobby; now Tom and I went to a nearby garden and talked about the almost breathtaking progress China had made since the death of Mao Tse-tung.

But economic reforms and technological advances had as yet been unmatched by *political* changes. China still lived under the old-line, hard-line Marxist-Leninist-Maoist government. By this time the world had seen glasnost and perestroika in the Soviet Union, and the policies of openness and restructuring were giving people new ideas all over the Eastern Bloc. But the Chinese leadership didn't seem to have heard the rumblings that would soon lead to the fall of the Berlin Wall and the collapse of the Soviet Empire.

I couldn't put my finger on it, but I sensed that the Chinese people, unlike their leaders, wanted more change, faster: I could almost feel the tremors beneath my feet.

One of the curses of Tom's job was that he often had to listen to my nonstop narrations. But this time he was clearly interested. "If you're right," he said, "this could be one of the great stories of our lifetime."

CBS News producer Susan Zirinsky reminded us about the Purple Bamboo Park, where people flocked on Sundays to a special corner, not unlike Hyde Park in London. The Chinese students and intellectuals came to talk and argue among themselves about ideas, and some came to practice their English on each other. This was Sunday afternoon: Why not go now? With producer Harry Radliffe, I went directly to Purple Bamboo Park.

To my surprise the people were talking about freedom, about democracy, about Leninism, Stalinism, and all the -isms, openly and matter-of-factly. They were talking about communism being obsolete politically, discredited intellectually, and unmanageable economically. They were excited about Gorbachev and had a sketchy idea of what he was doing. There was a consensus in this marketplace of ideas, in this small corner of China, that China needed to move more rapidly to change socially and politically. The Soviet Union's reforms, however, were not a map for China; China must find its own way.

A CBS News camera crew recorded many of these conversations, and thanks to satellite technology, within hours CBS would report that there was something that looked like a democracy movement stirring in China.

When we left China, Tom and I were convinced that we had put a marker down. Things sometimes go unnoticed on the Sunday news, but we were excited, in the way reporters are when they think they are onto a big story and onto it early. Ours was an almost childlike excitement. When I lose the ability to feel that way, I will know it's time to quit.

We gurgled out sentences that overran each other's speech. We knew we had to come back to China, and soon. We packed for our stop in South Korea the next day, and then I don't think we slept at all on the eighteen-hour flight home on the White House press charter. Neither could we shut up, despite the encouragement of those seated around us. It was one of those flights where you could get drunk twice and sober up three times. Other newspeople were shouting, "Will you shut up back there?"

We had talked David Burke into approving a long iffy visit to Japan, and now we talked about doing the same thing with China. Tom admonished me: "This is where you need discipline. You can't come home and start babbling about a China trip. It's like a big bank heist where you can't start circulating the money. Let's have a personal news blackout. Take the temperature. See the reaction to the Japan trip. Get some sleep. Clear our heads. Plan a little."

Tom, always the practical one, made sense, and logic told me that CBS would probably not send us on a crosstown bus for a year after all this. But I knew Tom and I were both dreaming as fast as we could. Gorbachev and Deng were planning the first Sino-Soviet summit since Stalin and Mao—maybe *then* we could make our move. We had left a great story building there, and we wondered how we could get back to China and get it on the air.

And so we waited. The Japan trip received better overall reviews than we had originally heard, and had gotten an unexpected boost from an unexpected source. Several somebodies had mentioned at several parties to Larry Tisch that they had liked our coverage. Here is a lesson it has taken me a lifetime to learn. A remark to the boss from his peers is worth more than a barrel of ink. If he had read this in a newspaper, Tisch might not have been impressed. But his peers said they learned from it, and Tisch mentioned this to his man and his man passed the word on to David Burke.

The story from Purple Bamboo Park had gone unnoticed. No disappointment there. All that meant was that we still had a clear track. Bettag laid out a budget, penciled in the details, and pulled a few trustworthy people from the *Evening News* into his circle of planning. We began slipping discreet memos to Burke, mentioning our reports on "The Changing Face of Communism" and how they might continue. And gently reminding him of our conviction that something was bubbling up from the bottom in China.

Soon we began to see scattered notes in the newspapers; students in China were staging mini-protests. It was written off as the traditional spring unrest. Tom and I smiled like deacons with four aces, convinced it was much more.

This went on for a few days, then Burke called me into his office. It was nearly 5:00 P.M., too close to airtime for me to be comfortable. But he got my attention.

He brought up the negotiations in 1980, when he was with ABC and Roone Arledge had made an offer I nearly accepted. "One of the reasons Roonie and I tried to hire you," said Burke, "was partly because we talked to some people, and had seen for ourselves that you have as good a nose for a story as anyone in broadcasting. We know you're rough and raw around the edges and sometimes you get carried away. But this experience in Japan confirms to me that your instincts can be trusted. Now tell me what you really think about China because I can't see it. And you don't know what I had to go through to get us to Japan."

I leaned over his desk and said, "David, I've never felt stronger about any story at any time. Not only should we go, we have to go. I don't know what's there, but I know it's big and it's coming. And

I'm so afraid it will happen before we get there, I can't express it to you."

He said, "Then we're going to go." Just like that. I could not have been more astonished if Princess Diana had ridden through the room on a giraffe. I told him I appreciated it and he wouldn't regret this decision. Then I asked, "How are we going to pay for it?"

He said, "That's for me to work out. Your job is to make this trip everything you've imagined, and my job is to handle the finances and upper management."

A year later, Burke would be forced to resign. Though it was denied at the corporate offices, the rumor was that he had fought too many budget battles. I hoped that was not the case, but in any event I respected David Burke even more for putting his hand in the fire for us.

If you worry enough about budgets and ratings, you will wind up with no news, bad news, or severe whiplash. In the end, the test is whether CBS got its money's worth. In this case, we did.

In May 1989, we were ready to strike out for China, lining up a top-notch team that included Bette Bao Lord, the brilliant American writer born in China, who would act as our special CBS News consultant for the trip. But then something happened that caught me up short. Probably in an attempt to intimidate the Panamanian dictator Manuel Noriega, the United States began to mobilize its forces in Panama and deploy additional forces. (Noriega, as it turned out, didn't budge until Christmastime, when the United States moved in and ousted him. The eventual December invasion was still a long time in the future, and in May we had no way of knowing what these U.S. troop movements meant.) So I had to ponder, and worry.

The prospect of drastic change in China is a big story, but for an American reporter there can be few stories any bigger than American service people readying for war. Should we be going to Panama instead of China?

Part of my quandary would be familiar behavior to any producer who's ever worked with me. Because news never breaks out in one place at a time, I am always asking, "Where else should we be?" This can drive a producer crazy when he has worked for weeks preparing a story. If we are in Russia for the Clinton-Yeltsin summit, I ask if we ought not to be in Mexico for the guerrilla uprisings. If we are in South Africa for the first multiracial elections in that country's history, I ask if we ought not to be in the Middle East. And so on. This is sometimes a practical exercise. In January 1994, for example, we did go from the Clinton-Yeltsin summit to the Los Angeles earthquake with barely a pause. But this kind of thinking is also a guard against complacency, trying to keep ourselves sharp: If we have to change coverage plans quickly, how can we do it?

But in May 1989, this was no exercise. We were proposing to go halfway around the world for a story that had only hinted at happening—while America's sons and daughters were about to put themselves in harm's way on our doorstep.

I already suspected what our competitors thought of the China trip, because I'd talked directly with Peter Jennings and Tom Brokaw. When the Soviet leader Mikhail Gorbachev had recently gone to Cuba to meet with Fidel Castro, all three network anchors wound up in Havana to cover the summit. Although Peter, Tom, and I like and respect one another, we seldom have the opportunity to sit around and shoot the bull. Halley's comet comes around more often. But by chance during the Gorbachev-Castro summit, we had a mini-summit of our own, putting back some truly terrible rum drinks and comparing notes at a press party.

The subject of Gorbachev's pending trip to China came up. Both Tom and Peter indicated they had no intention of going. Tom pointed out that *The Today Show* had just spent a week in China; that and his own inclinations had him saying there was little to be gained from another trip. Peter said flatly, "We're not sure anything's going to happen in China."

Those words were ringing in my ears that May as we got ready to go to China—and the United States seemed to get ready to go to war in Panama. Finally Tom Bettag and I went to David Burke's office. The scene was almost a duplicate of the previous meeting in which Tom and I had set out all the reasons to go to China—only now I was setting out all the reasons *not* to go to China. "David," I said, "we run the risk of being Wrong-Way Corrigans on this story."

I admit I felt a little foolish, not quite the boy who cried wolf, but closer than I care to be. Burke, however, was iron and oak. He listened patiently, and then replied in a steady, low voice, "You told me you believed in your instincts. You told me you believed China was one of the great stories of our time. I believed you. I'm going to ask you this question: In your heart, which do *you* believe is the more important story? You and Tom are trained reporters with a lot of overseas experience. I'm not. What does your heart tell you?

What does your gut tell you? What does your experience tell you?"

Tom and I looked at each other. If Tom had ever wavered on this story, it was only because his anxious anchorman was a bad influence on him. Now he put his foot down. "They all still say China," said Tom.

"China," I echoed. Now I *really* felt as though I'd been sent to the principal's office.

Burke said, "Trust your own instincts. Get out of here."

So we set out for China. That meant missing the Overseas Press Club awards dinner, where the *CBS Evening News* won a prize for its reporting from the Soviet Union. Peter Jennings was handing out the prizes. He announced that Tom Bettag and I couldn't accept the award because we were on our way to China. Then, according to friends who were there, Peter added, "I hope you'll be watching ABC. We'll be covering the *real* story—American troops in Panama."

Peter's justifiably famous for his witty remarks, but I believe that's one he now regrets. As big as the Panama story was, China would turn out to be bigger. And CBS had more than a headstart.

We flew eastward to China, not across the Pacific and into Japan. We scheduled stops in Paris and New Delhi, catching a few winks in both cities before flying into Beijing. Any experienced TV correspondent knows to catch all the rest you can on the way to a story. When the plane door opens, you need a surge of energy and stamina.

After we landed in Beijing, we dropped off our bags and went right to the heart of Tiananmen Square. We wanted to see and listen and find out what had changed in the past two months. The students from the universities had started their demonstration; at that point, it was nothing more than that—a student demonstration. In our imaginations, our hypotheses did not stretch far enough to see what it would become.

There is nothing in the world quite like Tiananmen Square. The Great Hall of the People is on one side, this huge mausoleum of a building. In the days of Mao, the people were not allowed to enter and to a large degree this is still true. At the top of the square is Tiananmen Gate, which leads from the square directly into the ancient Forbidden City. Above the gate is the huge portrait of Mao, forty feet by twenty-four, three stories high, that so dominates the entire square.

On the other side is the Museum of the People, and right in the middle of the square is the Monument of the Heroes, slightly phallic in shape, a kind of miniature Washington Monument, with inscriptions along the base of it honoring heroes back to antiquity. You had to climb a long flight of stairs to reach the entrance. At the base of the monument the students had established their headquarters. It was a long and laborious process to get there; they had already set up some loose checkpoints, a series of four circles, with fifty yards separating each one from the next. Part of what they were guarding against was being infiltrated by plainclothes police and local intelligence agents. Each circle was color-coded, and the last was red.

In the square itself, not many police or soldiers were in evidence. When we arrived that night, the scene was not particularly tense. There was no sense of danger. We did want to get some footage, but mostly we wanted information. Experience tells you to get there early and find out who the leaders are. Later, that task always becomes much more difficult.

When we first began talking to the leaders of the demonstration, one thing soon became clear: Something big was indeed brewing. We confirmed in our own minds that this was a beginning, not an ending.

Several of the students spoke English; the less well-off of the leadership did not. Those who had a second language tended to speak Russian, or a kind of pidgin Russian. At the checkpoints, we were asked a few times, "Russky?" And we replied, "No, no Russky." We had to keep repeating ourselves, explaining what we were doing there. Some suspected that we were CIA, or double agents of the Chinese government. Some couldn't make out whether we were British or American, TV or newspaper. A few said, "Oh, CBS, American TV."

One of our first steps was, and almost always is, to organize a support group. We used two or three interpreters, including Mike Lam, a young man who had flown in from Hong Kong, who was a paid CBS staffer. Mike was a wonder, setting up most of our operation in an instant. Then you can usually find certain types, among them The Scrounger and The Scholar. We found and kept with us a brilliant young American student, Bob Orr, who was happy to work for what we were able to offer: two meals and low pay. He was the son of two California schoolteachers, had never made less than an A in his life. He was designated as my guide and facilitator. Tom's interpreter was Lisa Weaver, a tall, freckle-faced, red-haired American woman from Minnesota, around twenty-six, who had been a student at Beijing University and stayed on to live with her Chinese boyfriend, an artist.

Americans living in China tended to be remarkable people, and she was one of them. The thing that shocks a lot of visitors to China is that you are never alone. When she moved in with her boyfriend, she moved in with three generations of his family, including uncles, aunts, and cousins.

There is a different sense of personal privacy from what we know in the West. The people touch you, feel you, touch your hair. When our redhead was talking our way through the checkpoints, working like hell, she wheeled around once and obviously started scolding a Chinese man standing behind her. I asked her, "What did you tell him?" And she said, without cracking a smile, "I told him to get his hand off my ass."

We referred to our three recruits as the Redhead, the Superkid and the Hong Kong Hustler. The Superkid got us right through to the top echelon of the student leadership. They spoke with animation to each other, quickly, words tumbling on top of each other, gesturing vigorously. They tended to interrupt each other, explaining what their movement was about, what they hoped to accomplish.

Here is what they were saying: They had a passion for self-determination. China had embarked on major, fundamental changes. More than any other single thought was their conviction—it was everywhere, palpable, in their voices, their eyes—that the system and the society were going to change and soon, rather than later.

The Richard Nixons, the Henry Kissingers, the George Bushes of the world all talk to the top. They don't talk to these people; they don't see or hear what is happening at ground level. If George Bush had talked to any of these students, he would not have later sent Brent Scowcroft to Beijing to clink glasses with China's old guard. The few American diplomats who know China, who see China, bump their heads against the same mentality ceiling that has been in place forever. It is the "I know China; I met with Mao Tse-tung or Lin Pao" Syndrome. We experienced the same problem in Iran, when our top people got all their information from the shah and his inner circle, and never sensed the volcano that was about to erupt.

One of the Chinese students started quoting Thomas Paine. When we talk about students in China, we talk about the treasure of the nation. To even enter a university in China, you have to demonstrate absolute brilliance, or have strong political connections. A student has special standing in Chinese society. We were talking to young people nineteen, twenty, and twenty-one years old. What they knew about our Constitution, our civil rights, Jefferson and

Lincoln and Tom Paine, fewer than 10 percent of American students know.

Do you get the picture? I hope I am never so blasé that I can stand in the middle of a square and not be impressed when I hear a twenty-one-year old foreign student quoting Tom Paine to me. I am not too proud to admit that I can't quote Tom Paine.

They knew what they believed in, knew what they were willing to die for, and how many such people do you meet in a lifetime? They believed it was a time to stand, and that was what leaped out of their eyes and faces. After about three hours in the square, I began to feel that the government would respond with violence. I have covered a few and I have learned some things about the dynamics of demonstrations. You cover one at the U.N., and you go away thinking, "This is interesting, but their hearts aren't in it."

One didn't need long to figure out what the boiling point would be in the square. Either the government would cave in, fold, and compromise in a way it had never done before, or there would be real violence here. Part of what went through my mind in those hours was the power of the individual, of one person with a conviction. In modern life it is fairly easy to forget how much power is there, or to say it was once true but no more.

There was an echo in what the students were saying of Martin Luther, who uttered these unforgettable words: "Here I stand. I cannot do otherwise." The students spoke of the need, what they called the imperative, of change. They gave full credit to Deng Xiaoping and those around him for making economic changes over the past ten years. All the while, they underscored their belief that even faster *governmental* changes were needed.

Their core argument, which they argued so fervently, was the need for change in the whole system. Marxism, Stalinism, and Maoism were dead, had been dead for a long time. They were arguing among themselves. This is what many people missed: They did not see the U.S.A. as the personification of all that was good. They did not want a United States of China. They wanted something uniquely Chinese; yet they were riveted by the ideas of liberty and freedom and a representative government. Their government was corrupt and unresponsive. The aging Chinese leadership knew nothing of real life. These students were patriots who loved their country.

We talked until dawn, and videotaped only a fraction of what we observed. At first, they didn't know or care who I was, didn't always grasp that we were journalists. Later, after the movement took traction, and they realized they were being watched by the rest of the world, signs appeared in English. They had studied the techniques of shaping public opinion and believed in it.

Mark it well, they considered themselves Communists. It was all they had ever known. And this is where the conversation grew complicated, got confusing and hard to fathom, all the more fascinating and intriguing because this was so. They wanted a whole new system that was uniquely Chinese, Marxism blended with liberty, freedom, democracy.

Several times, and my notes reflect this, the leaders would say it in just this way: "Liberty (pause)—freedom (pause)—democracy." They knew a lot about the Soviet system, and could discuss with you the Soviet dialectic. One woman student argued that Communism had brought some benefit to China because it attempted to bring justice. As an economic system it was not worth a damn and as a political system it didn't get anything done. They didn't want to be ruled by a dictatorship right or left, they said. They had this sense that they needed a government that addressed the complaints of the people.

Corruption was high on their list of complaints. Corruption was deep and abiding in China, with long tentacles and historical roots. They needed a way to deal with it. They described the party elite as getting privileges that the people as a whole not only didn't have, but in many cases had no conception of them. No one but members of the elite could get a job, buy a good train ticket, or get a library pass without paying off someone.

The students wanted to eliminate corruption, or at least reduce it. They wanted those entrusted with power to be accountable to the people. They wanted a little more freedom of the press, for example, and they recognized that this included radio and television. They saw this as a way of exposing corruption and holding the ruling class accountable. My sense was that they understood this better than many Americans understand it.

There were several TV networks in China, but all were owned and operated by the government. There were many newspapers, all government controlled on a regional basis. The one newspaper that carried extensive news from the outside world was circulated only to the highest officials. The press wasn't going to expose corruption; it was a part of it.

What was so clear was how much comparative shopping the students had done. They knew in detail the Bill of Rights. They quoted Karl Marx and the Little Red Book of Chairman Mao. They were familiar with Pushkin's poetry. And they understood the British parliamentary system and the advantage of having one head of state and one head of parliament.

Question: How many Americans discuss, even around Harvard Square, the relative merits of these philosophies? Not very many, I would suggest, despite the pretenses.

There was venom in their voices when they talked about the "party elite." They jumped to their feet, and equated it with the Mafia, gangsters riding on the running boards of '37 Fords with Tommy guns. I sensed they had seen some old Edward G. Robinson movies.

One of the main complaints about the corruption was that parents couldn't get their children into schools without a payoff. This was a complaint also heard inside the Soviet Union. The message: People care about schools no matter where they are. Parents will do anything to get their kids into a decent school.

When the revolution comes, it will start with the P.T.A.

What you saw in Tiananmen Square was simply at first a student protest. Would there be a metamorphosis? Would it catch on, spill over into a movement? The students were hopeful that with Gorbachev's presence their demands would get attention. There was no open concern yet about violence, and no sign that any violence had been threatened. Given what was going on out there, the government had shown some restraint.

The Gorbachev visit was not the reason we had come to Beijing, but it had served as a convenient cover. Now we had to start making decisions—how much of our resources to commit to the summit and how much to what we saw as the main "rail" of the story, the students.

We went back to the Hotel Mandarin, once more past the Chinese orchestra in tuxedos in the lobby, and began to reestablish our base camp. We had our satellite dish and our nerve center in place and all we needed now was the next twist in whatever the story was going to be. We were working against the clock, aware that we would be hard-pressed to stay many more days, if any, once the Russian premier left. As the test pilots were fond of saying, we were already pushing the envelope. I had assured Burke we would not get carried away on his time or Mr. Tisch's money. It wasn't open-ended.

My personal feeling was that the meeting of the two troubled Communist giants had already paled. China was different. Ideology, governments, even epics and ages come and go, but China somehow stayed a mystery. When I had first gone there in 1972, an old China hand had told me to think of the country as a huge glacier that seems motionless for centuries, so slight is the movement. Suddenly, there is an avalanche and the glacier grinds and crashes and stirs with a terrible violence. Then the glacier is quiet once more. So moved China.

Coming off the square, I thought, this is the avalanche. It is coming. I had no illusions about our being able to define or explain China. We had been trying to understand China as a nation, as a people, for 150 years. Ever since the old Yankee clipper ships sailed into the harbors, journalists had been among the foremost providers of information about China to the outside world. Diplomats and scholars, missionaries in the beginning, and correspondents, particularly Americans, had clung to the tradition of trying to explain China as best we could. Not all had been distinguished, but there was a rich legacy of American reporting on China by Thomas Miller, Edgar Snow, Theodore White. These thoughts were muddling around in my brain even as we reexamined China through the lens of the electronic age. White had written a breakthrough book at the end of World War II. Snow had been accused of being a Communist and an apologist for Mao. But he saw Mao as engineering a powerful effort to change China.

Here we were in 1989, working along the same themes: despots at the top, a churning, volcanic rumbling coming from below. What had triggered the protest was the death in April of that year of Hu Yaobang, the closest the politburo had to a pro-reform member. His death sent many students into mourning, and the mourning had turned into demonstrations, and these were evolving into a movement.

At one point, Hu Yaobang had been the heir apparent to Deng. He was a dedicated Communist, a scholar who rose to the top. There had been student protests in 1986, centered in Shanghai, culturally the most Western of Chinese cities. Hu was accused of being soft on the radicals, and this turned into the fatal mistake of his career. Now what the police feared most was that by cracking down too hard, they would transform him into a martyr for the students. The fear was legitimate. The same kind of solidarity movement that started in Poland could be sparked by this latest round of unrest.

I believe we were about the only ones in television who from the very start tried to unravel the central conflict: The goal of the Chinese leadership was to prevent the students' fervor from spreading to the workers, and then to the peasants. These were the basic layers of Chinese society, and as long as the government kept them separated, the party was secure. If two of the three started going in the wrong direction, the uprising would be difficult to stop.

As Tom and I talked over green herbal tea, Gorbachev was driving through the streets of Beijing. He was in for a shock, of that we were confident. First, there was food in China. At some corners fruit and vegetables were stacked higher than your head. You didn't see that in the Soviet Union. If Gorby was going to be gapemouthed at the sight of so much produce, his eyes were going to be spinning when he saw the throngs of students assembled in Tiananmen Square. No Communist leader had ever seen that many students urging the workers to unite behind their cause.

Frankly, I still couldn't figure out how to handle his trip. Our dilemma was how to deal with it in the existing time frame. And this is where the Chinese leaders blew it. The masses in the square had little or nothing to do with Gorbachev. But they elected to take no chances. He was given a tour of the suburbs in Beijing, which like suburbs anywhere else were not all that interesting. Here was the photo opportunity of their dreams, Gorby Does China, and they give him the "B" tour. No disrespect intended, but it would be sort of like a visiting dignitary coming to New York, and the mayor telling him, "Look, we're having a little trouble at Rockefeller Center, so we're going to show you Queens."

This was one of the stranger public appearances I had seen. They kind of whisked him in and out of the Great Hall of the People, and managed to have him pose for the mandatory picture beneath the huge portrait of Mao—but barely. His hosts did not want to risk his having any interaction with the students and, contrary to popular belief, I had the impression he wasn't really eager for an encounter, either. The visit had its comic aspect: Welcome, glad you're here, but can't wait to get you out of here because this town may blow at any moment.

I do not exaggerate the fleeting glimpses one had of Gorby, and that was all one had. He seemed bug-eyed and slack-jawed at what he was seeing. I had a sense that he had no idea what he was getting into, or what was going on. For roughly the first two weeks in May, many reporters had just concentrated on the Gorbachev visit. There was a lesson here. All of us had gotten accustomed to making a major or maximum effort with anything related to the word "summit." Didn't the politicians know it and, my, didn't they jerk our chains at each opportunity.

Gorby, for all his red-star-rising celebrity, had been reduced to a member of the supporting cast, and a minor one at that. While it certainly wasn't intended to do so, his high-speed, Chaplinesque swing through town provided a springboard for the students to multiply, and gave new energy and fuel to the protest movement.

One thing we suspected, which turned out to be true, was that the government was refusing to crack down while Gorbachev was its guest. *Time* magazine suffered somewhat by reporting that the Chinese had softened their line on the students. Not so. They were merely minding their manners, and biding their time.

I had heard that before Gorbachev arrived there had been some unusual troop movements. This was our first inkling that the army might be called in. The government had issued several warnings, and in some areas the police had actually busted some heads. Then it stopped. The boycott of university classes continued; the students and Party officials broke off whatever dialogue they had tried to develop. Some of the student leaders were vowing to stage a hunger strike. This was a new thrust by the students. A hunger strike in the Far East has a special significance. Anyone who has studied Mahatma Gandhi understands that a hunger strike is a fearsome weapon and carries a unique connotation. There was also the first semblance of a real split in the student leadership, with some in favor of the strike, some not. In the end, they decided to do it.

There is a danger in covering such things—the tendency to react as each new rumor replaces the previous one. There was the report that the army might move in, if not tonight, maybe tomorrow. In ours, an open society, you can check such reports. In China, you cannot. All Americans need to be reminded of the new turn in history that the United States brought forth, which is civilian control of the military. In China, there is no civilian oversight. It is an army of the Party, a tool of the Party. In the Soviet Union, the same was true.

The hunger strike and the climax of the Gorbachev visit had overlapped and dominated the news in the middle of May. Here were the leaders of the two Communist monoliths meeting at the pinnacle for the first time in thirty years. Then came the incredible scene of the seventeenth of May, the massive march that brought into the streets entire workforces, including some government ministries and maverick army units.

And out of the blue, amid questions about his age and health, Deng, the eighty-four-year-old hard-liner, the squatty little survivor, came down from his tower and made clear that he was still running the country. Nevertheless, the movement was gaining speed faster than we could have imagined. Gorbachev left town almost literally scratching his head. The look on his face when he left the airport—and I went out to see it—was priceless. Very quickly, as Gorby departed, the events tumbled one on top of another. The cataclysm was here.

Gorbachev was the one who eventually revealed that Zhao Ziyang, the Party chief, had told him Deng was indeed in charge. The government tried very quickly to arrange three meetings with the students: at a hospital where the hunger strikers were being monitored, at the Great Hall of the People, and in Tiananmen Square itself. The scene at the foot of the Great Hall was incredible, if you can appreciate what respect for authority means in China.

The number of students in the square was swelling each day. They came by foot, bicycle, bus, and truckloads. Once Gorbachev left, you had to know the government was going to crack down. Age is revered in China, but the students were hammering away that the leadership was old and out of touch. The students were prepared to die for their beliefs, they said, but they didn't think it would come to that if only they could be heard. But they were sadly, fatally wrong.

China's experience with the Red Guards in the 1960s and early '70s was one of the main reasons communism had been discredited. Deng had been a victim of the Red Guards. The students knew that history, but felt no fear. Their movement was spontaneous and nonviolent. The Red Guards were young people manipulated by the Party—they were the Hitler youth of China. The students were very much aware of the difference.

Now the demonstration had moved to the next phase. The students had decided to target two leaders for specific criticism, Li Ruihuan and Deng himself. And behind the scenes a terrific power struggle had taken place, reinforcing the power of Deng Xiaoping and purging the one potential peacemaker who was saying, "You ought to talk to the students. Permit them to release some of the steam." Zhao Ziyang was purged and removed from his position as head of the Party.

Then came the decision to send in the army, and the tanks were standing by on the outskirts of the city. There were reports of splits inside the army: "They may do it, may not." To eliminate the uncertainty, Deng called in a unit from way out in the provinces, one that barely spoke Mandarin.

Which led to the absolutely unforgettable spectacle of the people of Beijing blocking truckloads of troops with their bodies. And the image most indelibly burned into the memories of people around the world, was the solitary, slender, short-sleeved young man who stopped a column of tanks from rolling into Tiananmen Square by walking slowly in front of the lead vehicle and standing there. The tank commanders popped out of their turrets like gophers and stared at him with a blend of confusion and bemusement.

He was later arrested, his fate unknown. He was identified by human rights groups as Wang Weilin, the nineteen-year-old son of a Beijing factory worker.

By this time the home office was on record as being thrilled with the coverage. That's always nice to hear. But Jean Rather was saying, by overseas phone lines from New York, "Yes, but you are coming home, aren't you?" You can't stay on the story forever, no matter how much the adrenaline is pumping. You recognize a sensation known as falling in love with the story. I would argue that not to do so would lessen your chances of being good, much less great, at telling the story.

On the other hand, David Burke was depending mightily on my giving him an honest, professional reading on everything from some semblance of budget control to watching out for the safety of our people. This is China. Red Guards and Boxer Rebellions. The sense of being an alien in an alien place. In China that sense becomes very real. Burke expressed his concern. How do we protect our people? How many ways do you deal with tear gas? If shots are fired, do you stay at your post, hit the ground, call 911? Do you flee, and if so, where do you go and how do you get there?

Beijing is an enormous city. It sometimes took hours to get from our base camp at the hotel to the square. The streets were swarming with people, including vigilante security units. The dangers may have been real or imagined, but the emotions were running wild.

We had people who were among the best in the business at what they did, the ones who really made CBS tick. Some worked thirty-six to forty hours straight through. I passed the word that the situation had turned dangerous and might get more so. They had all volunteered to come, and anyone who didn't want to stay needed only to tell me, no questions asked. No judgments. We wanted them out of harm's way. I delivered that message on three separate occasions between the fifteenth of May and the middle of June. No one wanted to leave their posts because something might happen, and they were afraid of missing it.

Twice within an hour in Tiananmen Square I saw two of our people faint under sharply different conditions. One CBS person simply wanted to go to a rest room. Now, a rest room in a hotel is one thing. But a rest room in most of China is quite another. This was classified as an emergency nature call, and so I took him to one of the places around the square, a long, wide series of slit trenches, from which the stench was indescribable. There was nothing but a sea of people taking care of their vital personal body disposals. This staffer, a grown man—and I understood—took one look, inhaled one whiff, and fell over backward in a dead faint. He looked like a jackknifed oil derrick. If I had not been there every day, had not grown somewhat accustomed to the environment, I'm sure I would have keeled over the same way.

A short time later I noticed one of our cameramen weaving on top of a truck. Our technical team had done a marvelous job of improvising. We needed more camera positions, and we had been splitting them like amoebas. We wound up with one mobile unit that had been jury-rigged, and resembled a fugitive from somebody's destruction derby. I asked if the truck was German or Japanese. "Well, Mr. Rather," one technician said, "it's some of both." They had cannibalized a couple of old trucks, bought parts on the unofficial market, and created what looked like a relic of World War II.

The cameraman was standing on the roof, which fresh rain had made as slick as deer guts. He had positioned a tripod to have the camera in the center of the rooftop, and it kept slipping. He had been up there hour after hour, and at this moment we were live, on the air. I saw him first weave and waver and then just drop from exhaustion. This kind of dedication money can't buy. In my opinion, he was going to slide off the truck, but miraculously he did not. He was just sprawled there, out cold, finally getting some rest.

It began to get really rough at the beginning of the third week. They were closing airports and seaports with some regularity, and you can't determine when the last one will be shut down. I mean, you can't turn on Channel 11 and learn that the airports have closed down.

At Tiananmen Square, the noose had tightened and everyone knew it. There were arrests. There were rumors of executions. In the end, there would be indiscriminate gunfire into the crowds. The army had been engaging in heavy psychological warfare with the students and everyone else in the square. One more step, you sensed, and this would be a full-blown revolution.

The army had been spreading rumors that they were coming in strength from the southeast. Provocateurs circulated in the crowd.

Then the army started using the helicopters. The copters would just pop up out of nowhere, flying low over the square, in an attempt to panic the students and play with their minds. I know it certainly worked well enough on us. Were they going to strafe us, drop tear-gas canisters, or were they just scouting the area? Everyone was jumpy, all compounded by the fact that no one slept.

We knew they would come soon to shut down our ability to tele-cast from Tiananmen Square, and then would come the pulling of the plugs of all foreign satellite installations, including ours. But for now we kept working. At the same time, a U.S. Navy warship, anchored at Shanghai on a long-scheduled maneuver, canceled shore leave. The sailors were going to have Spam in the mess hall that night. And Betty Bao Lord with great enterprise kept calling every province in China to check and see if any demonstrations had broken out. Under the best of conditions, phone service was poor and slow. She confirmed protests in seventeen provinces and in time the number spread to all twenty-three. Hard to judge how big the demonstrations were, but they were happening.

By this time we had seen the first army units right on the edge of the square, the staging area. Soon the soldiers had shown up at the hotel, and our personnel were sounding edgy. I knew we were working against time and the bureaucrats. Tom Bettag and I hurried back to the hotel and found that CBS had interrupted a live broadcast to announce that Chinese authorities had pulled the plug from the square. And, indeed, they were intent now on shutting down our satellite.

We had two broadcasting positions, one outside in the garden and one inside. The troops were closing in, had blocked off the streets, while crowds gathered and chided them with cries of "Shame, shame on you." The soldiers had shown great restraint and discipline on several occasions, but there were also short, ugly, clubbing scenes. We didn't know what to expect. We wove our way through the army's loose encirclement and went immediately to our facility outside in the garden. Our hearts sank because we saw no one there. I feared we had already been shut down, but the contractor who had put up our satellite dish was still operating it. He had hidden himself in the shadows; now he emerged from his hiding place and gave us the hand signal: *Upstairs.*

I was relieved to see the satellite contractor, and not just because he was a nice guy. To transmit anything to the United States, we had to get material to that satellite dish at the Mandarin Hotel. We had links from Tiananmen Square to the hotel, but those links were controlled by Chinese television—government-controlled Chinese television—which had just broken the connections. We had video-tape pieces by correspondent Barry Petersen and myself, and we knew that we could beam them to New York, provided our satellite dish was still operating. Apparently the army hadn't shut down our satellite—*yet*.

Tom and I ran up to our control room and there correspondent Susan Spencer and Lane Venardos, the producer in charge, were broadcasting live. When I ducked in they were explaining to a government official that our main person, Mr. Dan Rather, was not here, and they—Susan and Lane—had no authority to let them pull the plug on any of our transmissions.

They were broadcasting, viewed by the American audience as they spoke. This was thanks to the adept planning of Tom Bettag, Lane Venardos, producer Susan Zirinsky, and Linda Mason, the executive producer of *Weekend News*. And back in New York, David Burke had seen the transmission and immediately called Howard Stringer, president of the CBS Broadcast Group. On Burke's recommendation, Stringer had put our broadcast from Beijing on the air live, interrupting a surefire prime-time ratings winner: the last-ever episode of *Dallas*. This is one of those occasions when you say you're glad you work at CBS. I can't know but have to wonder whether any other network executive would have made the call Howard did that night. (The fact that Howard came up in news, and we were way out in front on the story, probably helped.)

I walked into the room, live on the screen, and asked what was going on. Of course it was pretty clear what was going on. But I was stalling for time to get our new videotape transmitted back to the States. So I spoke very carefully, and pointed out that I had just arrived, so would these representatives of the Chinese government please explain to me the nature of the problem. Going through this discussion also enabled me to explain to the viewers exactly what was about to happen.

Over the shoulders of the Chinese gentlemen, I could see a small monitor. The videotapes were playing. I recognized Petersen's foot-age of Chinese citizens stopping army trucks and asking, "How can you do this?" Bettag wasn't taking any chances that the Chinese might see the tape, though. He positioned himself to block the entrance to the control room. CBS viewers couldn't see these machinations.

I went through a very polite and deliberate review of the paper the Chinese government had given us, authorizing our broadcasts. The paper was worthless now, of course. Finally, Bettag gave me a thumbs-up: The videotapes had been successfully transmitted to New York. Just in time, because the Chinese wouldn't be stalled any longer.

I insisted that if we were to be shut down, one of the Chinese would have to do it. I would not be put in the position of pulling the switch on our own telecast. Neither would anyone from CBS.

We danced briefly around the question of where the switch was, and I told the CBS audience that our policy was to obey the law. In China, this representative of the government was the law. And so we were going to be taken off the air now, with obvious regret. With that, the picture went to scramble.

Burke insisted that we leave; there were two flights still operating, and CBS had arranged for tickets to get us on board and out of the country.

But we had a little time before the planes left, and we wanted to get back to Tiananmen Square. We had no facility to broadcast live, but we could perhaps ship tapes to Tokyo or Hong Kong, and we could still get the story out by radio and cellular phone.

Tom Bettag and I and a crew piled into a car with the one and only driver still willing to violate the government-imposed curfew and make this trip at 1:00 A.M. (This fellow didn't speak much English, but the first day he drove for us he noticed that I had turned up the collar on my bush jacket. When we got back to the car, he had turned up his collar, too.) Now we told him through an interpreter that we wanted him to drive fast and hard. We pantomimed: "On the sidewalks." He got it—let us know he'd seen American cop shows and knew just what to do.

The mood at Tiananmen Square was tense. Everyone was awake, but you heard few conversations going on. Passing the checkpoints looked to be tougher. The guards seemed more than usually suspicious of strangers, especially Westerners. But then we said the magic word: *May-gwo,* American. We were reporters. We wanted to get the story back to the United States.

Suspicion melted instantly into sad smiles. The students knew what was going on, saw and heard the Red Army pulling into position around the city. They fully expected the government crackdown any minute. They weren't going to back down. The only thing they feared was that no one would ever know of the stand they'd taken, the sacrifice they'd made. They knew that within China, press restrictions would return, the society would close again, and word would not get out. But here we were, Americans, and we would tell the story.

And so they told us the story one last time. Their desires for an end to corruption and oppression, their dreams of liberty, democracy, freedom, not a carbon copy of the United States but a truly Chinese democracy. They pointed to the makeshift statue of the goddess of democracy that had been erected in the square. You knew she had a kindred spirit with the American Statue of Liberty, but she was all Chinese. That was what the students were trying to achieve.

We shot almost every tape we had, returned to the hotel, and flew out with our stories to Japan.

This was May 20. The army would move in with force around June 4. We left more than our normal bureau in place, but less than our maximum strength. Perhaps needless to say, these people were all exceptionally brave, including former CBS News correspondent Richard Roth, who was taken prisoner and roughed up by the Chinese during the June 4 crackdown.

Lacking support from, among others, the U.S. government, China's student-led movement for freedom and democracy was beaten down and back. It wasn't killed, it didn't die. Overpowered and wounded, it was forced to fall back, go underground, and await another time.

Later, President Bush secretly sent a high emissary, Brent Scowcroft, to toast with champagne China's victorious old-line, hardline Communist leaders. When the secret, including pictures, came out, no one in the United States said much. I believe it was because we were, as a nation, embarrassed by what had been done in our name—and what had not.

The final verdicts on the role of the U.S. government in acquiescing to the guardians of China's past will come with time. The irony is that we Americans used our influence to encourage the Chinese to change their economic system, which they did in the 1970s. But when a chance arose to make a statement about political freedom, America's leaders did nothing.

No one knows for certain how many died during the crackdown, but Amnesty International had the figure most believed, a toll of one thousand. The story won't end there, of course. China will always have more students, burning with more ideas, with or without the cameras rolling. And if the spirit of Tiananmen Square can stay alive, someday in China freedom will ring.

outtake

Franny

W E DON'T LIKE TO ADMIT IT, BUT IT'S TRUE: TELEVISION NEWS IS still television. And, yes, we sometimes wear makeup, too, just like everybody else on television.

Frances Arvold made me up my first day with the network. She continued to make me up for nearly thirty years. And when I was on the road and out of her reach, she'd be calling me up, reminding me to cover my beard line or attend to some other part of my face that was suffering without her ministrations.

Sometimes people tried to call her the Makeup Lady. She was a lady, past question. But she was a Makeup *Artist.*

She worked on entertainment programs. She worked on news programs. I can't list the faces she made presentable for the cameras. We used to say she'd do everything short of plastic surgery.

But let's start with a few names. Edward R. Murrow. Eric Sevareid. Judy Garland. Every president of the United States since Truman.

At the Kennedy-Nixon debate in 1960, however, Richard Nixon turned down Franny's assistance. Years later the story cropped up that Franny had somehow sabotaged Nixon's makeup, made him look swarthy and sweaty while Jack Kennedy looked healthy, vigorous, handsome. Franny was an artist, but she was also a journalist, with a journalist's ethics. She made up every face *accurately*. She didn't editorialize with her pencils and sponges, she gave you the straight face. And she didn't like this rumor about Nixon's makeup one bit.

So she wrote to Mr. Nixon, asked him if he recalled the hectic hours before the debate, and if he remembered that she'd sabotaged his makeup.

Richard Nixon wrote back. No, he said, he'd declined her help—and regretted it ever since.

Franny was satisfied—but only for a minute. And then went back to work.

She was small and gentle, with a sweet lilt to her voice that could melt the snows in her native North Dakota. At *CBS Evening News* Christmas parties, she'd dance for six hours in a row, wearing out the kids a third her age. Mike Wallace and Ed Bradley used to delight in swapping *slightly* dirty stories in front of her, just to tease her. "That Mike is such a rascal," she'd say.

She had a way of calming you down, talking quietly about things that were important. Your family. Her family—her beloved sister and brother and their families in Fargo. Franny remembered names. She remembered the times you'd shared. And she'd talk about these things, pulling out little stories like little stones from a bag, and turning them over to show you.

Then during a broadcast she'd be just off to one side, watching the monitor to make sure that her work met her exacting standards. And she'd joke with the camera operators and production secretaries and stage managers, who loved her dearly.

Franny left CBS a few years before she died, leaving New York for the warmth of her family and friends in the Dakotas. We missed her—but we weren't lonely for her, because we'd call her up, and she'd send clippings from the paper, or pictures of the deer that used to come right up into the yard at her niece's house.

Franny was an artist. Franny was, sitting right there behind the camera, a witness to American history. Franny was a friend. Now Franny is gone . . . and the time for being lonely starts.

SIX

The Party's Over: Gorbachev and the Fall of the Wall

IN CHINA, THE UNTHINKABLE WAS NOW A CHERISHED DREAM. BUT IN the Soviet Bloc, the unthinkable would soon be a reality.

By the autumn of 1989, the scene was almost like the commercials, where all the people in the crowded restaurant or train station drop everything to eavesdrop on the investment advice two people are discussing between themselves: The private conversation becomes the communal conversation. Everywhere I went in New York and around the country, I heard people discussing exactly the same subject, and sooner or later they'd all say exactly the same thing: "I can't believe it's happening *so fast!*"

"It" of course was the collapse of Soviet communism. Starting in the spring, what two generations of Cold Warriors had warned us about—the Domino Theory—actually happened in reverse. The dominos fell over there: Poland, Hungary, East Germany, Czechoslovakia, Bulgaria, Romania. The Baltic states wanted more than glasnost: They wanted their independence. And from Yugoslavia to Azerbaijan, no matter how much blood had to be shed, people were starting to want something called ethnic purity.

The man at center stage in this drama was Mikhail Gorbachev. He is unquestionably a historic figure. But I am not absolutely convinced that Gorbachev really meant to change the world, or even to change Mother Russia. His policies of glasnost ("openness") and perestroika ("restructuring") may have been meant as a fresh coat of paint for the mammoth Soviet system, to placate the grumblers just enough and then stay the course—forever. Others hoped Gorbachev meant to overhaul or reinvent Soviet communism, but surely he didn't mean to set in motion the forces that would implode the Communist empire over which he ruled.

Many if not all of his "restructuring" reforms were reactions to demands that had reached a dangerous potential among the varied populations of the Soviet Union, including the Russian people. The Kremlin was long accustomed to ignoring or suppressing many demands of the other Soviet states, but the government could not ignore for long the storm of dissatisfaction building from within Mother Russia itself. The storm reached such a point that the government had two choices: placate the people or crack down. Despite the objections of the Party hard-liners (who would later try to depose him), Gorbachev tried first to placate.

Gorbachev should not be credited then with tremendous initiative, but he should be credited with recognizing a problem. He had a decided vision of what would be required to address the problem, but had great difficulties in carrying out his vision. Yes, he met with resistance from the Party elite. However, there is considerable question about how committed Gorbachev was to democracy and genuinely representative government, which many in the West believed were the logical and intended ends of the reforms he instituted. Later, it became clear that Gorbachev had no immediate intention of abolishing one-party rule, or of relinquishing control of that one party.

About his moves to reform the economy, there are even more serious questions. With the economy, he moved slowly, cautiously, in fits and starts and jerks, and never demonstrated that he understood what a market-based economy was. (Chinese leaders did; Gorbachev did not.) The best example of this may be his refusal even to consider moving effectively to private ownership of land. As a lifelong Communist, as the model of the "New Soviet Man," he seemingly could not conceive of widespread individually owned land and other major property.

Later events demonstrated that Boris Yeltsin does understand—at a minimum, he understands better than Gorbachev did.

We at CBS News believed that the storm that had been building among rank-and-file Soviet citizens was nearing some kind of climax, that Gorbachev was the man at the center of the storm, and that our audience needed to be alerted to the changing face of communism—whatever that face turned out to be. And "The Changing Face of Communism" would become the umbrella title for a series of CBS News reports over a period of several years. For our coverage, we had a remarkable asset in two of the finest experts on the Soviet Union serving as CBS News consultants: Jonathan Sanders of Columbia University (now a CBS News Moscow correspondent) and Stephen Cohen of Princeton University. Between them, they know everything and everyone. Although they sometimes disagreed on particulars, Sanders and Cohen were both certain that Gorbachev bore close monitoring by CBS News.

The irony then, and later, was the fact that Gorbachev was more popular in the West than he was in the Soviet Union, where perestroika had brought disorder and more shortages. Many Americans, including our political leaders, were intrigued and even charmed by him. He is a bold man: How else could he rise so high in the Kremlin as an advocate of reform (and what must have seemed like drastic reform to some of the ossified apparatchiks around him)? He's sophisticated, the first Russian premier in memory whose suits fit. And he has an attractive wife. Although Westerners were never great fans of the speeches of Soviet leaders, most believed that Gorbachev was an interesting and intelligent (if long-winded) speaker—but *we* heard him in translation. Friends who are Russian speakers tell me Gorbachev has a thick country accent and was never a match for Boris Yeltsin's oratory. Russians mocked Gorbachev's speaking style.

A telling detail. Because as Gorbachev balanced himself on the high wire of a new global reality in 1988, reaching out for the hands of his country's old enemies in the West, his favorable ratings at home fell to 12 percent. The rating of his rival and eventual replacement, Boris Yeltsin, was 70 percent.

In a society where the people are conditioned *not* to share their personal political opinions, the survey might not mean much. But you didn't have to read the polls to understand that the mood in the

Soviet Union was changing. You could go a long way just listening to the jokes, like this one that was making the rounds in Russia in 1988: "What's the difference between the Soviet Union and the United States?"

Answer: "In the United States, Gorbachev could be elected president."

As it happened, there was a presidential election in the United States in 1988. It had become almost a ritual for any president to visit the Soviet Union, at least to shore up public confidence in his foreign policy and ideally to launch some kind of a campaign, taking a page from Nixon's dramatic trip to China in 1972.

Ronald Reagan was leaving office, but he was launching a campaign nevertheless: to solidify his future place in the history books. His crafty advisers had prepared a long good-bye for the Gipper, and the centerpiece of this farewell tour was to be Reagan signing an arms-control agreement that would seemingly join the United States and the Soviet Union in a new solidarity. Ronald Reagan, a man who spent most of his political career cursing what he'd come to call the "Evil Empire," would stand tall in the shadow of the Kremlin and announce this treaty with the Soviets for the good of all mankind. It would be a historic photo op.

What a picture! You may remember it from your TV screen or the cover of the weekly newsmagazines: Reagan in front of St. Basil's Cathedral at night, with the Hammer and Sickle and Old Glory in the background. What was that about strange bedfellows? There was Reagan, whose ability to forgive was surpassed perhaps only by his ability to forget, praising the Soviet Union and its leader. By implication, he had made himself a kind of unofficial manager of the campaign to keep Gorbachev in power.

Politics had replaced golf as the world's most bewildering entertainment.

I had been amazed for some time, and would remain so, by how wrong, how out of touch, and how behind the Carter and (perhaps to a greater degree) Reagan and Bush administrations were about the real developments within the Soviet Union. Again and again, American leaders and diplomats seemed to be wholly unaware of what the press couldn't escape: the rising pressure among ordinary Soviet citizens calling for drastic change. (This in turn leads to serious questions about the effectiveness of the Central Intelligence Agency and the rest of the U.S. intelligence community.)

Naturally we had White House and Moscow correspondents already in place. But well in advance, CBS had committed to assign not just a few reporters but a CBS News army to cover Reagan's trip to Moscow. We crammed the world's largest hotel, the Hotel Rossiya (which we promptly renamed The Roach Motel), with our personnel and equipment. The hallways in the Rossiya run longer than most city blocks, but a Marine boot camp would have been proud of the obstacle courses we created: With all the cases, cables, and crates, you had to play hop, skip, and jump just to get through the corridors.

As we would later do in China, we picked a theme and used it as an umbrella over the full range of CBS News, morning, evening, weekend, and Sunday. At this time, we chose as our working title "The Changing Face of Communism." But naming the story was the least of our problems. How do we tell it? As most people know, television has a problem with context and depth. But our challenges weren't only intellectual, they were practical. Television without pictures is not television, and how do you get pictures of social change? Even more challenging, how do you get pictures of social change in a closed society?

I went through a checklist of what I knew and believed about the Soviet Union, a country I first visited in the late 1960s. I had been back seventeen or eighteen times and I hasten to add that such travel does not an expert make. But I have a notebook and I keep a journal and I get paid to be a witness, to listen and observe. From my very first trip, I had the impression that the Soviet Union was not even a Third World country, but a kind of Fourth World country with the Bomb.

Each time I went back, I found myself wishing that more of my countrymen could see this place. Not many did. It would have no doubt been dangerous to say so in the Soviet Union, but the only things that seemed to work there were the KGB and the army. So many little things did not work at all, and that was the continuing impression on successive trips.

In 1987, CBS News made a documentary based on an unprecedented trip to the Soviet Union—seven whole days. At the time this was access as in-depth as any Western news organization had been able to obtain from the Soviet government, and I'm proud to say that under the supervision of producers David Buksbaum and Lane Venardos, we rose to the occasion. One of our segment producers was Andrew Heyward, who within a year would be the first executive producer of CBS News's weekly documentary series *48 Hours;* we used the same approach for *Seven Days in May:* Have a team of reporters fan out for mega-intensive coverage of different aspects of the same subject over a short period of time. You have to run fast to keep up with Andrew, but the results are worth the effort. Our documentary was like a series of clear snapshots adding up to a rounded portrait (my wife, Jean, points out that David Hockney uses this technique in still photography). In *Seven Days in May,* we captured daily life in the Soviet Union, with its discontent and dissent, talking frankly with leading intellectuals and rank-and-file Soviet citizens. CBS interviewed the chief of the Communist party in Moscow (a kind of super-mayor), a little-known figure named Boris Yeltsin. The documentary really contributed a great deal to the viewer's understanding of the realities of life in the Soviet Union—and it contributed plenty to my own understanding. Memories of *Seven Days in May* were fresh in my mind as I prepared to cover Reagan's visit in 1988.

In 1987, it was clear even to me that the economy was collapsing. I'm no economist, can barely balance a checkbook. But there was nothing to buy if you had money to spend. What few goods you could find in the stores or the markets were shoddy or damaged.

People had become so desperate that the desperation could not be concealed. Except for big interviews, reporters don't usually deal with the top level of any society. We deal with the middle and bottom levels. This was true in the Soviet Union, too. We weren't having breakfast with Gorbachev every morning. For ordinary Soviet citizens, the people we talked to every day, fear of the KGB was still rampant and well founded. At this level of society, people were still unwilling to criticize their leaders directly, but they couldn't keep on hiding their discontent, even their hunger. They'd gripe about shabby materials or shoddy services. Their eyes spoke of worry. Diplomats, unlike reporters, deal with the top level of society most of the time, and in the Soviet Union, things were not so bad at the top. Government officials could still reserve the best goods and distribute privileges among themselves and their families, with special shops and extra rations of vodka and caviar all around. Since these were the realities the U.S. diplomats saw in the Soviet Union every day, it was unclear to me what messages they could be sending back to Washington.

I am not suggesting that bottom-fishing is the best way to gather news in a foreign land, but for most reporters it is the only way. We talk to the lower levels of society because those are the only people available.

I knew from my own experience that the blood of the Soviet army was making the roads slick in Afghanistan. There went half of what worked, leaving only the KGB. A government that can boast of nothing more than an efficient secret police force is not going to endure comfortably.

And when we returned to the Soviet Union in 1988, the economy was free-falling. I barely remember the Great Depression, but when Reagan came to office the Soviet Union was already in a depression more devastating than the one that panicked the United States in the 1930s. We had a viable society and our Great Depression nearly caved us in. So what must this depression be doing, I wondered, to the Soviets?

When we weren't reporting from the scene, we divided our time between the Roach Motel and the bureau. Our CBS News Moscow bureau is a cramped, beige and gray pigeon cote, Graham Greene-esque offices stuffed one on top of the other, filled with loose documents and tangled wires. Presiding over our establishment was Mila Taubkina, a fixer, translator, and associate producer. If they ever bring back the Russian Empire, the job of tsarina is already filled— by Mila, for whom no task is impossible, before whom armed guards tremble, and from whom Jeanne Moreau could learn a thing or two about chic.

It was raining in Moscow that spring of 1988. Rain only adds to the drabness and the dullness of the Russian capital. I don't think most Americans realized that Moscow was then a closed city, not only to foreigners but to Soviets. You didn't live in Moscow unless you had permission. You could not travel to Moscow from another Soviet city and spend the night without receiving authority to do so.

The people in Moscow dressed better than they did when I first traveled there. They were a little more open, a bit more willing to talk to strangers. Yet the city itself remained a weary, dreary place—closed emotionally as well as legally. And even under today's freer conditions, the people are still not very outgoing (few people in any big city really are).

I found it irresistible to compare the sense of motion, energy, and optimism of Japan (where we had just been to cover the funeral of Emperor Hirohito) with the almost opposite atmosphere in the U.S.S.R. Even with Gorbachev's promises of the first rays of democratic reform, the people were basically cynical and defeated. You walked along the streets in Moscow and you saw an awful lot of people looking down. You walked the streets of Tokyo and the eyes of the Japanese were either level or raised—looking ahead. Why not? Japan was the Land of the Rising Sun, everything looking fresh and bright and working well.

In Tokyo, hope abounds. In Moscow, hope had been squeezed out of the people for too long. The most pervasive feeling was this sense of malaise and despondency. What we would call the work ethic was lacking. You would, on occasion, see people in the Soviet Union working quite hard. You rarely saw them working with efficiency. For one reason: There was no ambition, no incentive.

On my first trips to Moscow, I saw few cars and trucks, and the ones I saw were ancient. On the drive from the airport into the city, the sides of the roads were littered with carcasses of old cars and trucks that had broken down. People worked on some. But most had been abandoned.

And the lines. Muscovites waited for hours in lines that stretched for six blocks. There was a dry Russian joke that went: "What are you waiting for?" "I don't know, but if there's a line, it must be for something." In reality, there was a line for everything. They waited for bread, soap, toilet paper. But by 1988, waiting did not mean receiving what you'd waited for.

Once, there had been some spirit, some faith that hardships like lousy cars and long lines must be endured, but that there was an end to the tunnel. In the 1960s and 1970s, communism was still a kind of religion for these people, and they clung to the belief that communism would triumph in the world as an economic system, as a military power, and as a means to end poverty. But now I contrasted that mood with the mood I found in the late 1980s. Now there were more automobiles and better clothing, but melancholia had set in. The man on the farm and in the shop no longer believed communism was going to triumph, now or at any other time. Things were not going to get better. No amount of propaganda was going to persuade him differently.

A friend of mine who worked at TASS, the Russian wire service, had trotted out some figures from the Soviet census bureau. In a nation of 150 gazillion people, there were umpteen jillion television sets, not including those in the better hotels. My friend smiled a wry smile and said, "Of course, none of them are any damned good." When I said I thought that the KGB had bugged my room and that I was being followed (other journalists had gone through that, especially those posted to Moscow), he almost laughed. He said, "The greatest danger for you is not the KGB, it's burning to death. The firefighting equipment here is poor. Fire-resistant materials are relatively unknown here. There have been huge hotel fires with large loss of life, kept secret. If you want to worry about something, worry about burning to death—or being taken to a Soviet hospital."

I immediately saw the connection between the television sets and the fires. Many years ago I had been a police reporter in Houston when there had been a small epidemic of TV sets exploding. They were sold by a salesman who called himself "Mad Man Muntz." So the threat of spontaneously combusting TV sets in the hotel made some sense to me, even though my friend seemed to be half joking.

But I am, when encouraged, a fair worrier. So I checked out this information. I talked with some of the police departments and they verified it. "Oh, yes," an officer told me, "it is quite a problem." A KGB agent said he had jury-rigged a corrugated tin shield around his TV set for fear it would blow up. And we worry about violence and American TV.

About the Soviet hospitals, I had already been worried. I finally received permission to visit a showcase hospital in Moscow. I had read somewhere that John Reed, the American who wrote a riveting account of the Russian revolution, *Ten Days That Shook the World,* had died in a Soviet hospital and received first-class treatment (his story is the subject of Warren Beatty's film *Reds*). Many Soviet physicians were well trained, and quite good in working with spinal-cord injuries (they had seen so many during World War II), artificial limbs, and cataract surgery.

I was impressed up to the point when we happened upon women in white uniforms washing needles with soap and water. Mind you, the AIDS epidemic was well under way. I asked what these orderlies were doing. The interpreter said, "They are washing needles."

"And why would they do this?" I asked.

The interpreter looked at me as if astonished that anyone from a civilized country could be so ignorant of basic hygiene. "Naturally, they clean the needles before reusing them," he said.

This confirmed for me something I've felt strongly for a long time. At the risk of insulting the rest of the world, there are two places where I have always hoped to hear an American voice. One is from the cockpit of whatever airplane I am on, and the other from someone leaning over me on an operating table. Whenever people about to visit Russia for the first time ask me what to do if they get sick, I tell them, "Don't call an ambulance—call an airplane."

The Soviet hospitals were shockingly short of basic medicines: baby aspirin, for example. In a state-managed economy, strange things happen. Over the years, I had come to know a few Russian people fairly well, and before my trips I would call and say, "If you need anything, I'll try to bring what I can." At times I could. Each trip it was something different. One year it was American blue jeans. One of life's mysteries: Why would anyone in a "socialist worker's paradise" want to dress like oppressed, decadent, capitalist American farmers and rock musicians?

Other shortages were harder to explain. By and large, Russian women are shy and modest. One asked to talk with one of my staffers. What was on the Russian woman's mind? Well, you see, it was awkward to say, but there was a shortage of sanitary napkins, and could the staffer help to send . . . ?

You wondered, how can any country that produces rockets that soar into outer space, and tanks that can demolish cities, not produce the basics of daily living? After Gorbachev began urging the people to face the hard truths, an unofficial poll was taken to learn what Russians wanted. High on the list was brassieres.

Many journalists never understood that in spite of his brilliance, Gorbachev recognized the roots of Soviet despair only when he was forced to do so. After all, he was and is a dedicated Marxist, handpicked by the KGB (among others) and repackaged as the New Soviet Man. But in trying to salvage the old Soviet system, Gorbachev gambled, peeling back the Iron Curtain and exposing to the people all the old failures, as they'd never seen them before. People were confronted with the cruelties that had been practiced on a scale unhealthy to dwell upon. The Soviets were trying to grapple with the malignancy of Stalin and Brezhnev at the same time they were confronting the incompetency at Chernobyl, corruption in the bureaucracy, and shortages in the market. With the openness of glasnost, Soviets had a better idea of the wonders of Western, market-based economies—and a much clearer idea of the failure of their own economy. Now they had a whiff of what was really going on, compared to the past promises of happy times to come.

An electrified mass of feelings and events was turned loose that neither Gorbachev nor anyone else could control. This scared the hell out of Gorbachev because, in the end, he had in his heart more faith in the Party than in the people. Thus he was afraid to initiate the next phase of reforms (as Yeltsin would later try to do, with mixed and bloody results). His position was the opposite of China's: He took the political risk, but not the economic one.

Gorbachev was then widely seen the world over as the picture of glamour and success. But from another view, you could paint him as a tragic figure who led his country to the lip of the cup and then stopped. He could not break with his ideology and training, could not declare himself in favor of private ownership and individual incentives as fuel for the economy.

But for the moment, he was seen as a key interview, the top of the list for almost any reporter in the world, including this one. But how to get to him?

I admit that I wasn't as successful as I'd like to have been. Especially because Gorbachev had granted an unusually long interview to a competing network, which had run the conversation in prime time. Okay, I was jealous, and my pride was only a little assuaged by the flattering report that Gorbachev was turning down CBS's requests for an interview because he thought I'd ask too many tough questions, including some about Afghanistan. Of course I value a reputation for tough questions—but I really wanted the interview.

I did land a solid interview with Boris Yeltsin, the man outside, shut out by Gorbachev and the hard-line Marxists for his open desire to reform the state. Yeltsin was glad to keep his profile high in the United States. Gorbachev, though, kept turning us down.

But one of Gorbachev's favorite demonstrations of the new openness was to get out of the limousine and walk around. He did this famously in Washington, of course, jumping out of the car to work the crowds, much to the consternation of the Secret Service but to the delight of the American people. What many people don't realize is that Gorbachev very seldom worked the crowds inside the Soviet Union—not without tight crowd control. Ah, but there were fine spring days when he liked to stroll, and there were spots where, if you positioned yourself just right . . .

Actually, we had no idea we'd see him. We happened to be inside the Kremlin (which is not a single building but a complex of beautiful old palaces and churches and gardens within one big fortress wall), taking advantage of special authorization from the government to shoot a few stand-ups in one of the most famous but least photographed locations in the world.

Tom Bettag was producing, with Richie Mutschler directing the camera crew (sometimes we let Richie out of the studio on good behavior), and David Buksbaum and my assistant, Suzanne Meirowitz, standing by. The shoot was going well, when suddenly Suzanne cried out, "There he is!"

Nobody needed to say who "he" was—and we were like a shot out of a cannon, tearing across the quad as if we were a single body, calling out to Gorbachev.

I barely know how it all happened—or how David and Richie and I moved so fast, each of us far from the first bloom of youth—or why Gorbachev's bodyguards didn't kill us on the spot. David is an old-school newshound, with sharp elbows and the savvy to use them, and Suzanne speaks Russian very well, and by the time Richie had the cameras rolling, Gorbachev knew he couldn't duck us. If he tried to get out of the interview, he'd look bad on American television. We had him.

A little lesson: Fancy journalism degrees are well and good, but in the end it comes down to luck, reflexes, and shoe leather.

For the people at the top of your wish list of interview subjects, you've always got at least half a dozen questions prepared. Don't need your notebook, you've got it all on the tip of your tongue and ready to ask. Maybe the information minister will finally wear down and give you the green light for an interview with the president-for-life. Or who knows? Maybe you'll run into the pope at the Quik Mart. The point is that you've always got a few questions ahead of time, because you've been dreaming of just this opportunity.

So I had no trouble thinking of what I'd ask Gorbachev; the only question was who would translate. But Gorbachev happened to have with him a trusted unofficial translator, one of the top members of his government, Yegor Ligachev, whose English may be better than mine. During the entire conversation, Ligachev had a bemused smile, as if tickled to see somebody put the Big Boss on the spot.

We talked about the arms race and superpower relations, and Gorbachev was pleasant and reasonably forthcoming. After several minutes, he excused himself; he'd be late for a meeting if he didn't go now. The conversation didn't last long, but it shed a little light and it gave me a kick to get, even briefly, the exclusive interview I'd been refused.

Actually, this was only the first of a few times that I managed to land Gorbachev as a "Man on the Street" interview—and one of the times Gorbachev realized there could be unanticipated consequences to the openness of glasnost.

Already, Gorbachev was allying himself with the hard-liners, the military and the KGB. Already he was falling back from glasnost and perestroika, dumping Yeltsin and trying to prop up the crumbling Soviet system. But the rumblings were spreading throughout the Soviet Union and all through Eastern Europe.

* * *

In early February of 1989, I flew to Munich—as curious as this may sound—to attend a seminar on defense spending. I also wanted to take a look at the Berlin Wall. A knowledgeable U.S. senator had said to me, "Gorbachev loves surprises, loves the bold move."

"Yes, he does," I said, thinking of our interview, "so long as he's the one moving boldly."

"If you study him closely, what he usually does is size up what is going to happen anyway, and then he goes ahead, does the inevitable a little early, and then takes credit for a gutsy move. You know, he could announce that he is going to take down the Wall."

I expressed doubts, reservations, astonishment, but the senator continued: "I'm not predicting he will, but if he could do it, it would be another star in his crown."

One side of me was already prescribing a rest cure for the senator. But the Hildy Johnson side of me couldn't resist the tip. I decided to do a radio and television report from the Wall. I can't point with any great pride to that decision. There was nothing prophetic about it, and nothing happened while I was there. But at least we could say that CBS News had raised a question, sent up a flare, suggested the possibility of historic change in the wind.

I didn't have any more solid lead on the Wall, but I returned from Munich and Berlin with one surprising discovery: the strength of the undercurrent in favor of the reunification of the two Germanies. I was now prepared to go out on a limb and say reunification would come before the end of the century.

I went back to Moscow in midsummer for the Communist Party Congress, the first time that event had ever been open to the foreign press. I also landed my second "Man on the Street" interview with Mikhail Gorbachev, proving that lightning does strike twice if you know where to look. (A friend drew me a little cartoon of a highly perturbed Gorbachev saying, "Mr. Rather, we've got to stop meeting like this.")

The interview was a scoop, but, oh, so suddenly events would remind me that today's big win is tomorrow's forgotten story. TV news is even more perishable than print news—you can't wrap fish in ours.

We were starting a new television season, and in news the season begins on Labor Day and ends on Memorial Day. The ratings game is basically played out in the long, dark winter months, when the sets in use stay on later and the audiences are the largest. This is where you make and break careers in the squirrelly business called television.

Just in time for the new season, strange things began happening around the Wall and inside Berlin itself. Pictures started rolling of people from East Germany actually crawling over the Wall. In the past, people making such attempts had been shot. This raised the question, where were the East German guards? If they were still at their posts, how were the defectors getting past them? A trickle can turn quickly into a stream, and rumors flashed across East and West Berlin that something was happening at the Wall. People began to gather on both sides of the Wall—not yet to celebrate but lured by curiosity as much as anything else.

The Wall was not down, but it was beginning to totter.

After the newscast one night, Tom Bettag and I caught the next plane for Berlin.

We were a little ahead of ourselves, however. To my surprise, we had outrun our own logistics, and there was no CBS camera crew on the ground yet. They were coming hell-for-leather on their way to us, but for the moment I had no camera to talk into and Tom had no broadcast to produce. Such minor details couldn't delay us from going to the Wall.

The trickle of defectors had indeed turned into a stream. It was growing more obvious by the minute that the Wall was coming down, emotionally if not yet literally. No part of the Wall had been torn down physically, and while that was more than a formality, it was clearly a matter of time.

Willy Brandt, the former chancellor of West Germany and one-time mayor of West Berlin, was there, and one could not help but try to imagine what that day must have been like for him. I said to Tom, "Let's get him."

In that methodical way of his, Tom said, "How do you propose doing that?" He was probably trying to figure out whether I'd gone nuts, talking about a big interview without a camera or micro-phone.

But I pointed out that Brandt was being interviewed already by a variety of reporters. I said, "I'll try to keep him talking, and keep the interview going, while you round up our camera crew."

We got our interview: I managed to stall Brandt long enough without having to ask for his favorite recipe for sauerbraten, and Bettag charged up in the nick of time, like the cavalry over the hill, with the camera rolling.

The interview boosted our morale, but in terms of camera loca-tions and our ability to transmit, we found we were starting well behind on a huge story. Bettag was quietly planning for that night's broadcast, live at the Wall, which we knew would be our location for at least the next few days. But every television network in the known world, and a few no one had ever heard of, were lined up like ducks in front of the Brandenburg Gate. All had camera platforms or were in the process of constructing them. And we didn't even have a space we could claim as our own. For once, we'd have thought ourselves lucky if we'd gotten a shot that looked exactly like everybody else's. It wasn't as if we were trying to find 50-yard-line seats to the Super Bowl, but there was a good deal of jostling and jockeying going on.

We were staring at another monumental story, and this time we were not in front. We hadn't been hurt and were not very far behind. But our concentration was on how to get something—and, best of all, something the others didn't have. All the good positions were gone. All that remained was second-tier. We could buy into the Dutch network's position and get half of their meager space. But that seemed like a pretty dismal prospect.

From somewhere came the echo of a fundamental of television news big-event coverage: "Get high and shoot low."

"Tom," I said, "we need a high shot." We both spun around and realized the area in front of the Brandenburg Gate was like a park. There were no tall buildings. There was barbed wire at the foot of the Wall, and pavement twenty feet beyond.

"Good idea," said Bettag. "How are we going to do that?"

We needed to shoot from the highest elevation we could find, and we couldn't even find a little elevation. We would have to improvise. I said to Tom, "Drop whatever you're doing, stop everything, and find me a cherry picker."

I was talking about the kind of truck that has a forklift with a space where workers can stand and be raised up to change street-lights and do repairs on power lines. And the next thing I know, here is a perfectly handsome cherry picker chugging into place directly behind all the other networks' platforms, lined up like duck blinds, and Bettag sitting in the cab like Mike Mulligan with his steam shovel. For the first time since we reached Berlin, I could smile.

It wasn't checkmate. It wasn't even check. But it was a nice, helpful move and brought us into play. The good positions are all taken? No problem; we'll create one.

We instructed the man who owned or operated the picker to attach a little bucket—I suppose we could get fancy and call it a gondola. What this gave us was a tricky way to house, and to hoist, our crew. We knew it would be crowded with three of us in there: the cameraman, the soundman, and myself. But when the picker raised us, we got a fabulous shot of the Brandenburg Gate, the milling crowd below, and the other anchor positions. As soon as we were up in the air, photographers and runners from other networks started lining up, asking what it was, where we found it, and offering us $500 and more to take them up.

All I knew was that Bettag had found the only one around, and we had contracted for its exclusive services. I don't want to think about how much it cost. We did allow a few still photographers and other people to go up, after we finished for the night. We felt as if we were running a carnival concession.

It was one of those rare times when work is more fun than fun. The bucket was about five feet long by two and a half feet wide, and steady enough. A small part of the crowd around us stood back and watched. Some Germans oohed and aahed. Some laughed. The anchorman, meaning me, had to lean as far back as possible. The cameraman positioned himself at the other end, setting his butt on the edge and leaning back in order to focus the lens. The soundman just leaned out of the way and prayed the cable didn't break.

One of our competitors stopped by and said, "Good try, Rather, but it won't work." He didn't believe the police would let us stay; we were bound to be breaking a dozen or so ordinances. Any number of grizzled old newspaper people would scoff at this stunt, and they would be entitled. On the other hand . . . this is television.

We did our live broadcast at midnight, Berlin time. After we had finished and added the West Coast updates, Bettag said, "Whew. What next?"

I said, "Well, we got the picture. Now let's concentrate on the story."

It is a small point, but one worth adding, that the music that led into the broadcast was Beethoven—the "Ode to Joy" from the Ninth Symphony. "Joy" is an overused and overworked word, and we're lucky to feel the real thing six or seven times in our lives, but this was one occasion I thought the word was apt. The music soared like a skyburst of fireworks and rockets, and it was nothing compared to what the Germans were feeling that night.

Still, one particular moment brought me up short, and sticks with me now and always. The next day I wanted to get up on the Wall itself, and so I did. No videotaped piece to be used later; that was not what motivated me. I just wanted to share what I saw happening all around me. The Wall was filled with Germans, East and

West, some drinking champagne, some weeping, some laughing almost uncontrollably, hugging, singing, even engaging the East German border guards in conversation. People reached down to help others climb the Wall. I just wanted to sit and savor the moment, to soak it up for a few minutes.

I turned and saw that I had perched myself beside a German woman with two children. She was blond, not beautiful but pretty, about forty years old. The children were blue-eyed and towheaded, one about nine, the other I guessed maybe six. I smiled at the children and said to her, "Do you speak English?"

Nearly everyone in West Berlin did. She smiled back and said, "Of course."

I said, simply, "What do you think?"

She clenched her fists and said, "My heart has exploded."

Her eyes glimmered, and I said, "That's really beautiful."

Then she hardened around the triangle of her eyes and nose. "The Russians will soon be gone," she said, and with a look that was icy, added, "and I can't wait for the rest of you to be gone."

I must have looked like someone who had been hit with a sledgehammer. She went on, "I don't dislike Americans, much less hate them as I hate the Russians. But you Americans don't know what it is to have foreigners occupy your soil, your fatherland." And we just looked at each other, until she turned her gaze once again across the expanse of concrete outside the Brandenburg Gate and into East Germany.

Her words and her eyes stayed with me. I began to wonder about other borders where unwelcome Soviet guests might soon be leaving. When I climbed down, I knew I needed to talk to General Vernon Walters, at that time the ambassador to West Germany. I imagine a lot of what he would call his "conservative friends" would be surprised to learn that he and I have enjoyed a mutual respect. Certainly, my respect flowed his way and he knew it. I consider him a great American.

Part of our connection is simply that over the years we wound up in a lot of countries together. Walters speaks twelve languages, and during the Nixon administration often served as the president's official interpreter. As a final cap on a long and varied and wonderful career, he had been appointed our ambassador to Bonn.

Vernon Walters also happened to be the brother of a onetime CBS director named Vinnie Walters, one of the first I ever worked with as a young network reporter. But my friendship with the general stood on its own. I don't think we ever discussed Vinnie, although there was no reason to avoid him as a topic of conversation. Over a period of time I had made it a point to check with General Walters anytime I had an overseas assignment. The request usually went, "General, this is Dan Rather and I have some homework to do. If you can help me, I'd very much appreciate it."

He was never a news source of mine. If I had to depend on Vernon Walters for information to make a living, I'd starve. I don't think he was ever a source for anybody. He is a square shooter, and I hope he thinks the same of me. Which isn't to say that he always agrees with me.

This had to be a hectic and time-consuming period for him, but he made a little time to see me. I went to the American Consulate in Berlin and we put General Walters on camera for a brief interview. Then I said, "Mr. Ambassador, if you would, I'd like to take just a minute more of your time." He was agreeable, so I turned to Bettag and our crew and others in the room and asked them to give us a minute of privacy.

When the room had cleared I thanked General Walters and said, "I can understand if you don't answer this, but I'm wondering what's next. Where do you think this story goes from here?"

Vernon Walters was then seventy-two, not as light on his feet as he had been, but a man who had been everywhere, done everything, and I doubt for one instant in his life ever felt bored. He cut right through the haze and said, "I'd get to Czechoslovakia as fast as I could."

The firmness with which he spoke took me back a bit, because we had just arrived in Berlin. I tried not to let my confusion show, smiled, thanked him again, and shook his hand. As we walked outside, Tom Bettag said, "Where are we going?"

I said, "To Czechoslovakia."

"What do you mean? We just got here and we're already leaving?"

"Yeah," I said, "but I have a hunch. Something tells me we need to get to Prague."

Tom said, "I'll make some calls. Maybe we can get there next week."

"No, you and I and this driver are going there now."

"Like, right now?"

"You got it. Right now."

We highballed our way to the border between West Germany and Czechoslovakia and talked our way through, accidentally dropping a few bills in the sentry boxes. Prague was one of the best-kept secrets in Europe, an absolutely lovely city with grand architecture. Mozart adored Prague, and the movie *Amadeus* was filmed there. You can almost hear his music around every corner. In the center of Prague you are transported back into medieval times, to a city of a hundred cathedrals. I had been slow to learn that Prague was the only European city that did not suffer extensive bombing damage from one side or the other, or both, in World War II. It was just out of range of the German bombers, and then Hitler and his army walked in. So it was left intact, not greatly changed since the days when Franz Kafka roamed its narrow streets.

Unfortunately, a layer of fog, smog, and bone-biting chill had settled over the city. Bettag, ever the organizer, had called ahead and had our stringer book hotel rooms for us. The stringer, an absolutely unflappable young man named Tomas Vavrosek, helped us immediately begin setting up a mini-bureau in the hotel. When we checked in with the bosses in New York, and they asked what we were doing, Tom said, "We're following our noses."

The truth was, we were following the cryptic, coded message of General Walters. We had been operating on about one hour's sleep out of the past sixty, so I told Tom I needed to have a quick cold shower and maybe a glass of sarsaparilla to revive me. I asked him to call the American Embassy and see if we could talk to the political officer.

Tom made the call, came back, and said, "Good news, bad news. The good news is that the political officer will talk to you. The bad news is that there's a price: You have to interview the ambassador and put her on the air."

I muttered an expletive deleted. The ambassador was Shirley Temple Black. I loved her in *Bright Eyes* and *Curly Top* when I was in grade school, but was not in thrall to her diplomatic credentials, despite her previous appointments in Ghana and as the White House chief of protocol. I said, "If we do the interview, is it a deal?" Tom said, "It's a deal."

We drove to the U.S. Embassy, where we had our pictures taken with some very squared-away Marine guards. I was a little embarrassed when one of them said, "Mr. Rather, you're a Marine, aren't you?" In truth, my Marine Corps duty was cut short by a medical discharge, and I have too much respect for the Corps to go around bragging about service that didn't amount to much. But sometimes Marines choose to recognize my record and call me a brother Marine, and this young guard confided in me now. "Don't tell anybody I told you," he said, "but things are getting a little nervous around the edges here."

We had our briefing with the political officer, a very good State Department product, who did his job: He did not tell us one damned thing. Then we went in for our interview with the ambassador from the United States, recently appointed to this extremely sensitive post in Prague. Shirley Temple Black could not have been nicer. This was a gracious woman, but I was impatient to get the interview out of the way. She settled herself in a grand antique chair from which her feet didn't touch the floor. She was looking for what correspondents call "face time," and we all understood it.

In answer to the first few questions, Mrs. Black proceeded to tell me that it was all very interesting what was happening in Berlin, but in Prague everything was tranquil. "I myself," she said, "have just within recent hours talked to the archbishop and the foreign minister, and some very important people in the Party. They all assured me that nothing like that could occur here."

On our way to the embassy, we passed people celebrating in the streets. Dissidents were coming up from the basement. Vaclav Havel, the playwright and leader of the democracy movement, was stirring the populace with his words and his example. He'd been imprisoned several times.

Now, inside the embassy, I couldn't believe what I was hearing. In the back of the room, the political officer wore the look of a man whose underwear is too tight. At one point, Mrs. Black said there were only five thousand Soviet troops in the country. During a break, while we were changing videotapes, the officer coughed and said, "Mr. Rather, Madame Ambassador, the number is actually *fifty-five* thousand."

We finished the interview in time for *CBS This Morning.* I received a message later that the ambassador was not pleased with the results. But even as we were speaking, the Communist government was collapsing; within a matter of days it had fallen, and the nearly bloodless "Velvet Revolution" eventually resulted in Havel's rising to the presidency of the Czech Republic.

I thought of how much Vernon Walters could convey by looking you in the eye. He was the epitome of what one hoped a U.S. ambassador would be—impossible to stampede, nervy, a respecter of straight answers. A striking contrast to the American in charge in Prague.

Dialogue with the Dictator

Once, RIDING THE CUBAN COUNTRYSIDE IN HIS JEEP, FIDEL CASTRO told me he could never understand why African Americans in the United States had not turned to communism in large numbers.

He acknowledged that once, over a period of years in the 1960s and '70s, he had spent a lot of money (most of it supplied by the Soviets) trying to prime the Marxist-Leninist pump among blacks in the United States. But a surge to communism among North American blacks never happened, never even came close.

Castro said he had never understood it, never would. One of the many things about the United States and its people he found inexplicable.

With that in mind, I sometimes think of Eldridge Cleaver, the self-described black revolutionary. During the 1960s, Cleaver sought political asylum in Cuba. Castro loved that. He was pleased to have such a well-known North American join his team. He welcomed Cleaver to Havana.

Cleaver might have thought his troubles were over, but they were just beginning. The reason was that Cleaver was a "morning person," functioning best when he got an early start, but fading as nighttime fell, and switching off around 10:30 or 11:00 P.M.

Fidel is the direct opposite. He rarely gets in high gear before 10:30 or so at night. And he is a world-class talker. I am not referring to speeches, although Castro is famous for long ones, over many hours, sometimes days. In this he has rivals throughout the old Soviet and Chinese Communist guard, and in South Africa, the Zulu leader Mangosuthu Buthelezi has logged some impressive records for long, boring speeches. But Fidel has no rivals when it comes to sitting down and shooting the breeze with a couple of cigars and a bottle of Chivas Regal. (For image reasons and the fact that Cuba exports rum, he doesn't flaunt this, but he prefers Scotch. And for health reasons he has officially stopped smoking cigars in recent years.) In these bull sessions, he goes on and on, seldom dull, often scintillating, always challenging and aggressive. He'll talk nonstop for hours about everything from boxing to the Marxist dialectic to why the United States is doomed to fail. ("Any country that spends billions of dollars just to advertise mouthwash and deodorant cannot survive," he once told me, presiding over an economy that cannot produce enough toilet paper.) Among interview subjects he's a one-man marathon. Fidel can talk—can he ever!—and prefers to talk all night long. If he's talking to you, you'd better listen—all night long.

Eldridge Cleaver didn't do it, apparently couldn't. He fell sound asleep right in the middle of a three-hour sound bite. El Presidente para la Vida was not amused.

Cleaver was warned. One can imagine his trying, but try as he might he just could not stay awake. So Castro banished him. The ungrateful guest was forced to leave Cuba for Algeria.

That's the story told to me by several high-level Cuban diplomats. I have no trouble believing it. I've had several encounters with the "night person" Castro myself, including two lengthy interviews for *60 Minutes.* And I had the circles under my eyes to prove it.

And you know what? In spite of everything, the man is a great interview. Always a challenge. Pithy when he chooses to be. Generally interesting. Outrageous sometimes, often infuriating. But even when he is wrong (and he has been wrong about the United States, about the Soviets and communism, about Latin America, about many things), an interview with him can make for lively, informative television.

In the vernacular of my trade, he could make it as an anchor in a major market, probably even on a network.

For one of our most recent interviews, in 1985, I brought along producer Al Ortiz, a former Associated Press man whose skills in foreign news are such that he became our CBS News foreign editor and is, at present, London bureau chief. Al's family is Puerto Rican; he speaks fluent Spanish and is invaluable whenever we report from Cuba. We were accompanied by Terri Belli, now a producer but at the time my assistant. Al and I may have made a little too much of the Eldridge Cleaver story, because Terri, usually fearless under any circumstances, admitted she'd grown nervous that she'd fall asleep in the middle of our Castro all-nighter and be deported or thrown in a Cuban jail. Whether her fears were groundless or not, we all popped No Doz like truck drivers and poured down a lot of strong Cuban coffee before the interview.

But Fidel wasn't taking any chances on losing the full and undivided attention of our CBS News crew. He's a great student of the United States—tried to move here as a professional baseball player in his youth—and watches a great deal of television. Although I don't pretend he's a great student of Dan Rather, it's true you don't have to know much about me to know I love a scoop. And Fidel had one all ready for me.

At the time, financier Robert Vesco was on the lam after an embezzling scheme went sour in the early 1980s. Vesco also was widely suspected of having connections to the drug trade. Officials all over the world were looking for him. "Oh, yes," Fidel said blithely. "He's here—in Cuba."

My eyes probably widened. There it was: my scoop, the lead for my story, a good day's work in a single sentence. Our cameras and microphones weren't set up yet; I was already planning a sequence of questions to draw out more information about the Vesco story over the course of the interview. But Fidel wasn't through with me yet.

"Of course, I'll never say so on camera, and I'll deny it if you quote me."

For the rest of the interview, I was wide awake, all right—and fuming.

I suppose that if Fidel Castro governed as effectively as he jerks people's chains, Cuba would be a very different place.

SEVEN

Iraq: Sleeping with the Enemy

A VACATION IS TO A NEWSCASTER WHAT A TRAILER PARK IS TO A TOR-nado. They attract havoc. The theory may have no scientific basis, but there is nothing in my experience to disprove that a relationship exists.

In thirty years with CBS, I had never taken a month's vacation. I am entitled to six or seven weeks, I'm not even sure how many. But in the summer of 1990, Jean and I were taking the plunge. With Tom Bettag and his wife, Claire, we had been invited by friends to spend most of August in France, and part of that time fishing in the lower region of the French Alps.

Everything started off according to plan. Jean and Claire had gone ahead in late July, taking a leisurely drive through Normandy.

Tom and I joined them after our most recent passage to the Soviet Union.

Our hosts were Jean-Claude and Martine Christiane, and we celebrated our reunion over dinner, with wine and music, on the banks of Lake Annecy. We were all but giddy at the prospect of a holiday. Free, free at last! Gonna have some time off after a really incredible year and a half, which had started with the journey to Japan and carried us through Tiananmen Square, the fall of the Berlin Wall, the convulsions of Eastern Europe, the invasion of Panama, and multiple trips to the Soviet Union.

Jean-Claude had booked our fishing trip nine months in advance, to a very special place that required reservations. We were to leave the next morning on this wonderful excursion to the interior of France, part fishing, part sightseeing. At 7:30 in the morning, the Land Rover was loaded with fishing gear and we had our suitcases in the driveway. As Jean-Claude backed into the road, we listened to the 8:00 A.M. broadcast of the Voice of America, which is standard procedure when we are overseas. And the first report was the news that Saddam Hussein had sent his Iraqi troops across the border and invaded Kuwait.

Tom looked at me and I looked at Tom and Jean-Claude looked at the both of us. I said, "Stop. Stop right now. You have to take us to Geneva." The nearest large airport was in Geneva, ninety minutes away. Our wives said nothing. Jean and Claire had tolerated a lifetime of this and they knew. They knew.

So we quickly unloaded their luggage and let Claire and Jean out of the Land Rover. Our friend, bless him, grasped the situation immediately and from that moment on we considered ourselves in a race against time and distance to get inside Kuwait before the gates slammed shut. It was going to get difficult, if not impossible, but we felt we had to try.

If we hurried and the fates smiled and our luck held, we might be able to get through before all access to Kuwait was sealed off. We knew we didn't have long. Still, if we couldn't get into Kuwait, we could get close, into Saudi Arabia or Jordan.

We were barely under way when Jean-Claude reminded us that there was a small local airport twenty minutes from Annecy. If we were unable to charter a plane there, we could work the phones, try to get a charter or commercial flight from Geneva to Kuwait.

For the rest of that day, and into the night, we tried to get clearance to fly from Annecy or Geneva to Kuwait. Nobody wanted to fly anywhere near a war zone. At one point, we had the clearance and we had a charter waiting in Geneva. But before we could board a chopper to Geneva, the charter's clearance had been pulled.

Those were irritable, tension-filled hours at the little Annecy airport, and Jean-Claude shared them. We had blown a fishing trip he had been planning for nine months, and he had a business of his own to run, but he wouldn't leave us.

By then what we knew was this: Iraqi troops had crossed the border and effectively occupied Kuwait in twelve hours. The action was both audacious and astonishing. The Soviet Union no longer could be relied on as Iraq's patron and, in fact, was poised for the first time since World War II to cooperate with the United States.

The border dispute with Kuwait was not a new one; Saddam had referred to the sheikdom as Iraq's nineteenth colony. Now he had also retaken the Rumaila oil field, which straddled the disputed boundary of both countries. He accused Kuwait of depressing the price of oil by wildly overproducing during the eight years Iraq had been at war with Iran. It was in reference to these complaints that the U.S. State Department, in a message it later regretted and tried to deny, maintained that the United States had no interest in intra-Arab squabbles.

In the predawn dark of Thursday, August 2, 1990, a force estimated at over one hundred thousand soldiers poured south into Kuwait. In four hours, the first of the troops rolled unchallenged along the thirty-seven miles of superhighway that led to the capital, Kuwait City.

Our reports were that Iraq's heavy armor included three hundred tanks, fifty of which surrounded the emir's palace and the nearby U.S. Embassy. The emir, Sheik Jaber al-Ahmed al-Sabah, and his family had already fled by helicopter to Saudi Arabia.

Meanwhile, I was on and off the phone with CBS News in New York, where decisions were being made against a backdrop of corporate intrigue. David Burke was literally in the last hours of his presidency of CBS News, a fact unknown even to him at the time Bettag and I left New York. When we reached him that morning, he knew, but he never let on to us.

Back and forth we debated the options. Was it a smart idea to get on a plane even if we might not be able to get to Kuwait? Or should we return home and anchor the broadcast from New York?

Tom and I argued strongly in favor of getting to the scene. But this debate is a continuing one; should your anchorman be on top of a big story, or is his place in the studio?

I was then and am now dedicated to the idea of being there, seeing, hearing, touching, sniffing the story. When you slip back into your anchor shoes, you at least have a knowledge of the story—and the credibility—you could not get any other way.

From a visceral standpoint, which shouldn't count but does, what reporter would want to be anyplace else? Every instinct you have tells you to follow the fire trucks.

Burke, and the people around him, were raising the questions they were paid to raise. What did good judgment demand? How long were the odds against us?

Tom never wavered, but I did. The Middle East tends to pull you in, trap you in quicksand from which some people never emerge. It is a region filled with illusion. You have to be wary of believing you know the answer. There are no answers, only new problems.

In New York, the attitude was that the invasion was a one- or two-day wonder. A similar debate, we suspected then and confirmed later, was taking place among our major competitors, but they were less inclined to move.

Now Bettag made the persuading argument. "We have a chance," he said, "to be on the front edge of a great story. We have a huge advantage. We have a one-leg jump. If anybody can get to Kuwait, we can. If we're close, we'll figure a way to get in there."

My contribution was a fairly educated guess. I said, "There is going to be a war and the United States will send in troops. George Bush will go to war over this."

Candor requires an admission: I have seen big stories out on the horizon and by the time I got there they had faded into the shadows. But I knew I wasn't wrong on this one, and I wasn't relying on my own radar.

I was simply remembering a tip from Senator Bill Cohen, the moderate Republican from Maine. In the spring of that year, we had met in a coffee shop on Third Avenue, where we sometimes meet and chat when he is in New York. We had become friends after I left Washington and the White House beat.

It isn't easy, or even recommended, for a senator and a reporter to become friends in Washington. You need a certain air space between you. I kept up with Bill Cohen when he was a congressman and later a senator, and a fine one. We became friends for reasons that require no apology. He is a published poet and novelist, as well as one of the most effective politicians in the country. He has the capacity to feel passionate about issues that matter.

So I listened carefully when he said, that day in the coffee shop,

"You ought to be doing something on Saddam Hussein."

I said, "Well, what do you have in mind?" I knew who Saddam Hussein was. I knew the rough outline of what had been going on with the U.S. courtship of Iraq and the really strange double deal—our secretly sending our best missiles to Iran, at the same time we were slipping classified satellite photographs to the Iraqis. The more serpentine tales would emerge later.

Whatever was left of my reporter's nose, I understood that Bill Cohen was putting me onto a story. At the time, the White House was tilted completely toward Saddam Hussein. We were shipping him billions of dollars' worth of aid and weapons, not all of it legally. Through private channels, the government was encouraging various businesspeople to conduct all kinds of advantageous deals with Iraq. And here was Senator Cohen, saying, "The guy is a madman. He may be the single most dangerous person in the world."

Cohen had been saying these things to the annoyance of the Bush administration, but few in the Senate and fewer in the media were listening. The whole momentum of U.S. policy was going in the opposite direction.

Bill had made himself an expert on the Soviet Union and the Middle East. He is one of those rare senators who actually enjoys reading. Politicians, like journalists, are often good at faking it, some better than others. Bill doesn't fake it.

He serves on the Senate Intelligence Committee and is among the last of the independent thinkers, a quality that hasn't endeared him to party leadership. He isn't one who will obediently hew the line. Bill Cohen didn't defend Richard Nixon in Watergate. He wouldn't give Ronald Reagan a pass on the Iran-contra scandal. And he practically needs a press badge to get into a Republican convention.

Let me make it clear that he wasn't leaking any goodies from the Senate Intelligence files to me. Cohen was telling me that if I wanted a challenge, I ought to take a hard look at Saddam Hussein and the company he kept. He said, "This guy is taking us to the cleaners. He is making suckers out of us. He's getting all of this military hardware—tanks from the Soviet Union, artillery from Argentina, Mirage jet fighters from the French, and computers and weapons systems from us. On the one hand, he is stirring up Muslim fundamentalism, and on the other he presents himself as a secular Arab leader with whom we can do business. He is playing all ends against the middle, and his dream is to lead a triumphant Arab army into

Jerusalem. He sees himself as the new Saladin [the great Muslim warrior of the twelfth century]."

Our coffees usually ran fifteen to twenty minutes. That day we talked for more than an hour. I took it all in and sort of said to myself, "Hmmm, interesting . . . if true."

Enter Bruce Kaufmann, a free-lance writer and reporter based in Washington, who worked on some of my radio pieces. A few days later, I was on the phone with Bruce, another insatiable reader, a guy who devours newspapers, magazines, newsletters, pamphlets on dental hygiene, everything. Out of nowhere, he said, "What about doing something on Saddam Hussein?"

If I had not already spoken to Senator Cohen, I would have probably said, forget it. But instead, what ran through my mind was "What the hell is going on here?"

The net effect of these conversations was to focus my attention on Saddam Hussein. I did some homework, brought myself up to date. And I had to eat a few words. In 1981, the Israelis were sharply criticized when a precise, low-level bombing raid knocked out Iraq's nuclear reactor. I'm not going to be a hypocrite about it; at the time I thought the raid was overkill. The Reagan administration was hostile *in extremis,* with Vice President Bush leading the charge. Iraq as a nuclear menace was quickly dismissed; Israel's outlaw mentality was decried.

I did the radio script with Bruce, and mentally, I marked Saddam Hussein as a future candidate for the role of global mischief-maker. Through May and June and into July, Gorbachev's perilous effort to reform the Soviet Union dominated the news. It was from there that Tom Bettag and I had come to France for the first real vacation either of us had taken in at least two years. And it had lasted less than a day.

As we waited to see if we could charter a plane, clear a flight plan, and get New York's approval, Tom was the one who kept pushing. He threw back at me one of my pet expressions, "Think end zone." I take some needling because of my sports references, but they are part of my language and part of my broadcast experience, and it is way too late to start making excuses for my speech habits.

The phrase means to go deep, to look for the big play, and try to score. Now Tom used it to prop me up. "You've been telling me for months to watch this guy," he said, "and I wasn't listening. Now I am and I tell you, we have to think end zone."

This dialogue fascinated Jean-Claude, whose English was fairly good. "Ah," he said, "you mean 'endgame,' yes?"

I said, "No, end zone."

Bettag said, "I'll explain it to you later."

Near the end of the day our prospects were shrinking. We had to rule out a charter flight to Kuwait. Planes were forbidden to fly over Saudi Arabia and no insurer would cover them. There was one other small detail: We didn't have visas. By nightfall we had two choices: fly home to New York, or catch a plane to London and take our chances. In my mind, I heard a clock ticking and it wasn't the intro to *60 Minutes.*

There was almost no hope of getting into Kuwait by air. But I told myself that if we could get near enough, to Saudi Arabia, Syria, Turkey, Jordan, or even Iran, we might walk in. The reaction from CBS News in New York was "That's out of the question." I didn't say it, but I was thinking, "Well, that was what you said about Afghanistan and we walked in and we walked out." Kuwait had long borders, and not even an army could cover every mile of them.

Tom said, "Let's go to London. That way we don't completely give up our advantage. We can keep swinging and we can do tonight's broadcast from there."

Management's reaction from New York was: "Isn't it going to look odd for us to be broadcasting out of London?"

Tom countered: "No, it will look better than doing it out of New York. London is a center of Middle East diplomacy and scholarship. It gives us a chance to keep getting closer to the war."

All the while, Tom and I were throwing sports metaphors at each other. New York meant playing for a tie. If we went to London, we were still playing to win. To normal people, this may sound like so much locker-room bullfeathers, and it may be, but it was part of keeping each other pumped up.

The charter, the one we had hoped to take to Kuwait, landed in London, where that night I anchored the *CBS Evening News.* As soon as the broadcast ended, we climbed back aboard the plane and took off for destinations unknown. Our best bet appeared to be Amman, Jordan. If you look at a map of the Middle East, you will quickly see why: Jordan has a border with Syria, Saudi Arabia, and Iraq. Amman long has been a listening post for diplomats and journalists and spies, an Istanbul for today's war junkies. For the moment, it was as close as we were going to get and it was a move in the right direction.

I credit David Burke for giving us the go-ahead—with reluctance. He said he wasn't convinced about the wisdom of our going to Japan, or China, but we went and both trips turned out well. "If this is what you want," he said, "if you think this is where you need to be, then go."

In retrospect, it was a bigger, bolder decision than it seemed at the time. Burke was on his way out, signing off, and our trip would involve a hefty amount of money. There was also some risk in terms of where his anchorman was and where the broadcast would be coming from.

I hadn't given up on sneaking into Kuwait. At the least, I thought we could set down in Amman and make our way across the top of Saudi Arabia, through the desert, Lawrence of Arabia country. We talked about having our contact in Jordan start looking to hire four-wheel-drive vehicles, motorcycles, and, yes, camels. Someway, somehow, we would get there.

We flew on to Amman and it was from there that we did the next night's *CBS Evening News,* virtually all of which dealt with the invasion of Kuwait. We were operating on no sleep at all, driven by what tomorrow would bring.

"It could all be over in a few days," predicted Tom. Increasingly, it looked as if Saddam had crushed them without any opposition, the classic lightning strike.

"Maybe so," I said, "but the next question is, will he invade Saudi Arabia? If he's smart, he will. It's a bold move, but if he keeps going now he can get the major Saudi oil fields, probably without much of a fight. The other question is whether the United States moves and how quickly."

I was absolutely convinced that we would intervene. My reasoning was simple: In the Reagan years, the United States had spent more than two trillion dollars building up the military. Many Americans were not opposed to seeing it used. True, Bush had a public-relations problem. Earlier presidents went to war to make the world safe for democracy. Restoring the emir of Kuwait to his plush throne and repressive rule didn't quite compute. Nor did the idea of holding down the price of oil put you on the side of the angels. But a crisis can make everything seem larger and more important, including the president. I believed the moral objections would be overcome.

George Bush could push some hot buttons. There was the need to keep the Middle East from becoming less stable. America had a history, though a selective one, of rejecting acts of aggression. The trump card would be a call to reduce the threat of Iraq's becoming a nuclear power. The White House had good reason to know what was in its military and chemical inventory.

After the newscast Tom insisted that we venture into what was called the Arab Street. "Let's talk to real people," he said, "about how they feel and what they think will happen."

We wanted to talk with as many people as we could, plumb every source we could tap, from King Hussein in the royal court, through the Bedouin and Palestinian leaders, to the Iraqi ambassador to Jordan. The street was filled with ordinary men and women, a melting pot of Egyptians, Syrians, Moroccans, Algerians. While many of them hated Saddam Hussein and detested what he had done in Kuwait, they were also torn by Arab pride. In their hearts, at least, here was an Arab warrior who had put it on the line, who had stunned the West and the Israelis, and for the moment appeared to have won. He was an Arab who had done something. We wound up doing an Arab "street piece."

We learned that while the Arab governments might eventually take a bite from the American carrot, at ground level the early sentiment was with "the thief of Baghdad." It was not what we had expected.

I was not the only one surprised. Many diplomats, especially the U.S. diplomats, did not want to believe that Saddam had support among the Arab masses. But you didn't have to stay very long on the streets, or in the little cafés and watering holes of Amman, to get a sense and feel for it. In the very thin air of network anchor company, you tend to forget fundamental things. This is the reason you go, your reason for being there. You get to do the reporting. You get to step out of the glass cage and talk to people.

Now this wasn't in-depth reporting and we didn't represent it as such. But it was as much as or more than anyone else was doing at the moment. And it provided a clue that the official line—of Arabs united against Saddam—wasn't entirely honest.

The street piece aired on the second night of what we were calling "The Road to War" broadcasts, and no sooner did we sign off than the complaints began rolling into the CBS offices in New York from the highest levels of the U.S. government. We were accused of taking sides, of being pro-Saddam, pro-Iraq. I considered the charges outrageous. The invasion was an act of naked aggression and there was no other way to report it. Our interviews did not constitute an endorsement.

Then there was the case, strange to me then and strange now, of the visitor who identified himself as a "security officer" for the U.S. Embassy, who appeared at our little makeshift bureau. I say "bureau" with a smile: two hotel rooms and a handful of people who had been conscripted to answer the phones and run errands.

When the security snoop showed up, I happened to be with Tom at the Iraqi Embassy, inquiring about our chances of getting into Baghdad. When we returned we were told that he had left a threatening message: The piece was irresponsible and unpatriotic. "You don't know what you are doing, and you will be wise not to do it again."

Tom and I had the same reaction—total disbelief. In my usual sensitive way, I wanted to rush right over to the U.S. Embassy and drop an egg on someone's desk. Bettag said, "Listen, we can't afford the time."

I said, "Dammit, Tom, this character works for me. He's an employee of the American government and I don't need him coming over here and trying to intimidate us."

"Dan, that's the least of what we're going to catch. Forget it. If we get where we want to go, he's just a fly on the windshield." Our goal was still to get to the war zone.

We had organized a small support group in Amman. We had a stringer there, and we found a combination driver-fixer, a scavenger type. A window had opened in Dubai, and our plan was to broadcast from there, if we could, and use Amman as a base camp. Tom had checked into chartering a boat, but it was soon obvious that we had no chance of making our way up the Persian Gulf and slipping into Kuwait from the sea.

When you are chasing a story, trying to keep track of the time is like waking from a fever, and not being sure if you've slept for minutes or hours. The Iraqi raid had taken place on the second of August. We broadcast from London on the third, Amman on the fourth, and now Dubai on the fifth, under circumstances that might best be described as unpredictable.

Dubai is one of the Arab emirates, a bright and gleaming city-state with a population of around four hundred twenty thousand. It is Muslim to the core, but more open to the West than most of the Middle East.

From the start, the Dubai government was eager to cooperate. As luck would have it, a key official had been educated at Arizona State. He even greeted us wearing an Arizona State T-shirt. He was helpful but had to enforce one restriction. I could do a stand-up in front of any backdrop, so long as it was not obvious that we were broadcasting from Dubai. Now, in other instances—I'm not proud of this, but it's true—I have smiled and nodded and felt free to ignore such a stipulation. When the camera rolled it was, screw you,

Jack, and "Welcome to the banks of the River Nile . . ."

Bettag is not that way. He is very much of the old school, and a noble son of Notre Dame, and he shames me. If you give your word, even to a government flack, that is important to him. So he spent a considerable amount of time seeking out neutral backgrounds that consisted mostly of water and sky. There was no way we were going to violate the pledge we had made to Mr. Arizona State.

So for the next three days, what the CBS viewers heard was "Dan Rather reporting, from somewhere in the Persian Gulf . . ."

I knew that I was getting second-guessed at home by friends and foes. I was doing some of my own. Even as all the signs around you scream that a war is coming, you wonder if you are reading the signs correctly. Are you overplaying the story? Are we too far out on the edge?

During the first week, I heard later, NBC News President Michael Gartner told his people to forget it; the story was like everything else in the Middle East. It was just going to blow up, look big, and then fade away. Rather and CBS, he said, have made a classic mistake. Rather has plunged and they are going to pay the price. They are going to look like fools when the story disappears.

In the midst of that planetary adventure called war, it may seem vain and petty to be monitoring the competition. But it works that way on every level, at every television station I know anything about. Right or wrong, for most of a week we had a reasonably clear field. In New York, the other networks were sniping at me in quotations (usually blind) in newspaper and magazine articles. My favorite was an unidentified source's claim that "The only action Dan Rather has seen in Jordan is a fight between housekeeping and room service in the Intercontinental Hotel. He's just watching Jordanian TV."

I knew, and so did Tom Bettag, that soon enough we were going to have company. When we flew into Dubai, Tom had scribbled a list of early goals into his notebook, and then he wrote them in mine. One was to get to the battlefront. Two was to get to Baghdad. Three was to interview Saddam Hussein. Four was to interview as many other principals as we could reach, including Hosni Mubarak of Egypt and Jordan's King Hussein.

The picture on your screen, the order on the set, conceals the craziness around you. It isn't the stress that grinds you down, it is the need to constantly adjust your emotions. We all have our methods of dealing with the fear of failure.

I sometimes feel like a character in a Dan Jenkins novel—Astronaut Jones. He was the state 100-yard dash champion three years in a row, and winning became so routine that by his senior year he attached a small white handkerchief to a string in the back of his shorts. As he crossed the finish line he would yank it out, like one of the parachutes used to slow the descent of a space capsule. And so the sportswriters nicknamed him Astronaut Jones.

As a basketball player, he was not quite as good as he was a sprinter. He was famous for coming across the midcourt line and shouting, as he launched a high, rainbow shot, "Tryin' one!" And immediately follow with another confident call to his teammates, "Fall back!"

Bettag worried about what he called my getting "zoned" on a story, locking out everything else. His way of relieving the pressure was to tell me, "Hey, relax, you're just tryin' one."

A week to ten days passed before NBC News sent in a crew, and one of their ablest correspondents. He turned out to be Ed Rabel, an old friend and former CBS hand. I was in the lobby of our hotel in Amman when he arrived. We shook hands, said hello and little else. He didn't have to say much. His eyes gave him away. Rabel was too experienced not to know that this was a big story and getting bigger.

The war had moved to the television screen, whether the country wanted it there or not. When newspapers dominated the information industry, a William Randolph Hearst could start his own war. The network rivalries, and the widening presence of CNN, would assure that this one wouldn't go unnoticed.

I have a suspicion that most viewers couldn't care less about these intramural games of ours—who gets the story first, who gets it best, who draws the numbers. But they matter to us, and the critics, and the advertisers, and therefore they do matter.

We were still trying to move up the coast, at least as far as Bahrain. A time or two, we thought we had arranged for someone to drive us there, but the roads kept closing. We returned to Amman after word reached us that we had been granted our request to interview King Hussein.

On a Sunday, I went to the palace and met with His Royal Highness, with whom I had no special relationship, and about whom I had no special knowledge, although we had met. The atmosphere around that interview was as interesting as any I have ever experienced. Hussein has a reputation of being very guarded, not surprising for a monarch whose grandfather was murdered, whose father was schizophrenic, and who has survived forty years of intrigue and danger.

I found him heavyhearted, pensive, and willing to talk with a candor for which I was not prepared. Before the interview, I shared with him my own early and limited impressions because I wanted to get his reactions. "I have been here only a few days," I said, "and unlike a lot of people you have seen and will see, Your Majesty, I did not pretend to come here as an expert on the Middle East. I am here to educate myself."

He smiled, for possibly the only time I was in his company, and said, "Many before and many to follow may pass themselves off as experts."

"Having conceded that," I went on, "and with the little I know about the region, my instinct is that war is inevitable."

To my surprise, he said, "I fear you are right."

There was no evasion, no doubt in his words, and so I pressed on: "Your Majesty, there is a widespread belief in Washington, even at the highest levels, that Saddam Hussein is bluffing."

He looked at me with eyes that were chilling. I think probably only royalty is capable of so icy a look. He paused and let the full frigidity of the look sink in, and then said: "Mr. Rather, I will tell you that Saddam Hussein does not bluff, he is not now bluffing, and it is for that reason I believe there will be a war."

Shortly, we rearranged ourselves and did the interview, and I left the palace in a state that was nearly hypnotic. I was amazed by the nakedness of his feelings. He was morose and fatalistic, and I believe he had revealed himself as he had rarely done before or since.

After we finished, he invited me into his private study and it was clear he wanted to talk more. He told me about his most recent meeting with Saddam Hussein. He cautioned me about Hosni Mubarak, the Egyptian president, who had lied—his word, not mine—to the White House and, at the least, was dealing in sophistry.

Mubarak had been quoted as saying that Iraq would not invade Kuwait. After the fact, he said that Saddam had assured him he would not. Now, King Hussein was telling me that Mubarak had been told no such thing. We may never know the truth of who was told what before the invasion, but the king of Jordan left no doubt about what he believed. He was convinced that Hosni Mubarak wanted the United States to go to war with Saddam Hussein, and he was going to get his wish.

Still, the king said he was trying to arrange another meeting with the Iraqi dictator, in the hope of finding an "Arab Solution." Time was short, the hope was slender, but he felt it was possible, depending on whether President Bush really wanted a peaceful solution.

Of course, not all of this was on camera, but King Hussein's despair and weariness were. The life of his country, and his rule, were hanging in the balance.

Tom and I looked at the interview twice, and then I placed a call to Don Hewitt at his home in the Hamptons, on what should have been a well-deserved Sunday off.

Hewitt is a legend in television news, and not only as the man who invented *60 Minutes.* It was an extraordinary thing for me to do, calling him in such a way, on notice so short. I said, "Don, I know you have the show all locked up, and I know everybody thinks we're overplaying this story. But we have just done an interview with King Hussein and would you, please, just go in and look at it?"

Hewitt said, "I don't have to see it. Dan, if you tell me that it's good, we'll put it on the air. I'm coming in and I will edit it."

The interview ran on that night's edition of *60 Minutes.* I was again indebted to Hewitt. Much has been written about him, but often missing an essential point. He is somewhere north of seventy, but his youthful enthusiasm and exuberance for the news has never abated. Don and I go a long way back, but I knew the reality. He was a producer with a show already done, and it was Sunday. But Hewitt never hesitated. He sliced right through it.

Judging from the reaction, I do not believe I oversold him. David Hume Kennerly, an acclaimed photographer, who knew King Hussein and had photographed him for many magazine layouts, saw the show and immediately booked a flight to Jordan. What he heard the king say, and how he said it, had convinced David that the Persian Gulf was about to erupt. He was from that cut of journalists and photographers who follow wars, as moths to the flame.

The interview with King Hussein had other consequences. It angered America's policymakers, and if his position didn't change they were prepared to punish him. If anything, Jordan's brooding monarch was trying to buy time before the lines had hardened on both sides. He knew that Saddam Hussein could not be bluffed. He wasn't sure that Washington knew it and this made him fearful. In his own mind, he could not go against Saddam, he had no other option, and this was his lament.

ABC News suddenly showed up in Jordan in force. After hearing the king analyze the prospects for war, it was harder to say that this story was going to blow over—although NBC had placed its initial bet that way.

For our part, I think the interview sent a clear signal. We had been telling our Arab contacts: We are here. We are going to stay here. We want to be fair. We want to be right. We will keep our word. We want to be treated seriously.

Once, when I recited a variation of this code, a Palestinian smiled and said, "Yes, but you are an American."

I replied, politely, "Yes, sir, I am, proudly so, and I see things from an American viewpoint." I hope I would not mislead anyone about that. I am reporting primarily to an American audience. Even in the sense that we reach an audience that is increasingly worldwide, it is because they want to see what Americans are seeing. But I am also a journalist, I told him, and our tradition is to be independent and open-minded.

I don't know how much this attitude was believed, or what weight it carried, if any. Most of the news organizations of the world were on hand for the Arab summit, in Cairo, and stayed on to file reports. But only CBS was there with the anchorperson for its evening news.

Tom Bettag and I had returned to Amman from Dubai to get our light, twin-engine charter serviced for the flight to Cairo. It was no frills, but the plane met our needs and the price was right. The two of us had been traveling alone, picking up a camera crew as we went.

Meanwhile, Ted Koppel had flown in from Rome on a 707, with twenty-three people and a full load of camera and satellite gear. I looked at Tom and we both looked at the 707 and allowed ourselves a smug little smile: When you come late, you tend to come heavy. I had enough respect for Koppel to know we were in for a scrap. Also, I knew what it cost to charter a 707 and to support a traveling squad of twenty-three. We had to enjoy our edge while we still had one. (Bettag is now brilliantly ensconced as Koppel's executive producer at *Nightline*.)

The summit broke up with the Iraqi diplomats and at least one other delegation throwing pieces of bread at one another. There is a timeless resentment of the "Lawrence of Arabia" stereotype, of Arabs constantly quarreling among themselves, of being unable to get organized, or stay together. Sadly, that stereotype was not banished this day. The summit, which had been arranged quickly, ended quickly, and badly.

Before we left Cairo, the rumor surfaced that Koppel had met with Tariq Aziz, the Iraqi ambassador to Washington, and firmed up a deal to get ABC into Baghdad. I flew back to Amman and went directly to the Iraqi Embassy, where we had applied for our visas. By now, the Iraqi Embassy was beginning to be a zoo. It was dealing with a tidal wave of refugees, and journalists, and even diplomats from around the world wanting to know what was going on.

The embassy was understaffed and badly overworked. You had to fight your way through milling crowds just to get to the front gate. Once there you had to wait a couple of hours to get a message to anyone inside. Tom and I finally maneuvered our way to the desk of the second-in-command, the deputy to the ambassador, who had been in Washington a short time earlier.

He confirmed that Koppel and his staff were heading for Baghdad to do their *Nightline* telecasts. I came at him hard. We were on the scene first, I roared. CBS had been promised by the embassy in Washington that if and when Iraq began to let in Western reporters, we would be at the front of the line. He gave me as many sympathetic shrugs as his shoulders could manage, and then we got down to practical matters.

We made a lot of calls from his office, virtually spent the night there, and left with our visas to allow us into Baghdad.

At the airport in Amman, the scene was right out of the Old Testament. Refugees choked the road around the airport. People were fighting over bread. Women and small children huddled and slept with their dogs and camels. It was a sight to behold and to break you. In and around Amman, and on the borders of Iraq and Kuwait, life was spiraling into chaos.

There was only one way to fly into Baghdad, and that was on an Iraqi aircraft, which made one flight a day. I have to admit, the prospect didn't thrill me. Certain questions danced in my brain: Who maintains this plane? How do I know that one of the other passengers isn't a terrorist? What assurance do we have that someone is not going to blow it out of the sky?

In short, the questions you often ask yourself when you board a flight to the Middle East. And in each instance there was no answer. These were government flights filled mostly with Iraqis, diplomats, or intelligence agents. They truly looked no more menacing than any planeload of people. Nevertheless, the worries were on my mind, and not easily dismissed.

In the week after the invasion, an interesting paradox was being acted out at home. President Bush had decided not to break off his vacation in Maine, where he was photographed casting for bluefish.

This signal was meant to assure the American people (and Saddam) that the crisis would not consume him. At the same time, the largest air- and sealift since D-Day was taking shape. By August 8, the first of a half million American military personnel were landing in Saudi Arabia, along with a billion pounds of equipment and 150,000 bottles of sunscreen.

At the same time, frustration was fairly general among the media. Journalists were not being allowed into Saudi Arabia, except as part of the Pentagon pool out of Washington.

At one point, Bettag and I drove to the border north of Amman and talked to the Bedouins about the possibility of guiding us into Iraq. Until very recently, the Bedouins have lived as their ancestors did for millennia; they still move from place to place, campfire to campfire, the great nomadic tribe.

We had stopped at a spot just off the Baghdad road, and I remember looking out and asking, "Well, which way is it?" They pointed to a shepherd's fence about fifty yards out, and then beyond the fence the great desert stretched on and on. I found myself thinking, *that* would really be trying one. As I understood the translation, they said, yes, we could attempt to walk into Iraq, but at best it would take twelve to twenty-five days, and more likely we would be buried in the desert. This news had a dampening effect on our plans.

CBS did not win the race to Baghdad. Koppel was able to use his connection with Tariq Aziz to get the invitation to Baghdad. He was hoping to interview Saddam, of course, but instead had to settle for one with the ambassador.

We were ten hours behind them, and in this kind of competition ten hours is a lifetime. I was disappointed. We thought we had worked hard enough to catch a break. But you can work hard and work smart and the cards still won't fall your way. In the long run, ours did. To my astonishment, the interview with Tariq Aziz was less than Koppel at his best. It was, I thought, a kissy interview. Aziz pulled the strings. Koppel didn't press him. Once I got into Baghdad myself, I could see why. The city was really hairy.

ABC came in with a burst, did some things reasonably well and then, inexplicably to me, the *Nightline* team pulled out. What they had done was to heighten the challenge and the pressure on us. There was no battlefront now, and no resistance to report. All of Kuwait had been secured. But there was one story, one prize, still worth going after: Saddam Hussein himself.

outtake

Winged Victory

A SURPRISINGLY UNDERREPORTED STORY OF THE PERSIAN GULF War involved an F-15 fighter wing whose very presence may have kept Saddam Hussein from moving on Saudi Arabia.

This was the chronology: The Iraqi forces whipped across the border into Kuwait on the second of August. My crew and I arrived in the region on the fourth, even as the *Independence* carrier battle group was speeding toward the Gulf.

We were tipped off by David Martin, our Pentagon correspondent, that a wing of F-15s was being moved. A lot has been said about reporters fuzzing the line on national security. David isn't one of them. He told us all he could on our overseas calls, but much less than he knew.

"I'm going to work on some people here," said Martin. "You

work that end. What you should do is to get to this F-15 wing. Nobody has done them. The commanding officer is a Colonel John McBroom. And you need to know: He thinks Dan Rather is a left-wing, antimilitary pinko."

What else was new? Even though, during the Korean War, I volunteered first for the Army Reserves and then the Marines, I am somehow labeled an antimilitary agitator. I believe the label was first applied when I reported what I saw in Vietnam, and they tried to adhere the label even more firmly when I asked President Nixon questions about Watergate. What the latter had to do with the nation's defense isn't clear, but in the early '70s there were still disciples of Joe McCarthy who thought if you could spell "Stolichnaya" you were a Communist dupe, at the least.

Martin got in touch with Pete Williams at the Pentagon, and through him to Dick Cheney, the secretary of defense. Although we disagreed on many things, Cheney had in the past judged me on the only record I care about: as a reporter who tries to be fair and accurate.

They convinced McBroom to let me interview him. They did it, I believe, by saying: Look, we want to see those F-15s on television—all over television. We want Saddam to see them. We want them to look big and dangerous to the Iraqis, to the Saudis, to the Soviets, and yes, to the American public. Rather is there. He isn't going to do a little three-minute stand-up. He will build a whole broadcast around it: "This is the *CBS Evening News* tonight, with the First Tactical Fighter Wing in Dhahran, Saudi Arabia. . . ."

When McBroom hesitated, they said, "Colonel, we're not asking you to do this. We're telling you."

I took an instant liking to him. He had checked around and heard that, no, I was not the "wrong kind of reporter" in Vietnam. I never quite knew what that means, but his attitude changed. When we finished the interview, he waved off an invitation to review the tape. He said, "I'll tell you something. I didn't want to do this. Didn't think I would. But you're welcome back here at any time."

McBroom was silver-haired, jut-jawed, with unblinking blue eyes. He was everything you would expect a warrior to be: smart, tough, prepared to put his own life on the line. He had great esprit among his own troops. He made Tom Cruise's character in *Top Gun* look like a kid in the Soap Box Derby.

There were only twenty-four planes on the ground, but moving those F-15s was a critical decision. The F-15 is the basic fighter-bomber of the U.S. Air Force and the standard the world over.

In those early days of August, we had a good deal of air power at sea around the Middle East, but not much of it actually in the Persian Gulf. And carrier-based planes were limited in range.

The F-15s had left Langley, Virginia, on the seventh of August and had flown straight through to Dhahran. They refueled in the air. The moment they touched down, the price for Saddam Hussein to take the next step soared.

When I first saw them on the ground, they were out in the open with little protective cover. Airfields are vulnerable until you move in the troops with such weapons as the Patriot missiles. Land-based aircraft are never left exposed and in the open, a lesson we learned at Pearl Harbor. But these were. There were not even decent anti-aircraft batteries available, and McBroom knew it. After one visit, I knew it.

Yet their arrival was a tremendous lift to the Saudi spirit and a downer for the Iraqis. If Saddam had kept rolling through Kuwait, had immediately sent his tanks down the Persian Gulf highway and moved on the Saudi oil fields, he probably could have succeeded. But the price of poker had gone way up.

Iraq had hesitated just long enough for the F-15s to slip in. Historians may long debate whether Saddam ever intended to roll out of Kuwait and into Saudi Arabia. I was one who believed he did. He still had time to make a Pattonesque run, but by the time he checked his hole card the window had closed. The 82nd Airborne was soon on the scene in force.

You can make the case that this was the first war decided almost entirely by air power. And the point of the spear was one bold and uncelebrated wing of F-15s.

It is one of the eternal truths: Wars are often won not by the armies you have, but by the armies your enemy thinks you have.

EIGHT

The Search for Saddam Hussein

I FLEW INTO BAGHDAD AT TWILIGHT ON THE FOURTEENTH OF AU-
gust, into an airport that quickly emptied. It doesn't take long to
clear customs when there is only one flight a day. I would have enjoyed the ease of movement, the absence of the harried throngs, if
our privacy had been not quite so complete.

The other passengers were gone in a flash, leaving us in a kind of
holding area. Tom Bettag, cameramen Kurt Hoeffler and Jürgen
Normand, technical wizard John Smith, and I were alone now, except for a few custodians and the airport security officers. The security officers had no idea who we were, or why we had come. They
only knew that we couldn't leave.

There didn't seem to be any cause for alarm, except that we had
been told that someone would meet us and escort us into the city. I

remembered a man I'll call Hamoud, the one person I knew in the Iraqi government, and began looking for a phone. I eventually found one, and eventually figured out how it worked, and five hours later we were on our way to the Hotel Palestine.

There was no sense of entering a country that had become a fortress. But as we began our descent, I had spotted what appeared to be ground-to-air missile sites, although I couldn't be certain.

On the drive into town, we passed Iraq's Tomb of the Unknown Soldier, where armed soldiers walked their post. We were not likely to stumble across any military secrets on our ride into town, but armored convoys rolled along the roadways. Above us, we saw antiaircraft batteries hoisted by helicopters with slings, to be lowered onto the rooftops of key buildings. Still, I would find that the Iraqis were almost matter-of-fact about the threat of an American air attack, which they expected at any moment. The city had been seasoned by the murderous, eight-year conflict with Iran.

A "handler" from the Foreign Ministry was waiting for us when we checked into the hotel. His name was Ali Abdul-Rashad, a man of medium height, pudgy, a bureaucrat trying to hold down his weight. Politely, he told us we were not allowed to leave the hotel. We were absolutely forbidden to take photographs or film of any kind.

Whereupon we engaged in what no doubt will strike people as a series of foolish negotiations. It is impossible to convey how petty and torturous they were, and yet, how necessary. We were in Baghdad for the purpose of broadcasting the evening news, not just to churn out a daily piece.

I will say this for our baby-sitter/observer. He made it clear that he would do nothing to jeopardize the security of Iraq or Saddam Hussein or, for that matter, himself. But within limits he would give us whatever help he could. So our first negotiation was to loosen the prohibition against pictures. Television tends to lose something without pictures.

Tom convinced him to let the cameraman film me on the balcony outside our room, framed against the sky. There would be no shots of the Tigris River, no mosque in the background, nothing that was clearly identifiable. Of course, we needed to take our videotape to the television station, and have them put it on the bird (satellite) for us.

It took hours to get him to agree to this, but he did, and we were assured of a Baghdad dateline. More hours were spent getting into the station, which was surrounded by armed guards. Keep in mind that in many countries, certainly in the Third World, the three most important locations are the presidential palace, the airport, and the television station.

I was less concerned with the armed guards than with a woman we called the Tiger Lady. She was a member of the ruling Ba'ath party and in charge of the station. Each day you were subject to censorship; there was a censor sitting there with his hand literally on the plug. If you said anything that they disapproved, out it came. It was a potential nightmare.

After we had moved our first day's tape, we dropped by the U. S. Embassy, where I met Joe Wilson III, whom I consider one of the unsung heroes of the Gulf War. He had been left in charge after April Glaspie, the American ambassador, had returned to Washington shortly before the invasion. It was Glaspie who, during an interview with Saddam, seemed to assure him of "U.S. neutrality in Arab border disputes." Her message was disclosed in a now-notorious State Department cable, in which she said: "President Bush, too, wants friendship, as he had written . . . on the occasion of Iraq's national day. Saddam interrupted to say he had been touched by those messages." She went on to describe the dictator as ". . . cordial, reasonable and even warm. . . . His emphasis that he wants a peaceful settlement is surely sincere."

Either the ambassador suffered from a fatal case of naïveté, or she merely reflected the Bush administration's desire to humor the man they then viewed as protecting the balance of power in the region.

We could not have coped in Baghdad without Joe Wilson. He made it clear from the beginning: "Glad to see you, glad you're here, understand why you are here, and I will help you all I can. But that won't be much. I've got my hands full.

"And now, let me put on my official hat as a representative of the United States government, and tell you that as a U.S. citizen you are in peril here."

That very day, an Iraqi government official called at the hotel and said, "Let's take a ride." I thought, well, that's unusual. What I said was: "Where are we going?"

"Oh, just to ride around town a bit," he said. Keep in mind, we all but needed a note from our mother to get out of the hotel. And there was always a chance that your room and phone were bugged. We climbed into his car and started riding. Another Iraqi was at the wheel.

The government man said, "I am not supposed to tell you this, but I think you should know, our leader is considering taking and holding some foreigners, including and perhaps especially Americans. They will be regarded as guests."

I should have figured out that code very quickly, but in the context of the time I merely said, "What do you mean, 'guests'?" We were all, in a sense, guests, I thought. There were thousands of Americans living and working in Kuwait, most with oil companies, and hundreds in Iraq.

With no dissembling, he said they would be taken as hostages, and dispersed to selected locations as targets. "Human shields, if you will."

My reaction was just utter shock. I returned to the hotel and told Tom, who said, "My God, I can't believe it." I said, "Well, I believe it. I think we just had a story laid on us."

No one in Iraq told you anything they were not supposed to tell you. But Bettag reminded me that we needed more than one source. I said, "Well, this source is pretty good, and in a country like this I'm not sure a policy of having two sources is going to work. Besides, they all feed from the same trough."

He said, "Just the same, we need to get it confirmed."

So I put through a call to Hamoud, my contact in the Iraqi government. There were the usual delays, and we were getting closer and closer to broadcast time. I was sitting on information I knew to be explosive, and I felt reasonably sure no one else had it. We had been given a desk at the U.S. Embassy, and I had been overheard talking by one of the staff—not Joe Wilson. He called me aside and said, "I'm going to say it once and only once. I think this is true. Joe is acting on his own, and he has sent out people from the embassy to warn as many Americans as they can find, and get as many as we can under the umbrella of the U.S. government."

He made it clear that they were trying to bring Americans into the compound, and into the embassy residences, rather than the embassy itself, where space and facilities were already overburdened.

I was more desperate than ever to reach Hamoud. I thought about driving over to the Foreign Ministry and was turned back. I had no luck on the phone, and I believed that he was ducking my calls because he did not want to confirm or deny the story.

In short, we were in Never-Never-Land. The clock was running. We were in a beleaguered country that might soon be at war with our own, and already had a multitude of reasons, real or imagined, to be hostile. It was a country that had been the cradle of civilization, and had sunk into centuries of ignorance, poverty, and upheavals. They were talking about taking American hostages, and I knew the color of my passport.

Of course, I was concerned on a personal level. I was responsible for a team of people, including my friend Tom Bettag, a cameraman, soundman, and technician, all of whom depended on me in one way or another to look after their interests. They were tough pros, but they didn't know what I knew.

And if you set aside the fact that it was a lunatic move on Saddam Hussein's part, certain to inflame even those parts of the world willing to cut him some slack, it made a certain twisted sense. If you were going to grab anyone, detain or intern them, it might be useful to snatch a few who were the employees of an organization with the power to make things happen. All of these thoughts crossed my mind.

The *CBS Evening News* was to go on the air at two in the morning, Baghdad time. By 10:30 P.M., we hadn't reached Hamoud or anyone else to confirm the story. And, frankly, at the other end of the phone in New York, our colleagues were telling us, don't worry about filing the story, just get out of there. We were talking on a telephone line from the U.S. Embassy, into the control room at CBS. When David Burke picked up the phone and raised the subject, I had to tell him, "David, it's better that we not talk on this line." It wasn't a secure phone. And all I could really say was that we knew the risks and did not intend to be foolish.

Then, within the hour, Hamoud finally took my call. We used a couple of repertorial techniques that are not uncommon. One was: I have this story. I don't know whether to go with it or not, but the one thing I don't want to do is be inaccurate.

Hamoud said, "Well, what is the story?" I had a feeling that he knew quite clearly what the story was, but I said, "I would prefer to talk about it with you in person. It is a very sensitive subject and involves the lives and perhaps the deaths of many innocent people."

He said meeting with me would not be possible. He knew the ways of Washington well enough that I knew, under direct questioning, he wouldn't give me anything. I said, "Let me put it to you . . . let me ask you this, Mr. Hamoud. I am going to read you the first three paragraphs of my story, and if there is anything wrong with it, please correct me. And your silence will also tell me a good deal."

He said, "I cannot encourage you to do that."

I said, "Well, let me do it anyway." And before he could interrupt, I proceeded to read him the first three paragraphs, which basically said that the government of Saddam Hussein was considering the possibility of taking foreigners, including Americans, as what they preferred to call "guests," but what other countries would surely recognize as hostages. With the clear inference that they would be used as human shields and potential targets in the event of bombing raids on Iraqi soil.

There was a long silence. I said, "Mr. Hamoud, I need to do my broadcast, unless you have anything further to say." There was a second long silence. I said, "Thank you very much, and I may need to get back to you before we go on the air."

He said, "I am not sure I will be available."

That stopped me from putting the phone down. "I told you when I came here," I said, "that the one thing I wanted to do was be accurate. I certainly feel strongly about keeping that commitment in terms of the information I now have. I beg of you, don't let me broadcast it if what I have is inaccurate."

There was another silence. I waited . . . and waited . . . and waited. I wanted to be as sure as I could that I knew what that silence meant. Then I rang off, and I told Tom, "It's confirmed. I have the second source."

He said, "Did Hamoud confirm it?"

I said, "Not in so many words, but I consider that he did."

Bettag, a very prudent journalist, shook his head. "I would be a lot more comfortable if he actually told you, yes, the story is true."

The clock was ticking down and I was getting itchy. The story was huge and I wanted to unload it, because there is nothing worse than being a day late with a story you had first. But Tom kept yapping at me and working on me, and I finally called him back.

I said, "This story is of such importance that I think I need to talk to the foreign minister, Mr. Aziz, or at least the deputy foreign minister."

And Hamoud said, "That will not be possible."

"Then let me say this. You control the telephones, you control the country"—he kind of chuckled—"and I need you to tell me that this story is true."

He said, "I told you so three times in our previous conversation." Then he added, only half joking, "Mr. Rather, I thought you were a big-time Washington reporter. Do I have to come and color in your book?"

And I laughed, and said, "I owe you one. Thanks a lot." Before I could ring off, he said, this time sharply: "I think I do not have to draw you a picture of how important it is that my name not be associated with this story in any way."

I gave him my standard line: "Listen, when necessary I make my living by being a tomb of silence." With that, I heard the phone click at his end.

We led the nightly broadcast with the story. Over the next few days, there was so much in the way of rumors and speculation about the hostages that an American with any visibility at all had to be wary. We made it a point not to be careless, not to be stupid about our movements.

Up to this point, the global temper was more or less unchanged. Saddam Hussein had said, in effect, that he had made his point. He had taken from the Arab rich to give to the Arab poor, casting himself as a desert descendant of Robin Hood. He had been prepared to withdraw his troops and leave in place a broad-based government. Now, with President Bush rattling his sword—Saddam's view—and demanding the return of the Kuwaiti royal family to the throne, the equation had changed. Kuwait and Iraq were one nation, indivisible, with oil and dinars for all.

President Bush was continuing the military buildup, and heating up the rhetoric, having compared the Iraqi dictator to Adolf Hitler. Meanwhile, Secretary of State James Baker rallied our allies in Europe and the Middle East, forging what would become a most improbable coalition. Sanctions were already in place; a deadline for the Iraqi withdrawal was in the making.

My daily reports on CBS Radio allowed me a freedom not always available within the structure of a network newscast: I could interpret what I was told. I could conjecture.

From Baghdad, August 15: ". . . People here think there will be an invasion. If there is, one Iraqi told me, 'We do not fear it.' There is concern about food shortages. Americans are lectured on how inhumane it was of President Bush to cut off food to the people. . . . Baghdad radio and television are filled with what can best be described as patriotic audios and videos, programs intended to prepare the country for a possible long siege. . . ."

And on August 16: ". . . Events have tumbled one on top of another today in Baghdad. None of the portents are encouraging. The most important have been, in no particular order: 1) The ordering of the British and Americans in Kuwait City to an undisclosed hotel, which many diplomats here fear may mean some kind of internment, possibly in Iraq; 2) President Saddam Hussein's tough, vitriolic speech accusing President Bush of having insulted him and calling Bush a liar; 3) the Americans now held in Baghdad see no light, no hope, of gaining their freedom of movement.

"One diplomat, who has been here for a period of time and knows the situation well, offered a cautionary note: 'Do not jump to too many conclusions. Both sides are doing a lot of posturing.' If true, it is posturing that leaves one with the conclusion that the situation is extremely volatile and the end of it is not in sight. . . ."

And on August 17: "Dan Rather reporting from Baghdad, where the big question is, Where are the Americans?

"We are talking, in this instance, about forty-one Americans, among the three to four hundred who are known to be in Iraq. Of these forty-one, thirty-five were originally in Kuwait, brought to Baghdad, and kept in the Rashid Hotel. Six others were on a religious pilgrimage, and were kept in a hotel along the Tigris River. Where these Americans are, and what the Iraqis have in mind for them, is the big mystery, the big concern, the major fear here in Baghdad tonight. . . ."

And on August 20: "Armed squads of soldiers have been seen knocking on doors on Baghdad's side streets. It is believed that what they are doing is looking for Americans and other Westerners. This development came after it was announced on Baghdad radio and television that all foreigners were required to report their whereabouts. Iraqis were advised to let authorities know of any foreigners living in their neighborhoods. . . .

"In Kuwait, all embassies will be closed as of noon Friday, in a move widely interpreted by diplomats to mean that the four to five thousand American and British citizens there will be transported to Iraq as part of Saddam Hussein's hostages-as-human-shields strategy. It has been known for several days that Americans and other Westerners were being placed at key sites around the country. . . . CBS News was told by Iraqi sources tonight that they could be dispersed to as many as one hundred military and industrial sites."

Saddam had made a colossal error, compounded later by the television appearance in which he rubbed the head of a little British boy. He had with one ominous stroke turned world opinion into a solid bloc. At first, President Bush had avoided using the word "hostages," a label that had so wounded and haunted Jimmy Carter. But as the shock and anger mounted, words became a weapon. Within a week, Saddam released the women and children, but acted on his threat to disperse the men to potential military targets. The use of the phrase "human shields" suggested an image of the helpless captives spread-eagled across the hood of an armored car.

It wasn't long before we looked around and discovered that our ranks were growing thinner. An Iraqi source told us that he knew of only three or four Western reporters—we are talking full-time staff people—who remained. ABC had left behind a skeleton crew. CNN still had one or two staffers in place, and a French camera crew had flown in and out before anyone knew they were there. I found out about them from the Sudanese steward who cleaned our hotel rooms. In the time-honored way, if you treat people decently and tip what I call responsibly, you might pick up some information when you need it. So one morning, one of our Sudanese friends checked the hallway, looked in both directions, and whispered, "There is a Frenchman with a camera staying at the Sheraton Hotel."

But the French came and went, arriving on a plane owned by a construction company that did business with Saddam, and taking home with them a little girl. That was all I learned, and more than I needed to know, but it reflected the mind-set among what was left of the press corps. You were hungry for news, and not quite reduced to reading empty gum wrappers.

Some reporters left at the insistence of the Iraqi government, some on instructions from their home offices, and some because they thought, rightly, that the danger was increasing. During the next thirty-six hours, on the one hand we had the best story in the world almost to ourselves. On the other, it was getting lonely and there was a sense that: This is not a movie; this is real and it is frightening.

I made it a point to see as much, as I could of Joe Wilson, and I stayed in touch with Hamoud, knowing that I might require his help at any time. I finally managed to see him, alone, and made a hard pitch for the interview with Saddam Hussein.

I pointed out that ABC's interview with Tariq Aziz went nowhere, receiving little or no press coverage. I said I wasn't trying to criticize my competition—although obviously I was. I said, "You're telling me that Saddam is misunderstood, his policies and intentions are misunderstood. And you tell me this is dangerous for the world.

"I can give him one hour of prime time. He should speak to the people himself. That is his best chance, it may be his only chance, if indeed he is misunderstood as you say and if his policies have been distorted. We are the people to do it: CBS. I am here. I am going to be here. I'll stay in Baghdad for as long as I can. I'm not leaving until you tell me I have to leave. And even when we do, I'm going to be as near as Amman."

So our basic message, again, was: We're serious about this. We're here to stay. Here's our best proposal. The only condition we insist on is the right to edit the interview. We may or may not, but we reserve that right. The best I can tell you is that it will be in context and it will be in depth and it will run an hour.

I like to think that even the people who may dislike me, for one reason or another, will agree that I am a reasonably tough questioner. I told Hamoud there would be no cream-puff questions, and that would give Saddam Hussein his best chance of answering what was really on the minds of most Americans.

Hamoud took it all in, and he said, "I will try," which encouraged me greatly. There were several moments when we thought we were really close, and then suddenly it went away. Hamoud called and said, "It could happen at any time, but I do not think it will happen on this trip." A day or two later, he called and said, "It is time for you to go."

I said, "I'd rather not."

He replied, "It is not for you to say. You must leave."

I was of the impression that Saddam was not then in Baghdad; that he was moving around the country, trying to keep U.S. intelligence agents guessing. I think the Iraqis were concerned about leading anyone to where he was and, in addition, the Iraqis had a natural reluctance to allow anyone to stay long enough to build up contacts. The policy was, keep them moving, keep them off balance. Get in a new group, fresh and enthusiastic, and you can dump the same old fertilizer on them.

We left, but not disheartened. Tom and I both had a hunch that we would be back. On our return to Amman, we asked for an interview with Hosni Mubarak, whose role in the crisis held some fascination for me. I had been warned of his alleged deceitfulness by Jordan's King Hussein, who distrusted him.

We flew to Alexandria, the ancient city by the sea, where once the oldest library in the world was located. I had been there on other occasions and always felt it was one of the world's enchanted cities. Again, this was a touch-and-go interview, with a lot of players competing for it. I don't mean to make each of these forays sound like Stanley tracking down Dr. Livingston. But anytime the head of a state tells you to step forward, you don't dally. There is in each of these journeys an investment in time, money, energy, ego, and nerves . . . and always the risk that it will fall through at the last instant.

Mubarak had a home by the sea, and when we arrived I was pleased to find an old friend, Dean Fisher, a writer who had flown in to do a cover story for *Time* magazine. We had both been assigned to the White House in 1964, during the presidency of Lyndon Johnson. Dean's interview wouldn't run until the following week. Ours would be on the air the next night.

I had met Mubarak, but had never really talked to him. We had a leisurely conversation, and a good one, which can be counterproductive. Too often you can't get the subject to repeat for the camera a provocative comment made in private.

There is a squareness about his appearance, the set of his face and shoulders. He has a strong and sturdy look, with thick black hair and the hands of a laborer. He asked me how things were in Baghdad, and in Saudi Arabia, and in the timeless ritual between journalist and source, particularly a high-level source, you have to give something to get something. It is an interesting exercise and one I rather like.

We both knew the game. I told him of King Hussein's accusation. He did not seem offended, but insisted that he had not lied about what Saddam Hussein had told him. Then he said, "How long is Bush going to wait?"

I suppose the implication that I was in a position to know what George Bush was thinking surprised me. "Wait for what?" I asked.

"To go to war," he said.

"Mr. President, I'm not sure he will."

"Oh, yes," he said. "He will. And he ought to go soon."

During our actual interview, he was far more cautious, but he expressed a concern that President Bush might wait too long to engage Saddam Hussein. After we had finished filming, and removed our microphones, he returned to the subject. "The longer he waits," he said, "the more difficult it could be. Saddam Hussein does not have a strong army. It is a myth. Who around President Bush has built up so strongly his army?"

Dick Cheney, the secretary of defense, had kept referring to the Iraqi army as the fourth most powerful in the world, which made you wonder if the ratings were provided by the same people who voted in the college football polls. China, Russia, and the United States were one-two-three, that was a given. So what had happened to East Germany, Cuba, Israel, Great Britain, France, North Korea, South Africa, India, Syria, even Egypt? Had we missed something? Had any of them lost a big one lately?

"Yes, Iraq has a lot of equipment," said Mubarak. "But the equipment is not as good as has been advertised. Secondly, the best equipment in the world is only as good as the people who operate it." Then he told me that during one of the decisive battles of the war with Iran, when the Iraqis were about to be overrun, Egypt had sent in artillery forces to support Iraq and helped turn the tide.

"I am telling you," he said, "if it is an air war, it will last three to four weeks. If it is a ground war, ten days to two weeks, at the outside."

This was in late August, four and a half months before the bombs would fall. I said, respectfully, that his estimate was not what I had been hearing from the U.S. military. But I was impressed with his confidence, his forcefulness. He was saying flat out that Saddam Hussein and his forces were vastly overrated. While they had fought the Iranians to a standstill, the Iranians were not very good, either.

I knew that Hosni Mubarak had come to power out of the Egyptian air force. He knew about modern equipment and he knew how good the American weapons were. He had seen them firsthand. We had conducted military maneuvers in the Egyptian desert. He knew what our fighters and bombers could do.

He was the second Arab leader in two weeks who had said to me, "Saddam Hussein will not bluff. You have to show him the steel. But once you show it to him, he will fold. His army will fold."

He was perplexed that President Bush was waiting, was willing to give Saddam a deadline. I said, almost defensively, "My understanding is that they don't have the decent stuff in place yet. They don't really have much in the way of armor and offensive weapons on the ground yet."

He waved a hand and said, "It is not going to take all that much offense. Nor much defense. I hope he [Bush] goes sooner as opposed to later, and it will be over quicker than anybody knows."

In his judgment of King Hussein, he was as devastating as the Jordanian king had been toward him. "He is of no consequence," said Mubarak. "He believes if you feed a lion meat, he will become your friend. But what you get is a lion you cannot stop feeding."

We left Alexandria feeling fairly pleased. We had gotten an exclusive interview with the president of Egypt, the first he had given on the crisis in the Persian Gulf, and we thought it would play well. But in the way of television news, we wound up with breakfast food on our chins. Through the kind of mixup that doesn't happen often, which is a source of wonderment right there, only two and a half minutes of the interview ran on *60 Minutes.* They thought most of it would run on the *Evening News,* and so they just gave a taste, rather than a full segment, which it deserved.

We blew off much of the prestige of having landed him, and I took it as a setback. Having said that, we were working seven days a week, virtually around the clock, napping on planes and in between broadcasts. This is how it really is; you are working on the edges and on the margins so much of the time, you are surprised when nothing goes wrong.

People have, I think, this perception of a television network, a giant organization such as CBS, with people everywhere operating at peak efficiency. And yet the confusion factor is out there where the meter doesn't register. When you are operating out of a place like Cairo or Amman or Baghdad, you are literally depending on two hotel stewards holding wires together in a back room. And if one of them tries to light a cigarette, you're in a world of trouble.

In a twenty-four-hour period, we had gone from Baghdad to Amman to Alexandria and on to Dhahran, Saudi Arabia. At the airport we were met by a representative of the company that leased us the plane, Arab Wings, and as soon as they lowered the ramp he ran right up and popped his head inside and said, "Mr. Rather, you must call your office in Amman. They want you to call immediately."

Bettag and I got off the plane and walked into the airport, apprehensive about the call and the urgency of it. We were operating on maybe an hour and a half of sleep over the past forty-eight hours. It took awhile to get a call through to Amman, but I finally reached Kathy Sciere, a senior producer for the *Evening News,* who said: "We've had a strange call. Your man in Baghdad says that he might be able to show you some sights if you come back to Baghdad as quickly as you can." I hung up the phone, turned to Tom, and said, "The Saddam interview."

We sprinted back to the plane, where we had a bit of difficulty with the crew. They were over the international limit for flying hours, but we worked that out, and they turned the plane around. We had not been there even long enough for the ground crew to put blocks under the wheels. We told the pilot, in effect, to shovel in a little more coal and get us back to Amman. We had to claw our way through the airport scene, and then to the Iraqi Embassy to have our passports stamped with our new visas for Baghdad. Then we had to wade through the crowd outside the embassy, and one more time through the flood of refugees at the airport, and hustle aboard the Iraqi government plane.

Our anticipation was high, but we still had no certain knowledge of what lay ahead. Bettag and I were met at the airport by our original handler, Ali Abdul-Rashad, which we took as a favorable sign. This time he even had an assistant, a driver, who we concluded, rightly or wrongly, was *his* handler and eavesdropper. I long ago forgot his name, but simply called him Cassius, for his lean and hungry look.

In truth, both struck us as fairly decent people. To our delight we found we had been upgraded: They drove us to the newly redecorated Sheraton Hotel. We were no longer consigned to the Hotel Palestine, with its run-down, faded hints of an elegance long gone. We accepted this as another hopeful sign. Our second trip to Baghdad was off to a swift start.

There were more reporters pouring into the city now every day, many from Europe and even Africa. Astonishing to me, the American newspapers of record, *The New York Times* and *The Washington Post,* waited three to six weeks before sending in a correspondent.

NBC had finally appeared, in the person of a good man, Keith Miller. But back in the States, the critics were still saying CBS was too far out on the story, and not doing a very good job, at that. I bit my lip a few times at the insinuation that I was hyping the story. This wasn't Chad, after all. This was where a good many analysts thought Armageddon could take place.

All I can say is that we had started the month of August way back in the ratings. We finished the month within one tenth of a point off the top. My position on the ratings has been that I don't believe them when they go down, so consistency requires me to say that I don't believe them when they go up. But if I did believe them, I would have to regard that as a dramatic rise. It told me the audience was there.

We had been in Baghdad two days, on this second trip, and I was having trouble getting through to Hamoud. I was asking myself what the hell was going on here. I had been told to get there quickly, and now nobody was telling us anything.

The mood of the city had changed dramatically since our first visit. It was almost self-congratulatory. The people had expected to be bombed in early August, and when it didn't come they thought the Americans had backed down.

My own mood was made no easier by the fact that I had caught a cold, complicated by a strep throat. I like to think I am as durable as the next guy, but everyone has a weak point and mine is the throat. Just the weakness you would pick if your living depended in large part on your ability to speak.

I nearly always carry an antibiotic with me, erythromycin, but when I opened my bag the container was missing. You couldn't fill a prescription in Baghdad, and I was running a fever of between 101 and 104. I knew that 104 was a kind of medical breakoff point, and when you had a fever that high you had to do something. I was taking Tylenol, calling around, trying to find erythromycin at any price. I felt really punk.

We were still reporting, getting stories out—in particular, following up on the hostages and those Americans who had taken refuge in the compound of the U.S. Embassy. We did all the obligatory things. We went to the office of the information minister, and followed the routine. You checked in at the downstairs reception desk. They sent your name to the second floor. Then you went up one flight and had tea with the deputy minister. And if all the tea leaves fell into place on that particular day, you would be invited to go all the way upstairs to meet with the minister himself.

It took awhile to figure it out, but there were some turf and entitlement battles going on among the information minister, the Foreign Ministry, the Intelligence Branch, the Ba'ath party, the military, and the palace. We came to believe that in the end, Saddam Hussein made his own decisions, but the single most important character was the information minister.

The reason he had this status was a tale in itself. He had been in prison with Saddam during their days as revolutionaries, and he had done Saddam's laundry for him. So we began to pay him more attention than most others had done.

On our fifth day back in Baghdad, our handler stopped by the hotel around noon and told us, "The information minister wants to see you." That hadn't happened before, and so we dropped whatever we were doing and went straight to his office. We went through the usual formalities, and drank more cups of tea, the authentic Persian tea that is as close to kerosene as any liquid I know.

But the end result was somewhat disappointing. He said, through a translator, "I can't promise you anything, but I would like you to stay in your hotel for the remainder of the day."

I said, "Fine, we will be happy to do that, Mr. Minister. Thank you very much." And we were out the door.

Back at the hotel, I took my temperature and it was still pushing 104. I was having difficulty talking and every two or three hours I broke into a cold sweat. I had gone through these sweats the preceding day, which told me the fever was peaking at precisely the wrong moment, as far as I was concerned. So we dug in at the hotel and I decided to run a bath, but there was no hot water. No surprise. There were many days when we had no water at all.

But I thought a hot bath would help, and I tried to bribe the kitchen help to heat some buckets of water and bring them to my room, but it didn't quite work. So I kept popping Tylenol, tried to gargle, and napped all I could. And I said a little prayer that it not get worse because this could be the day.

Another member of our team, technician John Smith—his real name—was suffering with the symptoms and more. He had been a combat cameraman for CBS, and we brought him in because he could do just about anything. He knew how to shoot film and edit. He could work the sound, access the satellite, and repair anything electrical. You know the type. The eternal next-door neighbor of all those of us who can't work with our hands.

But John had a fever, and a sore throat, and he couldn't keep any food down. The hotel eventually got an alleged doctor to see him, and he somehow produced some alleged erythromycin. My own instinct told me the man who saw John was not a doctor, and whatever he gave him, at a hundred dollars a tablet, was not erythromycin. But I borrowed a tablet and hoped for the best.

By now the daylight had begun to fade and so had our hopes. We hadn't left the hotel and the word was spreading, "It looks like CBS." People called and others dropped by and poked around a little. Several print reporters asked if we would take them along. I was candid from the start: I can't afford to gamble, I don't know that we're in, but if we are we're going on our own. I didn't know how true that would be.

The twilight passed, and I really felt like hell. As darkness came, I found myself sort of hoping that this wasn't the day; if I could get a full night's sleep maybe I would feel better tomorrow.

But right then I felt worse. By 9:30 P.M., we had waited all day and heard nothing. Tom said, "I think we ought to call somebody." So we called the deputy minister at home and he said, "Oh, didn't somebody tell you? I don't know that it is going to happen at all, but it certainly isn't going to happen today."

That was the first we had heard of that and our hearts dropped a little, but to be honest I felt relieved. John Smith was already out cold, and I told Tom, "I'm going to pack it in and hope I can get a good night's sleep. But I'm worried that we are in the same basic shape as the last time we were here. That is, close but no cigar."

That was about 10:00 P.M. I went to my room and had one of those shivering sweats, and when it subsided I dropped off to sleep. Shortly after eleven, there was a knock at the door and I staggered out of bed, opened it, and saw two uniformed guards standing there. I was in my undershorts and a T-shirt, groggy and unwell and still half asleep.

One of them said, in broken English, "Mr. Rather, you are wanted at the Foreign Ministry." I knew that Hamoud was a late-night person, and this had happened once or twice before, a knock at the door close to midnight.

But this time I said, "I'm not really up to it. I'm not feeling just terrific and if you don't mind I would prefer to do it in the morning."

He said, "No, no, you must come now. Foreign Ministry. You are expected."

Looking back, one might think I would have brightened right up at that. But I didn't. In the context of all we had been through, and what we had been told, I really believed we were going to the Foreign Ministry, and I was irritated. I had not shaved since early morning, had not bathed after going through two or three of these cold sweats, felt grubby and intended to stay that way. I didn't bother to put on a fresh shirt. You didn't get laundry done all that easily, so I put on a white one I had worn before, wrinkled and a little soiled around the collar. I almost didn't put on a tie, but at the last moment I did, as a concession to respectability, I suppose.

Unshaven, disheveled, looking and feeling crummy, I slipped into my coat. I figured I was going to see Hamoud and he would understand. The guards—soldiers, police, I wasn't sure—kept telling me to hurry. I said I had to get my producer, and the one who spoke English shouted, "No, nobody else."

I thought I really needed Tom, and he heard the noise and came out of his room. He walked me to the elevator, trying to slow them down and not cause a ruckus, but asking, "Would you please tell us what this is all about?" My escorts were walking me by the elbows by then, and it dawned on Tom that they might be taking me to one of those "guest" lodgings.

Part of the scene didn't look right to him, and he knew I was ill and looked as if I had dressed myself in the dark. All of this took place in a minute and a half, and as I stepped into the elevator I told Tom, "It's okay. I'm probably meeting Hamoud. They probably want to lay the groundwork for the interview. Don't worry about it."

Of course, we had no choice. We walked outside, and I got in the back while the two Iraqis sat in front. Both were wearing sidearms, I noticed. The one in the passenger seat also had an AK-47 submachine gun at his feet.

It was now between eleven and midnight, and as we drove along I realized we were not heading in the direction of the Foreign Ministry. I was reasonably well oriented because our hotel was right by the Tigris River, and you are either going upriver or downriver. You either cross it or you don't.

I was still fuzzy-headed, but then we started running into roadblocks and checkpoints. The car would stop and the two guards would show their ID cards, and the soldiers would stick their heads into the car and look me over. Naturally I didn't understand a word of what anyone was saying. I finally leaned over and asked the one who had done the talking, "We are headed for the Foreign Ministry, are we not?"

He said nothing. Before I could really zero in on the other possibilities, we circled around and stopped in front of a large building. When they opened the back door, I realized, "Wait a minute, this looks like the Baghdad Palace." I had never seen the palace except at a great distance, but my head began to clear and I knew it had to be.

Yet it still had not dawned on me that I was going to meet Saddam Hussein. I already had it firmly in my mind that the interview had been postponed to another day.

As we climbed the steps, I thought, maybe it's his staff, the last hurdle, and they need to check me out. Maybe they want me to meet Saddam and let him get to know me before the actual interview. I was mentally cursing myself for not having shaved, or showered, or found a fresh shirt. I'm trying to soak up every detail, even counting the number of steps that led to the palace, what the door looked like, and then the hallway, with the long, plush red carpet.

And then something came back to me that I had said to Hamoud when I made my initial request. I told him I fully understood the need for security and I would go anywhere, anytime, under any conditions to do the interview. I had even said, "If you think it's necessary, blindfold me, put me in the trunk of a car, whatever." At the time, he didn't smile, he didn't frown, he just sat there.

I had said any conditions, and I had no squawk coming.

I am no authority on palaces, but this one, I thought, met the old-fashioned image. It had been built in the 1940s for the Iraqi royalty, who had been put on the throne by the British and desposed in the revolution of the late 1950s. It is a world-class palace, not in a class with Buckingham Palace, but large and ostentatious, with the high ceilings and marble columns and marble floors that the aristocracy like so much.

I *knew* Saddam Hussein was there. I could feel it. First, the security was extremely heavy. There was a guard with a weapon every fifteen feet. My two escorts led me into a combination office and study. The one said, "Please, sit down." And almost immediately, Saddam Hussein's personal interpreter appeared, although I did not know his identity at the time.

He was obviously well educated, his English was perfect, he had a nice smile and manners that were almost excessively polite. He put me at ease right away. He said, "Welcome to the palace. You are going to interview the president and he will be with you in a few moments."

I said, "Well, I'm really pleased to hear that. I'd like to call my producer and camera crew and get them moving right away."

He said, "No, there's no time for that."

I was stunned. I said, "Well, I have to have them."

He smiled and said, pleasantly, "It will be done with our cameras. We will provide everything you need."

I don't want to put too fine a point on it, but I was thinking, it is after midnight, they say they want me to interview Saddam and I can't use my own producer and crew. Is this a setup? A propaganda trap? Am I being used? Did they intend to edit the interview?

I said, "I respectfully submit, I must have my producer and my crew, and while I recognize you are a high-ranking official, I would ask you to appeal to someone higher."

We argued a while, and he said, simply, that there was no appeal. In the end, he said, "Mr. Rather, you said you would go anyplace, anytime, and the president is waiting. He is ready for you. You may do the interview now, or you may go."

So I took a deep breath and said, "In that case, we will do it your way. But I want to say, and I would appreciate your repeating it, I must have assurances from the president himself. I say this respectfully. First of all, if you are doing this with your cameras, I must be given every millimeter of videotape, from however many cameras you are using. And I want his assurance that I will be allowed to feed every millimeter of it to the United States."

He said, "That is our intention."

I said, "Again, with respect, I would like to hear that from the president."

He said, "Then you may ask him yourself."

With that we took what I thought was an exceptionally long walk over the red carpets, deep into the palace, to a room that appeared to be a small but adequate study, actually quite a bit larger than the study just off the Oval Office at the White House.

I was ushered into the room and, indeed, at one end was Saddam Hussein. Near him, smiling, was the information minister. The first thing that struck me was the number of people in the room whom I had seen under other circumstances, including, I now realized, the translator. I knew several of them to be Western-educated, with fine intellects. But in that room, they all literally clicked their heels and tended to bow to Saddam when they addressed him. It was more than a little unsettling. The only one who did not seem scared, in a word, sheetless of him was our friend the information minister, the onetime prison laundryman.

I mean, he was at his heel-clicking best, but his body language and the tone of his voice said that he was not in awe of Saddam.

Saddam had the firm handshake, the eye contact, and through his translator, he said, "Welcome."

The everlasting first impression that attached to my mind's eye was not of the desert warrior, or the Abominable Sandman, but of a man who did not look a great deal different from a successful, well-tailored merchant.

I had noticed quickly that everyone in the room, including Saddam, appeared to have just shaved, showered, or bathed, and had on freshly pressed clothing. Most of them were in civilian dress, and Saddam, whom I had seen only on television in nothing but self-designed military uniforms, was wearing a dark blue suit, with a light blue shirt and a striped tie.

I was both looking and feeling as if I had been rode hard and put to bed wet. The information minister made a point of saying to me that I looked tired, and smiled. But my mind was turning now, clicking ahead, trying to put together in my mind the serious questions I needed to ask. I was close to being distracted by the idea that they might be trying to trap me. I wasn't sure why, or what form it would take, but I kept looking around the room, wondering what could go wrong.

As we talked, I said through the interpreter, "Mr. President, I want to get one thing cleared up from the beginning. This is highly unusual to do the interview this way."

His eyebrows seemed to arch and he said, "What do you mean?"

I said, "Well, to do the interview by myself, with no camera crew."

He said, "But we have several camera crews. It has all been arranged."

I said, "I understand that, and I want to do this interview. I consider it important, and I think it can contribute quite a bit to understanding on all sides. But I can't do it unless I have your word that I get every inch of tape from all the cameras, the ones I see and the ones I don't see. And I want to know if this broadcast is going to be live."

When my question was repeated, he smiled and said, "Iraqi television is off the air now."

I said, "I would like to have your assurance on these things. It is important to the integrity of the interview to do this." He didn't even glance at the information minister, which I thought he might, before he answered: "You have my word."

I didn't think about it then, but I had the word of a man who had just gobbled up a neighboring, small Arab country; who had gassed undefended villages and executed some of his closest friends. He had been called a madman, and compared to Hitler, and even as we talked he was holding hostage the citizens of a dozen other countries.

At times, I will tell myself to lighten up, it's only television. But this wasn't one of those times. A principle had been involved and I had not compromised on it. And on that note, I looked at my watch, and thought about what I would ask the man who, at that moment, was the villain of the world, the man who took so lightly the spilling of blood in the sand.

During the interview, we talked mostly about why Saddam had invaded Kuwait, what he intended to do now (less than a month after the invasion), how he thought things might play themselves out, and what he wanted U.S. leaders and the American people to know.

That night in Baghdad, on camera and off, Saddam emphasized that he would not withdraw from Kuwait, that he would go to war with the United States if necessary, that he was "not bluffing." And he wanted President Bush and the American people to know that. He warned of much bloodshed and many U.S. casualties.

Throughout the on-camera, hourlong interview, he never took his eyes off me. He answered every question slowly and deliberately. His interpreter and right-hand man was quick and brilliant. The man selected to interpret for me was—surprise!—slow and, frankly, thick. Saddam's interpreter sat on his left, mine on my right, and Saddam's man frequently corrected my interpreter. The translation setup was not, to put it mildly, conducive to a good interview climate. Not for me, anyway.

The only time I thought I saw Saddam's eyes flicker, even for a minute, was when I asked him how he answered criticisms that he and his regime were similar to Hitler's leadership of Nazi Germany. Saddam didn't like the question. (He wasn't supposed to.) And his main man gave me a look as if to say, "I can't believe you asked him that." He probably couldn't. In Iraq, nobody asks Saddam tough questions. Certainly not in public, and for sure not on television.

When Saddam answered, it was with a stare and a voice thrown deeper. He said that anybody who suggested that he was anything like Hitler, or that what he had done was similar to Nazi Germany's conquest of weaker neighbors in the 1930s, just didn't understand. Didn't understand him, Iraq, or the region.

One of his themes throughout the interview, and during our private conversations, was that Americans, and President Bush in particular, were "ignorant" about his history, the history of Iraq and all of the Middle East. He repeatedly criticized what he said was an "insulting and dangerous" lack of knowledge about Iraqi character and culture.

As he went through this, I silently reminded myself that this was coming from a man who had seldom traveled out of Iraq, whose only in-person brush with the West was two short trips to Paris. The greatest danger, I thought, was *his* misunderstanding, his miscalculations about America, Americans, and American character and culture.

"America is big and strong," he said repeatedly, "but you cannot take the blood," meaning Americans would not support a war with heavy casualties. "America has great power," he said, "but it has no staying power." And he convinced me that he believed this.

I came away more convinced than ever that there would be a war. I thought at the time and I believe now that Saddam's ignorance, his lack of understanding of the United States, made war inevitable.

I could see that America's role in the Vietnam War was one very big factor in Saddam's belief that Americans "couldn't take the blood" and had "no staying power." Any suggestion (and I made several in our time off-camera) that Vietnam had, in fact, demonstrated just the opposite—had demonstrated the United States' ability to stick with a war for a decade despite terrible casualties—was dismissed by Saddam.

But more important than Vietnam in his miscalculations, I believe, was Lebanon. In 1983, President Reagan had responded to the terrorist attack on the Marine barracks (in which 241 American servicemen were killed) by immediately withdrawing all American troops from the peace-keeping mission. Whether Saddam had anything to do with the bombing or not, he took away an important lesson from the attack: that the United States would run from a tough fight. It was the wrong lesson, but he took it. So did many others throughout the Middle East, including the Iranians and Hafez Assad in Syria.

Vietnam plus Lebanon, and the latter even more than the former, had led Saddam Hussein to the mother of all miscalculations.

outtake

Reporting Desert Storm

Hıstory ıs trıcky. It ıs elusıve, ambıguous, and sometımes un-fathomable. As Stanford historian James J. Sheehan has written: "History often seems to lie just beyond our reach. But at the same time, it is all around us, shaping the way we view the world and insinuating its lessons for the future. And this can be dangerous."

Let's take the Persian Gulf War as an example. The history of the Persian Gulf War is already badly skewed, and at risk of being forever skewed in many ways. For example: the interrelationship between Special Forces operating inside Iraq *before* the main ground offensive started; the success of vertical envelopment attack; and the use of air power with the eventual flanking operation to the west of Kuwait. These were all part of the *heart* of the victory, which, along with the Marines' stab up the coast road into Kuwait City, pierced the soul of the enemy. It broke his will and his ability to pursue the war further. This is the kind of thing of which legends are made, from the ringing windy plains of Troy to Normandy and Inchon: doing the impossible, and doing it in record time.

But *over*-censorship and control of the press hid much of the accomplishment at the time, and has shrouded much of it since then. The shroud includes a weave of confusion and uncertainty caused by the fact that so little *independent,* firsthand record was allowed to be compiled by independent witnesses.

History may not give this victory the full measure of what those who earned it *deserve* because the record, especially the picture record, is sparse, and what there is of it is confused and confusing and not compiled by independent sources.

There are many reasons. Some of them accidental and simply the luck of the draw. There are many other reasons having to do with personalities, bureaucracy, interservice rivalries, and battles for budget dollars.

For the purposes of this discussion, just note that too much censorship, too many unnecessary controls and ill-conceived policies concerning the flow of information, fogged up a story of great courage, great strategy that worked, and a mighty triumph.

And this is a reminder that an overemphasis on censorship and control of information has many dangers for the country and for the military itself.

Consider now the limitations of history in preparing for war—including how the press is to fit in.

It can be dangerous to apply the lessons from past battles to the future. This is because what are believed to be "lessons" may be the wrong lessons. It can even be dangerous to apply the lessons from past wars about propaganda and press relations. Or as the military prefers—I do not—"media" relations.

Just as many lessons that military historians believe were learned from one previous war or another about fighting turn out to be wrong, so it is with many lessons about news and propaganda.

British historian Michael Howard put forward this general thesis brilliantly in his book *Lessons of History.* In a section entitled "Men Against Fire," he writes that on the eve of World War I the leaders of every European army frantically searched recent history for clues to what was about to happen and how to deal with it. The war between Russia and Japan in 1904 was closely studied for the lessons it supposedly taught. European generals believed that war demonstrated that well-disciplined and well-led troops could generally triumph over firepower. This turned out to be wrong, given the improved weaponry that was developed after the Russo-Japanese War and before World War I. The belief cost many lives, helping to open doors to disaster on World War I battlefields. The military's vaunted historical studies were of little use in the 1914 to 1918 slaughter.

Generalizing from false premises based on inadequate evidence is dangerous. It was dangerous in the aftermath of the Vietnam War. It is dangerous now in the wake of the Persian Gulf War. Both as applied to the way the war was fought—and to the way the war was reported.

What the U.S. military believes it learned about news coverage and how to handle the reporting of war from the Persian Gulf experience is not likely to be of nearly as much value in the next war as many of our political and military leaders now seem to believe. We would do well to remember a few points.

- The technology of news coverage is changing so much, so quickly.
- The internationalization of news coverage is spreading so far and wide, so quickly.
- This was a short war, with few casualties on the Allied side. (Also, the other most recent episodes of extreme press restrictions, Panama and Grenada, were comparative skirmishes.) The next war in which we are involved may be similar, but odds are that it will not be. Certainly not all future wars will be. (Yes, I too pray that we may never have to fight another war. And I too pray that if there must be another war it will be short, with few American casualties. But I am talking here not about prayer but preparedness, in case reality turns out some other way.)
- The press will almost certainly behave differently, under different leadership, than it did during the most recent conflict. Put another way, the next war will not be happening so closely behind the Vietnam experience, with all of the Vietnam War's ramifications on the attitudes of the public and on those of political, military, and press leaders.

About the changing technology of news coverage, consider that miniaturization of equipment and other advances are making everything from cameras to the electronics of reaching satellites much more adaptable to battlefield conditions than anything available in the Persian Gulf War. CBS News had some of the smallest, most up-to-date equipment for live, on-scene coverage. It is part of what made CBS the first to report with live pictures and sound from Kuwait City. It fit on the back of a jeep. Very soon, one correspondent will be able to carry all that it takes inside a backpack. And soon after that, it will all fit in the pocket of a bush jacket.

Besides this, there is the fact that independent pictures of battlefields and other strategic sites taken from satellites are increasingly available to news organizations—not just to the military and intelligence agencies.

All of this and more in the exploding world of new, smaller, better technology has ramifications wide and deep for how much and how little control any commander may have over what is and is not covered.

This is especially true when you consider the rapid internationalization of news coverage—including mergers of international news organizations and cooperative newsgathering efforts by news organizations of different nations.

Quick, decisive wars with few casualties on your side make it comparatively easy to get control and keep control of news coverage. Stonewalling, sophistry, even outright lying may work, may hold for a short time—especially when the euphoria of victory overwhelms all. Long, bloody wars, in which the outcome dangles in doubt, make it much harder. I believe they make it impossible in a society such as ours.

That, let there be no doubt, I believe is an *advantage* for our warriors. Military leaders and journalists may agree to disagree about this. But I do fervently believe that in a constitutional republic based on democratic principles, a high degree of communicable trust between the leadership and the led is absolutely essential—especially in time of crisis, such as war.

This, I believe, is *the* great lesson of the Vietnam War, one that will stand the test of time. There is an old cliché: "In war, truth is the first casualty." It doesn't have to be. And one of Rather's Rules of War Coverage is: It had better *not* be, not when the United States of America has fighting men and women in the field. For our country, I believe, in war truth is our best weapon. Even the tough truths. Even the truth, when it *is* true, that we are getting the hell kicked out of us.

I do not say that every commander in every circumstance must tell every reporter the truth, the whole truth, and nothing but the truth in any and all circumstances. I do say that it is best not to lie; it is best to tell as much of the truth as possible, as quickly as possible. In the United States of America, only an informed citizenry can and will defend itself. In our beloved country, only an informed citizenry will send its young people to fight and die for any extended period—and only then if American citizens are convinced that the cause is just and worth the price, and that no other reasonable course is open.

It is one man's opinion, clearly labeled—this man's—but I believe any military commander who tries to mislead about the truth very much for very long is doomed—and there is high probability that the forces he leads are doomed as well.

In war, truth is the first necessity.

But in war, as in so much else in life, the easy wrong is tempting in the face of the tough right.

Political leadership is especially susceptible to this.

Example: It was the easy wrong to make the American people believe during the Vietnam War that the entire country did not need to go all-out, with everybody making major sacrifices in order to win. In the short run, it worked. In the long run, it was a grievous error.

The officers and men who actually had to fight the Vietnam War knew from early on how difficult it was, and that an all-out effort was necessary if the United States was to prevail. So did journalists who covered the fighting firsthand. But the top political leadership of the country, Republican and Democrat, was determined to have the people believe otherwise. And I'm sorry to say a few top flag-rank officers went along to get along, and—as the saying goes—the rest is history.

This much we must not forget; we—military people, journalists, and citizens in general—forget it at our peril. The consent of the governed is basic to American democracy. If the governed are misled, if they are not told the truth, or if through official unnecessary secrecy and deception they lack information on which to base intelligent decisions, then the system—some system—may go on. But not as a constitutional republic based on the principles of democracy. Political leadership may survive the politics of lying, at least for relatively short periods. The country may *not* survive sustained politics of lying, not for long anyway. And the ultimate military mission—war—cannot be sustained for long and cannot be victorious in a society such as ours if the military systematically engages in the politics of lying.

I believe the military and the press agree on the basics: the need to get the American people the truth and straight information about their fellow Americans in uniform. It is in the nature of political leadership to want to wedge us. I see us as partners in patriotism, each needing the other to fulfill our different roles—roles that sometimes place us in adversarial positions, but partners in trying to get the truth to our fellow citizens. We should be alert to and resist efforts to wedge us. In that spirit, together, the military and journalism, two great American professions, can work out ways to work together, whatever the new and different demands are for keeping the peace and fighting the next war.

Somalia: The Politics of Hunger

I CAN SEE HER FACE NOW, CAN SKETCH EVERY DETAIL IN MY MIND: THE eyes deep and hollow as ashtrays, the cheeks so sunken you appear to be looking directly into a skull. It is the face of a small girl. It is the face of Somalia, of every parched and barren land where life was once, and may be again, worth less than a bowl of rice infested with flies.

Any reporter who hangs around long enough will cover them all: famine, flood, war, and death, not quite the Four Horsemen of the Apocalypse, but close enough. For sheer horror and helplessness famine rarely ranks less than a tie for first.

For years I had been struck, as had others around me, by the harrowing stories of starving masses in Africa: in Mozambique, Sudan, Ethiopia. Somalia was arguably the worst, but even the thought of comparing misery on such a scale is pointless.

From time to time, CBS made an effort to bring this story to the attention of our viewers, on the *Evening News* and other broadcasts. We used our own correspondents when we could, bought footage from outside sources when we could not. But no matter what we did, none of us was ever satisfied with the result. We moaned about the dilemma of so many stories to cover, so little time and so few resources.

This is the endless, ageless problem of journalism. How do you choose to allocate your resources? And you *must* choose. The world is never going to run short of wars and plagues and other crises. You cannot focus on every one. On almost any day, you can stick a pin in a map and cue up a videotape and see these haunting pictures of people dying of hunger.

I ought to say up front that I have spent more than a few working lunches sitting in a dark screening room, in the air-conditioning, in my nice suit, with a thick sandwich and chips on a paper plate. I was bothered by the transposition; everyone I worked with was bothered by it. But we ate our sandwiches.

Trying to report this story is a sure formula for guilt and frustration. I do not mean to be existential. Everyone in television news has shared these feelings. I traveled to Mozambique years ago, taking a stab at showing the pictures and capturing how merciless the story really was. But a television camera is like a flashlight. You can show what's at the focus of the light as long as the beam is fixed upon it. We are horrified—and then the beam moves on.

The story comes and goes. We take our numbness with us and turn to other subjects. Part of the problem is that we—reporters and viewers—become desensitized. It seems so far away, so unreal. Half a million people dying of hunger and thirst? Dial an 800 number, make a donation, send oatmeal to a child in Rwanda.

In 1992, an election year, most of our resources, psychic and otherwise, were committed to the presidential campaign. Still, a few of us who were nearly obsessed with the idea promised ourselves that before the year ended we would make an all-out effort to bring home the story of the African famine.

In August, Bob Arnot, who had been among those chomping to go, went to Somalia for *CBS Morning News,* and Ed Bradley went for *60 Minutes.* The numbers of those dying had been large for a very long time, but there was always someone around to say, "Listen, it's Africa. No one gives a damn. Starving children have been around since biblical times. There are no ratings for it. No audience."

Arnot, a medical doctor, and Bradley came back with stories that pierced the heart. I was determined now to make the trip. Somalia saddened and outraged me. While I had never traveled to that area, I became something of a student of Somalia during the Persian Gulf War. It was strategically placed, a Cold War battleground.

I knew that Somalia should have been able to feed itself. The shortage of food, the masses of starving people, these were conditions created by gangsters. In different times, India and parts of Africa had been unable to raise the crops to feed their populations. This was different. This was war between clans and people denied food as a form of terrorism.

Life in rural Somalia was little different in the 1990s than it was in the fifth century before Christ. Nomads crossed and recrossed the land. A hundred generations had survived drought and famine, but nothing had prepared the Somalis for modern civil war.

Colonialism had come to Somalia in the late nineteenth century, when Britain took the northern third and Italy the south. Independence, which had been delayed by World War II, was declared in 1960 and the clans quickly seized power. Into the 1980s, the United States and Soviet Union armed the different factions to the teeth, battling for control of the region and its access to the Indian Ocean and Persian Gulf. When the superpowers pulled out, the warlords kept their arsenals. Food was to them what whiskey was to Al Capone. The clans that controlled the two big ports, Mogadishu and Kismayu, took a 15-percent rake-off on whatever passed through them.

In November 1992, Bill Clinton won the American election, and I began doing my homework, not just on Somalia but on the four or five parts of Africa threatened by famine. It appeared that the earliest I could get there would be late February or March, after the Clinton inauguration.

Then I began to pick up the muffled drums of the Pentagon, in mid-November. What I heard was that the United States might just "do something" in either Bosnia or Somalia. President Bush was now a lame duck. His administration had been criticized for acting too slowly to help the Kurds in northern Iraq, and for allowing the Serbs to begin their genocide in Bosnia.

It had been a lesser issue in the campaign, but the White House was stung by charges that the United States had simply winked when the Germans gave formal recognition to Croatia, which helped set off the Balkan war. There had been a peace treaty on the table, but the Muslims rejected it. They were led to believe, their negotiators said, that the United States would get them a "better deal."

So in the waning weeks of his presidency, Bush and his team were criticized for indecision, confusion, and a general lack of leadership on Bosnia and Somalia. Now, after the humiliation of losing a campaign they could and should have won, George Bush, Jim Baker, and the State Department were in danger of going home as double losers.

Bosnia was viewed as a bottomless pit, Somalia as quicksand. Both were going from bad to worse, but Bosnia posed a risk of longer term. This was Europe, with a history of trained, fully equipped armies and long wars. I called a flag-rank officer I had known in Vietnam, who knew the area well. "Frankly," he said, "I don't know if they are going to do either one, but if they do it will be Somalia. Why? Because it's a three-fer. The U.S. military is looking for a role in the post-Communist world. If they don't find one, there is no way they can justify their budget. Somalia is much closer. It's doable, particularly if they get in quickly and out quickly. And our presence there would put the lie to the smear that America doesn't care about black Africans and doesn't care about Muslims."

Logic told me that if the troops were going to Somalia, they would start moving two weeks or so before Christmas. It would be pretty hard for Americans to argue with a humanitarian mission to save starving children during Christmas. We had meetings at CBS twice a day for about ten days, and finally I said, "If we're going, let's adopt the U.S. military strategy. Let's go early and in strength, and if I'm wrong you can put pins under my fingernails."

We geared up to go and attacked our first problem: getting there. Somalia had no airline service. You flew to Nairobi, Kenya, chartered a private plane, and hired the best bush pilot you could find. There was no American Embassy in Somalia, no economy, no police force, no food you could depend on that was edible, no water, no sewage system worthy of the name, and no courts. In short, there was no government. And everybody had a gun. Ten-year-olds carried automatic weapons.

I thought, if I ever needed to know what anarchy looked like, this must be it. CBS made discreet inquiries to the State Department about what assistance we might expect if we sent a crew to Somalia. A CBS executive gave me their answer. "They say, don't go. They say, you're crazy if you do. You need to understand, there are people who will kill you for the sport of it. There are, of course, many decent Somalis, but they are helpless. If you go in, don't expect any help from the U.S. government. They say they are not capable of giving you any help even if they wanted to and, Dan, in your case they might not want to. . . ."

Believe me, I am no more a fan of hardship than the next person. But this is the trade-off you have to make. You don't cover a famine from one of Donald Trump's hotels.

For good measure, we knew we were heading into a country that was absolutely disease-ridden. So we had to be totally self-contained. I didn't plan to pop in there and do two stand-ups and get out. The plan was to get in, survive, and wait for the American ground forces to arrive.

We started making our arrangements before President Bush announced that the United States would join the United Nations peacekeeping force in Somalia. Operation Restore Hope would call upon 28,000 U.S. troops to provide an armed escort for the safe delivery of food to the towns and countryside.

It was a small risk, but still a risk. The army didn't send us a telegram saying they would go. There was no guarantee. We had made a commitment to fly halfway around the world on a hunch and some information from our Pentagon correspondent David Martin. That may not have been a prudent business decision, but it is often the only way to get out in front of a story. (It was reassuring to remember that Martin, one of the best reporters this network has ever known, last made a mistake sometime around Caesar's Gallic campaign.)

We had to provide our own food, water, medical supplies, and protection. You handpick your crew for an assignment of this kind, and you want people who can do several jobs, do them under pressure, and have worked before in tight corners.

Once we made the decision to go, the clock started ticking. If an anchor is off the air for a day, the competition will ask a few questions. Two days, and the competition will ask lots of questions.

As a first step, we took Lucy Fox out of our outpost in Cyprus and sent her to Nairobi to set up our base camp. Lucy is British, short, with red hair, green eyes, and freckles, and with a very precise accent and a confidence that reminds you why the British Empire lasted four hundred years. She was to be our fixer, a role I've described before, one that is essential in any overseas broadcast we attempt. When I was covering the civil rights movement in the

South in the 1960s, fixers were known in the trade as "dog robbers." If you needed someone to steal a dog, or kick a competitor's camera bag into a corner, they did the job and kept their lips sealed.

In Nairobi, Lucy hired our pilot, a daredevil who had to fly us into an airport that wasn't open. The Mogadishu airport lies hard by the sea. It was the largest airport in the country, but hadn't operated in years and had no control tower. Private planes that attempted to land nearly always drew sporadic gunfire.

So you had to hire a bush pilot to fly you in. None of them came cheap. The trick was not to barter with them on the money, but to find one who was good and trustworthy and fearless. Since the airport wasn't operating, he had to carry his own drums of aviation fuel in the cabin of the airplane, so he could refuel and fly out.

We had to have additional gasoline of our own, knowing we were not likely to find a Texaco station to serve the vehicles we would be renting. When we boarded we were literally sitting among the cans of fuel. There were twelve of us in the original contingent, with ten to follow. Four had gone ahead to Mogadishu, including Allen Pizzey, one of our most experienced and toughest correspondents. The advance party would set up some kind of camp and at least try to figure out a way to get us from the airport to the interior of the city.

Pizzey and I had not always gotten along that well. I would hope it speaks well for both of us that he was willing to go and I wanted to have him.

There was no place to stay in Mogadishu, so far as we knew, and we were prepared to sleep outdoors on the ground. We had sleeping bags and a few personal articles, but mostly I carried lots of U.S. currency and some gold coins. The cash was in denominations up to a thousand dollars. My experience is that while the dollar is still almighty in many remote places, when you absolutely, positively, have to pay for what you can't do without, gold is better. From the most brutal warlord to the smallest street urchin, everyone knows gold.

We took off for Mogadishu, the capital of Somalia, on December 4, 1992, on a billowing, cloudy day. The pilot immediately told us the air was rough and we might not get in. "What I'll try to do," he said, over the the wind and the hum of the propellers, "is fly halfway, and at that point if the weather doesn't look any better we'll turn around and go back to Nairobi."

Now this was a pilot right out of *The Great Waldo Pepper* and the era of the aerial circus. If he didn't want to fly, my reaction was that I better check my hole cards. The clock was running, the competition couldn't be far behind, and CBS had a heavy bet down on this whole road show.

I subscribe blindly to the anchorman code of being frequently wrong but never in doubt. Under no circumstances did I want to return and spend the night in Nairobi. We had to set up a broadcast facility in Mogadishu, and we had to do it without local electricity. We were carrying our own generators. We had everything we needed for a small base camp, including tents and lanterns. All we needed to do next was locate whatever gunmen we had hired.

I'm not being cute about this decision. I am not a gun toter, despite what Morley Safer and others have said. I did not tote a gun in Vietnam, with a bandolier across my shoulder. Yes, in a tight place I know how to use one. I have hunted, and I know what damage a gun can do. I do not carry a gun on my assignments and have no intention of ever doing so.

We reached the halfway point in our flight and the pilot said the weather wasn't getting any better. By now, the gasoline drums were bouncing around, and none of us were feeling too frisky. I've flown to a lot of desolate places and in hairy situations. But I don't like flying in what amounts to a big egg filled with gasoline and my stomach was queasy, too.

I said, "Look, you're the pilot. If we have to turn back, we turn back. But it's pretty important that we go on if we can."

He said, "How important is it?"

I slapped down a thousand-dollar bill on the instrument panel. The accountants at CBS may or may not be pleased with my negotiating style, but you have to carry the big bills because now and then you need to make a big statement. I'm not certain in what expense category one would list this kind of bonus, but I prefer to call it incentive money. Americans believe in the incentive system.

I told the pilot, "We want to get in there badly enough that if we can land, you'll get another one just like it."

We had a contract with him, and he was good enough to say, "Aw, that's not necessary."

"You're doing a heckuva job," I assured him, "and that's what it's for."

Within seconds, we had broken through the cloud cover, and then we saw below us the beautiful Indian Ocean, lapping up against the outer reaches of the airport. And we saw the airport itself. "Hot damn, we're here," I said to myself. My colleagues in the cabin had other expressions, such as, "Our Father who art in heaven," and "Hail Mary, mother of God . . ." Someone may have invoked the god of Abraham, Isaac, and Jacob.

As we started a long descent to the airstrip, the pilot suddenly veered off and jerked the plane straight up and off to the right. Gasoline drums rattled around and the prayers were coming faster and louder. I shouted, "What the hell is going on here?" The pilot replied with one word: "Gunfire."

And it was. Then I heard it, fairly steady firepower, too. We learned later that a small band of Pakistani troops, under the U.N. flag, were trying to hold the airport and were under constant harassment by one or more of the clans.

At that time they actually controlled very little of the field. They controlled the warehouses, but not the entry to the airport, meaning that they could not provide a secure landing for small aircraft.

It was a classic case of being too few in number and outgunned. But I give the Pakistanis credit. They were brave men, very disciplined. The gunmen they had ousted just two months ago had moved back only fifty feet or so. Half a mile away, semi-starving refugees subsisted on the charity of a small aid agency. They had to be wet-fed, given food already cooked, so it couldn't be looted. Relief officials were hoping the U.S. Marines could quickly take control of the main road leading to the remote districts where thousands of starving people were clinging to life.

The bandits wanted to keep the airport closed, and reinforcements out, so they could run their food extortion machine. The ones firing on us were loyal to Mohammed Farrah Aidid, the clan leader who would soon have a bounty on his head. Aidid would gain more notoriety when his gangsters ambushed and killed eighteen American soldiers.

At that moment, I was, to put it mildly, ambivalent about what to do next. I thought, damn, to come this far and get through the weather, with a full day's advantage on the clock, and now this. The pilot was worried, quite properly, about how much fuel he had. Even if we landed safely, he had to fly out of there in bad weather. Yes, he did this for a living. He knew Mogadishu was likely to get busy and he wanted more of our business. Still, I was worried that he might not try to put the plane down.

"You understand," he said, "that if one bullet hits this aircraft in the right place, we're a ball of flame."

Now that he put it so delicately, I shrank a bit from my gung-ho, plant-the-flag mentality. I mean, as we circled the airport I thought about Jeannie, my children, Danjack and Robin, and about the people flying with me. They had families, too. We were not there to get ourselves killed. One is acutely aware at such moments that life is not a movie.

None of us had any delusions about being John Wayne. Mogadishu was a certified hellhole; the Michelin Guide gave it five pitchforks. But this was the job. We had come so far and now we were so close. I always think we can make it, that we can catch lightning in a specimen jar if need be. But I will be the first to admit it: That attitude can be dangerous and it can be deadly. What if we did get in, then what? Would we be under fire? Could we get unloaded? Could the pilot take off again?

I was trying to make sense of this big kaleidoscope, when the pilot leaned back and said casually, "It seems to have settled down." This was daytime and the shots were sporadic. The firefights might go on all night. The pilot looked around to see if there were any mortars shelling the strip and he saw none. To my surprise, he said, "We'll try it one more time."

He circled his way around, got very low, skimmed just over the beach and nearly brushed the sand dunes, and brought us in. There was no control tower, but the Pakistanis had radios and he made contact with them on his last approach. The Pakistanis asked what nationality we were. He told them, and they said to come on in. There were a few scattered shots in the distance as we touched down, and light applause broke out inside the plane.

We were not surprised to see racing toward us, across the tarmac, what were known as "technicals"—ancient and badly battered pickup trucks, on occasion a half-wrecked Toyota. They had guns mounted behind the cab, sometimes a .30-caliber, sometimes a .50-caliber, occasionally a 20-millimeter. These were lightly armored, Mad Max kind of vehicles of a very low grade. The backs of the pickups were packed with guys carrying M-16 rifles, Russian Kalashnikovs, and all kind of small arms. Some of the gunmen wore crisscrossed bandoliers, looking like a Somali version of those old sepia photos of Pancho Villa.

Before the plane had finished taxiing, three or four of these vehicles were moving toward us, so the reasonable question was, what were their intentions? The possibilities were endless, including petty theft. In previous weeks, several airplanes owned by relief agencies had been stripped, their radios, seats, and tires taken—virtually anything that could be torn loose and carried off. Our pilot was armed but he would be no match for this crowd.

The plane came to a stop and we opened the door not knowing what to expect. It turned out that this small convoy that greeted us was a mixture. A couple of the trucks contained thugs who were looking to see what the plane had that was worth stealing. A couple had been hired by a relief agency, and Allen Pizzey had arranged with them to send in these trucks in the hope of getting us off the plane, off the tarmac, and into town.

The United Nations refugee teams and the Red Cross had done a terrific job of feeding the people they could reach. They would prefer not to say anything about having to hire guns to protect the food and themselves, but that was the reality. On a selective basis, they would help newspeople if they could.

Then there were a couple of technicals that just circled the plane, giving new meaning to the phrase "balance of power." I never did find out who these buzzards were. I came to believe they were just more scavengers, weighing their options: Could this be a big kill, or just some grungy reporters?

From the window of the plane, to my immediate relief, I had spotted a telltale grapefruit bag in one of the trucks—used for shipping CBS News film and videotape. So I figured that at least one of the vehicles was our own, or had just been stolen from us. Almost from the moment we swung open the door and started clattering down the steps of the ladder, a relief agency official was calling to us. "Get all your people and all your stuff off as fast as you can," he yelled. "Did you bring any gasoline?"

I said yes. Quickly, and under cover, four trucks—two of ours and two from the relief agency—formed a cordon around the plane and we unloaded our equipment, supplies, and people. The pilot kept the plane running, got right out, and immediately went to the off wing and started pouring fuel into his tanks.

We hadn't gotten all of our supplies off the plane when the relief man, an Australian, gave me the signal to stop. "We can't tarry here," he said. "We have to get the hell out." The plan was to drive quickly away from the plane while the pilot took off, then fall back to the abandoned airline terminal to gather ourselves for running the gauntlet from the airport to downtown Mogadishu.

When we reached the edge of the terminal, we moved to an unoccupied corner of the building. The Pakistanis were at one end, and various ominous-looking people were eyeing us from locations just inside the main gate. At that point, I had a bright idea. I turned to Al Berman, a senior producer of the *Evening News* and our commander in the field, and said, "You know, we've got a chance to make tonight's newscast if I can do the anchor stuff right here, and we can get it on the airplane before he leaves."

So one of the technicals raced back out to the runway and our crew asked the pilot, "Can you give us eight or ten minutes?" He said, "I can't give you a damned thing, but it will take me that long to get all the gasoline in the tanks. When I get them filled, I'm gone."

Three members of what we called the PFM crew—Pretty Frigging Magic—were already setting up their small and highly portable equipment. To the uninitiated, it looked like the hardware for an extraterrestrial movie. There were microwaves and strange robotics, gauges, machines that made weird sounds and seemed half human. I do not profess to understand any of it and will confess to you that I dislike, in an irrational way, being around it. I am notorious for walking a wide path around this equipment, as if you might become sterile or impotent if you got too close. To me it was weird stuff.

But the engineers understand every fuse and wire and knob. They love it. To them it is like sleeping with the lions at the zoo. And for all my skittishness, I admire their panache. You give them an hour and they literally give you the world. They start with whatever they can pack into a saddlebag, this magical piece of gear. They send pictures up to a satellite, and another satellite back in New York or London reaches up and pulls in those pictures. I have no idea how that happens. They simply reach for the stars.

They are all recognizable as types, all built like offensive linemen. There are no two alike and they do not blend into a crowd. One strapping guy from London had a habit of always wearing a headband. He was nearly always smiling, a most likable fellow, but you couldn't touch him. No slap on the back, no arm around the shoulder. His code of the road was, call him anything, but touch him and you were liable to be hurt and you might die.

Videotape editor Paul Bellinger looked as if he had stepped out of the pages of *Hunting World.* He wore a crisp bush jacket and was always immaculate with his tools, always squared away.

We quickly did the following: I had the crew put a camera on me and I ad-libbed an opening. I knew which correspondents were doing what pieces that night—"and now we go to Susan Spencer at the White House"—but we had Bob Schieffer in the studio in New York to do the newscast if everything went wrong. If we got anything on the air, it would be a miracle. If we ad-libbed the whole newscast, it was going to be a miracle plus luck.

This was the opening:

> This is the *CBS Evening News.* Dan Rather reporting tonight from Mogadishu, Somalia. Good evening.

This is your quintessential hellhole. There is no government, no police, only anarchy and chaos, danger and death. We are at the airport. Just arrived here a few minutes ago. There was a firefight at the end of the runway as our plane came in. Early reports: Pakistani troops engaged in a firefight with one of a kind of Mad Max vehicle with a machine gun strapped to its side that the bandits and thugs and gang leaders in this part of the world specialize in sending to test perimeter defenses. The Pakistanis' main role has been to keep this airport open and under United Nations control.

About one thousand people die every twenty-four hours here from gunfire, disease, starvation. One person will die roughly every two, two and a half minutes while this broadcast is on the air. This is the kind of situation the Marines, followed by the U.S. Army, will be coming into.

For the official version of what President Bush is planning, we go to our Defense Department and correspondent David Martin.

It worked. In seven and a half minutes, that videotape was back on the airplane and bound for Nairobi. In Nairobi, we had what amounted to a miniature television transmitting station in a hotel. The staff there sent it off to New York and that night's *CBS Evening News* had a broadcast anchored from Mogadishu.

I probably use a half dozen variations of what I am about to say now, but you have to keep saying it. Ours is a small planet where most people measure their lives in little victories and defeats. We were there because this was an important story to tell, but our morale required a little victory, and as insiders we cheered. I do think you should avoid doing moonwalks in the end zone. But we felt good about ourselves. The best story in the world is worthless if you can't get it out. I knew Pizzey would have a piece from inside the town, and with our PFM gadgets we'd transmit that one, too.

We climbed onto our trucks and began taking the back roads into Mogadishu. The main street was sealed off with roadblocks. We had not gone very far when the nostrils picked up a hellish stench, and off to one side as far as the eye could see, there were shallow graves, mostly of people who had starved, some who had been shot. The stench of death was as thick as the draperies in an old English castle. The smell of human decay was worse than I thought, or remembered. Part of me said, yeah, this story is going to be something. But the really depressing part was the sight of people living out in the open, sleeping in bags, with no water, no sewage, sleeping next to this hideous graveyard with the toxic odors.

The trip was a short one. The great majority of the people we saw were women and children, many of them totally naked. This was a Muslim country and to view even a woman's bare arm or leg was once uncommon. They were skeletal, the walking dead—at least, the ones who were walking. Kurt Hoeffler videotaped it all.

Kurt is one of the world's best cameramen, a blockish man with a great eye, who served a long apprenticeship and became a craftsman in the German mold, a breed now all but gone. He is fearless, smart as hell, can take a camera apart and put it back together blindfolded. But he is addicted to German sausage. He has a cast-iron stomach, and no matter how stark a place he may find himself in, if he has his sausage and water, he can survive indefinitely. On the flight into Mogadishu, while nearly everyone else was saying his prayers, Kurt sat calmly in the back of the plane, cutting off little slices of sausage and washing them down with sips from his canteen. This is Hoeffler wherever you go. Even now.

I couldn't pull my eyes away from the women and children and the shallow graves. It was around two in the afternoon, and the clouds overhead indicated that we would have a sprinkle of rain later. The day was hot, humid, and rancid, and all around us was this indescribable raw sewage mixed with death, corpses of four-year-olds waiting to be buried in the dry, unyielding earth.

The Somalis who had the energy looked at us as if we were the advance column of the army of deliverance. Some, we learned later, thought we were and raised a hand or uttered a timid cheer.

This was not the time to worry about being inconspicuous. I had on my person enough food and water for two days. I wore a pair of lace-up boots that came up over the ankles, the better to avoid a sprain if I had to jump out of a plane or a truck. I had on thick socks to absorb the moisture and keep my feet from rubbing. I always carried an extra pair of clean socks, a lesson learned in Vietnam, and I wore a pair of fatigues with large pockets. None of my clothing had camouflage markings. The less military you looked the better off you were. Ideally, you wanted to look like a civilian or a camper.

I also had an old-fashioned web belt with a system of web suspenders, two canteens, and a butt pack. If this sounds like a description of a guy preparing for a survival camp, so be it. I have found that this was the best rig for me if I have to walk a long way, or live in my clothes. In the butt pack, I keep an old-fashioned army poncho and a hammock, especially welcome if the ground is cold or hard. My food staples are the usual tubes of peanut butter, cans of Vienna sausage, and ordinary trail bars. The only other weight is allocated to a reporter's notepad and pencils—unlike fountain pens, they are dependable and don't leak all over you. If I need a hat, I prefer a baseball or fishing cap.

We had tense moments at several roadblocks and talked and bluffed our way past them. At one point, we had to jump all over one of our PFM guys—Steve Sando. The Somalis will put their hands all over you and, even as the truck is moving, they are reaching in, hands darting, trying to steal your sunglasses, or whatever. If you slap their hands away, you have to do it with a flick. Sando slapped the hell out of them. These were people with itchy fingers. As I said, a ten-year-old with a semi-automatic weapon is a very dangerous individual. Partly by keeping the truck rolling, partly with chatter, partly with threats and payoffs and by restraining Sando, our friend from the refugee agency led us to where Allen Pizzey was.

Here we fell into a huge break, based mostly on the resourcefulness of Andy Clarke, who had been brought in from the London bureau. Andy was a former officer in Her Majesty's Navy, but when the life turned out not to be what he expected, he resigned and went begging for a job at CBS. He started out as nothing and worked his way up to become one of the best field producers the network has.

Sandy-haired, of medium build, Clarke is relentless. He was one of the four in Pizzey's group who had flown in early and scouted the landscape. He talked to several people and I suppose a few dollars changed hands, which led him to a former low- to mid-level Egyptian diplomat who owned what was left of a very small villa in Mogadishu, with a two-story stucco house and a patch of yard enclosed behind a shell-battered stucco wall.

The place looked like something out of Beirut during the worst of the bombing in the early eighties. Part of the wall had been knocked down, and elsewhere there were holes the size of satellite dishes.

But finding Mr. Egypt was a coup, because he was exactly what we needed in this situation. He was worldly, an intellectual, the only one I met in Somalia, and not averse to making a dollar. He was curious about everything, especially television. Clarke talked him into letting us come in and set up our equipment in his yard. While the fence and gate didn't provide any real protection, it was better than leaving equipment in the open. Mr. Egypt had a few connections with the clans and a lot of connections with the street people.

Mogadishu had its Keynesian side and our man was plugged into it. If we needed dependable runners he could find one, none more than nine years old perhaps, but reliable. If we needed to hire guns—euphemistically called "security"—he knew where to find them. It was never really clear to me whether we were better off with or without these guards. In all matters, the wage scale was interesting. It went up hourly.

The Egyptian knew about all of these things, and was willing to allow our small contingent to take over his home—for a small fee, of course. I was still a little suspicious the first night and slept outside. Nevertheless, the advantages were soon apparent. He had a makeshift generator of his own. He also had the closest thing to his own septic tank—better in the telling than in fact. The tank was rudimentary and showed no sign of ever having been cleaned. He had his own water well. It wasn't much as wells go, and I was not about to taste a drop of his water without adding a few purification tablets.

But we recognized our overall good fortune and had the extra advantage of Andy's military experience. He set up an outer perimeter and an inner perimeter and an inner sanctum, where only the Americans could go. This latter precaution was to keep our equipment from being ripped off, piece by piece.

When Andy asked our host if he could set up any kind of eating facility, he said, yes, he could do that. He had a woman who baked bread, the highlight of each meal, and he ran a twenty-four-hour kitchen. The house had two large rooms on the first floor and two smaller rooms upstairs. We basically turned it into a coed dormitory.

The quarters were tight—sleeping space on the floor and that was it. I was not aware of this at the time, but Pizzey went to Mr. Egypt and told him, "Our top man is coming in and he is perfectly prepared to sleep outside, but what can you do for him?" He replied, graciously, that he would move out of his own bedroom. He moved into what amounted to the maid's quarters—I don't know what happened to the maid, but he explained that this would enable him to be closer to the kitchen.

The key to this relationship was what courtesies our PFM lads could provide in return. There was no electricity in Mogadishu, but in addition to getting up the television pictures, the crew had brought along self-contained telephones. Since there was no government, and no laws, no permission was needed to set up a small dish in the backyard and attach it to one of their electronic gadgets, then search until they found a satellite. Bingo. We had mobile phones.

There were still just a dozen of us, but in two days we had created an infrastructure that functioned like a small town. As our host's curiosity about our equipment grew, I sensed a deal in the making. The price of poker was going up on the half hour now, and I understood that it had been a very long time since he had talked to his dear mother in Egypt. I made a proposal: What if we give you the phone in our off-hours? Here's the area code for Cairo. Be my guest.

From that moment on, he was bonded with CBS, which led to unexpected benefits. He had weapons of his own, which he did not advertise, to protect his home and hearth. Al Berman had served in the National Guard. He checked out the weapons and cleaned them. Then Al and I sat down and talked about what we would do if an effort was made to storm the compound. We kept the key to Mr. Egypt's gun closet, which contained guns of varying description, nothing automatic, one semi-automatic, and not much, but some, ammunition.

Talking about doling out bullets can be sobering, but there is something reassuring about contingency plans, especially when you don't need them. The story is still what counts and I never lose sight of that central point. Counting bullets in Somalia wasn't about risk. It wasn't about courage or even foolhardiness. It was about doing the job on days when you don't punch in at nine and leave at five.

I was able to close the broadcast that first night (the fourth of December) with a satellite feed from our new headquarters. I don't believe I misrepresented anything, but I did give our facilities the benefit of the doubt:

"We've moved from the airport," I said, ". . . a short distance away into what is called our CBS compound. What it is, is an abandoned former ambassador's residence. The residence has been completely shot up . . . bullet holes all over it. There is a wall with jagged broken glass at the top, barbed wire over it.

"As we drove from the airport to this compound, we passed many recent, very shallow graves butted right up against a vast area where people who've been knocked out of their homes are living in the open. No plumbing, no sewage, no water. There's some gunfire just over our shoulder . . . and the stench of death in that area was everywhere."

I walked over to our Mad Maxmobile. "This is the kind of vehicle that the warring gangs here use. This is a newly redecorated and outfitted four-wheel-drive Toyota and it has at the top, if you notice, a heavy-caliber machine gun. Now that machine gun may look to you like it's something out of a museum . . . but this is what is used in the Somali version of a drive-by shooting. And this will be the danger for U.S. troops as they move in. This, and the fact that so many people have weapons here that they can just fade back into their homes, put the weapons right under the bed and wait to see what happens with the U.S. military.

"Part of our world tonight . . . Dan Rather for *CBS Evening News.* Reporting from Mogadishu, Somalia. Good night."

Out in the Indian Ocean, several miles offshore, waited the Marine amphibious vessel, the U.S.S. *Juneau.* CBS had correspondent Bob Simon on board, and from the deck he reported they could see the lights of Mogadishu. A Marine commander told Simon they didn't expect any opposition, but if anyone challenged the Marines, "they will be killed." Their orders were neither to disarm the population, nor to tolerate the presence of weapons in any area the Marines controlled. The strategy was to smile and carry a big stick; to arrive on shore with such an overwhelming show of force that any potential resistance would evaporate into the thin desert air.

Tens of thousands of leaflets would be dropped in the next day or two, advising the Somalis that the Marines were there to help, to feed, to care for the sick and starving. Success would be judged, the commander said, by shots not fired, by casualties not taken.

On Monday, December 7, I filed the following report on radio for CBS News:

> I do not intend to tell you today about millions of starving people. I do intend to tell you about *two.* West of Mogadishu there is a woman and her child. They are starving. They are waiting, bravely, staging a battle for time. . . .
>
> They have heard that the Yanks are coming, coming over here. Incredible, unbelievable, but true, they are told. This mother and child hope the Americans hurry. They are Muslim. They pray to their God that the Americans come soon. Probably Wednesday. Perhaps here, they are told, where they are . . . but it may be later.
>
> The mother's eyes respond: Later, for *this* child, my child, later may be too late. The child is a girl . . . Harita Mohammed. One of two living children now of a mother who once had six.

Four others of her children died in her arms—disease and lack of food. Now, this child is dying, little Harita, seven years old, height about three feet, weight now down to about eighteen pounds.

Mother and child are in a refugee camp. There is a feeding area nearby. They are too weak to get to the area and it is too dangerous for anyone to take them. The feeding area itself is cut off, isolated; has been for a while. Warlords and their gangsters of the brush decreed this. They kill, rob, intimidate, extort. There is no law in Mogadishu and no law west of Mogadishu. For Harita Mohammed and her mother, no mercy.

The message from Mogadishu is: Hurry! For Harita and her mother, it may already be too late. . . .

Soon, many of our own sons and daughters, many of America's best, will come pouring into this hellhole of a country. When someone, anyone, asks you why, tell them . . . to save the children.

The Marines landed at dawn on Wednesday morning, December 9, 1992, and the situation was well in hand—no resistance, so far everything going according to plan.

I was broadcasting live and direct from atop the old terminal building at the Mogadishu airport in Somalia. Just behind me was what used to be the control tower, now bombed out and abandoned. Down in the dark, the Marines were seeking to secure a landing strip about 150 yards inside the beach, on the edge of the Indian Ocean.

The Navy SEALS (Sea, Air and Land Service) had swept ashore several hours ahead of schedule. The job of the SEALS was to clear the way for the Marines, to make sure no mines were strewn in the water or on the beach to maim and kill them.

And, yes, the television cameras were there—sort of Hollywoodish, almost cartoonish. But planned, all of it, by those behind the task force. If viewers at home were saying, well, this looks silly, in some ways they were surely correct. But the cameras were there by invitation. And as inappropriate as it may seem for an assault by sea, under cover of darkness, few TV cameras can operate without lights.

It did give the operation the character of a performance, with comic overtones, and I sympathized with the surprise and consternation the SEALS expressed. They had the look of cat burglars pinned in a searchlight. I believe some language may have aired not normally recommended for family audiences. If there had been any resistance, this would have been a setting for tragedy. But the landing was well scripted and nothing tragic happened. In the end, those involved continued to go about their business.

For the U.S. military it was a deadly serious business. Once they entered Mogadishu—never mind the interior of the country—no one knew how grim it might get. Hard behind the SEALS, the Marine reconnaissance units were the next to come ashore. They skidded onto the beach in their rubber boats to be greeted by members of the Pakistani forces in the blue berets of the United Nations. Within two hours, the entire Marine battalion would land in the dark to secure the airfield and the port. The helicopters would flutter in at first light.

The airport was to be the linchpin of the entire operation, and the Marines' first job would be to get it ready to handle a steady stream of military transports. The first transport plane landed around noon the next day, carrying the personnel and equipment needed to turn the airfield into a twenty-four-hour-a-day air-cargo terminal. For now, it operated only in daylight and could handle only two transports at a time.

But planes alone could never bring in all the equipment that would be needed. Most of it would come by ship. The first to dock at the port was the *Lummus,* loaded with electrical generators, water purification units, trucks and fuel tanks to support the Marines ashore. Three more cargo ships were waiting off the Somali coast, but the port was big enough to handle only one at a time.

On Thursday, the first combat troops from the United States, the Marines from Camp Pendleton, started arriving in Mogadishu and began moving into the interior, first to Baidoa, another boneyard of starvation and the scene of fierce gun battles between rival clans. The best estimate was that another week would pass before the relief agencies could deliver significant quantities of food to the starving. You tried not to think about how many more thousands would die in the meantime.

U.S. officials had stressed over and over again that Operation Restore Hope was a humanitarian mission, with the primary aim of feeding the hungry. But that is not all that it was. Reality check: The first task, of necessity, had to be to establish at least a minimum level of law and order in a place that would make the old Wild West look tame.

The young men who cruised on the technicals were the unpredictable element confronting the Marines. One wrong move on either side could turn a peacekeeping mission into a bloodbath.

The guns were simply everywhere. Merchants had their own militias. Even car-rental agencies included a gunman in the deal. This was such a way of life for the Somalis that two of them could argue for fifteen minutes, pointing a gun at each other, and not come close to pulling the trigger.

But when a CBS cameraman was spotted taking pictures, a Somali put a gun to the back of his head. The Somali backed off when our gunman threatened to shoot first.

The technicals working for the humanitarian agencies were kept off the streets for the first forty-eight hours after the Marines landed, in an effort to "prevent misunderstandings." A major problem was that the young men who rode the technicals didn't have any other way to make a living, and they needed the money to support a drug habit that, by late afternoon, left them dangerous and unpredictable. The drug they use is called khat. It had been a part of the social fabric there for years, but the civil wars turned teenagers into chronic khat abusers. If a kid high on khat was killed by a nervous Marine, there was a distinct danger that such an incident could spark a vendetta by the young man's clan, with every foreigner considered a legitimate target. No one dared forget that clan warfare was what had brought the country to the point where the Marines were needed to save Somalia from itself.

You do not settle into a routine on such stories, in such places. You start over every day. Sometimes you follow the blood.

After the Marines came ashore, I took a crew to a town even more violent than Mogadishu. It was at the southern corner of the triangle of death, where the suffering was the worst. No one had heard much about it because journalists seldom traveled there. The town was Kismayu, the second largest in Somalia. Almost no relief shipments were allowed in by the local gunmen, either by sea or air. A UNICEF plane had been robbed at gunpoint, even the pilot and crew relieved of their cash and valuables.

Kismayu's top clan boss was Colonel Omar Gess and word had reached us that he was annoyed this day because he had not been consulted about the American military intervention. He suspected that the United States, and certainly the United Nations, were plotting once again to bring Somalia under foreign rule.

"I will never accept to be colonized again," he told me, on camera, "and I do not see the solution to my people that, you know, a certain group comes and dictate to them and make them, you know, a colony. We believe that is not the solution. We will fight anybody who wants to colonize us. We want to be independent and free. We will not accept to be colonized by anybody."

The colonel gave us a tour of Kismayu's port, built with American aid in the 1960s. Shiploads of cigarettes, diesel fuel, and sugar managed to pass through, but no food-relief ships had docked for the last two months. The colonel said that was not his fault.

"I want to understand," I said. "You have not kept food out of this port?"

"Never," said Gess. "Never have done it."

"And you didn't loot ships in this port?"

"We never looted ships," said Gess, "and we never prohibited ships to anchor here in our port, and we don't know why it was this propaganda was made by some people, but it never happened."

I noticed that the colonel's motorcade featured a truck topped with a rocket-launcher from an old Soviet MiG-23, a relic of Somalia's past as a pawn in the Cold War.

Later, he showed me some khat, from Kenya, and I asked him if he chewed any. "Sometimes," he said, "when we are—when we want to work a lot of time." He added that it was not illegal, partly because nothing was illegal in a land where no laws existed.

"Well, I have heard people say," I told him, "that when the American troops come, they must be very careful in the afternoon because many people chew on khat and maybe get reckless."

"No," he said, "it is not like whiskey."

On the second day of Operation Restore Hope, nearly a week after CBS had begun its coverage, the first shooting casualties were reported. On a day of soaking monsoon rains, first the French and then U.S. troops were involved in shooting incidents. The official version was that a truckload of Somalis accelerated at a checkpoint. The French took that to be a possibly hostile act and opened fire.

U.S. forces then followed with more fire. Two Somalis were killed, seven others wounded, two seriously. The only weapon found in the truck turned out to be a large knife. U.S. forces evacuated the wounded and flew them to a hospital.

Back on land, flares popped over the capital as U.S. troops traded fire with gunmen near another checkpoint. Meanwhile, the Americans quietly extended their reach inside Somalia. Sixty miles inland from Mogadishu, U.S. Army Special Forces secured the largest open airfield in the country, easily overwhelming a small security force of clan gunmen.

U.S. soldiers said everything went smoothly. Through an interpreter, a Somali guard said they were shocked: "We came to greet them, to turn over our base, but the Americans just take our weapons."

The Marines were coming under sniper fire virtually anytime they moved. Relief workers were frustrated by the slow pace of setting up a system for delivering food, but the Marines were moving with caution. They were, Bob Simon reported from Mogadishu, "still in the hearts and minds business."

The French didn't bother with hearts or minds. They knew this part of the world. They used to own some of it. They used a different approach. Gentlemen of the French Foreign Legion had neither flak jackets nor strict rules of engagement. In Mogadishu, they always assumed the worst and were often right. They were carting weapons all day long. The first blood had been shed, and a few assumptions were changing. The conventional wisdom was that the Americans and the Europeans would be welcome at first, that the trouble would start later. Later began on day two of the operation.

We were home again in January 1993 when Bill Clinton was inaugurated as president. The United States had sent 28,000 troops to the Horn of Africa, and by June Clinton had brought home all but 4,000, some 1,300 as a rapid deployment unit. The U.N. was now paying the bills, providing most of the soldiers and shedding most of the blood.

By then, the plague of death by hunger among Somalis had lessened, and the U.N. estimated that hundreds of thousands of lives had been saved. But it was still a country without a government, without laws, without structure.

In October, U.S. soldiers were pinned down for nine hours and eighteen died in an attempt to rescue a trapped Pakistani unit. It was a fraction of the number killed in Beirut and in the Persian Gulf, fewer than in the invasions of Grenada and Panama. Yet they died during what had been hailed as a humanitarian cause, and Americans were angry and bitter.

We fed the children and brought home our troops, eighteen of them in coffins. The armed clans still roam a land where anything worth stealing has to be brought in from the outside.

After not many months had passed, there were few pictures on television of people starving in Africa, and few stories in the newspapers and magazines. The politicians still argued about who deserved the blame for which decision, but the rest of the country had moved on to other issues, other problems, other pictures.

outtake

Heroes

THE NEWS ON AUGUST 10, 1993, WAS EXACTLY THE KIND I HATE TO hear. The deaths of American soldiers on foreign soil are never easy to report, but in this case, the circumstances were especially sad.

These four young Americans—Sergeant Christopher Hilgert, Sergeant Ronald N. Richerson, Specialist Keith Pearson, and Specialist Mark Gutting—were killed by a command-detonated mine near the Mogadishu Airport. "Command-detonated" means that the mine was deliberately set. Someone waited in ambush until the soldiers' vehicle passed over the pre-positioned mine. Then that someone set off the mine. Then the ambushers opened fire on the other vehicles in the convoy.

Anyone who was in Vietnam recognizes this as a classic convoy ambush. Preferably, the second vehicle in the convoy is hit by the mine; then the stalled convoy is sprayed with fire from all sides.

These were soldiers who'd been sent to help—to save children—on a humanitarian mission. Yet they had died, evidently at the hands of the neighbors of the people they'd been sent to save. It made me sick to think about it.

And the other circumstances of the mission in Somalia were by this time no more encouraging.

After a bold start and the best of intentions, the Somalia rescue mission had begun to seem like America's forgotten war—yet our service personnel were still on the ground. As "Operation Restore Hope" was expanded to include "nation-building" and other assignments (for which I believe the military of any nation will always be unsuited), public interest seemed to decline in direct proportion.

Part of the lack of interest was easily understood. More and more when I talked to Americans who weren't in the news business, they described a "blizzard" of news—it seemed as though there were more important stories coming at them all at the same time than there had ever been before—and many of them were in corners of the world their geography classes forgot to teach. Grabbing hold of a story, digesting it, and learning more—this seemed almost impossible in the ceaseless flow of news and information.

But I believe the roots also lay elsewhere for the American public's lack of awareness about the mission in Somalia. We journalists were at fault: We'd come over in strength just before the Marine landing, and stayed in strength a few weeks. But by this time our resources had dwindled. CBS always had a camera crew based in Mogadishu, but there were several nervous days when we didn't have a correspondent in Somalia. A correspondent hungry for airtime makes an effective advocate for coverage of any story, and the good ones are always looking for ways to make each story different from the rest. Our ability to pitch a story in the newsroom was thus challenged. Our ability to grab the attention of the audience was even more severely challenged.

The debate was beginning to be heard that American television had "gotten us into Somalia"—a debate whose utter wrongness didn't seem to preclude its getting rewritten every couple of weeks on the op-ed pages of most newspapers in the country. (I wrote and spoke often for the opposing viewpoint, but I'd have needed to make a full-time job of it just to keep up with the chorus blaming television for America's involvement and perceived failures in Somalia.) They said our pictures so disturbed the American people that intervention was necessary: I pointed out that much worse pictures from Bosnia had never inspired such a strong reaction. The American people don't make the call to arms lightly; they need more than a picture to send their sons and daughters to fight and die.

The outgoing Bush administration and incoming Clinton administration had allowed the mission in Somalia to become diffuse, even turning our entire military force into a detective force (when three or four New York City detectives could have located and detained the Somalia warlord Mohammed Farrah Aidid in a couple of days). Both administrations took advantage of the American public's difficulties in focusing for long on the story. What the government hoped to gain in Somalia while (as they perceived it) no one back home was looking, I don't know.

I knew that the American men and women in harm's way in Somalia needed to feel that the folks back home knew and cared about what was going on—not just when things were going badly, but all the time. Otherwise, why should they be there?

So on August 10, 1993, I was honestly upset to learn of these four young Americans making the ultimate sacrifice far from home.

The death of Fred Woodruff, a U.S. intelligence operative, in the Republic of Georgia the same day only compounded my sadness. I knew that the Georgian president, Eduard Shevardnadze, had made a valiant attempt to maintain independence from Russia after the collapse of the Soviet Union (of which Shevardnadze was once foreign minister). Georgia should have had an easy time of it: Its agribusiness is legendary, its climate inviting, its tourism and other businesses promising. But the "ethnic purity" campaigns had started up again—and many believe the Russians instigated the campaigns. Within months there was bloody civil war in Georgia. The U.S. intelligence operative had been sent to advise and to protect Shevardnadze—and had been killed in an attack on a motorcade from which Shevardnadze himself only narrowly escaped.

I believed Georgia was about to be swallowed up by Russia again—that Shevardnadze would be forced to "invite" the Russian army into the country to keep the peace—and he did make that invitation shortly thereafter.

The ability of the former Soviet states to maintain their independence and their new, hard-won democratic forms of government is an important story on which I'm always trying to focus attention (in January 1994, producer George Osterkamp guided me back to Tbilisi for interviews with Shevardnadze and a survey of the scene). I knew that one way to help Americans understand what's going on in other countries is to start by concentrating on what other Americans are doing in foreign countries. So, with only a few minutes to airtime, I prepared a radio essay paying tribute to the five Americans who died.

"One does not need to know the details to know this: All five of these men were Americans far from home, in lonely places, doing lonely duty," I wrote, "dangerous missions in dangerous places. All five were in the service of their country, in the service of their fellow Americans. . . .

"This we do know: They died heroes. And attention needs to be paid.

"There was a time not long ago when heroes abounded in this country. Now there are few, a precious few. Why and how this came to be is an important question. But this we do know, and have been reminded in recent hours: There are, still are, Americans who believe in the fundamental American dream, in the American ideal—and are willing to fight for it, and die for it."

I wouldn't have minded a little extra time to polish my thoughts, but the radio microphone never blinks either, and deadline was upon me. I was glad at least that I'd spoken up, recognized the service and the sacrifice these men had made.

But a short time later I had the all-too-rare opportunity to make my point again, once it had simmered and stewed a little.

A listener in California wrote to say that while he was sorry these men had died and was sure they were good people deserving of some kind of tribute, the word "hero" was so overused as to be nearly meaningless these days. These soldiers had only been doing their duty, acting on orders—nothing heroic in that, said the listener. The word "hero" ought to be reserved, he said, for "ordinary people" who risk their lives, save others, perform truly heroic actions. Next time, he suggested, I ought not be so hasty—and I ought to use another word.

I have to admit I am always pleased by this kind of letter: It indicates that the writer has really listened and thought about my reporting, and respects my intelligence enough (and knows I'll respect his or hers) to offer specific, constructive criticisms. That this criticism centered on word choice also pleased me: Eric Sevareid used to get letters from listeners praising the beauty of his writing. I'll bet not five other electronic journalists in history have gotten many letters like that; I certainly don't. But this letter, addressed to me not just as a reporter but as a writer, was as close as I'm likely to get most days.

So I wrote back.

"Dear Sir: Thank you for your letter of 12 August, and for taking the time to share your kind words and provocative thoughts. While it's clear that some words like 'hero' risk being cheapened through overuse, I cannot agree with you that the Americans I named don't fit that term.

"Take as an example the American soldiers killed in Somalia. Anyone who was in Somalia before the Marines landed in December can tell you precisely what kind of heroes our service people are in the eyes of those they came to help. I walked among the refugees, many of whom were dying of hunger in their besieged campsites, and even the most jaded American would have been moved by their longing for a rescue and their absolute faith that the Americans could and would provide that rescue—if only it wasn't too late. When word spread that the Yanks were coming, hope was reborn in a country where hope had died.

"By every standard you yourself name in your letter, the five Americans I cited were heroes: 'ordinary' people risking their lives, saving others, performing truly heroic actions. Each of the five (including the CIA agent in Georgia) died trying to bring peace to a needy, troubled part of the world: I call that heroism, too.

"Much of heroism comes from recognition of and obedience to one's duty. That these men gave their lives in the service of that duty does not deny but *confirms* their heroism."

In my radio essays I've tried to call attention to the services rendered by America's unsung heroes—soldiers, yes, but also police and firefighters, teachers, nurses—and all the people without whom suffering and misery would never end. A tip of the hat, a little expression of respect and appreciation.

Every now and then, somebody listens—and sometimes I even get to speak my piece—*twice.*

TEN

Vietnam Revisited

T HE MEMORY IS A KIND OF MUSEUM, WITH EXHIBITS YOU CAN STUDY at your leisure, at any time, then move on and come back to them. Some exhibits are refurbished regularly, and always put in the best light. All my most flattering self-portraits are on permanent display. But other memories are closed off. Access denied. Special admission required.

And then you come back to the place, the person, the song or the taste or the smell that breaks open the locks, bursts open the doors, and throws you headlong into the memory.

I came back to Vietnam in March 1993, for a *CBS Reports* documentary with retired General H. Norman Schwarzkopf. Neither of us had returned to the country since before the war ended.

The purpose of the documentary was to record the impressions and reactions of General Schwarzkopf, along with several other veterans who were also making a return trip to Vietnam. Coming to terms with the past and the present, the memories and the realities.

It was my assignment to help draw out the general. That turned out to be the easiest part of the job. The general is a big man with a good German-American face, but not a stereotypical blustery warrior. He's gracious and thoughtful, with a constantly searching mind. He's had to mull over some big issues in his day, and he enjoys talking many of them out. "Stormin' Norman," "Norman the Conqueror," isn't afraid of letting you know that he's got emotions and flaws and vulnerabilities—and frankly, he's the stronger for his honesty. He certainly doesn't lose a whit of his dignity. We've become friends over time: When we get together, we get to talking so thick and fast, usually rehashing strategy from long-ago campaigns, that our companions struggle to fit a word in edgewise.

When we landed and went through passport control, the general looked up and saw a portrait of Ho Chi Minh on the wall. I could see his hackles rise. This wasn't going to be an easy trip for him, and his misgivings were especially strong now, at the start. At first he was none too convinced that participating in the documentary was a good idea, but General Schwarzkopf gradually warmed to the project, opening up and sharing a wealth of feeling. So for me, the hard part of the trip wasn't dealing with the general's memories.

The hard part was discovering and dealing with so many memories of my own. Seeing places I had forgotten, seeing other places I *hadn't* forgotten, where events had taken place that would haunt my dreams for twenty years or more.

Jean Rather is a voracious reader and spent one breathless, delighted summer reading Marcel Proust's *Remembrance of Things Past.* We could barely get her to eat or sleep; she didn't want to let go of the books. Even on the strength of Jean's recommendations I haven't yet mustered the gumption to plow through a thousand pages of the minute reflections of some turn-of-the-century French aesthete. But a lot of the things she's tried to explain to me about Proust's notions of memory and the past have become clear and make a good deal of sense.

Proust says that there is no such thing as the place, only the name we give to the place, because a place is defined by the time and the people who are there. If you try to go back, the place will have changed, and it will have become another place. You can only go back to the name you gave the place when you were there before.

To see the real place, which is the backdrop for the past, and to see that the remembered event isn't taking place anymore—that's how to start coming to terms with your past.

When I come home to Houston now, I *expect* the city to have changed. I spent many years there, nearly half my life, and I've seen firsthand how fast that city can change. When I was a little boy, there was only *one* Downtown Houston. Now there are three.

The city changed in relation to me, too. Buildings got shorter as I got taller. My old neighborhood, the Heights Annex, doesn't officially exist anymore. But when I go back I can still feel the blazing heat of childhood adventures—the ambition of young manhood—the stunning miracle of fatherhood—ticking them all off like my height on a growth chart.

I was in Vietnam not for half a lifetime but for chapters. These were long periods which consumed my consciousness while I was there, but which ended. Other chapters got written in other places. I moved on—literally. I went to other places, and didn't go back to Vietnam. I had nothing to measure the passing of time in Vietnam, no reality against which to hold my memories.

To me, to the general, and to most American veterans of the Vietnam War, the opportunity to measure the memories was denied for a very long time.

But in 1993 as our plane approaches the Saigon airport, the memories come flooding back.

Ghosts walk in, including the ghosts of who and what I was, and the ghosts of personal illusions shattered and dreams unfulfilled.

I remember the first time I flew into Saigon, in 1964. How green the place seemed to me then! A lovely, deep emerald green.

The color would change for me during the war. In 1964, Vietnam was already a green jungle hell, a seething caldron of real mud, real blood, real death, and the screams of the wounded. It was to get worse while I was there that first time, and even worse still as I returned over the years during the war.

But the first glimpse was one of lush beauty, viewed almost innocently, unaware of the horrors (and, yes, the heroism) that went on under the canopy of leaves. I was excited that first time in 1964. The green so vivid—the place so strange—the job so new.

Now, in 1993, with the war long ended, there is no excitement, not for me (and not for the general, either, I believe). I am curious, apprehensive. The museum of my memories is beginning to open up.

Once on the ground, General Schwarzkopf and I begin a tour of postwar Vietnam: Saigon, Cu Chi, Da Nang, China Beach, Tam

Ky, Hue, Hanoi. Each was a big-story wartime dateline. In the war, I had reported from each of these places except Hanoi—and I had reported plenty *about* Hanoi.

Everywhere we go, there are images I'd forgotten, sounds I hadn't remembered, events that had been closed off for me.

Saigon, where I covered a massive firefight in the street alongside Eric Sevareid—the great Sevareid clad only in his silk robe and bedroom slippers.

Eric has been dead not quite a year by March 1993.

Cu Chi, where I covered a long-forgotten, bloody "Battle for the Treeline" with a camera mounted on the back of a jeep, and later reported one of the first stories out of Vietnam on the "Tunnel War."

Da Nang, with the old Marine "Press Camp" headquartered in a former brothel, where, after "The Battle of the Pagoda," we walked out so dangerously, waving a white flag and pointing at ourselves a portable battery-powered light called a Frezzy, as if by being well lit we'd make it clear we didn't want to be shot. Only making a better target of ourselves for the Vietcong.

China Beach, where an old woman and a child tried (and almost succeeded) in blowing up young Marines with a booby-trapped cooking pot.

Tam Ky, where I very nearly died pinned down on my back in the muck of a rice paddy when the VC and North Vietnamese troops ambushed a detachment of Marines within hours of my arrival in Vietnam.

Hue, where I spent several warm and fragrant nights in the sampan houseboats on Hue's "Perfume River," long before showdown house-to-house, pagoda-to-pagoda fighting wrecked the ancient capital.

Hanoi, the unreachable during the war. I've written elsewhere about the time I spent in Laos trying to help arrange a visa to Hanoi for the late Charles Collingwood—that's when Collingwood taught me to "always wear a dark suit, white shirt and tie when asking for something from Asian officials," to show your respect.

In our hotel in Da Nang in 1993, there is a gift shop where they sell old cigarette lighters taken off dead GIs and Marines. History, mystery, anger, and paradox race through my mind as I flee the place. I can't stand it.

Everywhere in Saigon there is proof that while the South lost the war, it was not conquered. Nobody calls Saigon Ho Chi Minh City (not even most people I will come across in the North). Saigon has grown by an estimated one third since the war ended. Many expensive homes have been built since I was last here, including many for top Communist party officials and the rapidly increasing number of rich capitalist businesspeople.

Posh (and not-so-posh) bars, restaurants, and new hotels are multiplying. So is pickpocketing and general street hustling.

Saigon today is in constant movement, up all hours, an exotic blend of cheap modernism, entrepreneurialism, capitalism, good, evil, decadence, and traditionalism, the old, the very old.

We go back to the U.S. Embassy. Memories of the desperate faces pressed against the front gate at the time of the Great Exodus at the end of the war. I was in the States when Saigon fell in April 1975, but I remember watching the reports, recognizing the place from my visits to the embassy, fearful I'd recognize some person I knew in the seething mob of helpless panic at the gate. Even watching strangers, the urge to reach out and help was agonizing. But there was nothing you could do, not from your safety and comfort thousands of miles away. The gate remained closed.

Now the gate is opened for us and we go through.

Spooky, ghostly pale now. The embassy has been kept up, a little. All of the empty rooms inside, all of those offices large and small where once I interviewed American officials, high and low. The ambassadors, most memorably the elegant patrician Henry Cabot Lodge; the military attachés, the secretaries, and the CIA men. All gone now, the offices empty except for the cobwebs and the ghosts.

We go up to the roof where the last U.S. helicopters lingered before Vietnamese took the city. We walk around, thinking and remembering. I had been on the roof once or twice. You seek rooftops in Vietnam, trying to catch a little breeze. I look out over the city, at the old Catholic Cathedral, at the pagodas, at the tree-lined streets, and over to the Caravelle Hotel where I had lived.

General Schwarzkopf and I conduct one of our first interviews up on that embassy roof. The general is a patriot; I think he would prefer not to start off at the site of an American retreat. He tells me he watched the reports of the fall of Saigon, too, from his posting in Alaska. And went out and got drunk. The fall of Saigon was not an easy time for anyone who cared about South Vietnam—or the United States.

The *CBS Reports* documentary is produced by Joel Bernstein, an old friend from *60 Minutes* and the *Evening News,* now assigned to the revitalized documentary unit. Supervising the whole project is Linda Mason, CBS News vice president for public affairs programming, an Ivy Leaguer, one of the smartest people ever to work for the News Division, someone I trust and admire. I am reminded of her smarts many times on this trip, but especially in this regard: I have forgotten my makeup kit. Linda has brought a backup kit for me.

I remember the difficulty of finding "my" shade of face powder in the American South during the civil rights struggles. It takes the nerve of two Clint Eastwoods to walk into a small Southern drugstore and ask for a compact of Gay Whisper. But in Vietnam, there's none of this brand of makeup to be had. Faces don't look right on camera without some makeup, especially faces with a beard line as heavy as mine. If Linda hadn't brought these supplies, we'd be in trouble: "The Werewolf Returns to Vietnam."

We go to Cholon, the Chinese section of Saigon. It was a favorite hangout for me and our CBS News team during the war. It had and still has some of the best restaurants. I always liked its character, the Chinese overlaid with all that is Vietnamese. I think of the scenes in the gambling den in the movie *The Deerhunter,* and I am reminded of Cholon. Intriguing, strange place. And is still.

We go to President Thieu's palace. I interviewed the South Vietnamese president there during the war. Remember how he always put oil or cream on his face to soften it—how he loved the "face oil." Thieu was a very proud man and a determined fighter, which no one remembers now because he lost. You can now have your picture taken at his desk for a handful of change.

We carry loads of U.S. greenbacks. Security for it, protecting it, is a constant problem. Carry it in our shoes, strap it deep inside our thighs, tuck it in money belts, and spread it out among bags and equipment. No American credit cards are allowed in Vietnam.

(And, as always when traveling in dicey places, I am carrying some gold coins on my person.)

In 1994, for reasons best known to himself, President Clinton will break the promise he made to the families of America's Missing, and he will lift the embargo before Hanoi has rendered a full accounting of the whereabouts of all the Americans who fought, may have died, disappeared, or been captured, and never came home. But now, in 1993, there are no diplomatic relations between the United States and Vietnam—not yet. So if you get into trouble, you're on your own, especially in the countryside and outlying areas.

We have also brought cigarettes. Sometimes better than gold. Marlboros in the old U.S.S.R. Kents in Romania at the height of the Cold War. "555" cigarettes are the ticket in Vietnam. Why I never know. But a few packs of "555s" can work wonders at a road-block or in customs.

I go alone to the Museum of American War Crimes. The general, of course, isn't about to go. Nobody even mentions it to him. It is a cheap, disgusting, outrageous propaganda palace. And I think it would be seen that way by the most objective people not American. But about it I do not claim to be objective, and I am American.

The museum does not, by the way, give any indication of Japanese, Chinese, or French war crimes in Indochina—much less Vietnamese. About not having any mention of Vietnamese atrocities (disemboweling political and military opponents and leaving their corpses out as a warning to others), I can understand. About failing to mention the war crimes of other countries, I do not.

Soon after we arrive in Saigon, Schwarzkopf surveys the New Vietnam. "I came over here," he recalls, "for God, country, Mom, and apple pie. I came over here to fight for the liberty of a small, friendly country. The South Vietnamese airborne was a superb military organization with a lot of genuine patriots in it. So we joined them one hundred percent. We went where they went, slept where they slept. We ate what they ate, didn't carry C rations with us or anything like that. And we wore their uniform. We really 'went native,' if you want to call it that. . . . For probably the first time in my entire life, I was serving where I really got no personal return whatsoever other than the satisfaction of serving a cause. And that does something to you." He says his first tour of duty "really was one of the happiest periods in my entire life."

Before he left for Vietnam, Schwarzkopf was given a crash course at Fort Bragg, N.C. He had been on the faculty at West Point, and had received a last-minute approval of his request for combat duty.

That strikes me: He *requested* to serve in a war that would come to be dreaded and despised by many Americans. But it was never his way to duck a duty. He went from teaching engineering, through a couple of weeks of military tactics, a few words of Vietnamese, and then found himself on a transport bound for Tan Son Nhut airport in Saigon. Determined to do his best, and proud of what he was able to do for others.

When I came to report the war, I found a lot of Americans like Norm Schwarzkopf. And I admit to a kind of bias. The Rathers were brought up to respect service, and service to one's country and one's God above all. We were taught, my brother and sister and I, that there was no higher calling than to turn your effort to the needs of the land that made you—and we were taught it so long that it's no use trying to persuade us any differently now. My brother and sister have given years of public service through teaching; I believe that, on my best days, my reporting provides a public service. With most of the soldiers you met in the Vietnam War, the commitment to service was as strongly felt, and as obvious, as the commitment young Norm Schwarzkopf felt, to the cause, to his own country, and to the country of South Vietnam.

Perhaps that paved the way to disappointment for many soldiers. Even for General Schwarzkopf, the war didn't continue as it began.

Saigon, like Hue of old, is still filled with warm and fragrant nights in 1993. The rustle of bamboo. Gentle breezes come in off the Saigon River.

One evening I stand on the edge of the roof garden atop the Majestic Hotel and weep. Alone. Weep for the dead, for the names on The Wall. And for the memories.

Of all the memories of Vietnam, this may be the strongest, the one that stays with me the longest. It already has been with me a long, long time.

Members of its cast were the most frequent players in my nightmares when I came home from my first year of covering the war. They came back every time I returned to report from the war zone.

I have met them many times since. While walking moonlit nights in the woods along my favorite trout stream. When watching the stars at night, all big and bright, over Texas. At odd times in the quiet of my library, and amid the hustle and bustle of the newsroom. And every time I even come close, even riding by in a car, to The Wall.

The time was 1965, late at night. The place was a hospital ship somewhere off the South Vietnamese coast near Qui Nhon. We were looking for a specific interview and had come to the ship seeking it. But the person we sought had already left.

I asked to be shown around, and to be taken below, to see what was there, since I had never been aboard a hospital ship before. So as we descended the ship's interior ladders, I had no idea of what I would find.

They took me several decks down, into a room that effectively took up the entire deck at this level. As we entered, the room was so dark—just a few subdued lights here and there—I had to struggle to get my eyes adjusted to see.

What I saw was the recovery room for young men, brave young Americans, with fresh amputations. There were dozens of them. Heroes all. Each had at least one fresh amputation. Many had multiple wounds; some had multiple amputations.

They were warriors caught up in the terrors of war. The shock was great, this scene that appeared to be something out of Dante's hellish circles, so great that I cannot imagine anyone's seeing it for the first time and not reacting as I did: with a step back, repelled, almost as if I had been blown back, accompanied by a rush of tears.

Nurses moved, almost floated it seemed to me, row to row, bed to bed. The only sounds were those of water lapping at the side of the ship, coming low, almost imperceptibly through the steel—and the moans, groans, and quiet weeping, with the occasional crying out, a low scream of pain.

I was there, what? Maybe fifteen minutes. Standing transfixed, almost suspended in time and in space and in my own very personal state of shock.

I've recalled in other places Eric Sevareid's saying that the essence of youth is believing things last forever. Here was proof that the belief was wrong, and the beginning of the loss of the last remnants of my own youth. Never before had I experienced anything even approaching this. And never since. And I hope never, ever again.

During the whole time I was there, only one word was spoken. It was spoken over and over; first you could hear it there, then over here, now back there. It was spoken in whispers by some, in moans by others, and, in a few cases, as a low shout.

The word was "mother."

No one, not one of these valiant young men in their desperate hours, suffering, spared from death but perhaps not for very long, in the bowels of a dark and lonely ship, spoke any other word. None called for father, or for doctor or nurse. Only mother.

Until such a moment, we can still think of the human body as whole: the fine graceful machine, in the image of God. We can still think of war as "exciting," an adventure, a test of bravery and strength.

But at such a moment, we are stripped of such notions, and we cling to the first person we ever knew, who brought us the first love we ever knew, the first idea we ever knew: Mother. I thought of Jeannie and our son, Danjack, then four years old, and the perfect movement of his fingers and toes as he ran after balls and bugs in the yard.

I thought of my own mother, wondered if she'd ever imagined me in such a ship, during my brief career in the Marines.

I wondered if any of the mothers of these men could have imagined such a ship—and the feats they'd have performed to keep their sons out of this place.

I could not leave the recovery room fast enough, but I have returned to the hospital ship a thousand times in my memory.

Saigon at sunset brings tears. So does sunrise at Da Nang. I watch from the balcony of the Bach Dang Hotel, overlooking the Da Nang River. I once fished the lower reaches of the Da Nang. Later vomited when we had to wade through a blood- and body-filled part of the river's upper reaches.

In Saigon I eat rice mixed with shrimp and *nuc-mom* sauce, the "dead fish sauce" that's a staple of Vietnamese cooking. I throw in some of my own Tabasco sauce, for old time's sake. Favorite when I was here before.

In Hanoi I eat *pho*—broth, vegetables, meat, and noodles mixed together. During the war this was a favorite of mine. I ate it often in Hue and Da Nang.

The food tastes the way I remember it. It hasn't changed.

Before going to Vietnam, I take the following shots: diphtheria, tetanus, polio, gamma globulin (a BEEG needle and the shot good for only three months—supposedly sometimes protects against hepatitis A), typhoid shots, and shots against Japanese encephalitis. Also get flu shots (Vietnamese rural areas, especially, are said to be teeming with all kinds of weird flus). I begin doses of malaria pills before the trip and I continue throughout the trip.

Lots of people go to Vietnam and never take all of these shots. But experience—including war experience in Indochina—has taught me to be a believer in shots.

I get all of these at a fancy New York place specializing in precautions against and treatment of Exotic Diseases. After my sequence of shots, the efficient, middle-aged nurse opines: "You have a good butt."

She smiles and I have to admit I am pleased. After all, this good woman has seen a few. Then she adds, "That is, you *had* one before I marked it up with my needles. *Now* it has more little holes than a window screen." 'Tain't funny, Ratchet.

In Saigon the general and I meet with a group of veterans who have come back to Vietnam. We shoot the discussion atop the old Rex Hotel. This is where the U.S. Military Command's daily briefings were held during the war, the infamous Five O'Clock Follies, so named by reporters because they were scheduled at 5:00 P.M. each day and degenerated into such farces: deceptive, upbeat "reports" that, unfortunately and no joy in saying so, often featured outright lying designed to mislead the American public. More often the military was simply misleading and deluding itself.

Atop the Rex on this return trip I think about the Follies and the difference between deception and self-deception. Accurate information is essential in conducting a war, but in Vietnam the military had tremendous problems with its information. Many of these problems were of the military's own making, releasing deceptive information that would be believed by those outside the military. But, in the end, those who believed were policymakers and those inside the military.

Some in the military acted out of a desire to do what the White House and Defense Department wanted done and wanted to hear. Some just wanted to "please up," but some acted on direct orders and political PR strategy from above. Some of it came from self-deception.

The White House, Defense Department, and the very top U.S. military brass during the war have a lot to answer for about the Follies.

But in wartime, almost everybody has a lot to answer for about something.

The Rex Hotel looks out on the Saigon River on one side, wonderfully lighted now at night, and a choked traffic circle directly below on the other side.

Traffic in the circle gets especially heavy in the early evening, along about twilight and just beyond. Motor scooters and bikes and cars circle round and round on "C-runs"—just seeing what they can see. Nearly every motor scooter or bike has a young couple on it.

The rooftop of the Rex Hotel is decorated with brightly colored lights, palm trees and bamboo, caged birds and tropical animals. We gather around a big round table as if we were tourists at a resort. But we aren't tourists.

At this time, the Vietnamese government has decided to let small numbers of American veterans come to visit—on condition that they perform some kind of community service work, and the government would prefer that the service rendered have some kind of link to the war. If the Americans blew up a building, let them come back and rebuild. That may sound manipulative, playing on veterans' emotional needs and extracting work in return. Candidly, I believe it is. But in practice it can also be a positive experience. My new friends have been working hard all day on building a health clinic.

They are a cross-section, representatives of the different kinds of Americans who came to the war in Vietnam. Like most, these are good people, trying to do right, trying to understand. I haven't met any of them before tonight, but I feel I know them already.

One man was an M-60 machine-gunner, wounded at Khe Sanh on the day the siege officially ended there. His best friend was killed trying to save his life. And he spent the next thirty-four months of his life in military hospitals in the States.

Another served on riverboats in the Mekong Delta—for three consecutive tours of duty. Another was a rifleman, whose tour ended about six months after his second Purple Heart. Another was a special forces medic. Yet another started as a medic, was wounded, and was brought back again and again to fight with the First Cavalry Division, and one more time "because I'm such a good target." The last is a woman, who came to Vietnam as a Red Cross volunteer, one of the recreation workers nicknamed the "doughnut dollies." She is still gathering the words and the confidence to say what she wants to say, and requests that I wait before asking her to talk.

The others talk about the need for completion, to come full circle, to bind up wounds and finish the job. One speaks of the disparity between his memories and the present realities: "There is no war here," he says, with a kind of wonderment in his voice.

I'm struck by how many of them came to care about the Vietnamese people. The Special Forces medic talks movingly about living and working among the Vietnamese, learning some of their language, and developing an abiding respect and affection for them. The war's aftermath has kept him apart from these people who were, in a time of incredible stress, friends to him. Now he has come back to find them, and he finds that the qualities he admired in the Vietnamese endure.

Some of the veterans are walking now among other veterans of the war, veterans who fought in the same battles—veterans from the other side, VC and North Vietnamese. There's a feeling like surprise when the Americans find that "the enemy" mourn their dead, have struggled to build families and a normal life in peacetime. One veteran has gone into the homes of some of "the enemy," been welcomed as a guest: "I think it's one of the most healing things that I've ever done," he says.

As I listen, I know that not all the Vietnamese can be good and kind. But I believe it is true that most people, in any country, even in a terrible war, want to be good, are trying to be kind. And perhaps we love peace best because it is a little easier then to call on the kindness within ourselves.

One of the veterans seems to echo some of my thoughts when he says, "I think the war just went bad. The war was bad. But the people in the country were very good."

He tells me he came back to Vietnam for the first time in 1989 because he found himself playing Russian roulette three to five nights out of the week. "Although I was going for treatment, I wasn't stopping what I was doing. I was wanting to be dead," he says. "And I thought that I needed to take a real gamble to break the habit that I got myself into."

That gamble, he decided, was to come back to Vietnam. And he has come again and again. This is his fifth trip since the war. He says he still feels he is missing something, speaks of searching crowds for familiar faces, although he realizes that after three decades the faces must have changed. But, he says, he is transforming his memories from a "horror show" and "getting a peace over me."

I know the horror show he's talking about. I see it myself, sometimes before I go to sleep. But I'm not here to talk about myself, and I have the feeling, more strongly now in the company of these people who have sacrificed so much for their country, that my experiences don't measure up. I am, rightly, denied entrance to Valhalla; there's no epic poetry dedicated to the war correspondent who knew when he was flying in, when he was flying home, and never had to pull a trigger. I keep my counsel and listen to the tales of bravery and pain, of rising awareness and the certainty of triumph over sorrow, someday. These veterans are heroes still engaged in a battle, longer than any they ever fought in Vietnam.

The machine-gunner talks about survivor guilt—his best friend dies saving his life, and within a few months, he says, more than forty other members of his company were killed. For a time he became deeply involved with the group Vietnam Veterans Against the War. But his problems grew: post-traumatic stress disorder, drinking, family problems, and still the guilt.

A friend—Nancy, the doughnut dolly who's sitting with us now—persuaded him to write to the parents of the friend who saved his life, to make sure they knew how brave their son had been and how much gratitude he felt. Now he has become close to that family, and opening up to them has made it easier to seek counseling. He's on the mend, and a real fighter. I admire his spirit.

I also admire Nancy, who helped this man understand how important the letter to his friend's family could be. Nancy knows how important, because she lost a brother in Vietnam. The loss is still raw to her; she can't talk about it.

She can tell me why she came to Vietnam: The reason is rage. She was angry toward the Vietnamese people, not just the government but the entire nation. She doesn't say so exactly, but I believe she blamed all of Vietnam for her brother's death. And she didn't like the anger within herself. So she came to Vietnam to heal the anger.

The first day working on her building project in Vietnam, she found herself teamed with a Vietnamese who had fought in the tunnels at Cu Chi, where Nancy had been during the Tet Offensive. She leaped to a conclusion which turned out to be correct: "This is the guy who lobbed mortars at me during Tet."

But talking with the man has brought Nancy closer to forgiveness; she sees this man not as a faceless enemy but as an individual who has also suffered many losses. And she sees that the Vietnamese don't hate her, don't hate Americans: "They say, 'Your government sent you over here. Many of you did not want to come, if not all of you. It was the government's war, not your war.' They don't hold us personally responsible at all."

Then, in a powerful rush, Nancy describes the process of mourning she's undergone since she arrived: "I was mourning the loss of Vietnam. I realized that I had to go through the process. I'd been in denial by thinking that Vietnam hadn't changed. That it was [still] the Vietnam that we left. And I came back here and there's nothing. There's no American presence. There's nothing. You can't fake it.

You can't pretend." And that's when the mourning kicked in.

She says that when she first asked to come to Vietnam, she wanted to work only with veterans, but now realizes that she was in the "bargaining phase" of mourning, trying to keep the past alive by doing something similar to what she had done during the war. Then she'd gone through the "anger phase," directing her hostility toward the Vietnamese people. Then there was depression. And then, she says, came "the shock of coming back to Vietnam, and it not being my Vietnam any more. It's their Vietnam. And once I realized that, it made a big difference, because I was able to start letting go of my Vietnam.

"I mean, that doesn't mean that I [won't] continue to think about Vietnam every day. Vietnam is not over for me, by any means. But the anger toward the Vietnamese people is gone. They did what they had to do."

Her face is alive with emotions, many of them conflicting. It is a face I have seen many times in my reporting, the face of the survivor. I have seen her after a storm or a shooting. She is still a little stunned by what has happened, but she is blinking back the tears, summoning her strength. She is going to survive. And she's going to do better than survive: She is going to flourish, show 'em all.

"About a week ago, I said I wasn't ready to give Vietnam back to the Vietnamese," she says. "But the way I feel now, it's done with me. I don't need to come back. It's theirs. They've earned it. They can have it. I don't want it."

There are nods of assent all around the table, and General Schwarzkopf says quietly, "Vietnam's never going to be over for me, either."

We talk for a long time, remembering the dead, recalling what we have done to keep living since the war ended. We talk about guilt and pride, and most of us feel something of each for the things we did and did not do during our time here. We talk about reconciliation: between past and present, dead and living, civilian and military, Vietnam and America.

I point out that there are some who believe the past is the past, should be let go, forgotten, buried.

One of the veterans snorts. "The people that say that—number one, most of them weren't here. And number two, to hell with them. To hell with them."

There's laughter, good rich laughter that comes from down deep inside. The laughter says that the past is the foundation of the present; it can't be buried or forgotten, not reliably. It must be shored up, made sturdy, to make the present and the future more secure. These people have come back to Vietnam trying to do just that.

It's been a long journey to the roof of the Rex Hotel, with the colored lights and the tropical birds all around, and the traffic spinning in the circle below. A long journey, but a necessary one.

Geography. We fly over Hue on this trip but don't visit it—not enough time. China Beach is adjacent to Da Nang, all long, blond sand along the wonderfully blue South China Sea. I still know die land well enough to walk it blindfolded—if such things were permitted. But where once there were guerrillas and snipers and mines, now there are government restrictions and the same old mines still waiting for someone to step there.

The Mekong Delta was, as most Americans know, one of the worst of the battle areas. Mangrove swamps, triple-canopied jungle cover in some places, beaches alongside jungle, an absolutely terrible place to fight. I don't have time to take the full Mekong River trip; I take a truncated version, alone with a guide.

Everybody who visits Vietnam now talks about their trips to Tay Ninh in the Delta. Tay Ninh was a blood- and sweat-soaked killing ground during the war. Now its Cao Bai Temple is a major draw. I think back to the Buddhist monks who used to protest the war, swarming the streets for demonstrations, some of them setting fire to themselves. Always struck, even frightened, by the passion of their ·commitment to peace—perhaps even stronger than the passion of soldiers to wage war. I used to go to a temple in Saigon to listen to the chanting, the warm droning sending me into a kind of trance that comforted me. There is music in Cao Bai Temple today, and worship services open to the public. The temple is beautifully decorated with carvings of spiritual leaders from Buddha to Victor Hugo.

Victor Hugo? The French influence on the former French colony is still evident.

But we feel that influence a little, too. The other day, General Schwarzkopf quoted the musical version of Hugo's *Les misérables,* in which the sole survivor of a rebellion wonders why he has lived when his comrades have fallen, and then sings, "Don't ask me what their sacrifice was for."

With the general at Cu Chi: This is difficult for me. Would be with or without the general. To put it bluntly, I saw many good men die in this area—Americans and Vietnamese. Women and children, too. But mostly fighting men in combat. Much of the worst of the Tet Offensive was fought here in 1968, and the infamous tunnel war, with guerrillas burrowing for miles, able to travel without being seen, to take cover and to pop up again and again to attack American troops.

The battleground has become a tourist attraction, much of it staged, poorly staged, and some of it strikes me as downright phony, a kind of cheap and chintzy "Disney World of the Jungle and Tunnels" quality to it, designed to emphasize how brave and brilliant the Vietcong and North Vietnamese Army were, and how dumb, foolish, and fooled the Americans were.

But when you see it you don't believe it. At least I don't. They were good, but not all *that* good.

Example: As you approach the "showplace" area, there is, just off the road, "preserved" in the jungle in full view the almost complete remains of a "shot-down" U.S. aircraft. I can't see any evidence that the aircraft really was shot down, or was shot down in this place, left there, and is the artifact it is purported to be.

There is also the odd helicopter leaned up, wrecked, at just the right angle in the jungle over there. For amusement, there's a firing range. You can fire a rifle at a buck a bullet, aiming at paper targets, silhouettes of animals.

And the tunnels themselves: Well, yes, there were *some* tunnels during the war. I was there, did some of the first reports on the tunnels. But I wonder if they really were as ingenious, as long, as widespread, and as effective as the Vietnamese government now claims. The *original* tunnels *did* have multilevel rooms for sleeping, medical care, communications, cooking, et cetera, but on a limited basis. I saw that at the time. But the limit was size. The originals I saw were much smaller, tighter, and not nearly as extensive as what is now shown. The general and I (and neither one of us shops in the Petite Juniors Department) are able to go down in the tunnels and explore. The general admits that, during the war, he was always afraid to go down in the tunnels—not because there might be VC or snakes or some other danger, but because he might have gotten wedged in and then subjected to the indignity of being tugged out, Pooh Bear style, by his men.

I believe the tunnels have been redone, reinforced, improved, extended, to make them much more impressive—and to make the Vietnamese seem more impressive, too. Can't prove it, but that's what I believe.

At Cu Chi, most guides claim to have fought the Americans here; most of them claim to have done so during the Tet Offensive. Again, to my ear it sounds a little too pat, too much like propaganda: I wonder that we stood a chance against so numerous an enemy.

Oh, well, maybe it's natural. History is written by the victors. Americans still make the British in our own Revolutionary War out to be dumber and more evil than they were in fact. So the old-line, hard-line Vietnamese Communists, eager to hang on to power awhile longer, hoping to pump themselves up to look like heroes, try to make Americans look dumb and evil. Part of you wants to shrug and say, so what? What difference does it make in the long run? Does it really matter? I doubt it.

But I do find it interesting that it is the Americans, not the French, not the Japanese, not the Chinese (who were much worse over a much longer time in what they did to Vietnam), who bear the brunt of all of this. This is part of what rings hollow in all the present talk of how much the current Vietnamese *government* really likes and "holds no grudge" toward Americans. The Vietnamese *people* are as warm and welcoming as they can be, but the *government* churns out propaganda, builds anti-American museums and tourist attractions. It makes me skeptical, even suspicious.

Listen, I think they want our money. Period. And what it is about now, as far as our government is concerned, is money. The embargo of Vietnam by the United States will continue to hold for almost a year after General Schwarzkopf and I finish our trip in 1993, but in the interval, the American and Vietnamese governments will talk, perhaps most often in terms of money, until President Clinton will lift the embargo in February 1994. And so it goes.

Coming to Hanoi is like stepping into the past—except that I've never been here before. The city is dominated by the old-fashioned French colonial architecture, none of it very many stories high, and is, as Anne Groer of the *Orlando Sentinel* has written, very much "a city trapped in amber," both because of the warm amber sunlight that holds the city close up and down the wide boulevards and among the overhanging trees and because here something seems to be caught motionless in the movement of history.

I come off the plane at Noi Ba Airport with the general, who is looking grim and uncomfortable. And we are off to the capital of the Socialist Republic, what was during the war the capital of the enemy, where the enemy's orders originated, where Jane Fonda came to be photographed with an antiaircraft gun.

Our ride into the city is punctuated by "soldier's rain," so called because it is light, the kind troops used to welcome because it broke the heat while not soaking them—infantrymen loved it. It is a rough, bumpy ride in an old Japanese car. Running through my mind are images of the times we'd go on board carriers and photograph U.S. pilots flying off the decks, destined for "missions north." Hanoi has grown up around numerous small lakes, crisscrossed with bridges. Many pilots were trying to knock out those bridges, then knock them out again after they had been repaired. Many pilots did not return.

We are swept into the city center on a long line of traffic. We hear the blare of horns, our driver's and those of others. We dodge pedestrians, animals, and vehicles of and beyond every description. Women in Vietnamese straw hats carry buckets of water on poles the old-fashioned way. Many other women and men carry large baskets balanced on their heads.

My friend John McCain, now a U.S. senator from Arizona, was held and captured in the "Hanoi Hilton," the notorious Hoa Lo Prison downtown. We are told the prison may be torn down for a high-rise.

Inside the city center, capitalism edges in on communism but does not, not yet anyway, consume, does not swallow up communism. The new capitalism is similar to what I have seen in Moscow, Eastern Europe, South America, China, but the character and pace of this capitalism are unique to the Vietnamese. While other countries run pell-mell, grasping at capitalism randomly, frantically, as if time is running out, the pace in Vietnam is slow, steady, almost rhythmic, the character cautious, measured, even grudging. There is a kind of collective individualism operating. While the individuality of the citizen is still not respected as it is in the West, Vietnam is determined to do things according to a distinct national character and tradition. Let the Chinese and the Russians go in some other direction; Vietnam is going Vietnam's way.

What most Westerners still do not grasp is how poor, utterly poor in material possessions, Vietnam is. The estimated annual income, on average, is about $200 per person.

And while we debate President Clinton's lifting the embargo, and the way the Vietnamese government has treated the American Missing and their families, what has been lost or deliberately shuffled into the background is the issue of how the Communist Vietnamese government treats its own people.

The Vietnamese work force is, in a word, oppressed. U.S. multinational business outfits have worked hard to keep this fact out of sight. Lane Kirkland, the chief of the AFL-CIO, is right when he says that U.S. multinational business interests have tried to deflect attention from working conditions in Vietnam, precisely because they hope to exploit the low-wage work force.

Human rights in Vietnam are a mess and an outrage. Vietnam is a police state. It does not have free elections worthy of the name. It does not tolerate public criticism or debate. Rank-and-file Vietnamese do not have any rights to speak, worship, or emigrate.

The Vietnam War is over. But the war of Vietnam's Communist elite against their own people continues.

Some American business interests are so eager to find another haven for low-cost, high-profit production that they have trumpeted "progress toward democracy in Vietnam" when they know it is not true, and promise that lifting the embargo will encourage the Vietnamese government to improve conditions there. All that has happened is that the Vietnamese government has cynically opened itself to making money, not to democracy or human rights.

Hanoi is where the government sits, but it is also where people live, riding rickshaws and motorbikes, conducting all kinds of business and daily affairs right on the street. They are outdoors simmering rice, barbecuing fish and chicken, the smells of food wafting along the streets. Selling gasoline from a two-liter jug: no self-service. There are outdoor barbershops: just a couple of chairs, a couple of mirrors hung from tree limbs. Straight-razor shaves are a specialty. I have one. Excellent. But they do need better shaving cream. An old toothless man gives me my shave. He does haircuts with scissors and a bowl over the head. A genuine soup-bowl haircut. He offers to give me one.

I wonder what the bosses in New York would say if I came home with a soup-bowl haircut. Linda Mason and Joel Bernstein aren't about to let me find out. I decline my barber's offer, respectfully.

Heavy loads are stacked sky-high on carts and bicycles. I realize this is how much of their military supplies traveled along the Ho Chi Minh Trail during the war. All kinds of goods are being transported along the streets of Hanoi: food, machinery, snakes. The snakes are to be eaten. There's at least one place deep inside the center city where you can pick the snake you want to eat and have it prepared to order—curbside, of course—and eat it right there. Mine tastes nothing like chicken.

I've eaten snake more often than most, perhaps, because there's a restaurant near Lake Travis, Texas, that specializes in rattlesnake steak. The place is called Hudson's on the Bend, and the chef, Jay Moore, knows a hundred ways to camouflage the taste of snake. But this snake in Hanoi does not use Jay's recipes.

I eat with my own chopsticks. This trip and in years past I have seen that dishwashing in Saigon and elsewhere has little to do with sanitation. Filthy water in the gutter of my curbside snake restaurant is definitely not up to Mother Rather's standards. Carrying one's own chopsticks has always seemed the least one can do. (In the countryside you can quickly make your own chopsticks out of bush or tree twigs.)

Hanoi has many rats, including some world-class large ones—comparable to those in New York and Washington. You see them on the streets, in the parks, and now and again in shops. One reason I always walked around with a stick. I called it a walking stick, but of course, what it was, was a rat-whomping stick. Among places I would prefer not to have to get rabies shots, Hanoi is high up there on the list.

There's a fine old tune called "The Sidewalks of New York." I think we'd need to write an oratorio to describe "The Sidewalks of Hanoi."

But we're not in Hanoi to sightsee. We're here to work. We look for locations.

There's a War Museum in Hanoi, and guess which war? There are some smashed U.S. planes and helicopters, some captured tanks. A bit junky and (again, to my American eye) very heavy-handed in its propaganda. There aren't many people around either time I go.

The wrecked vehicles are in the courtyard; inside there's a stack of GI combat jungle boots. I can see every man who wore them, and can't look anymore. I move away quickly.

The wreckage makes a dramatic picture, and Joel Bernstein hopes we can shoot an interview with the general here, but I tell him it will never happen. It doesn't. The general takes one look, then gives me a look, and we leave—pronto. He is steamed. We ride around Hoan Kiem Lake. I try to talk him down, and eventually he relaxes. I understand his feelings. This really was a mistake on our part.

* * *

I have imagined Hanoi for so many years that it is startling to find myself here for the first time at last. I want to explore, and I take many of my side trips on my own. One can travel faster that way. I grab quick moments during meal breaks, or at night when the crew has turned in. The general isn't interested in getting around very much. When he isn't working, he spends most of his time in and around the hotel.

I go to the mausoleum of Ho Chi Minh, which looks about like what you would expect: a huge monstrosity of a concrete and steel box designed (couldn't have been anybody else) by the Russians. It's surrounded by a park, wonderfully kept grounds, very green with lots of flowers, and nearby is the so-called Stilt House, where he is supposed to have lived. There's also a Ho museum, with plenty of artifacts, and a souvenir stand.

I don't know if scholars still debate whether history is made by great events, or by great ideas, or instead by great men. But looking at "Uncle Ho," I keep wondering: If it hadn't been for him, would history have been what it was? Or were his ideas so powerful and pervasive that others would have promoted them, and led Vietnam away from colonialism and into bloody wars with the West? The kind of debate better left to academics (or fortune-tellers), but in my mind this morning it all comes down to this: If Ho had never lived, how many of my friends would have died in Vietnam?

We stay in the Hotel Metropole, the unofficial hotel for foreigners. Run by the French, recently restored. Run like a first-class European hotel, or as close as you can get to it in this part of the world. The Vietnamese who work in the hotel have been superbly trained. Most speak French and English.

I am surprised at first to find how many Vietnamese bureaucrats speak German, but I am told that many of them were educated in East Germany.

I decide to give snake cuisine another try. I go to a joint frequented by the local folk; I checked. I can't get my colleagues to go with me—once was enough, thank you—and don't even tell them when I head for the most famous snake-food restaurant in town.

This is the real thing, small, and the menu is short: snake, snake, and snake. The snake is mashed up with spices and fried. It tastes about like it sounds.

The wine list is impressive, though: You pick from big glass jars filled with dead animals in alcohol. I pick the dead snake, a recommended vintage, because I believe snake is the proper drink to accompany snake.

I have had tequila straight from a bottle with a scorpion at the bottom in Mexican border towns (during my early years, my *Last Picture Show* days) and have drunk from bottles of brandy with alleged dead snakes in them high in the Alps. Those experiences do not compare with this.

And I won't tell you about the dreams I had, despite double doses of Alka-Seltzer and Tums. I was glad no one from the CBS News team knew I'd sneaked off to engage in such folly.

The whole meal, with drinks and tip included, costs five dollars. Who says you can't put a price on adventure?

Another night, dinner is in our honor, thrown at a big government place near the hotel, with the whole CBS team invited. The general understandably declines.

It is a long meal, three hours, stiff and formal. I have to carry most of the conversation. It isn't easy—there are tense moments. A ranking official, who had been junior negotiator at the Paris Peace Talks in the 1970s, now hopes to be the first Vietnamese representative in Washington when the trade embargo is lifted. He says, "If you think Vietnam *needs* American trade, you are badly mistaken. We can get along quite well without it."

I respond, "If you think the United States *needs* Vietnamese trade, you are also mistaken. We can get along quite well without it."

He smiles a very Vietnamese smile and repeats that he is confident America will lift the embargo—and soon. "It is simple," he says. "Americans want to make money. The urge is very strong. And so you will lift the embargo."

Translation: Americans value money over morality. I am angry. I am confident he is wrong.

In my hotel room this night in 1993, I am still angry about what the Vietnamese official has said. I remember a story General Schwarzkopf told me our first day in Vietnam: In 1964, just before he shipped in, he was given a guide to Vietnam, which stressed two points. The Vietnamese have been raised on a rice diet, and therefore do not have much endurance, the book said. And, the book went on, all Vietnamese are Buddhists and none of them drink alcohol.

The day after Schwarzkopf met his counterpart, a captain in the South Vietnamese Army, he was invited into the captain's office. The captain opened his drawer and pulled out a full bottle of Scotch, and they drank the whole bottle on the spot. "So much for *that* part of the little book," Schwarzkopf had said.

Shortly afterward, Schwarzkopf went on his first combat operation. He was in the field, moving from My Thanh past Vinh Quoi, in peak condition, and carrying only a radio. With him was a Vietnamese, slight of stature, raised on a rice diet just as the book said, and laden down with a hundred-pound pack.

"We were going down into these deep mud gullies, and then we'd have to climb out of them. There I was . . . panting, with my tongue hanging out. And that little Vietnamese, with that one hundred-pound pack on his back, would walk by and wave as he scampered on ahead. So much for the endurance thing. I came back and threw that book away."

He looked across the countryside. "I decided we really didn't know very much about this country . . . which turned out to be all too true."

I wonder if it isn't true even today—if the Vietnamese don't understand us better than we understand them.

For much of this trip, Schwarzkopf's experiences and memories overlap with mine. This is no *Rashomon,* where each witness has a different account of the same event. We have spoken at length about friends who died, battles that were fought, pain that was felt. There are strong similarities. But at the same time, neither of us has lost sight of the simple, drastic distinction that he was army, I was press. In the eyes of some American service personnel and others, the military's real enemy in Vietnam was the press. The press must be deceived, deterred, because the press was determined to undo the United States military operations.

To make matters even worse, perhaps: I was not merely press but *television* press, in what a number of people (including me) had called the Television War. *Our* pictures, broadcast into America's living rooms and dining rooms, supposedly turned the tide of public opinion against the war and brought about the American loss. Most reporters have never believed this theory. We see it as excuse making, blame shifting, oversimplifying of a very low order.

Now, in 1993, the general and I have been many days in Vietnam. Finally Schwarzkopf is ready to tackle the distinction between us. He begins by remembering the *first* time he returned to Vietnam, during the war, and I stand back and let him run.

Rotated home after two years of duty in 1964–65, Schwarzkopf volunteered to return to combat duty in 1969. Whereas his first tour had been "one of the happiest periods of [his] entire life," the difference in military climate in 1969–70 was almost shocking.

"I'm commanding an infantry battalion, and ninety-nine percent of the people in this battalion had been drafted. They hadn't asked to go to war. They had been drafted by their country and they had answered the call. They hadn't run away to Canada. But when they went to war, they were going to a war which they already knew was very unpopular in the eyes of the people at home.

"So, right away they were being asked to go off and die in a war that was unpopular. They got over here at a time when we had started sending U.S. units home, so they were out on the battlefield and one of their principal objectives just became 'I want to stay alive until I can go home. Other guys are going home now; why do I have to stay over here and fight?' At the same time, they were getting no public support from home. Quite the contrary.

"Then, amazingly, when they got back home, somehow the mood had turned and they were being *blamed* for the war. That was wrong. These were Americans who were doing their duty to their country, had been drafted, sent to war, came over here—willing or unwilling was irrelevant—but it wasn't their war. They hadn't started it. They were not the ones sustaining it. They certainly were not the ones who wanted to be here. And yet, when they got back home, suddenly they became the people who were receiving the blame.

"And that, I think more than anything else, contributes to the Vietnam Veterans Syndrome. You know, we went off to do our duty to our country, and we came back home and you all somehow made us the bad guy."

When Schwarzkopf says "you all," he doesn't mean the American civilians. He means the American press. He means my colleagues; he means *me*.

And there it is: the rift between us, the rift between the military and the press in Vietnam, out in the open, where Schwarzkopf and I can discuss it.

He continues: "I don't think anyone can say the press lost the war. The war was lost because of a bankrupt strategy. I think that in hindsight all of us fully understand that. Many of us, at the time, blamed the press for the attitude that the American people were adopting, which caused this to become a very unpopular war, and eventually caused the withdrawal and caused one of the most significant blows, and that was when the Congress of the United States in 1973 cut off all military aid to South Vietnam, which I think in fact caused the eventual fall of Saigon.

"I will confess to you that in 1965 and '66, I had a very good relation with the press. A few times, I ran into free-lancers who admitted to me, 'Nothing makes duller reading than a military battle well-planned and well-executed, but if you throw in civilian casualties or you throw in a few short bombs that land on your own troops, or something of the kind, it spices up the reading and I can sell my piece better that way.' Yes, obviously I had a knee-jerk reaction against that."

But over time and with the sensation that more and more reporters felt the way those free-lancers felt, Schwarzkopf's good relations with the press cooled. "Personally, I was anti-press because I felt that the reporting of my military operations was going to be slanted towards the direction that the American public had already taken on the war—and not a balanced presentation.

"Was I right? In hindsight, probably not. But at the time, I felt very strongly that I could not get a fair shake. So therefore, I just avoided the press whenever possible."

He looks at me now, a hard look. I have the feeling he hasn't expressed these things very often—certainly not to a representative of the press, with his crew standing by and cameras rolling. He is being honest, and I know that sometimes honesty requires the most bravery, even for a general. I want to respond in the same vein.

"I can't speak for the press as a whole," I say. "Who can? But my own experience was different. In the mid-1960s, I got along very well with everybody in the field. I got along with most military people wherever they were stationed. My only difficulty came with people at, or very near, the top, who time after time demonstrated that they were either dealing in sophistry or deliberately misleading the press and the American public.

"After the Tet Offensive, as public support at home withered in the face of the mounting casualties in 1970 and '71, I'll be candid with you—as you were with me—I resented being held responsible for the war's not going well. That was our counterpart of the military saying, 'Hey, we did our job, maybe we didn't do it perfectly, but don't blame us when things go wrong.' The press had its version of that."

Schwarzkopf nods and says, "Oh, I think so. I think we were both right and we were both wrong. It was just like anything else. In a very complicated situation like this was, nothing was all black and white. It was various shades of gray. As I say, the blame certainly cannot be placed on the press for losing the war. That's a gross oversimplification of a very complicated time, and I think that is a bum rap for the press to carry."

He keeps his eyes on me. In a strange way, we have just declared peace, we two representatives of the military and the press, by agreeing that the war was lost neither by those in the field nor by those in the press, but by those who directed a losing strategy.

Perhaps others—other soldiers, other reporters, other Americans of whatever profession—will not sign on to our peace. But I believe it is a just peace, and a genuine peace with honor.

One night in 1965 I was on the outskirts of Nha Trang, a beautiful city just off the South China Sea, although there was little beauty where we found ourselves. We were in a no-man's-land between a city held temporarily by the troops of the South Vietnamese, and a countryside controlled by "moving hats" (GI slang for the Vietcong guerrillas, so called because sometimes when the VC struck you caught only a glimpse of their hats moving away). Bill Stout, then the local anchor at the CBS-owned station in Los Angeles, had flown over and was sitting with me on the steps of a house the South Vietnamese government (the ARVN) used to question prisoners. After a hard day's reporting, Bill and I were relaxing, drinking bon-me-boms, Vietnamese for beer.

Then the screen door slammed, and out of the house stomped the South Vietnamese major in charge of this area. A Vietcong sniper had been captured after killing five or six of the major's troops. As the prisoner stumbled into the street, you could see his arms were bound in a sort of half-nelson. It all happened so quickly that we barely had time to look up. The major put a .45 between the prisoner's eyes and blew out his brains.

Bill and I were totally gape-mouthed. Our cameraman had caught some of it, not all, but the quick aftermath—the spray of brain tissue and the body on the ground. The major and the men around him couldn't care less that an American television crew had witnessed the execution, or that our film was running. The major turned around and walked right back into the house.

All along the way, I have had ghosts as my companions: Sevareid and Collingwood, the mentors, larger than life, with a nerve and a style that made a little boy of you, filling you with wonderment and admiration, and a yearning to grow up and play with the big boys.

The Vietnamese peasant woman who once aimed an ancient rifle at my heart because I'd entered her hut by accident.

The soldier from Tennessee, caught on a mine on Thanksgiving Day.

The GI who, without anyone's ordering him and while we watched dumbfounded, leaped up and single-handedly cleaned out a machine-gun nest that his whole unit had failed to finish off in half a day's fighting.

The good-hearted army nurse with a strange, braided pattern tattooed on her arm. She gave me a cup of coffee and a kind word.

The tribal chief who arrived riding on a little Cambodian elephant to negotiate with an American colonel.

My wife, sweet Jeannie, raising our children and wondering what was happening to her husband among the intrigues and atrocities of a nation at war, half a world away.

The faces of Vietnamese and French and Americans, friendly and unfriendly, trusting America, trusting the press, trusting me—or not. The faces still living, but changed—and the faces long since dead. Most persistent in their haunting are the ghosts of those who died beside me.

I am not a soldier, not the Marine I tried to be. A record of rheumatic fever and my own destiny saw to that. But I came to Vietnam, I saw a war. I have these memories, and these memories have become a part of me.

Since the war, I don't think I've ever seen a day in my life without thinking about Vietnam. But that doesn't mean that I had managed to put the past into perspective—that I had ever managed to understand the past *as* past. Mostly, my memories were stored away, not dealt with.

Much of the time, a journalist's memory is nothing more than a mental notebook, jotting things down just as we do during interviews or on the scene of a big story. Maybe we're not so different from anybody else; we put down a couple of quick lines here or there to be fleshed out later, when there's time—if there's time.

That's a shame, because our sense of the past, our sense of history, could and should contribute so much to our reporting. Eric Sevareid's best analyses abound with historical perspective—not only of the period he was reporting, but perspective gleaned from reading Herodotus and Holinshed and so on. And how much wiser the audience would be if we managed to share our sense of history. At the very least, we might convey a better image of ourselves as the kind of scholar-reporters Ed Murrow sought to develop at CBS—because he knew that listeners and viewers would trust the journalists, like Eric, who could tell not just *what,* but *why.*

But in the hectic atmosphere of deadlines and sound bites, history is all too often crowded out. We tell ourselves we'll come back and do the historical context, perspective, and analysis later. In this, we're probably no different from anyone else. We let ourselves believe we haven't got time for the past.

But the past keeps sneaking up on you. It is always there behind you, right over your shoulder.

Only by coming back to Vietnam was I able to experience the differences that change had wrought—in the country, in me, in my memory.

A lot of those who went to Vietnam years ago were soldiers. Many of us weren't—we were reporters, nurses, doctors, businesspeople. We were, all of us, *trying:* trying to help, trying to see, trying to make a name, make a buck or just get through it. But all of us had ample opportunity to witness and to act, to be a part of a war, with the extremes of human conduct playing out all around us. Extremes of horror and exultation, extremes of cowardice and valor, extremes of cruelty and compassion.

It takes a long time to absorb so many extremes, and in the shock of war, we didn't have a chance to absorb everything, not right away. Over time, many have been able to reconcile the Vietnam of the mind with the Vietnam that is actual—some have been able to do so without returning to Vietnam, as Norm Schwarzkopf and I had to do, as the veterans we met there had to do. We needed to return to Vietnam, to see that life has moved on for Vietnam and for us. We needed to smell the fish sauce in the streets and the fragrance of flowers on the water, to return to a country of death and pain and find that it's only another country.

outtake

Sevareid

Y OU COULD BE AROUND ERIC SEVAREID FOR HALF A DAY OR MORE, just the two of you, and he might not say anything. Oh, maybe mumble "Good morning" or something, but other than that, nothing.

It happened to me many times, riding with him up to hunt birds over dogs in Virginia, or on some plane ride, or working a story.

He wasn't mad or anything. That's just the way he was. Eric Sevareid, who died July 9, 1992, at seventy-nine, was eloquent on the air, but in person he was quiet. Given to silence. Long silence if he was thinking, or if he just didn't believe he had anything worth saying, or if he didn't feel like talking just then.

I remember the first time he invited me to go bird hunting with him. I had not been hunting anything for a while and was certainly lacking confidence about my ability to hit something as difficult as quail. So I brought along a 12-gauge automatic shotgun with a choke. It was in a carrying cover, so Eric didn't see it when he picked me up. We drove for two hours. Other than "Good morning," he said nothing.

When we finally got out of his car and began preparing to walk, I unsheathed the big 12-gauge. He uncovered a little 28-gauge double-barrel. He spoke not a word. But he looked at me like I was a hitchhiker with pets, looked at me with that big Nordic glare. Then he smiled, shook his head, and mumbled, "C'mon."

I felt foolish but forgiven. Eric always forgave you. We went on to have a great afternoon in the outdoors. I was constantly early and too far out front with my shots. "Patience," he counseled softly. "Patience." Pause. "And concentration."

He was even better when it came to pursuing trout.

He was out of Velva, N.D., by way of the University of Minnesota, Paris, and a thousand datelines long since forgotten. He had been many places, but he came home.

And he came home to Georgetown, to his own house, to die.

He knew he was dying. You could never fool Eric; he was too smart, too observant, too sensitive.

Like Edward R. Murrow, who hired him at CBS, Sevareid was a lifetime scholar. Murrow was the best reporter and broadcaster in the history of over-the-airwaves news. He was the classic scholar-correspondent. So was Sevareid. Eric also grew into being a philosopher-correspondent, the only one broadcast news has produced. And he is unquestionably the best writer to come out of electronic journalism.

The proof is not just in *Not So Wild a Dream,* one of the best autobiographies of his time and perhaps his defining work. There are also his essays, read on radio and television for almost half a century. No one of his generation wrote more or better essays—no one, print or broadcast. And they have stood the test of time. Much of what he wrote about America and what it meant to be an American in the post–World War II era is as interesting and instructive today as it was the day he wrote it. Sevareid is the only broadcast journalist I know who was a combat correspondent in the Spanish Civil War, World War II, Korea, and Vietnam. When I visited him for the last time, he sipped tea and told how he wished he could have gone to the Persian Gulf. "Sort of," he added, "but I guess I've seen enough wars."

My mind went back to a place near Hue, early in the Vietnam fighting. Sevareid was the first of the big-name American broadcasters to come and see for himself, firsthand, what we were getting ourselves into.

"I don't like it," Eric told me. "I don't like it partly because I don't believe anyone has thought this damn thing through."

Sevareid always thought things through. And partly because of that, he knew about an incredible range of things: how to lead quail, how to mend a fly-line, how to converse with a monarch or a showgirl, and how to stay alive in tight places.

Like Hemingway, he loved the outdoors. Like Hemingway, he was a man's man when that was still something you said, when that still meant something. He and Hemingway had a northern-midwestern stoicism, determination, and intellect. He went to Paris as Hemingway did (they knew each other there). And the two wrote in similar spare, lean styles. For my money, Sevareid did it better.

The man and his writings had a quiet authority, and the beauty of simplicity.

The excellence of his writing is part of the reason people who came late remember Eric Sevareid the elder statesman, the sage. But he was a combination of thought and action. Like André Malraux, the French philosopher, writer, and journalist whom he knew and admired, Sevareid traveled the world, seeing for himself, engaged, taking chances. And then he tried to think things through, write about them and philosophize about them.

He always seemed taller than he was, although he was well over six feet. He dominated rooms, seemed to dominate any landscape he occupied. He had charisma, and he was a star. But he was a quiet star, and he was not so much glamorous as he was compelling. When you heard him speak—on the radio, where I heard him first, and later on the television or in his office—you listened, and you thought.

There was, in person as over the air, a brooding quality about him. But his wife for the last thirteen years, Suzanne St. Pierre, brought him a calmness within and a happiness that had always seemed to have eluded him before. He also took great joy in his twin sons and a daughter from previous marriages.

When I saw him that last time, in his Georgetown house, with the sun shafting through the windows over a fountain-centered, small back garden, he seemed at peace. He knew, in that way that Eric always knew everything, that his work was done, his place secure. In the pantheon of broadcast journalism, only Ed Murrow himself ranks above Sevareid.

When Murrow died, Sevareid wrote (as usual) the best line: "He was a shooting star; we will live in his afterglow a very long time."

Now, the same might be said of Sevareid himself. But I prefer to think of him as a Northern Star, the Great Northern Star: constant and clear, the big, bright, quiet one.

And a Catfish Runs Through It

W HEN I RETURNED FROM SOMALIA, AT THE END OF 1992, I MADE MY-self two promises. One, I would never complain again (not realistic, but we try). And, two, I would get out of the office more and onto the cutting edge of the big stories.

You look in the eye of a hungry child, or you watch a doctor pry bullets and shrapnel from a baby, and you can't walk away as the same person you were—or even as the same journalist.

No doubt the budget makers at CBS believe that I travel quite enough as it is. But the simple truth is that the best stories do not make office calls. You have to go get them. When I sense a big one brewing, or it explodes in front of me, inside me there is this feeling of the caged cat.

As the years have rolled by—and many times they haven't so

much rolled as bumped—that feeling has increased. I know how that must sound: Stick a press card in my hatband and put me through to the City Desk. *I'm going to bust this town wide open.* In truth, there is an element of that anytime you chase a story. Big stories are the essence of good theater. Time is always running out. You don't know what the ending will be.

So in the summer of 1993, I arranged to cover the economic summit in Tokyo. I told my boss, Eric Ober, that I believed I had been to every summit since they started having them. I never knew one to make real news. They are basically a charade, with important people posing for pictures. But this was Bill Clinton's first overseas trip, a valid reason right there. And I had another angle. I wanted to tack on a trip to China behind it.

I have tried many times to explain the magnetic pull that China has on reporters. As an emerging economic superpower, China may well be the most important story of the post-Communist era. My instincts tell me that the chances are high that Hong Kong *and* Taiwan will be part of one China faster than people think.

The trouble with covering an economic summit is that everybody has to take enough people to fill a Verdi opera. I promised to keep it lean, keep it low-cost, and the bosses indulged me on China. That was the trade-off.

Out of the summit came what amounted to a mini-scoop, one made more interesting by events soon to unfold. We landed an exclusive interview with President Clinton, and we slipped in through a side door. The hook we used to get it were the floods building in the Midwest. There are few positions less attractive to a president than to be overseas when a disaster strikes at home, giving his critics a chance to say he doesn't care.

We were told before the summit that there would be no interviews until Friday, the closing day. I said, I know, I understand, there are things he can't talk about. But I don't want to ask him about economics. I want to ask him about the floods. Bingo. David Gergen, who had worked for Reagan, and as shrewd and fair as a Washington image maker can be, got right back to us. The interview was on.

It turned out to be no big deal, but it did bug our rivals for about twenty-four hours, so we sprang for an extra ration of sake for the troops. The summit ended and we quietly slipped off to Shanghai. I was really up, excited about being there, and by the quality of the help available to me. George Osterkamp, one of the best field producers anywhere, had been sent ahead to advance the trip. I had given him three or four story ideas to pursue and he had come up with a couple more. Zipping along the China coast, I reminded myself why I had seen the summit as a stepping-stone. Despite the effort of the president and his people to create the mirage of news, there was none. They had droned on and on about GATT. My definition of GATT was: General Agreement to Talk and Talk.

In the summer of 1993, Shanghai was the most interesting city in the world, a kind of new Klondike of the Orient. It was the engine that would pull China's train. I liked working with Osterkamp, a thoughtful man who fits the popular image of a college professor— favors tweed, wears glasses. We were just getting started when I felt a big tug from another direction.

While we were in Tokyo, I had assigned my main man, Bill Madison, to monitor the storms back in the States. I knew the floods were on the borderline of being a major story. My contacts at the National Weather Service had told me that El Niño comes over the Pacific every once in a while to cause some unusual weather patterns. Now it was sort of parked over the Midwest and wasn't moving. I told Bill his job was to keep me up to date, hour to hour, on the floods. While we had an investment in the summit, and China, I didn't want to be caught there playing with chopsticks, not if they were building arks back in America's heartland.

I am probably obligated to say that nature's fury has always been one of my obsessions. It was Hurricane Carla, which struck Galveston and the Gulf Coast in 1961, that more or less catapulted me to the network.

Sure enough, the story broke just a few hours after we landed in Shanghai. I said to Madison and Osterkamp, "I hate it, but we're going to have to fold the China cards and plug into the floods." I told Bill to book us on the next flight out, which happened to be on China Air at eight the next morning. It was now midnight and Osterkamp started to disagree politely. I said, "George, I love you, but this isn't a debating society. Bill and I are going back in the morning. You tell me what you absolutely must have and I'll do whatever I can." We laid out a plan to get up at 3:30 and tape enough stand-ups to flesh out the pieces we already had in progress.

This is what separates a major league producer from the others. George is halfway around the world, in one of the toughest possible places to work, with program segments of his own to produce and now with pieces he has to finish for his anchorperson. His time and his glands have all just collapsed. But he never skipped a beat. He stayed up all night, thinking ahead, arranging the pictures in his mind, planning and writing, making the pieces of the jigsaw puzzle fit. Our cameraman was Tom Rapier, who does his work with the spare movement of a great second baseman, ably assisted by sound-man Paul Sedia.

We left the newly decorated and beautiful Shanghai Hilton at 3:15 to go to what I call Good Earth country, after the book by Pearl Buck. This was far from the boom of Shanghai, out where rice paddies are the only business. We began working at daylight. Thanks to George's planning, between daylight and 7:30 we did the pieces we needed and then made our Daytona 500 run to the airport. Madison and I boarded the plane in trousers and shoes soaked from the fields, looking like Chinese peasants. Osterkamp and the rest of the team stayed behind. I hated having to break away, but in the United States the Midwest floods were the one hundred-year floods. This meant destruction writ large.

After I left Somalia, I should have made myself a third promise: to quit making trips to places like St. Louis by way of places like Shanghai. But that certainly seems to be one of my patterns and I have learned to live with it.

For years, journalists tried mightily to avoid flying on Chinese airlines. For one reason, the Chinese were unable to buy American aircraft for several decades, and their planes were generally old and repaired with spare parts from Cambodia or Mexico. We had no sooner settled in our seats than I experienced something absolutely unique in my travels. Just before they closed the door, I turned to watch the stewardesses working in the galley and, lo and behold, a rat scurried across the floor. A large rat. I don't know how many millions of miles I had flown, but I had tried most of the carriers of the world—North and South Vietnam, Aragona, Air Madagascar. But never in nearly half a century of flying had I seen a rat, not before or since. I nudged Bill Madison and said, "Take a good look. You might never see that again."

The hostesses did not appear to notice. The crew closed the doors, leaving me with the certain knowledge that a full-grown rat was aboard the plane. He did not reappear, but I must admit I did not sleep very well on the flight.

The trip from Shanghai to St. Louis lasted all day and night and the next morning. We flew through time zones and the international dateline and had a change of planes and a brief stop in Tokyo. I went to the gate and got instructions on how to make an international telephone call. What I had to do now was in my head. I had to seal off China and forget the small, handcrafted pieces I had planned to polish and hone for our audiences. Now I had to mobilize a much larger unit to cover a big, breaking domestic story and I had to do it on the fly, in short bursts by phone.

In addition to the daily coverage, I wanted a commitment to run a major piece on *48 Hours,* our weekly documentary series. This is prime-time, ferociously competitive; *48 Hours* is an hour of news competing with entertainment, and many are unwilling to tamper with its winning formula. And part of that formula, as is true for any documentary that adheres to the highest journalistic standards of integrity, is that much of the program must be planned well ahead. I had been trying for most of 1993 to convince my colleagues that we should do breaking news on *48 Hours,* a television version of "stop the presses."

It had been an uphill climb, and not the first since Howard Stringer, then a news producer, and I first began dreaming of restoring a prime-time documentary series to the network's schedule. In the early 1980s, we sent some of the wise owls of television into hoots of laughter: "Impossible! Just say the word 'documentary' and you'll hemorrhage ratings!" they insisted. In 1993, after five years on the air, *48 Hours* was generally considered one of the most successful news programs in television history, and nobody was laughing at us anymore. (You may want to consider that people weren't laughing at Stringer because by this time he had moved out of news to become president of the whole CBS broadcasting empire—his creative vision and his savvy management having taken him straight to the top just around the time *48 Hours* premiered in 1988.)

I have to admit that almost none of this was in my thoughts as I argued for *48 Hours* to cover the flood live with breaking reports. I had to keep focused on what was happening next. Now I said to News Division president Eric Ober, "Turn on a dime and we'll swarm this story. We have the team, we have the capability, and we have the story."

Ober gave *48 Hours* the green light. He wanted CBS to provide "saturation coverage," so called not because we were reporting on a flood but because every component of the news team would make a contribution, and every program we had would make a report. Eric and I don't always agree, but this time we were in lockstep, and you have to remember that, given the financial realities of the age, "saturation coverage" is a huge risk. Eric realized that this was a big, important story with significant impact on millions of Americans, and if anything warranted risk, it was the Great Flood of 1993.

That took care of *48 Hours,* at least for the moment. Under executive producer Cathy Lasiewicz and senior producer Al Briganti, our reports were in good hands. Now I had to think about the rest of our coverage, and how I could help.

If it is anything, my mind is compartmentalized. I have radio hourlies, the late news, overnight news, hour by hour hard news, each behind a different partition. There is a separate compartment for *48 Hours.* To get the journalistic aircraft carrier that is CBS News to move one degree requires many turns of the wheel.

I stood at the gate until the last second, shouting into the phone, taking orders, giving a few, trying to persuade, argue, debate, nudge, beg for the resources to cover the floods. The story was still breaking. There was no way of knowing how big it would get. I wanted a total commitment. As the big hunters of Ernest Hemingway's era would say, I wanted to bring enough gun. On summer weekends, that is not always easy to do. People are at the Hamptons, at their summer homes. The Chablis is being poured and the cheese is being sliced. You can't always reach the ones you need and when you do they are not always sober. In short, I wanted to franchise this story—if we could.

I didn't have enough time in Tokyo to finish making the arrangements, and the next chance I had to phone was from San Francisco. I remember being at the gate with a phone in each hand and Bill Madison holding a third. But this is why you get into this fruitcake business. This is it, your addiction, the adrenaline rush.

We were working out dozens of details, starting with hiring the best helicopter pilots available—at least two, and I sure would prefer three. I wanted one in St. Louis, one in Des Moines, and another anywhere along the great Mississippi, from the Illinois border to Missouri. On a story like the flood, the overhead shot is key. Ideally, what you look for is a retired Vietnam chopper pilot who is now flying fat cats to gambling casinos and business deals, is bored by it, and would like to relive a few of those landings in the combat zone. You pay him well and assure him he's going to have a damned good time.

On the other phone, I'm ticking off the names of the producers we want, how many cameras, and the people behind them. Lane Venardos, now vice president of the News Division, was already on top of the project by the time we reached San Francisco. The aircraft carrier is turning. There is a lot of talk in television circles about CBS not being as big as it once was. But we are still deep in experienced off-camera people: executives, middle news managers, producers, associate producers, researchers, writers, dog robbers and fixers, the people with Rolodex files who know where, in St. Louis, you find a former Vietnam helicopter pilot.

We had a forty-minute layover in San Francisco until our next flight, so there was a lot of telephoning back and forth. I was thinking, hot damn, it's going to work. We're going to get there. The story is still building. We're going to pop on the air on Monday with an anchor presence.

In a two-day period, I had been to Japan and China and was bound for middle America—the marvel of modern jet travel. Now I had a quick but hardly a minor decision to make in San Francisco. I was supposed to be on vacation as soon as my China reporting trip wrapped up. Sweet Jean Rather was even then waiting for me at our fishing camp outside Austin. I'm thinking, maybe, just maybe, if I work it right I can go to St. Louis via Austin, stop by the camp for a change of underwear, a home-cooked meal, and an opportunity to show my affection for the mother of my children. And I really had a clothes problem. I needed to take my foul-weather gear, including my wading boots, to St. Louis.

I took a chance and put my quandary in the hands of two customer-service reps with American and United airlines. A Far Pacific typhoon had swept through the West that Sunday, canceling a long list of flights. The reps were trying to ticket me to St. Louis through Denver. I asked them if it would be possible to get there from Austin. They were both fabulous, got into it instantly, had me ticketed in every direction on every flight that was still on the schedule. On rival airlines, even. They also accommodated us when I told them we needed three phones and hot coffee.

Lurking somewhere beneath this feverish activity was a memory half-buried. Some years ago, when *The Camera Never Blinks* was first published, I had to change the ending at literally the last moment. There was an anecdote that was mild and fairly tasteful even by the standards of the mid-1970s. I no longer remember how we happened to test the story on Jean's parents, but we did. And it struck them as "suggestive."

The Goebels lived, and still do, in the Texas town of Smithville, a lovely, quiet, neighborly town, sheltered from many of the problems of modern, big-city America. It was the kind of town where generations of proper young ladies would blush at the word "intersection."

Times have changed. Smithville now sits alongside a highway

that connects Houston and Austin. The people get cable and the story we deleted in *The Camera Never Blinks* wouldn't offend the Goebels today.

I had led into the story by admitting my guilt over how much time I was away from my family in 1962, the year I covered the civil rights struggle for CBS as head of our New Orleans bureau. I spent a total of twenty-six days with Jean and our two babies. I wasn't proud of it then and I'm less proud now, when I'm older and more aware that you can't replace the days you didn't spend with the people you love.

But we had agreed that Jean would stay in Houston with my mother, knowing how much time I would be spending on the road, in the famous datelines of that day—Oxford, Selma, Montgomery, Little Rock, Jackson. There was a safety factor, as well; I did not want Jean exposed to the phone calls and hate mail I might be getting. Reporters were not real popular in the worst of the Old South in the 1960s.

The understanding was that I would join them every weekend I could. Then on Friday, almost without fail, I would get word that a story I had been working on was about to break. There was going to be a march, a confrontation, a riot. Friday after Friday, I would call Jean, explain that I had to cancel my flight home in order to cover whatever was going to happen. And each week I would promise to be there the next time.

You find yourself needing to finish the story. You have to be there. You don't think anyone else can do it as well. And you keep making excuses until, suddenly, two or three months have passed.

That was pretty much the case when I called Jean, again, to tell her I was going to have to postpone my flight, but I would see her for sure the following Friday.

There was a long, heavy pause on the phone. Jean said, very deliberately, "Dan, I understand. What *you* have to understand is this: Saturday night there is going to be some lovemaking going on in this house. And if you want to get in on it, YOU BETTER BE HERE."

That weekend, I used my plane ticket to Houston. That story, someone else covered.

Now, in San Francisco, the customer rep at San Francisco was able to work out my detour and I jumped at it. At least, after twenty years, I had learned that much.

After a stop in Dallas and yet another change of planes, I finally got to Austin. A car and driver had been prearranged to meet me, and a good thing, too. I would've been unsafe at any speed. But an object in motion tends to remain in motion. By then I'd realized that my flood boots were in New York, but the flood was not and neither was I. So I bought a pair of boots, made a quick pit stop at our fishing camp, picked up the rest of my foul-weather gear, kissed Jean (who wasn't sure we'd ever met, but re-called having seen me on television a few times), and caught the next flight to St. Louis.

In St. Louis, a newsroom nerve center was already in the process of being set up, in the form of two connecting rooms at a Holiday Inn. From there we could assign the stories and direct the crews. Everything was coming together now. I had left China on a Sunday morning and by Monday I was ready to follow The Great Flood of '93.

It may have been my imagination, but I thought that as soon as Tom Brokaw and Peter Jennings found out I was in Missouri, they were out the door. That shoe has been on the other foot, but as a personal matter, Monday was a great day. The first thing I wanted to do was get to where I could give people an overview of the story. This goes directly to my own style of work. As part of my checklist, Bill Madison reminds me to describe what happened and tell what I learned from it. This is critical when you're covering something as vast as a flood; it's too large to fit the small screen.

To begin with, a hurricane is like a cobra. When it's ready it strikes quickly with an awesome force and killing power. A great flood is more like a python: huge, slow, but able to wrap itself around anything in its path and squeeze the life out of it.

The best way I knew to bring the viewer into the story, to recognize the vastness of the flood sweeping down the Mississippi, was from a helicopter. I've been in a few and I still feel some excitement—you don't anchor a newscast every day from a helicopter. The clear advantage is that you can cover a lot of ground in a hurry.

We took off early and I knew immediately that I was paired with a fabulous pilot, Gary Lusk. The good ones may not always hear the instructions of the FAA about maintaining a certain altitude. But they instinctively position you to use what I call God's light. So here is how we rigged ourselves inside the chopper:

First, it's tight. In the front there is space for two people, the pilot and our producer, Wayne Nelson, a Texas A&M product. In some ways Wayne is the antithesis of George Osterkamp. He doesn't try to be all that cerebral. He has a great heart for a story and he's your quintessential crash-and-burn producer. Maybe not a timely analogy, but I like his drive. The producer sits next to the pilot so he can explain to him what we are trying to do. By the way, Wayne is ten feet tall.

Right behind the cockpit, there is a compartment designed to seat four people. We have three—an anchor, a cameraman, and a soundman. Before we even took off, the cameraman hunkered down in the corner farthest back, facing the cockpit, with the sound man beside him. I'm catty-corner from the camera, wearing a standard, intra-helicopter headset. We had built in a microphone connected directly to our videotape because you must find a way to override the whir of the rotor blades.

Both doors were removed from the compartment and everyone was wearing two really strong, web safety belts. We also attached one of the cameraman's belts to the fuselage and put another around a thigh, with enough slack to allow him, if necessary, to get out the door and onto the skid of the helicopter. This would give him more range and latitude and a wider shot of the flood.

On the opposite side of the cabin, the anchorman (me) did the same thing, so I could get out on the skid and have a longer focal point between the two of us. And the cameraman would then be better able to frame me against the background of the shot.

For example, if you wanted to put the anchorman in the picture showing a house where just the tip of a chimney is visible, you can have the pilot bank the helicopter a certain way to get the best shot. As the chopper hovers and banks, the cameraman on one skid and the anchorman on the other can slide up or down, depending on how the helicopter tilts, to give you different angles and different shots. Otherwise, from inside the chopper you really don't have much leeway.

Our opening piece was going to be what is called the establishing shot, explaining to the viewer that "this is where the flooding Missouri meets the flooding Mississippi." There is an impersonality to these often distant, panoramic shots. So what you want is to take the viewer up close and personal. You can't stick a TelePrompTer out there on the skids, so my reports were ad-libbed, almost a running play-by-play. This is a sample:

"The Mississippi River is spreading like an epidemic now across Missouri, Illinois, and Iowa, with more states to be afflicted soon. I've flown over the area many times in the past few days, and I'm still trying to grasp the dimensions. The vast expanses of waters, hemmed in only by hills. At its worst, the water stretches from one horizon to the other. The natural inclination is to marvel at the physical dimensions of this disaster. But you can't ignore the human dimensions.

"Over there, that's not just a house in water up to the eaves—that is somebody's home and hard work. And over there, that's not just a flooded field. It's somebody's livelihood—and it might have been your supper.

"Understanding how much is at stake here, in human terms, makes it easier to appreciate another marvel of the Flood of '93. That marvel may be the greatest of them all: It's the way citizens have come together, helping neighbors and strangers, with bravery and good cheer.

"You know, Mark Twain used to say that the only good thing about a flood was that the streets were quiet. He said this before the development of the outboard motor. Now the streets up and down the Mississippi sound like a speedway, as neighbors zip back and forth with supplies and passengers."

On our first day of reconnaissance, July 9, we wanted to land someplace and we did, on the hilltop campus of Culver-Stockton College in Canton, Missouri. We prevailed on Amy Looten, public relations director for the school, to take us into town, where we rented a small boat with an outboard motor. Then we gave our viewers a tour of the flooded area from water level.

At the town of La Grange, the mayor, Harold Ludwig, joined us. As we passed the rooftop of one house, I remarked, "Boy, that place is really flooded out. Whose home is it?" The mayor said, "That's mine."

I asked him, with the camera running, if he would mind showing us around on the inside of the submerged house. He sort of paused and shrugged and said, "Well, yeah, I guess we can do that." He looked at the cameraman and asked, "Can you do it? You're carrying a lot of electric equipment."

He could and we did. I don't know how and I don't think I want to know. But we had filmed wide, tight, and medium shots from the air. Now we were going to take the viewer on a tour of a flooded home—with the person who owned it.

It may be unnecessary to say that we climbed out of the boat and onto the roof of the house very, very carefully. We eased ourselves into the water and tiptoed into the house. There was just enough air to keep our noses out of the water. I could see the mayor's eyes welling up a bit as he surveyed the damage. He pointed out the living room. Then we sort of felt our way along the ceiling until we reached the kitchen. "This," he said, "is what's left of my kitchen."

I suddenly felt something alive brush up against my leg. I was startled, to say the least, and my first frantic thought was, I hope it's not a snake or an eel. It turned out to be a big Mississippi catfish. They are bottom-feeding fish, and naturally he (or she) would be in the kitchen, looking for food.

Mayor Ludwig had made this tour several times since the flood began, and now he was nonchalant, as if the catfish were a family pet. But you could see he was pretty torn up. It was a fine old house, a two-story Victorian country home in which the Ludwigs had taken great pride. And the mayor was well aware that many of his constituents' homes and businesses were in the same shape.

The siege of Des Moines was under way, and so we split off part of our base camp on the outskirts of St. Louis, chartered a small plane and took off. On July 10, the Raccoon River hit a crest of twenty-five feet. It knocked out the Des Moines waterworks and flooded most of the major downtown areas. In this day and age, it is fairly unusual for the center of a metropolitan city to be threatened. Our flight was extremely rough getting there. We encountered a lot of thunder and rain and both our people and equipment were stacked to the ceiling. The plane started bouncing so much that ashtrays popped out of their sockets and sailed through the cabin, and only a few people kept their lunches down.

We made a decision to anchor *48 Hours* out of Des Moines, from the top of a van overlooking the army of people sandbagging the levee, trying to spare the rest of the inner city.

You kept coming back to the immensity of the problem—waves of water up to eight miles wide. You measure the height and width of the flood, the acres of crops ruined, the billions of dollars in devastation. You watch people cry and you weigh the tears.

There were at least a few glimmers of hope. As one farmer put it, "There's a hundred-year flood somewhere every year. This is a big country." And somehow the people always rebuild and move on.

Because of our mobility, we had the opportunity to see an awful lot in a compressed amount of time. The Mississippi River basin—Illinois, Iowa, Kansas, Minnesota, Missouri, Nebraska, South Dakota, and Wisconsin—contains close to 15 percent of the landmass of the United States. Eight months of rain had swelled the major rivers to record levels and brought the region to this catastrophe. People actually wondered if the floods were a sign that the world was ending. In St. Louis, callers to local radio stations wondered if Busch Stadium or the Gateway Arch might disappear.

"If a six-hundred-twenty-foot-tall structure were underwater," said one city official, "yes, we'd be close to the end of the world."

You saw the effects on people's dreams: water lapping over the curbs and into the homes that had been built on high ground in expensive neighborhoods; new cars ruined and new shrubs and plants floating away. In an hour, you saw individual farms wiped out, not just the crops and houses, but an entire family business and a way of life, gone and in many cases gone forever. Often, people would not have the insurance or the savings to reinvest and start over.

In part, what makes these stories of natural disasters so powerful is the realization that it can happen to us—you, me. A whole school of journalistic thought has emerged in recent years along the line that the wrath-of-nature stories are overplayed, especially on television. I do not subscribe to this. I think of the eruption of Mount St. Helens, Hurricane Andrew, the San Francisco and Los Angeles earthquakes. These are stories people identify with and they make a difference, certainly to the people whose lives are rearranged by them. Can anyone not think, "There but for the grace of God?" These disasters truly put life in perspective, how transient and ephemeral it really is. No one gets through unscathed.

All of that was compressed and synthesized in the story of the Great Flood of '93. When you see all the family photographs ruined by water, an heirloom piece of furniture washed away and lost forever, or a dog you can't get out of the kennel, a horse you can't get out of the corral, a cow you can't get out of the barn, or, indeed, a person who stayed too long or got caught in the wrong place . . . you feel humbled.

I was aware of one case where a man tried to climb over a slippery levee, had a mild heart attack, continued to struggle, and was struck by lightning. You tend to mentally throw up your hands.

Or it can be as simple as the words of a man who watched his favorite recliner floating off in the distance. "I sure liked that recliner," he said. "Had it since the day I was married."

Yet the setbacks, even the tragedies, are countered somewhat by heroic deeds to the left and right of us. The floods were a great leveler in the sense that you would find a six-figure advertising executive working alongside a homeless person. Most news organizations underplayed the story in the beginning, I thought. They missed the best part, the humanity of strangers waging a battle against a force you can't even get mad at—nature itself. Firefighters, police officers, national guard, volunteers, ordinary people, entire families, hour after hour, day after day, filling sandbags and stacking them, striving to build their last lines of defense. Such sights made your heart soar and, yes, a secret little part of you likes to think that, if called upon, you could do that and you would.

This may be the lesson of the Midwest floods, one we have to keep relearning. In hard and desperate times, you have to be able to depend on others, neighbors or strangers, as they did in Des Moines. Maybe my impression of what happened there is stronger because this is so deep in the heartland. This was a humane version of street-to-street, house-to-house fighting to beat back an enemy at the gates. The city was without running water for at least two weeks. The people had to jury-rig buckets and pull cords just to take a shower. When the waterworks plant was able to supply a limited amount of water, the residents were warned not to use it for drinking purposes for at least a month. The water was a vivid brown, like cold gravy.

One day I watched the sandbag line stretching out a quarter mile or more along the riverfront. I almost didn't notice a woman walking past us. She had bright red hair, green shorts, a red-striped blouse, and heavy work gloves. She carried a plastic bag. She was filling it with trash.

The sandbag line was a little like an outdoor rock concert. Even though the work was tough, a great party spirit pervaded, rock music pumped out—and the crowd generated an enormous amount of trash. This woman had designated herself the cleanup crew. She'd fill a huge plastic bag with trash, then go and get another bag, fill it, and keep coming back for more, each bag bigger than she was.

She did this for the whole day, long after dark, all by herself, and again the next day. Her name was Norma Buehlmann.

Finally I stopped to tell Mrs. Buehlmann I admired her dedication. She brushed aside the compliment. "I'm a mother," she said. "I'm used to picking up after people." She was doing this, she said, even though her house hadn't been flooded: It worried her to see so many of her neighbors in Des Moines affected, and she wanted to help any way she could. But she didn't have time to talk; she had to get back to work.

By the end of July, the flooding still had not abated. It had claimed more farmland, more homes, more businesses. The estimate of damages had risen beyond $10 billion. I went to West Quincy, Missouri, a town turned into a lake. The battle to defend the town from the rising river had failed. Telephone poles were knocked over like matchsticks. Streetlights were bent like pins.

And yet people who had lost most of what they had were sharing with those who had lost everything. In an era when the decline of community, and the sense of community, is so troubling, these events—floods, quakes, fires—force people to remember that we still need to be connected.

Hurricanes Then and Now

THEN: HURRICANE CARLA, 1961. I THOUGHT IT WOULD BE WORTH-while to chain myself to a tree in the middle of a hurricane. How could I report a hurricane if I'd never experienced one close up? And how could I get any closer than riding one out, lashed heroi-cally like Odysseus to his mast, with the wind and the water and the debris flying everywhere?

I tried it. It didn't work.

Now: Hurricane Emily, 1993. I am hanging my sixty-one-year-old rump halfway out of a helicopter flying over Cape Hatteras in the aftermath of Emily, a kinder, gentler hurricane to most of the world (especially compared to Hurricane Andrew the summer before), but not in Cape Hatteras, where she left behind winds a little higher than are really optimal for helicopter flights, especially flights when you are not, as I say, entirely *inside* the helicopter and you are no longer the twenty-nine-year-old who used to go around chaining himself to trees and, more to the point, your wife is no longer exactly enthusiastic about stunts like these, and you think she's probably right. I always say that you have to go up high to see what's going on, and seeing what's going on is what television news is all about. I am trying to concentrate on the story, but I keep coming back to a litany of high school football injuries, and why I had that extra cup of coffee at breakfast, and what it must be like to be a grandfather, provided I ever live that long and do not fall out of this helicopter as we sail over the broken matchsticks that used to be homes. And over there is a tree, uprooted and carried several yards, about the size of the tree to which I once chained myself—so securely, I thought at the time.

Then: When you are young and the hurricane is on its way, when lives are at stake, it's one thing to convince yourself to take a few risks.

Now: When you are, well, let's just say *mature,* and the hurricane has waltzed out to sea, a threat to nobody but a few seagulls, it is much more difficult to convince yourself to take risks. Such risks must include this trip to inspect the storm damage: Hanging out over the struts of the helicopter, flown by a pilot you don't know, strapped in with a seat belt you don't trust. My father always carried a length of rope in the backseat of our car, wherever he went, because you never knew when you might have to haul something or tie the radiator back on or capture Bonnie and Clyde. A rope is useful. I used to follow his example but fell out of the habit. Now I wish I'd brought some rope on this trip. Tie myself into the helicopter. Who cares if it makes the other passengers nervous? It's a long way down, and "dropping anchor" takes on new meaning at a time like this.

Then: It was as if no one had ever covered a hurricane before. In a conversation with me, my boss, Cal Jones, program director at KHOU in Houston, suddenly got the bright idea to put the radar on television as it tracked the course of Hurricane Carla—and to superimpose the radar image over a map. The viewers would be able to *see* the hurricane approach—for the first time in history. We were reporting to the tiny portion of television-owning households across a huge swath of the state of Texas ("KHOU: The Eyes of the Golden Gulf Coast"), and there were about three of us, and we were making it all up and getting away with it.

Now: I have stopped trying to count how many hurricanes I have covered. Over two dozen, under three dozen. For Hurricane Emily, I am accompanied by two other correspondents, Giselle Fernandez and Harry Smith, five television producers, one radio producer, four camera operators and four sound operators, one news writer, plus unnumbered satellite technicians and support staff. (These numbers are inexact, because we chased Hurricane Emily the length of the Atlantic Coast from Florida to Virginia, and folks joined us and dropped away when they were called to other assignments over the course of the week.) Compared to the grand and glorious expeditions of yesterday, this is a bare-bones crew. We have not brought along makeup artists or representatives of senior management, for example, both of whom would have been deemed essential as recently as ten years ago. The jugglers and minstrels, though, we quit bringing along in 1982.

Then: I already knew something about hurricanes. You don't grow up in Houston without knowing something about hurricanes. There's folk wisdom, but also the wisdom that comes from close observation over many years: You get pretty good at figuring the path of a hurricane. Not flawless, no one is. And you tend to take the National Weather Service's best estimate as more reliable than your own. But you start to figure out a few things about hurricanes.

Now: Members of the crew are coming up to me. "When's it gonna hit, Dan? What's going to happen?" As if I were the wizard Gandalf Greybeard and had certain answers. I give them a comforting smile and offer the most up-to-date analysis I have: "We know the storm won't hit Virginia Beach," I say.

"How do you know? What do you mean?"

"Well, the Reverend Pat Robertson has his headquarters in Virginia Beach," I say. "And he prays the hurricanes away."

Then: There are things in the air—charged particles, velocity, fear—that drive a young man. The instincts tell you to run fast and hard, but you're too young to know if your instincts are telling you to run away or just to run free. The hairs at the back of my neck would rise, my adrenaline would pump, my heart would thrill. The winds rose and buffeted me, and the sea splashed higher. This was dangerous, this was exciting.

Now: There is salt in the air, and my glasses are getting a thick coating every few minutes. I am wondering where I can find a little shelter to change into my contact lenses.

Then: I came to the attention of the network and was described as "Dan Rather, up to his ass in water moccasins" by Walter Cronkite, who did much of his growing up in Texas and knows his water moccasins. Hurricane reporting can be a genuine public service: You teach people how to prepare, warn people to get out of the way, and tell them when it's safe to go home. There aren't many stories you can report that are of more direct importance to people's lives. But, I thought at the time, it can also be good for your career.

Now: In a speech to college students in Chicago, I say, "Be sure to tell your parents: Dan Rather did not advise you to chain yourself to a tree in the middle of a hurricane just to advance your career."

TWELVE

The Accidental Tourist

I MAY HAVE ENJOYED, NO, ENDURED, ONE OF THE LONGEST FLASH-backs in television history when I traveled to the Balkans as part of a globe-straddling summer of '93.

My mind began returning to Yugoslavia not long after we had followed the floods along the Mississippi, and where my mind went my body usually followed. I knew the Balkans a bit. I had been in and out of there in the 1970s, including one six-week period when I was chasing after Tito, needing an interview for a *60 Minutes* story.

We almost had him—almost being one of the saddest words in the English language. Alas, he spent an extra day in the mud baths at Dubrovnik with his mistress, and the chance slipped away. I have to admit, my respect for the man was undiminished. Tito was then well into his eighties, preparing to come to the United States for what would be his last visit. The Cold War was winding down. He had undergone a series of face-lifts, shed a few pounds, gone on a diet, and in the final phase he and his mistress had retreated to the privacy of the ancient mud baths.

This was my connection to Dubrovnik and one of the worst memories of my life. One of my trips to Yugoslavia had been with President Nixon in 1972, as the CBS White House correspondent, a job I held for nearly ten years. It was my proud boast that in all that time I had never missed a press plane, even in the days when I stayed out all night and consumed too much soda pop.

Until Dubrovnik. I have my excuses, and even someone to blame it on, but I did miss the plane, once. That is just about the worst embarrassment that can befall a correspondent. It isn't so much that you are stranded, or have failed in the simplest responsibility, or wasted the company's money or, worse, your own. The greatest torment by far is the knowledge that the stories, whatever they may be, have flown off without you.

Two planeloads of press people usually traveled with Nixon, one plane was basically for the writers and the broadcasters, the other for technicians, now infamous in White House lore as "the zoo plane." Hunter Thompson wrote about it in his book, *Fear and Loathing on the Campaign Trail.* I can't actually confirm that anyone smoked dope on those planes, or that any White House staffer was actually bound and gagged. But I can't deny it, either.

Nixon's purpose in going to Yugoslavia, as it had been in Romania, was to woo the self-described nonaligned nations. Tito would have been the ultimate trophy. More than any other leader, he had tried to walk the tightrope between the superpowers. He was a Communist, true, but not a Russian Communist. He was born Croatian, but he came to embody all of Yugoslavia.

Traveling with the president has a big downside, but balanced, if not outweighed, by the upside. If you choose, you can enjoy the illusion of being someone special, and why wouldn't you? You are flying ahead of Air Force One. Sometimes, you get to be the pool reporter with a seat assignment on Air Force One itself.

But the press plane isn't bad, a flying country club with an atmosphere of privileges. If you aren't wary, you can buy right into that. You never go through immigration and rarely through customs. Everybody gives his or her passport to the clerk in charge of transportation and is relieved of those inconvenient details. All nice.

So we moved into Belgrade, as we moved into any of the dictatorial countries, with their secret police operations, but secure in our own cocoon. If you are with the White House press, you have a badge with your picture and a number on it. The word goes down to even the scruffiest of secret police: Don't touch him. Fragile. Handle with care.

In the larger scheme, this was the tightest of the hand-held, spoon-fed operations for which the Nixon administration was either praised or loathed. It perfected the closed environment. Every administration since then has tried to copy it. Whatever one thought of Haldeman, Ehrlichman, and Company, they were tireless in arranging photos against useful backdrops, and spoon-feeding a ration of news pabulum every day, never mind if it had any value or made any sense. This trip, I indulged as much as anyone. No news was going on. If there was, you couldn't pin it down. Your job was to act as a stakeout.

So you flew with the press plane. You filmed the president getting off the plane, appearing with Tito, and waited. Marty Schram, a very good reporter then with *Newsday,* was always trying to resist being on a leash. As the VIPs exchanged toasts at a state dinner, Marty stared into a jigger of White Label and said, "You know, it's a shame to come this far and be a part of the circus act and have to wonder, what's going on . . . really going on."

So we hooked up with an English-speaking cab driver and said, "We want to go outside the city to a village, to a nightclub, whatever, someplace where the people are passing the night." We wound up going to just such a place on the outskirts of Belgrade. I fully endorsed Marty's sentiments. I believed it was important to at least thumb your nose at this Cuisinart news operation. We had a helluva time and learned a lot. We also paid a price.

We drank this native liqueur, a plum brandy whose name, in Serbo-Croatian, means "paint thinner." It was a peculiar and distinctly lethal kind of freshly brewed Slavic fruit brandy. Along about 3:00 A.M. Marty said, "We probably ought to head back to town. I think the buses leave the hotel around five-thirty for the press plane, and we're due to take off around seven-thirty." So we had a nightcap, which we really didn't need, and headed back into town. I know this may shock some of the customers, but it is not uncommon for reporters to pass their evenings in this way, especially good reporters. Like politicians and hangmen, they usually do their best work after midnight.

For the parents of those students who are thinking of going into journalism, this information may fan their fears. But there we were, bouncing along on the road to Belgrade, which is not one of your major convention centers. The press corps had to be farmed out to several hotels, even though the White House preferred to keep us all in one. We represented the finest in herd journalism, and you like to keep the herd together.

Marty dropped me off at my hotel and briefly alluded to the fact that the buses would be leaving soon for the airport. Had we been at one hotel, I would have used the tried-and-true buddy system. But we were not, and Yugoslavia at that time had a telephone system that was a cut above two tin cans connected by wire. I thought of invoking a Rather rule: If you have an hour or less to sleep, sleep in the lobby. Then when your compadres come down to pay their bills, someone will notice and wake you.

Regrettably, the hotel did not have a lobby. It had a check-in counter and not much else, so I made the mistake of going to my room. My roommate was someone I had known a long time over a lot of miles. When I came in he was asleep, and I made another mistake. I didn't wake him. I took off my shoes and tiptoed in as quietly as I could. He was honking like a flight of geese, anyway. I quietly slipped off my clothes and decided to snooze for a fast hour.

I had said when I walked by the very sleepy clerk at the front desk, "Be sure to wake me at five-fifteen." Had I been in better shape, I might have recognized that he was unable to understand anything I said. I told myself, at worst I'll wake up when my roomie wakes up.

The bus left at 5:30 for the Belgrade airport, which was a fair distance from town. The press plane was to depart at 7:30. None of this was among my conscious thoughts, mainly because at that hour I wasn't having any. The maid walked into the room and I sat bolt upright as a shaft of sunlight fell over my face. I knew immediately I was in trouble. And as the maid backed up toward the door, I didn't need to speak the language to know she was saying, "Sorry, I thought you were all gone."

My roommate and his luggage were gone. In one sweep, I slipped on my shirt and trousers, stuffed my socks in a pocket, grabbed my shoes, and bolted out the door. I rode the lift down, cursed the guy at the desk, who wasn't the same one who had been there earlier, and threw myself in front of the first vehicle to pass the hotel. I mean, I spread-eagled my arms and legs like a drug-enforcement agent and all but shouted, "Stop! Freeze!" The driver lightly banked into my knees and stopped.

Unshaven, my shirt sticking out, carrying a suitcase, my shoes still in one hand, I ran around to the side of the car and demanded: "Do you speak any English?"

"A little," he said, clearly apprehensive. I said, "Turn this son of a bitch around and get me to the airport, anyway you can, for any price." And by then I had plopped myself in the passenger seat with my bag tossed in back. I pressed my hands to form a tent, the prayer sign, and whipped a few bills out of my wallet. "At least," I said, "take me to Hotel X." CBS had a small staff there and I knew I could get help from one of the women who ran the bureau. In fact, women pretty much ran all the bureaus. None of the men would let on or acknowledge it at that time, but we all depended on them. There was Pat Bernie in London, Frau Schultz in Germany, Mrs. Hashimoto in Tokyo, Marthe Schermen in Paris, and in Moscow Mila Taubkina. It may or may not be necessary to add that no romance was ever involved. These were the nuns of CBS. Men had been karate-chopped for suggesting dinner.

They were the spine, the backbone, the heart of the CBS overseas news. If not the whole heart, at least the left ventricle. I don't want to overstate this, but at the time I knew that if I could reach one of these extraordinary women, my troubles were over. They had contacts everywhere, had chips that could be called in, knew everything and said nothing. Frau Schultz was in charge in Belgrade, having flown down from Bonn.

My driver refused to go to the airport, so I persuaded him to drop me off at the hotel, the nerve center. We drove like we were answering a 911 call, and along the way I managed to tuck in my shirt and put on my shoes. I yanked my bag out of the backseat, threw a hundred-dollar bill at the driver and said, as earnestly as I could, thanks a million and I hope I can repay you someday. I often wonder what he thought that was all about.

The crew was still packing up when I got there. I figured, had hoped, that someone would miss me before the plane took off and would not allow the pilot to leave without me. At the least, I thought my roomie, that good and faithful warrior with whom I had traveled so many roads, would realize he had made a mistake by not making sure I was awake.

Wrong, wrong, and wrong, but I didn't know it then. I rushed into the lobby, much relieved to see a couple of the rooms we had been using still bustling with people. Streamers of paper and cables from disconnected machines snaked across the floor. There was Frau Schultz. I came through the door shouting and she looked at me as if she had seen an apparition. I blurted out, "Please, call the airport and contact the press plane."

She said, "They must be gone by now."

I said, "There is no way they could have gone without me."

A couple of frantic calls were put through to the airport. We tried the U.S. Embassy, which was virtually unstaffed. All the personnel were exhausted from handling the trip, and with the circus having come and gone, most of them had stayed home. No one seemed to be there except a Marine guard and a secretary.

The airport was a maze of no answers and do-not-knows. The only option left for me was to proceed directly to the airport. I asked Frau Schultz to lend me $500 in local money and $500 in greenbacks and please step outside, speak to a taxi driver in his native tongue, and put him on the accelerated incentive plan.

She promised the cabbie a hundred down and a hundred if I made the plane. As she finished the negotiation, she suggested that I put on my socks. She was Old World, kept shaking her head from side to side, but in control, organized, thinking about the next move. She said she would keep making phone calls, and try to reach the airport, the police, the embassy, the White House press corps. As long as the president is in a town, you can tell an operator to get you White House communications, and a call will go through.

We drove to the airport and I was alternately praying and cursing, thinking, this can't be happening to me, it's all a bad dream. And the guys with the hammers are working away inside my skull. We raced to the Belgrade airport, pulling up to the entrance with a mild degree of caution. You had to be careful. Soldiers with automatic weapons were standing around. This wasn't Cleveland. From a distance, I could see that there was no blue and white airplane on the runway, and no backup planes.

My heart took an optimistic beat because there, looming against the sky, was a big U.S. Air Force C-141 at the end of the runway and the engines were running. I told the cab driver to take me around to the plane and he shook his head, explaining in his very limited English that he was as close as he could get. I walked to a gate in a fence and talked to a couple of guards. I showed them my White House badge. They asked to see my passport. Of course, I no longer had it. The transportation office had it.

I found my way to the airport manager and asked him to please have someone radio that U.S. Air Force plane. He looked at me suspiciously, refused to call, but agreed to send me out in a car. We highballed it toward the C-141 and I thought, "Boy, I'm in luck."

Most of these planes are based in Frankfurt. The presidential party is already on its way to London and I'm a half day behind them. Bad, but not too bad. I was worried half sick that the plane would start to taxi just before we could get there, so I stood up in the Yugoslavian jeep, waving my hands, waving my badge, waving my White House travel bag, carrying on like a crazy person.

As we pulled up, the pilot leaned out and said, right off, "Dan Rather! What are you doing here?"

I said, "Thank God. You have to let me aboard and I'll tell you the whole story. I've been left behind and I'm at your mercy." I was smiling from ear to ear, silently making my amends, vowing never to leave the herd again, never to drink plum brandy again. I said to the pilot, "I can't tell you how glad I am to see you."

And he said, with a cheerful wave, "Hey, no problem. We're on our way to Libya. Should be there in six or seven hours."

I tried to talk him into making a brief stop in London, did some serious begging. But his flight plan was for Libya. From there, planes took off, oh, four or five times a month.

Unceremoniously, I slunk off the plane and took one of the longest walks of my life back to the terminal. There I kept trying to remember all those things Coach Camp, my high school football coach, used to tell us. There is no disgrace in being down, the disgrace is in not getting up. It isn't the size of the dog in the fight, it's the size of the fight in the dog. You can be outscored, but not defeated.

Well, I was feeling defeated. I trudged back and with every passing minute I knew the press plane was closer to London. I had not even begun to focus on the possible seriousness of my predicament. A gate was about to clang shut in a closed society. I had no passport, not much money, and no longer the protection of Air Force One. I didn't see this as being a very good career move.

Part of the shame was, I was not exactly the most popular reporter around the Nixon White House. I also knew I had my detractors around CBS, some of them for political reasons. The ones who thought I wasn't especially equipped to be the White House correspondent now had some fuel.

Inside the terminal, I glanced at the big board, indicating what planes were going where, and said, hello, what's this? A flight leaving for Rome in about twelve minutes on Yugoslav Airlines. Hot damn. Back in action. I knew the agent at the counter would ask for a passport. I didn't even have a reservation. So as nonchalantly as I could, I walked up to the counter, sporting a beard a day and a half old, and told them my sister was bringing my passport to the gate. I flashed my White House pass. They knew what I didn't at the time: Let's not get into a fight with this guy; someone will deal with him later. The usual Communist efficiency. So I bought a ticket and the agent said, "I'm going to send somebody to the gate and tell them to check your passport."

I walked to the gate and started thinking and planning. I had flown around the world, knew the procedures, didn't have a seat assignment. So I hovered in the background. Just before they closed the door, I came rushing up, all out of breath, and showed them my ticket. The gate agent looked at it, sort of fidgety, said nothing, and I boarded the plane. The plane is 85 percent full and I'm afraid someone will hear my heart calling Kong to the walls.

They closed the door and the plane took off and I said, under my breath, "Thank you, Lord." We began to climb, then leveled off, and the stewardess came back and asked if I would like a drink. *Would I like a drink?* So I began to relax and mentally count the hours. We would get to Rome in no time and I would find a phone. I would have missed a day in London, but that was no calamity. Mind you, we were a two-man team and my backup was Bob Pierpoint, a classy guy, not someone you had to worry about covering your back. I *was* worried about one CBS executive who, it turned out, was going to join us in London.

The flight to Rome had a stop in Dubrovnik, but at the time I didn't give it a thought. I had never heard of the place. When we started to land, I looked at a map and saw it was on the Adriatic coast. I asked someone if this was a scheduled stop. They said it was. I told myself, don't panic, steady, just stay on the plane.

We landed, and after a while there was a request in Yugoslavian and English for all passengers to get off the plane. I buried my head in a magazine, but the stewardess said, "Sir, I'm sorry, you have to get off."

I said, "But I'm going to Rome."

She said, "Yes, but you will be in transit."

The exit was at the rear of the plane and I immediately spotted the soldiers with automatic weapons. They were checking passports. This might or might not have been standard procedure—I had no way of knowing. Maybe they were doing spot checks for a week, a day, for this flight. I looked around and ducked into the lavatory. By now, I was at least in the category of being a suspicious character. The stewardess knocked on the door and called out, sweetly: "Sir, oh, sir."

I said, "Just a moment." When I came out, I was wiping my face with a paper towel, mumbling that I didn't feel well, kind of woozy, had been with President Nixon. White House. Television. Why don't I sit here for a moment and collect myself?

"No, no, sir. You must go down the stairs."

At the foot of the ladder, one of the guards asked for my passport. I said, "Well, I have a problem there. You see, I'm an American citizen . . ." And that was as far as I got. With a guard holding me under each arm, I was whisked to a small, windowless room, with bare walls except for a large picture of Marshal Tito.

"Where is your passport?" I was asked.

I said, "I can explain."

"We are not interested. Either you have a passport or you do not."

Hard to argue with that kind of logic. They asked where my luggage was, and I told them it was still on the plane. They went aboard and searched my carry-on bag and my Gurkha bag. Minutes later, the police arrived and I was told that I was under arrest. As we drove away from the airport, heading for the police station in downtown Dubrovnik, I heard the plane for Rome taking off. Squirrels were playing soccer in the pit of my stomach.

We reached the police station at about 10:30 or 11:00 in the morning. I sat there for the next four and a half hours, the conversation consisting of a police sergeant telling me at intervals, "Sit down and shut up."

I asked to go to the rest room, and a guard went with me. Now I was in the hands of the bureaucracy and I had a feeling close to hopelessness. I asked to speak to the officer in charge. "Sit down and shut up," I was told. Eventually, I was taken in to see the chief of that precinct, and damned if I didn't notice first thing that his breath stank of the same plum brandy that had indirectly led me to this sorry state of affairs.

For the first time, I was able to tell my story. Then he nodded at me and the two guards led me out into the hall and to a seat on a hard wooden bench. I sat there for three more hours.

It occurred to me that I needed to do something more creative. Only Frau Schultz knew that I had left for the airport. Unbeknownst to me, she was still in Belgrade, trying to make a little noise. She had covered for me wonderfully, said I had been taken ill, which wasn't that far from the truth. At the same time, she was trying to raise a few alarm bells. When the press plane and the backup flights got to London and I wasn't on them, she began to call all her contacts in Europe.

Although I had no way of knowing that Frau Schultz was working that end, I decided to make a fuss of my own. I knew that could go one of two ways. I could wind up with a knot on my head in a jail cell, or they could decide to let me talk to someone higher up on the food chain.

I told the precinct chief that I was through talking to him. "I want to talk to the chief of police," I said, "and I want to see him now. I have shown you, and I am showing you one more time, my official White House pass. I am with the official White House party. I have asked you repeatedly to contact the American embassy in Belgrade. If you do not take me to someone in authority, your job and the job of everybody around here will be in a world of trouble. I have met Marshal Tito. I have met the head of the Yugoslavian KGB"—and at that time I knew his name. It was a stretch, but I had been part of the pool that went with President Nixon when he posed for pictures with Tito, and the head of the Yugoslavian secret police was there.

I faulted myself for not having done this sooner. At the mention of Tito and the secret police, they began to confer, and would throw some side glances my way. After a while, the precinct chief said, "As you know, we have said all along, if you want to speak to someone at the American Embassy . . ."

Of course, they hadn't said that even once, but I figured now I was going to get my one phone call. And if I could get through to Frau Schultz, one call does it all. I knew darned well she would not leave Belgrade without knowing my whereabouts. But I was reluctant to call her. Having made these lofty statements, I couldn't back down, so I asked for the number of the American Embassy.

The clock was running. By now it was nighttime, and the eighteenth assistant attaché was on duty. I tried to explain who I was. He was very doubtful that he was speaking to Dan Rather or that the call was on the up-and-up. I was trying not to hit a high C. I begged him not to hang up. No matter who he thought I was, I asked him to get on another phone and call Frau Schultz and then get me the ambassador or the head of the KGB—I threw out the name—"because I'm not kidding, I'm in trouble here."

And in that maddening, typical American fashion, he said, "I don't respond to threats."

I wanted to climb through the phone and wring his weasely neck, but I stayed calm, and for whatever reason he called Frau Schultz. I knew there had been a breakthrough when the chief came in and inquired if I would like some tea. I said, "I just want to get the hell out of here."

He said, "Of course, you're free to go. I'm sorry you were detained. We have policies that . . ."

I did not hear the end of the sentence. I was out the door and hailing a taxi, and told him to take me straight to the airport. It was now past eleven o'clock at night and the airport was virtually deserted. There was no activity on the tarmac and none in the terminal, except for the guys with the waxers buffing the floors. I counted one person working in the coffee shop and two or three others at the counter.

I checked the arrival and departure board. There was one flight to Rome, but not until morning, so I walked into the coffee shop. It occurred to me that I hadn't eaten since the night before, with the exception of a day-old piece of bread I was given during my stay at the local jail. What, they quit serving gruel?

I ordered a cup of coffee and thought about calling London. I wanted to tell Pierpoint, or anyone with CBS, that I was coming. But I couldn't suck up the nerve to call because I was too embarrassed to say, "I need help." That was another mistake.

The lady from the coffee shop was doing her inventory, a woman maybe in her mid-thirties, tall, thin, hair back in a bun, clothes rather drab—but in those days not a lot of choice. She glanced at me curiously. So I offered a wan smile and asked if she spoke English. I was not surprised when she said, "Yes, I once taught English."

I had found myself a Yugoslavian version of Mary Poppins, without the music, with a plain but pleasant face. I said, "Well, I'm an American and I'm in a heap of trouble and looking for help." She tensed up the way people do when they think you are going to ask them for money. I said I needed an airplane; was there a charter service here?

I knew there wasn't, but I was hoping for any sort of small plane that might get me to any somewhat larger city. She said, "We have the tourist charters, but they don't leave until the morning." I soon learned that the tours were operated by a man named Freddie Laker, of later no-frills fame when he ran his discount charters between New York and London. Back then, in the early 1970s, he had gotten his start with charters to the coast of Yugoslavia.

She was visibly unsure of who I was or what my intentions were.

She stared at me and repeated the single most important words she knew: "If you have no ticket, you're not supposed to be on this flight."

I said, "Yes, I know that, but I will explain to the captain or I will explain to you."

After a slight hesitation, she said, "Okay, but you will have to wait a minute." She signaled another stewardess and told her to get the captain. "We have a little problem here."

The captain came and was quite polite. I repeated my litany: "I am not trouble. All I ask of you is to have somebody radio the U.S. Embassy, tell them I'm aboard and ask them to send somebody to meet this plane. You will have no immigration problem, I can assure you. I'm in your custody and if you'd like to search me, you may."

He looked at my White House press pass. I showed him my CBS identification card, my Washington, D.C., police card, and my American Express card. Basically, he took the attitude that he didn't want to know any more about this than he already did. It might be trouble. He said he wanted me to sit up front, in the jump seat, and told the stewardess to keep an eye on me.

Then the second officer came around and said, "We have been in contact with London. Someone from your embassy will meet you." They said not another word to me the rest of the flight. I could almost read their minds. They were concerned about the fact that I had been able to sneak aboard. They were afraid this intruder might cost them time and piles of paperwork.

It was, of course, a very strange scene, one that wouldn't happen today. If a guy jumped into the aisle with his hands up on a flight in 1994, there would be panic on the plane and the pilot would put down at the nearest airport. I'm not sure the other passengers knew, cared, or asked what was going on. We landed. I stepped off the plane and was met by a rep from the White House transportation office. I looked back to wave my thanks to the pilot and crew, and everyone had their backs to me. The guy who met me just shook his head, and got his jaw in the one-quarter-open position. I cut him off. "Bob Manning, don't open your mouth. Don't say a word."

Halfway into town, I leaned back and said, "Now, Bob, I'm prepared to talk. How bad is it?"

He said, "Everybody feels like hell."

I wasn't expecting that answer. "No," I said.

"Yes," he insisted. He named my roommate, who should have

awakened me. He said, "Your producer tried to get us not to take off, but we were already taxiing. We thought you had probably made the zoo plane. We were halfway to London before we contacted the other pilots and realized you were not on any plane. The only problem for you may be this CBS executive who showed up in London. He was doing some bitching about you."

I said, "Well, do me a favor. Get me my damned passport. Take me anyplace where I can take a quick bath and borrow a clean shirt." We went to his room in the hotel where the White House staff was staying, and a few minutes later I walked into the press room, smiling and nodding and saying hello.

There was a little burst of light applause. Bob Pierpoint rushed up with a big smile and said, "Boy, am I glad to see you. How the hell did you get here?"

I said, "It's a long story. You don't want to know how long. Give me a quick fill and let's go to work."

I gave my roomie a cold shoulder for the rest of the day. I was mad and he knew it. I accepted my reprimand from the CBS executive, agreed that there was no excuse, none, for missing a plane. Then I called Dick Salant, the president of the News Division in New York, and started to apologize. Dick said, "You don't need to apologize. These things happen. But I'd like to hear the full story when you get back." And he did.

In the end, the bottom line was that I had lost a day. Only a very few ever knew what actually happened. Bob Mead, an extraordinary producer and observer of the human species, was one of the few who actually understood it. He and I have joked about it many times over the years. Mead put out the word that Rather had cut away to work on something special. It wouldn't be on the air anytime soon—like, in the next twenty years.

My worst fears were not realized. Despite the fierce and sometimes cutthroat competition, my peers and colleagues in the press corps were overwhelmingly sympathetic—whatever had happened. The transportation people felt bad because their job is to get you there. My co-workers at CBS kept sidling up and telling me of the times they'd missed a flight and had been stranded. I began to adopt a philosophy. They hand you a bible and a minute-to-minute schedule, and if you don't violate either one you won't ever miss a plane. But you won't experience much, either.

I telexed a check and a nice note to the kind lady in the coffee shop, but never heard back. Still, when I think of Yugoslavia, and remember that night, I think of the Tennessee Williams line about depending on "the kindness of strangers."

In two or three days we were back in New York. I had borrowed some clothes and bought some clothes to get me through the week. I had left my carry-on bag containing three suits, shirts, ties and underwear, and my dopp kit at the airport in Dubrovnik.

outtake

Malik

MANY THINGS HAVE NOT CHANGED IN THE FORMER YUGOSLAVIA. You can still meet friendly people, offering a warm welcome to a traveler, no matter the political circumstances that may grip the country.

In Sarajevo in August 1993, I met a boy named Malik. He was nine. He was paraplegic. An artillery shell made him so: 122-millimeter. It was fired at close range. In artillery terms, point-blank range.

Malik was at breakfast in his home. It was just before school. Malik remembers the shell's scream. It crashed through the roof and ceiling thunderously. Then it exploded. The shell was more than a foot long. When it erupted, heavy hot metal filled the room with a quick lethal blizzard of jagged shrapnel. It burned and tore into Malik. His family remembers his screams. His mother hears them in her dreams, every night.

Malik was near death in the blood-and-metal hell-box his mother's kitchen had become. He was rushed to the hospital. The hospital itself had been hit by artillery and mortar fourteen times in recent months. Its sterilization room had been struck. So had its operating theater. The hospital was without running water and electricity much of the time.

Doctors operated by candlelight. They did their best. They saved Malik. He is now a paraplegic. He may be one forever.

By the time I arrived, nine thousand civilians had been killed in the siege of Sarajevo. About two thousand of them were children. Many thousands more children had been maimed. And Malik was one of them, because politicians and generals, supported by self-described intellectuals and theoreticians, far away in Belgrade and elsewhere, decided that Malik was of the "wrong" race, his parents of the "wrong" religion. Because of this, Malik was made a paraplegic.

Malik was excited to have visitors from America, and he mustered a weak smile in the sunlight of midmorning. It was a welcome I won't forget.

THIRTEEN

The Weapon in the Box

I HAVE BEEN DESCRIBED IN PRINT AS SOMEONE WITH A "NEVER-END-ing, consuming passion for news: what's news, what's going to be news, what's not news, what could be news, does anyone else have the same news, and how to keep it clean."

That description is dead solid perfect. I embody all of that and to a fault. When I stand back from myself, I think about how tiresome and boring it must be for anyone near me who doesn't share this addiction. Maybe not boring. By *definition,* news can't be boring or it isn't news.

In many ways, my career at CBS has been a puzzlement. I was tagged as too intense to be an anchorman, too inclined to get into a confrontation over the odd event, too bull-headed. Yet more than a dozen years have passed since I succeeded Walter Cronkite and, to the surprise of many, myself included, I am still here.

It is true that during that time, I have been guilty of several mis-judgments, but never of overconfidence. I have run scared. And if CBS had decided at any point that I was no longer needed, I would have walked away without a whimper. How close I have come to this actually happening, I cannot say. Probably closer than I care to know.

But I am among the blessed few who get to make a living acting out their childhood dream. I make no apology for how corny that may sound. Anchoring the news is a peculiar world of makeup and hair and the right necktie. You are under a huge magnifying glass, aware at all times that if the sun catches that glass at the wrong angle it can burn you to a crisp in a nanosecond.

Over these last thirteen years or so, we have gone through some ups and downs, TV news, CBS, and I. CBS survived hostile take-over attempts by Ted Turner and by the religious right, egged on by Senator Jesse Helms, witnessed the birth of an all-news cable net-work, and fell from grace in the eternal ratings battles.

By the end of 1988, NBC had been dominant for about four years. Its prime-time entertainment programs were sweeping the boards. A week didn't go by in 1988 that NBC didn't have fifteen of the top twenty entertainment shows. Some weeks CBS had one or two in the top twenty, usually *Murder, She Wrote* and *60 Minutes.*

As the 1989 calendar year started, CBS News was hanging on to first place, in spite of budget restraints and staff cutbacks and a morale problem that was rampant throughout the network but al-most at critical mass in our division. I am as proud of that first-place distinction as I am of anything in my career, even though I can't explain it, which may say something right there about the va-garies of television news. Tom Bettag pointed out that no network had ever before been first in the evening news and third in prime time.

By way of acknowledging this defiance of gravity, I was sum-moned to the aerie of the late William Paley. He was then eighty-seven and trying to renew his grip on the network he had founded. The effort wasn't working. Still, I felt the same sense of wonder I always felt when I walked into the only totally black granite sky-scraper in New York, at 51 West Fifty-second at Avenue of the Americas. Black Rock. I took the express elevator to the thirty-fifth floor and took a seat in his outer office, which was cavernous and plush.

I remembered the first time I sat there. I was thirty years old and had recently been made a CBS correspondent. I sat there with Charles Collingwood, Eric Sevareid and David Schoenbrun, Mr. Paley's other luncheon guests, three of "Murrow's Boys" and the network's top correspondents. Now I saw again the same painting I had studied that day, an American Gothic, a scene of industrial Pittsburgh in the early 1930s. I had been in awe that first time, sitting there with people out of the pantheon. I was clearly the new kid. The only reason I had been invited was because Mr. Paley had expressed interest in hearing about Martin Luther King, Jr., whose speeches and marches I had been covering in the South.

Now I was fifty-seven, the new kid no more. I had never in my life called William S. Paley anything but Mr. Chairman or, on occasion, Mr. Paley. I had not seen him in a while, and then he had been in a wheelchair, attended by a nurse. Today, as his secretary waved me into his office, I thought he looked better, stronger. I walked around his desk and shook his hand, and he told me to pull up a chair. He leaned toward me, tapped my knee lightly, in a grandfatherly way, and said, "Tell me what is going in the world. Give me a tour of the horizon."

And we talked. I gave him a rundown on Gorbachev, glasnost, Nelson Mandela's chances of getting out of prison, Israel and the Arabs, our fight with corporate Japan, and what was then forming up as the Bush Cabinet—elected but not yet in office.

He said, "Let's have lunch," and I realized it was only the second time I had ever had lunch alone with him. The other occasion was so he could reprimand me, and, no, it was not after the blackout in Miami. I had expected to get a call then, but I didn't. Instead, it had been shortly after I took over the newscast. He said I had strong eyes, but my failure to smile when I signed off was a negative. I remember telling him I wasn't a natural smiler. He thought my answer was strange, said he had never heard of such a thing. I replied that it was tough for me to pull off a smile that didn't look forced, but I'd try.

Now he was wheeled into the dining room and we continued to talk. Paley liked to gossip. We had a bottle of Iron Horse champagne with our veal piccata, and he said, "You know, for years I wouldn't touch this California stuff because I like only the best and I thought that meant French. I can truthfully say that California wine is among the best in the world."

With Mr. Paley, you always had to ask yourself what this was about. And it all led up this. He raised his glass, clinked his with mine, and said: "The *Evening News* is the only thing left at CBS that's on top now. I don't know why or how it is and neither does anybody else. But take great pride in that. Take time to look around. Take in the view and breathe deeply. You won't be this high very many times in your life."

He was right, of course. There would be darker and more difficult days ahead. I'd seen enough light and shadow in my own life, and I knew he'd seen more than I had. Something a little scary about his prophecy, except the faith that brighter days would follow the dark in turn. He made me think of the cycles of life that had once seen us young and now saw us older, that had brought CBS up and down so many times, that had taken all of broadcasting through countless evolutions and revolutions.

If anybody ever loved broadcasting, it was Mr. Paley. In many ways, Mr. Paley gave birth to broadcasting, but in other ways, it gave life to him. The electricity of radio and television coursed through his veins, and now he seemed to be trying to regain control of his network because he needed it to stay alive. It wasn't just a business to him. What we did on his network mattered to him personally: That's why he'd invited me to lunch.

The News Division had always been special to him. In London during the war, he'd experienced the glamour and necessity of Ed Murrow's reporting, seen the way a reporter could get the attention of a world leader—or, not unimportantly, of a pretty girl. The News Division had given him prestige, made the difference between an electronic sideshow operator and a powerful public figure, and made it possible for him to say with pride that he'd served the public. Now news was the only thing that was still on top at his network. Even he was no longer on top. "Take in the view," he said over his champagne glass.

And so the cycle turned. *ABC World News* was gaining, and had been for most of the 1980s. We saw it as the competition with the most resources.

Heading into the nineties, CBS News underwent yet another change in leadership. We would have four presidents in six years, seven presidents out of nine years. And the ownership had changed for the first time in CBS history, from Mr. Paley to Laurence Tisch. In 1989, Mr. Paley died.

So I had been storing up a few years' worth of observations, and concerns, about the business of news, when I was asked to speak to the Radio and Television News Directors Association and, in particular, to honor the memory of Ed Murrow, Mr. Paley's greatest employee, who had begun the traditions left in my custody. I began with these words from Shakespeare:

> *"Men at some time are masters of their fates:*
> *The fault, dear Brutus, is not in our stars,*
> *But in ourselves . . ."*
>
> Cassius, Julius Caesar,
> Act 1, Scene 2

Of course, it wasn't only Shakespeare I was quoting: Murrow used a line of that speech to conclude a famous broadcast about Senator Joseph McCarthy.

With that quotation hanging in the air, I looked out across my audience, the men and women who directed the news at stations throughout America, meeting now, in late September of 1993, in Miami. A commemorative stamp had been issued in the name of Ed Murrow. And to this group, decades earlier, he had given the best known speech he ever made, the greatest ever by any broadcaster.

As part of my appearance, I had been asked to introduce a videotape tribute to Murrow, the best reporter of his generation. "Almost sixty years after he started—almost thirty years after his death—he is still the best, in broadcasting or print," I said. "He reported, he led, he made the best broadcasts of his time, in radio or television.

"They include the *This Is London* broadcasts during the Battle of Britain, the radio reports from the death camp at Buchenwald, and the television programs on Joseph McCarthy and on the *Harvest of Shame.*

"Edward R. Murrow was not only the patron and founding saint of electronic news and the best-ever practitioner of it. He also set standards for excellence and courage that remain the standards the world over. Murrow was, in short, a hero. But we should, we must, remember this: He was a real, flesh-and-blood, flawed, vulnerable, mistake-making hero.

"With all of his triumphs, many and mighty, he also fought some fights he should not have fought and he sometimes, oftentimes, lost. Including losing at the end. In the end, his bosses and his competitors—inside as well as outside his own network—cut him up, cut him down, and, finally, cut him out.

"And not long after that, he died. Cancer was the cause, they say.

"Murrow made his memorable speech to the news directors not at the dawn, nor at midday, but in the twilight—in Chicago, October 15, 1958. In it, he criticized what commercial television was becoming, and challenged himself, his colleagues—and us, all of us—to do better.

"Ed Murrow said of television: 'This instrument can teach, it can illuminate; yes, and it can even inspire. But it can do so only to the extent that humans are determined to use it to those ends. Otherwise, it is merely wires and lights in a box. There is a great and perhaps decisive battle to be fought against ignorance, intolerance and indifference. This weapon of television could be useful.' "

With those words, the camera flashed upon the screen both a biography and a fond remembrance of Murrow, prepared by Charles Kuralt and producer Bernie Birnbaum. As I watched, I was thinking about Murrow's speech in Chicago in 1958. It was risky, and he knew it; a bold shot, and he knew it. That was part of the Murrow style and part of what has made the Murrow mystique. And so I shared those thoughts with the professional descendants of the people Murrow had addressed thirty-five years earlier:

> [Murrow] began [his 1958] speech with the modest speculation that, "This just might do nobody any good." I don't think Ed Murrow believed that. It was a call to arms—the most quoted line is the one about "wires and lights in a box," but the more important line is "This weapon of television." Ed Murrow had seen all kinds of battles, and if *he* lifted *his* voice in a battle cry, surely some of his own colleagues would hear him and heed him.
>
> As with many television and radio news people of my generation, that speech has crisscrossed the back roads of my memory through a lifetime in the business.
>
> I wasn't in Chicago that night. I was in Houston, serving my apprenticeship in news, a beginner in radio and television. I hadn't met Murrow yet. I could only read about his speech in the newspapers, but I absorbed every word. In my own little Texas bayou and pine tree world of journalism dreams, Murrow became protean, titanic, huge. (I still think that.) There were other great ones: William L. Shirer, Eric Sevareid, Charles Collingwood, and Douglas Edwards; and later Walter Cronkite—men of courage and skill and great intelligence. But Murrow was *their* leader.
>
> As he had been for many others, Murrow had been my hero

when I was just a boy. Across the radio, across the Atlantic, and across half the United States, his voice came, the deep rumble and the dramatic pause just when he said, "THIS . . . is London." I never got that voice out of my head. It was like a piece of music that has never stopped playing for me. Murrow told me tales of bravery in time of war, tales more thrilling than *Captain Midnight* or *Jack Armstrong* because these were *true.*

He talked about the bravery of soldiers and citizens. He never made a big fuss about his own bravery. But even as a little boy, I knew it took bravery just to stand on that rooftop, with the bombs raining down thunder and lightning all around him . . . or to go up in that plane—"D-for-Dog"—with the ack-ack and the Messerschmitts all about. And I never forgot that Murrow did all this because he wanted me and my family, and all of us back home in America, to know . . . the truth. For *that,* for our knowledge of the truth, he risked his life.

In my mind, then and now, neither Achilles nor King Arthur—not Pecos Bill or Davy Crockett—surpassed a hero like that.

The Murrow I met years later—person to person, if you will—the real Ed Murrow, was everything I wanted that hero to be. He was a quiet man: tall, strong, steady-eyed, not afraid of silence. What separated Ed Murrow from the rest of the pack was courage.

I know what you're thinking. I've gotten into trouble for using the word. Probably deserved it. Maybe I used it inappropriately. Maybe I'm a poor person to talk about it because I have so little myself. But I want to hear the word. I want to hear it praised, and the men and women who have courage elevated.

Ed Murrow had courage. He had the physical courage to face the Blitzkrieg in London and to ride D-for-Dog. He had the professional courage to tell the truth about McCarthyism. And he had the courage to stand before the Radio and Television News Directors Association, and to say some things those good people didn't want to hear, but needed to hear.

In our comfort and complacency, in our (dare we say it?) cowardice, we, none of us, want to hear the battle cry. Murrow had the courage to sound it anyway. And thirty-five years later, however uncomfortable, it's worth pausing to ask—how goes the battle?

In the constant scratching and scrambling for ever better

ratings and money and the boss's praise and a better job, it is
worth pausing to ask—how goes the real war, the really important battle of our professional lives? How goes the battle for
quality, for truth and justice, for programs worthy of the best
within ourselves and the audience? How goes the battle against
"ignorance, intolerance and indifference"? The battle not to be
merely "wires and lights in a box," the battle to make television not just entertaining but also, at least some little slice of
time, useful for higher, better things? How goes the battle?

The answer, we know, is "Not very well." In too many important ways, we have allowed this great instrument, this resource, this weapon for good, to be squandered and
cheapened. About this, the best among us hang their heads in
embarrassment, even shame. We all should be ashamed of
what we have and have not done, measured against what we
could do . . . ashamed of many of the things we have allowed
our craft, our profession, our life's work to become.

Our reputations have been reduced, our credibility cracked,
justifiably. This has happened because too often for too long
we have answered to the worst, not to the best, within ourselves
and within our audience. We are less because of this. Our audience is less, and so is our country.

Ed Murrow had faith in our country and in our country's
decision to emphasize, from the beginning, commercial broadcasting. He recognized commercial broadcasting's potential,
and its superiority over other possibilities. But even as he believed in the strength of market values and the freedom of commercial radio and television, Ed Murrow feared the rise of a
cult that worshiped at the shrine of the implacable idol, Ratings. He feared that the drive to sell, sell, sell—and nothing but
sell—was overwhelming the potential for good, the potential
for service of radio and television.

He decried the hours of prime time as being full of "decadence, escapism and insulation from the realities of the world
in which we live." As you let that sink in, let's remember that
he was talking about programs like *I Love Lucy* and *The
Honeymooners,* that are now esteemed on a par with the best
comedies of Plautus and Molière; Murrow singled out *The Ed
Sullivan Show,* which is now studied and praised as a modern-
day School of Athens, peopled by all the best minds and talent
of the time. These are the programs that had Ed Murrow worried.

He wasn't worried about, didn't live to see, *Full House* or *America's Funniest Home Videos* or *Fish Police.* He wasn't worried about, didn't live to see, the glut of inanities now in "Acess" time. He never lived to see the cynicism and greed that go into the decisions to put on much of that junk.

In 1958, Murrow was worried because he saw a trend setting in: avoiding the unpleasant or controversial or challenging. Shortening newscasts and jamming them with ever-increasing numbers of commercials. Throwing out background, context, and analysis, and relying just on headlines. Going for entertainment values over the values of good journalism, all in the belief that the public must be shielded, wouldn't accept anything other than the safe, the serene, and the self-evident.

Murrow knew that belief was wrong, and contrary to the principles on which this country was founded. He had seen how honest, mature, and responsible American listeners and viewers could be when programming itself was honest, mature, and responsible. Reducing the amount of real-world reality on television, Murrow argued, was unconscionable.

But Murrow did not just offer criticism. He also offered solutions. Importantly, Murrow proposed that news divisions and departments not be held to the same standards of ratings and profits as entertainment and sports. He recognized that news operations couldn't be run as philanthropies. But, he added, "I can find nothing in the Bill of Rights or the Communications Act which says that [news divisions] must increase their net points each year, lest the Republic collapse."

Murrow saw turmoil, danger, and opportunity in the world; and the best means of communicating the realities to the public—the communications innovation called television—was increasingly ignoring the realities. And those few Americans who had been given the privilege of owning and operating television stations and networks, the privilege of making great wealth from them, were beginning to reduce if not downright eliminate their responsibilities to public service.

Private profit from television is fine, but there *should* be a responsibility to news and public service that goes with it; this was the core of Murrow's case.

These were words which needed to be heard, then and now. I thought about coming here tonight—and you might have been better enlightened if I'd done this—to read you verbatim the text of Murrow's speech from 1958. It's a hell of a speech.

Much of it is more true, more dire, more needed now than it was when Murrow said it.

When Murrow spoke to your predecessors, he knew that they were not his problem. The people he wanted to hear and heed his speech were not in that Chicago ballroom. They worked in boardrooms, not newsrooms. Murrow's Chicago speech was a brave, bold bid to persuade corporate executives, both at stations and networks and at the advertising agencies and corporate sponsors.

He failed. Not long afterward, his position inside his own network was diminished. And not long after that, he was out.

Little has changed since Murrow gave that report from the battlefield and issued that call to arms. And much of what has changed has not been for the better. More people in television now than then are doing things that deny the public service of television, that ensure that the mighty weapon of television remains nothing more than wires and lights in a box.

Even the best among decision makers in television freely take an hour that might have been used for a documentary, and hand it over to an "entertainment special" about the discovery of Noah's Ark—that turns out to be a 100 percent hoax.

And the worst among the decision makers have got us all so afraid of our independence and integrity that at least one news director recently planned to have all his hirings reviewed by radical ideological and highly partisan political groups. (And he bragged about it.)

They've got another news director telling his staff that he didn't want stories on the pope's visit—he wanted stories, plural—on Madonna's sex book. It's the ratings, stupid.

And they've got us putting more and more fuzz and wuzz on the air, cop-shop stuff, so as to compete not with other news programs but with entertainment programs (including those posing as news programs) for dead bodies, mayhem, and lurid tales. They tell us international news is considered an expletive best deleted in most local station newsrooms and has fallen from favor even among networks.

Thoughtfully written analysis is out, "live pops" are in. "Action Jackson" is the cry. Hire lookers, not writers. Do powder-puff, not probing, interviews. Stay away from controversial subjects. Kiss ass, move with the mass, and for heaven and the ratings' sake don't make anybody mad—certainly not anybody that you're covering, and especially not the mayor, the governor, the senator, the president or vice president or *anybody* in a position of power. Make nice, not news.

This has become the new mantra. These have become the new rules. The post-Murrow generation of owners and managers have made them so. These people are, in some cases, our friends. They are, in all cases, our bosses. They aren't venal— they're afraid. They've got education and taste and good sense, they care about their country, but you'd never know it from the things that fear makes them do—from the things that fear makes them make *us* do.

It is fear of ratings slippage if not failure, fear that this quarter's bottom line will not be better than last quarter's— and a whole lot better than the same quarter's a year ago. A climate of fear, at all levels, has been created, without a fight. We—you and I—have allowed them to do it, and even helped them to do it.

The climate is now such that, when a few people at one news organization rig the results of a test to get better pictures—and are caught and rightly criticized—there is no rejoicing that a terrible, unusual journalistic practice has been caught, punished, and eradicated. Because we all know that, with only a slight relaxation of vigilance and a slight increase of fear, those journalistic sins could be visited upon us—we know that, as honorable and sensible as we, our friends, and our colleagues try to be—it could happen to us.

Now you would be absolutely justified in saying to me right now—"Excuse me, Mister Big Shot Anchorman, but what the hell do you expect me to do about it? If I go to my boss and talk about television as a weapon, and why don't you take *A Current Affair* or *Hard Copy* or *Inside Edition* off the air next week and let me put on a tell-it-like-it-is documentary about race relations—I *know* they're gonna put me on the unemployment line, and I'll be lucky if they don't put me on the funny farm."

Well, none of us is immune to self-preservation and opportunities for advancement. I'm not asking you for the kind of courage that risks your job, much less your whole career.

Ed Murrow had that kind of courage, and took that kind of risk several times. But you and I, reaching deep down inside ourselves, are unlikely to muster that kind of courage often, if ever.

But there are specific things we can do. They won't cost us

our jobs. But they will make a difference—a start—a warning shot that the battle is about to be joined.

Number one: Make a little noise. At least, question (though protest would be better) when something, anything, incompatible with your journalistic conscience is proposed. When it comes to ethics and the practice of journalism, silence is a killer.

No, you won't always be heeded or heard. And, yes, even to question may be a risk. But it is a wee, small risk, and a tiny price to pay to be worthy of the name "American journalist." To be a journalist is to ask questions. All the time. Even of the people we work for.

Number two: In any showdown between quality and substance on the one hand, and sleaze and glitz on the other, go with quality and substance. You know the difference. Every one of us in this room knows the difference because we've been there. We've all gone Hollywood—we've all succumbed to the Hollywoodization of the news—because we were afraid not to. We trivialize important subjects. We put videotape through a Cuisinart trying to come up with high-speed, MTV-style crosscuts. And just to cover our asses, we give the best slots to gossip and prurience.

But we can say, "No more." We can fight the fear that leads to Showbizification. We can *act* on our knowledge. You know that serious news—local and regional, national and international—doesn't have to be dull, not for one second. People will watch serious news, well written and well produced. The proof—it's all around, but I'll give you two examples. Look at *Sunday Morning* and *Nightline.* No glitz, no gossip. Just compelling information. You can produce your own *Nightline* or *Sunday Morning*—all that's required of you is determination and thought, taste and imagination. That's what Tom Bettag and Ted Koppel, that's what Linda Mason, Missie Rennie, Charles Kuralt, and their teams bring to work.

Number three: Try harder to get and keep minorities on the air and in off-camera, decision-making jobs. Try—and be determined to succeed.

I know there are market survey researchers who will bring you confusing numbers and tell you they add up to one thing: Your audience wants to see Ken and Barbie, and your audience doesn't want to see African Americans, or Arab Americans, or Latinos, or Asian Americans, or Gays or Lesbians or

Older Americans or Americans with Disabilities. So we give our audience plenty of Ken and Barbie, and we make the minorities we have hired so uncomfortable that they hold back on the perspective, the experience, the intelligence, the talent that they could have offered to make us wiser and stronger.

Those market researchers, with their surveys and focus groups, are playing games with you and me and with this entire country. We actually pay them money to fool us—money that I submit to you could be better spent on news coverage. Their so-called samples of opinion are no more accurate or reliable than my grandmother's big toe was when it came to predicting the weather. Your own knowledge of news and human nature, your own idealism and professionalism, will guide you more surely than any market researcher ever will. You and I know that market research can and often does cripple a newscast—pronto. But the market researchers will keep getting away with their games so long as you and I and the people we work for let them.

If we change the voice and the face of broadcasting, honestly and fairly, on the basis of excellence and ethics, talent and intelligence, we can shatter false and cheap notions about news; we can prove that our audience wants electronic journalism that is ethical, responsible, and of high quality—and that is as diverse, as different, as dynamic as America itself.

There is another thing we all can do, a difference we can make. One Word. More.

Let's do more to think more. Let's bring all the brilliance and imagination this industry has to bear. That's what Ed Murrow was talking about. Let's phase out fear. If we've got an idea, let's not hide it out of fear—the fear of doing things differently, the fear that says, "Stay low, stay silent. They can't fire you if they don't know you're there." That fear runs rampant through the corridors of radio and television today.

The people we work for are more fearful than we are. Fear leads them to depend on thoughtless, lifeless numbers to tell them what fear convinces them are facts. "American audiences won't put up with news from other countries. Americans won't put up with economic news. Americans won't put up with serious, substantive news of any kind."

Bull-feathers. We've gone on too long believing this nonsense. We've bought the lie that information is bad for news. We are told, and we are afraid to disbelieve, that people only want to be entertained. And we have gone so far down the Info-Tainment Trail that we'll be a long time getting back to where we started—if ever.

The more the people we work for believe this kind of nonsense, the less inclined we have been to prove them wrong. We go about our days, going along to get along. The fear factor freezes us. The greatest shortage on every beat, in every newsroom in America, is courage.

I believe, as Ed Murrow did, that the vast majority of the owners—and executives and managers—we work for are good people, responsible citizens, and patriotic Americans. I believe that the vast majority of the people in this room also fit that description. We all know what's at stake. We know that our beloved United States of America depends on the decisions we make in our newsrooms every day.

In the end, Murrow could not bring himself to believe that the battle about which he spoke so eloquently could be won. He left the electronic journalism he helped to create—believing that most, if not all, was already lost, that electronic news in America was doomed to be completely and forever overwhelmed by commercialism and entertainment values.

About that, I hope, I believe, Murrow was wrong. What is happening to us and our chosen field of work does not have to continue happening. The battle is dark and odds-against. But it is not irreversible—not yet. To prevent it from being so requires courage.

A few, just a few, good men and women with courage—the courage to practice the idealism that attracted most of us to the craft in the first place—can make a decisive difference. We need a few good men and women, with the courage of their convictions, to turn it around. We can be those men and women. If the people in this room tonight simply agreed, starting tomorrow, to turn it around—we would turn it around. What is required is courage.

I don't have to tell you, you already know, but it is important for me to say it to you anyway—I haven't always had that courage. I said earlier that to talk about Ed Murrow before you tonight was humbling. And perhaps that's true most of all in this respect: It is humbling to realize how little courage I have, compared to Murrow, who had so much, and how many opportunities I have already wasted.

But tomorrow is a new day. We toil and are proud to be in

this craft because of the way Edward R. Murrow brought it into being. We can be worthy of him—we can share his courage—or we can continue to work in complacency and fear.

Cassius was right: "Men at some time are masters of their fates: The fault, dear Brutus, is not in our stars, but in ourselves . . ."

The initial reaction was stunned silence, an almost robotic applause as I finished my remarks: "We're supposed to clap now."

I guess the audiences at RTNDA conventions expect to hear a lot of self-congratulation and blather. When you go back over Murrow's speech from 1958, it's hard to believe that anything so straightforward and sensible caused so many ripples and forced Murrow out of broadcasting. His most radical proposal was that Americans establish something which sounds a lot like PBS, and once you've seen PBS, that proposal doesn't seem radical at all.

My remarks weren't as eloquent as Murrow's—maybe not even so straightforward and sensible—but they were tougher than what many people expected. (One colleague asked, as I entered the auditorium that night, if I planned to regale the crowd with "funny Texas stories.") Now, as people absorbed what I'd said, what I'd tried to say, and why I'd said it, the immediate response was respectful, but not what you'd call enthusiastic.

My assistant was in the audience. He'd spent a lot of his youth working in the theater, and had seen plenty of standing ovations. A standing ovation, he says, starts with three or four people and then builds until everybody's up on their feet. But on the night of September 29, in Miami, the audience clapped dutifully for about thirty seconds—and then, as Bill Madison remembers, they rose all at once—as if they all understood at the same time and, whoosh, they were on their feet.

This is a flattering recollection that I can't actually verify: I was already halfway out the door. But they brought me back into the ballroom to see a genuine standing ovation, a warm and supporting gesture from the men and women I'm proud to call colleagues.

Outside the auditorium, it was pandemonium. Joe Peyronnin, a vice president of CBS News, ran forward and gave me a great big bear hug. Erik Sorenson grabbed me by the hand. Old friends and people I'd never seen before swarmed around, all asking questions and shouting things. The hotel's security surrounded me and started hustling me to my car. A young reporter from the Comedy Central Network tried to interview me on camera—I'm still not sure why she thought I'd be funny, at that moment or any other.

Starting almost immediately, we heard a variety of reactions. Not all of them were good. Murrow had expected to be accused of "fouling [his] own comfortable nest," and so had I—and I was. But most people, television critics, viewers, and my colleagues in the craft, understood what I was saying and why I felt it needed saying—especially to the specific group to whom it was said. I had offered criticism (and self-criticism first of all) only because it was important to stress exactly *why* it was so necessary that we return to the ideals and the idealism that brought us to journalism in the first place. Reporters from local stations and other networks called and wrote: "Right on, Dan," and that sort of thing. Some magazines and newspapers, from the *Miami Herald* to the Santa Rosa, California, *Democrat,* printed long verbatim portions of the talk—in a few places the whole thing was reprinted. C-Span carried the speech live when it was first delivered, and repeated it on tape in full for several days. And we had calls and letters from many viewers, including some who hadn't been viewers of CBS before then: "If that's the way Dan really feels, then his broadcast is the one for me," one said. In calling for higher standards in the product we offer, I'd struck a chord among those we are supposed to serve: a useful reminder that the audience would prefer *not* to be treated as if they were dumb and uncaring.

Within the Broadcast Center, friends and co-workers stopped me in the hall or came to my office, brought little notes (a few even sent flowers—whether as congratulations or condolences, I'm not sure!). One had tears in her eyes, and tried to explain: She'd gone a long time believing that the network didn't *want* for her to do her best, believing that there was no room or budget anymore for excellence, and the certainty that her best efforts wouldn't be appreciated had taken a toll.

The response from the rank and file inside CBS was overwhelmingly positive. It was humbling and in many ways made me ashamed, remorseful that I hadn't done my job better over the years, that I hadn't been a better leader, and regretful that I'd made so many big mistakes.

But the response from management was a little different. Not from Larry Tisch, the head of CBS, Inc. He never said a word to me about the talk, and if he ever said anything to anybody else, it never reached my ears. He may or may not have appreciated what I said, but I guess he respected my reasons for saying it and my right to say it. Not every head of every corporation would have felt that way. I appreciated that more than he may have known. What the president of CBS Broadcast Group, Howard Stringer, said publicly was also appreciated; without approving of all that I said, he was understanding.

Unfortunately, a very few in management below the top privately chose to hear the criticism as a personal attack. Some others chose simply to hear the criticism and ignore the plea for improvement. Some of them treated it simply as "Dan in one of his moods," instead of Dan trying to stick up for what he believes in, mood or no mood, every day of his life. A lot of egos were involved, certainly, and a couple suggested that they'd have felt better if they'd seen a text of the speech before it was delivered (although what that kind of supervision by managerial committee would have done to the content of the speech, I don't like to think—Eric Sevareid's remark about being "nibbled to death by ducks" comes to mind).

It's true I'd held the speech close to my vest all the way: Up until the day before I delivered my remarks, only Jean and the person who'd typed my nearly illegible notes had any clear idea what I was groping to put together, and I shared the text in its close-to-final draft with only three others before I walked into the ballroom in Miami. As I came into the ballroom, only I knew exactly what I was going to say, only I had the precise final speech, with the changes I had made in the car on the way over. But this wasn't just the worry that word would leak out or that somebody would try to talk me out of speaking from my heart. The truth is that the words I wanted to speak were so personal, so very much from and of my heart and my experience, that I didn't want to share them until I was ready. And I wasn't absolutely certain to share them the way I'd prepared them until just before I walked up to the microphone.

I haven't worked in journalism for more than forty-five years without caring how the work is done. My work is important to me, and the work that's done by others around me is important to me. Not only because I'm a professional, but because I'm an American.

I've been to countries where the people don't have a free press, where reporters with strict professional standards are thrown in jail or killed. It's sobering to pick up a paper and read nothing but the ruling-party line, to turn on the television and see, instead of an anchor, the rough equivalent of a government spokesperson. Those Americans who believe the American "Media" is biased, would do well to sample the newspapers, radio, and television of other countries. Nothing is left up to the journalists or the audience. All the tough decisions are made in advance: What's left for "news" is prescreened, preapproved, predigested, a simplified view of limited scope, only that part of the truth that somebody else wants you to know.

Through the years, Edward R. Murrow and other dedicated, responsible American journalists have believed the American people were mature enough and wise enough to handle the truth. That belief is one I fervently share. It got me into journalism, it's kept me in journalism, and it'll keep me here as long as I have my health and a story to report.

outtake

Happily Ever After

THE WEEKEND BEFORE VALENTINE'S DAY, 1994, YOUR REPORTER went to a wedding. My young friend Suzanne Meirowitz found the man of her dreams, Bob Nederlander, and had a storybook wedding. Suzanne couldn't have looked prettier, Bob couldn't have looked prouder, and together they were as happy as anyone I've ever seen, surrounded by loving family and friends. Outside there were cold and snow, one of the worst snowstorms of the impossibly snowy winter, but inside was a scene as warm and romantic as you could hope for.

I wish I could tell Suzanne it will always be so—and every wedding, don't you always think, "Maybe, maybe *this* time for *these* lovers it *will* always be so—maybe the joys of this moment can translate to a lifetime of love and happiness right out of the story-books'"?

But the storybooks almost always stop just *before* the wedding. Suzanne looked like a storybook princess—like Snow White, in fact—but you never find out how Snow White handled a career and raising kids. Snow White would've become Queen, you know—she *would* have had a career. You never find out how Snow White faced down the killer flu that swept through her whole family when she'd got a big report due at the office the next day. You never find out how Snow White and Prince Charming settled disagreements or what happened on days when Prince Charming . . . *wasn't.*

That weekend, at Bob and Suzanne's wedding, the rabbi said a lot of good things: about patience, about sticking out the tough times just the way we'd stuck out the snow. And having a clergy-man at a wedding does relieve even anchormen from the need to deliver advice and opinions to newlyweds. But you want young couples to learn, to have an easier time than you did. You want to be able to say that magic something that will let the storybook go on forever.

And then you remember that there is no magic in it. There's patience. There's sticking out the tough times. Just as the rabbi said. And there's togetherness, knowing that I'd never have been able to stick out the tough times if Jean hadn't been right there, patiently sticking them out beside me.

But there's also *dancing*—and for my newlywed friends on that Valentine's Day, that would have been my best gift. I'd tell my friends to take a minute to dance together whenever you can. At the wedding, I took a spin around the floor with my own dancing part-ner for most of four decades. And in my eyes, Jean wore glass slip-pers and a golden gown—a storybook bride all over again.

Real life is hard on storybook love. But sometimes the dreams really do come true.

The Men and Women of CBS News

JOURNALISM IS A COLLABORATIVE PROCESS, AND EVERY ONE OF OUR adventures is the result of the hard work and caring of dozens of people: producers, camera and sound operators, writers, researchers, technicians, managers, administrative staff, and all the rest. Without them, my work would go invisible, inaudible, and incomplete.

By necessity, the following list can only approximate a full accounting of all of the people who have contributed to my adventures. It was especially difficult for me to check the names of free-lancers and the crews working from overseas bureaus; I regret each and every omission. But I am proud to have worked with all of those here named and many others at CBS News in recent years.

MARY AARON

VICTOR ABALOS

DAVID ABBATE

K. R. ABDUS-SALAAM

FOUAD AJAMI

TARIF AL-AZEM

BOB ALBERTSON

SUZANNE ALLEN

MOSHE ALPERT

ALLEN ALTER

CYNTHIA ALTMAN

MARA ALTSCHULER

ROBERTO ALVAREZ

MANNY ALVAREZ

JOHN AMATO

ANDREA AMIEL

BOB ANDERSON

TOM ANDERSON

JIM ANDERSON

CRAIG ANDERSON

BOB ANGELELLI

HOWARD ARENSTEIN

BARBARA ARMSTRONG

INGRID ARNESEN

HAL ARONOW-THEIL

STEPHEN ARONSON

FRANCES ARVOLD

PENELOPE ASHMAN

RALPH AVIGLIANO

JAMES AVIS

SAMI AWAD

BOB BAHR

KEVIN BAILEY

MARGARET BAILEY

MARGERY BAKER

AL BARGAMIAN

AUBREY BARNARD

BOB BARRY

GAIL BARSKY

NEIL BARUCH

BONNIE BELLAMY

TERRI BELLI

CRAIG BENGSTON

VALENTINE BENSON

VICTORIA BENSON

CHARLOTTE BENSON

SCOTT BERGER

RANDY BERGMAN

AL BERMAN

JOE BERMEJO

JOEL BERNSTEIN

TOM BERTOLINO

STEVE BESNER

TOM BETTAG

ANN BIESTER

KATHLEEN BIGGINS

NANCY BILLIK

AMY BIRNBAUM

BERNIE BIRNBAUM

SISSEL BJERKE

CARL BLENCOWE

HUNTER BLOCH

PETER BLUFF

KATHLEEN BOLAND

NANCY BOLLING

GERMAN BONEFONT

TONY BORRELLO

KARL BOSTIC

GAVIN BOYCE

TOM BRADFORD

JAY BRENNAN

JAMES BRENNAN

LES BREWER

LESLIE BREY

RAY BRIBIESCA

AL BRIGANTI

FRANCOIS BRINGER

DAVID BROWN

DAVID BROWNING

PAUL BRUIN

JENNIFER BUKSBAUM

DAVID BUKSBAUM

PAT BUTLER

PAUL CABLE

ANNE CADEL

MIKE CADMAN

JUAN CALDERA

JACKIE CAMERON

JOE CANAVAN

SUSAN CARAHER

DAVID CARAVELLO

TERESA CARDENAS

LINNEA CARLSON

SHLOMO CARMON

SUSAN CARTER

MARILYN CARUTHERS

MAUREEN CASHIN

ALAN CASSELL

ANDY CATER

MARTHA CAUST-MORAN

AMY CHACON

JULIANNA CHALLENOR

MABLE CHAN

TOBY CHANDLER

ROY CHASE

LE JEN CHEN

CLAIRE CHIAPPETTA

ANDREW CHILDS

BETTY CHIN

GEORGE CHRISTIAN

DAVID CIFRINO

JERRY CIPRIANO

MARK CLARK

ANDY CLARKE

CHARLES CLARKSON

PAUL CLAXTON

RUTH CLEMENTS

JIMMY CLEVENGER

AL COBY

BARBARA COCHRAN

ELLIOT COHEN

RICHARD COHEN

MICHAEL COLE

TOM CONNOR

MARSHA COOKE

LARRY COOPER

LORI COOPER

VICTOR COOPER

LILA CORN

ALEXANDRA COSGROVE

TOM COSGROVE

LAURA COVERSON

LISA COX

THOMAS CRAVEN

BILL CRAWFORD

MICHAEL CREAN

GEN. GEORGE CRIST

KENNETH CROSS

BEBE CROUSE

SPENCER CRUMP

TIM CULP

P. G. CUONG

GLEN DACY

MARK DALY

ED DANKO

KATE D'ARCY

RONNEE DAVID

NANCY DAY

WALLY DEAN

MARIO DECARVALHO

DON DECESARE

ANDRE DEGRUY

GILBERT DEIZ

FRED DEL TORO

ANGELO DELUCIA

THOMAS DEMANIK

ELLEN DENTON

GAYLE DEPOLI

TRUSTUM DEVOE

WIM DEVOS

KEVIN DEYO

JANE DGEBUADZE

RICH DIEFENBACH

DARCEL DILLARD-SUITE

ARLENE DILLON

DENNIS DILON

PAT DILORENZO

CYNTHIA DINAN

JUDY DOLAN

GEORGE DOLAN

P. K. DON

TOM DONAHUE

CHRIS DONAHUE

DAVID DONOVAN

DAVID DORSETT

LARRY DOYLE

ELIZABETH DRIBBEN

AMBROSE DUBEK

JOE DUENAS

RAMONA DUNN

BOB DUNN

PETER DUNNIGAN

BRUCE DUNNING

MARY BETH DURKIN

LINDA DYER

LISA EDMISTON

JOHN EGGER

KENNETH EINHORN

BRIAN ELLIS

STUART EMENY

LOUIS ENAMORADO

PEGGY ENG

BOB ENRIONE

BOB EPSTEIN

MARGARET ERSHLER

AMNON EVENTOV

CHRIS EVERSON

MIA FABIUS

JEFF FAGER

DAVID FAIRWEATHER

MARK FARRINGTON

KAREN FARRIS

JEFF FASSINO

MICHAEL FAULKNER

STEVE FELDBERG

BILL FELLING

KEVIN FINNEGAN

VINCE FINOCCHIARO

PAUL FISCHER

HAL FISHER

DAVE FITZPATRICK

GAYLE FITZPATRICK

ALICIA TANZ FLAUM

PATRICIA FLETCHER

VINCENT FORESTA

JOE FORMATO

ED FOUHY

MICHAEL FOUNTAIN

JIMMY FOX

MICKEY FOX

JESSICA FRANK

STEVE FRANKEL

GARY FRIEDMAN

DAVID FRIFIELD

ROBIN FRITH

ALAN FRUTKIN

HAL FURMAN

BILL GALBRAITH

HUXLEY GALBRAITH

RUSS GAMMELL

JONATHAN GARBER

HARRIET GARBER

MANNY GARCIA

LIN GARLICK

KENT GARRETT

GAYANA GASHIAN

ROSEMARY GASSON

ANDY GATTO

JULIE GAUTIER

MIKE GAVSHON

MATTHEW GEERS

DAVID GELBER

MICHAEL GEORGE

KEN GERAGHTY

GENE GERLACH

MARK GIBBERT

CLARENCE GIBBONS

CORKY GIBBONS, SR.

Corky Gibbons, Jr.

Laurie Giesen

Joan Gilbertson

Phil Gillespie

Carl Ginsburg

Benson Ginsburg

Luigi Giuliani

Hinda Glasser

Steve Glauber

Sima Glickman

Franz Goess

Harvey Goldberg

Alan Golds

Mike Goldsmith

Vince Gonzales

Rene Gonzalez

Kyle Good

Peter Goodman

Tom Goodman

Frank Governale

Michael Gray

Bob Green

David Green

Joe Griffin

Richard Griffiths

Gary Grist

Beatrix Gruber

Ron Hagler

Joe Halderman

Cynthia Hand

Mark Harrington

John Harris

Neville Harris

Rome Hartman

Renee Hartman

Suzuko Hashimoto

Dennis Hatton

Brian Healy

Hugh Heckman

Gavri Hefer

Lance Heflin

Saul Held

Jim Helling

Clara Hemphill

Olga Henkel

Marcia Henning

Zeeva Herman

Mike Hernandez

Yacov Hershkovitaz

Dierdre Hester

Andrew Heyward

Tony Higgins

Lori Hillman

Thanong Hirunsi

P. B. Hoan

Kurt Hoeffler

Al Holder

Dwight Holland

Roberta Hollander

Tom Honeysett

Cookie Hood

Mark Hooper

DON HOOPER

MIKE HOOVER

TESSA HORAN

BOB HORNER

LASLO HORVATH

TIM HOULIHAN

SHARON HOUSTON

JOSH HOWARD

JACK HUBBARD

REGGIE HUFF

JOHN HUIE

CHRIS HULME

TOM HURXTHAL

HIROSHI IIZUKA

SUSIE INABA

TOM INESON

LUZ INTINTOLI

GEORGE IOANNIDES

MIKIO ITASAKA

JACQUELINE JABARA

STEVE JACKSON

BERNARD JACOBS

STEVE JACOBS

MIKE JACOBSON

JEFF JAMES

RONNIE JAMES

BROOKE JANIS

RAUL JARAMILLO

SIMON JARVIS

ARNE JENSEN

TOM JESTER

HENRY JOHNSON

DICK JOHNSON

DOUG JOHNSON

CLIFFORD JOHNSON

WARREN JONES

TYRONE JONES

DENNIS JONES

PERRY JONES

WENDY JONES

LYNNE JORDAL

ADRIENE JORDAN

GORDON JOSELOFF

RANDY JOYCE

LONNIE JULI

GREG KANDRA

JONATHAN KAPLAN

ROZ KARSON

MARK KATKOV

ROBERT KAUFMAN

KEITH KAY

ANDY KAY

SCOTT KEENAN

DAVID KELLER

GEORGE KELLOCK

PETER KENDAL

TIM KENNEDY

BILL KENNEDY

EDDIE KERRIGAN

ABDOULMAJEED KHALDOUN

GARY KIFFEL

TADASHI KIKUCHI

JANIS ANNE KINZIE

TANYA KITZROW

MARLEY KLAUS

LORI KNIGHT

BRIAN KNOBLOCK

MARK KNOLLER

NILS KONGSHAUG

LARS KONGSHAUG

PAT KOPCO

RICH KOPPEL

MARTY KOUGHAN

AL KOZAK

JAY KRAJEWSKI

JEFFREY KREINER

BERYL KREISEL

STAN KRODER

AnnMARIE KROSS

BRIAN LACEY

JEFF LAING

MIKE LAM

STEPHANIE LAMBIDAKIS

JILL LANDES

CATHY LASIEWICZ

MEL LEVINE

HENRY LAWLESS

HOBERT LAWSON

VAL LEBEDEFF

PAUL LEDERMAN

LOUIS LEDFORD

JAN LEGNITTO

WALT LEIDING

JANET LEISSNER

HENRY LENZ

OLIVER LEONARD

JON LESSNER

GIL LeVEQUE

DAVID LEVINE

RANDY LEVINE

NORM LEVINE

LIONEL LEVY

LEE LEVY

DANNY LEW

WARREN LEWIS

KEN LEWIS

CATHERINE LIBERATORE

JIM LIEU

BILL LINDEN

CAROLYN LIPPERT

YURI LOBOV

INEZ LOPARDO

MATTHEW LOWE

JIM LOY

MARK LUDLOW

VINCE LUGO

WARREN LUSTIG

VERONICA LUZURIAGA

PATRICIA MCBREARTY

HARRY MCCABE

MAXWELL MCCLELLAN

JOANNE MCDONOUGH

MICHAEL MCEACHERN

TOM MCENENY

KATHLEEN MCGANN

MARCY MCGINNIS

JIM MCGLINCHY

BRIAN MCGOVERN

FELICITY MCGRATH

KAREN MCINNIS

DAN MCKINNEY

KATHY MCMANUS

WILLIAM MADISON

JOE MAHONEY

ROLLIE MALICSI

JOANNE MALLIE

LUANN MANCINI

CHRIS MANZANILLA

MARY MAPES

MASSIMO MARIANI

CAL MARLIN

MICHAEL MARRIOTT

KAREN MARRYSHOW

LINDA MARTELLI

MARY MARTIN

TERRY MARTIN

SUSAN MARTINS

LINDA MASON

TOM MATTESKY

WALT MATWICHUK

STEPHANIE MAUER

MARIKAY MEAD

EVELYN MEENAHAN

PAUL MENENDEZ

VIVIANA MENNA

NATHANIEL MERRILL

SHARMAN MESARD

RICHARD MEYER

DICK MEYER

JON MEYERSOHN

JESSE MICHNICK

TOM MICKLAS

CLYDE MILES

PATTY MILLER

O. T. MILSAP

WENDY SUE MILTON

NATALIE MINES

ORLANDO MINGARELLI

PHILIP MIRANTE

TONY MIRANTE

JIM MOHAN

MESHACK MOKOENA

LOUIS MOLINA

VITO MONACO

JOHN MONDELLO

MARY MONTALBANO

JIM MOORE

JOHN MOORE

KATHY MOORE

NAIM MOR

ROBERTO MORENO

JOHN MORIARTY

SUZANNE MORRIS

JOHN MOSEDALE

VIRGINIA MOSELEY

ALISON MOSKOWITZ

Brian Moynihan

Bill Mumford

Brian Munday

Joe Murania

Jim Murphy

William Murphy

Anne Murray

Richard Mutschler

Simon Nasht

Rob Navias

Stan Nazimek

Suzanne Nederlander

Dean Nelson

Wayne Nelson

Quent Neufeld

Juergen Neumann

Maria Nicoletti

Bill Nieves

Brian Nolan

John Nolen

Peggy Noonan

Linda Norris

Vincent O'Connor

Patrick O'Dell

Nene Ofautey-Kodjoe

Peter O'Hara

Catherine Olian

Cecil O'Neal

Mike Orloff

Bob Orozovich

Al Ortiz

George Osterkamp

Arden Ostrander

Susan Ottalini

Bill Owens

Joyce Ozarchuk

Victor Paganuzzi

Lou Palisano

Larry Pancamo

Alan Parcell

John Parry

David Patsel

Kevin Patterson

Valerie Paul

Carol Pauli

John Paxson

Ruby Payumo

Mary Peatman

John Michael Pelech

John Peters

Johnny Peters

Gary Petrini

Ed Petrovits

Joe Peyronnin

Jyll Phillips

Tom Phillips

Gillian Phillips

Stacia Phillips

William Phypers

Tom Piccolo

Susan Pichini

Barbara Pierce

FRED JOHN PINCIARO

VIRGINIA PITTMAN-WALLER

TERRY PLANTINGA

TOM PLUMMER

SANDY POLSTER

THERESA PONTE

MARQUITA POOL

JERRY POSEY

RALPH POYNTZ

CAROL PRESSMAN

HOLLIS PRITCHARD

CHRIS PUSH

DIANA QUINN

JOHN QUIRK

PAUL QUODOMINE

HARRY RADLIFFE

DAN RADOVSKY

MICHAEL RADUTZKY

LEN RAFF

KAREN RAFFENSPERGER

ROB RAINEY

HUGH RAISKY

DALE RALEY

SIPHIWO RALO

LIANE RAMIREZ

CORKY RAMIREZ

BILL RANDELL

TOM RAPIER

AL RAUSCH

NICHOLAS RAWLUK

SUSAN REED

JOHN REID

SUZANNE REID

ANN REINGOLD

IRV REINHARD

JOE REISMAN

MISSIE RENNIE

ANN REYNOLDS

LIESBETH RIBBINK

RON RICCARDI

COLIN RICHARDSON

STACY RICHMAN

JOAN RICHMAN

RICHARD RICHTER

JOE RITCHEY

BRIAN ROBBINS

SAM ROBERTS

TERRY ROBINSON

KEVIN ROCHFORD

ANDRE RODRIGUEZ

MARY ROGERS

STAN ROMAINE

GABE ROMERO

BOB ROONEY

JILL ROSENBAUM

MICHAEL ROSENBAUM

AMY ROSNER

JOAN ROTH

DEBORAH RUBIN

SUSAN RUCCI

MARK RUCKHAUS

JANIS RUDEN

MICHAEL RUE

ROXANNE RUSSELL

DIERDRE RUSSELL

BOB RUTTENBERG

KATE RYDELL

JASON SACCA

MICHELLE SACHAROW

ELSIE SALBERG

FAWZAT SALLOUM

ANNE SAMPOGNA

STEVE SANDO

DOROTHY SARCHIAPONE

SUSAN SCHACKMAN

NATALIE SCHACTER

ROB SCHAFER

JUDY SCHAFFER

DAVID SCHILLING

DAVID SCHNEIDER

RICK SCHNEIDER

MAUREEN SCHOOS

HANK SCHROEDER

FRED SCHUH

MICHAEL SCHUSSEL

HERB SCHWARTZ

PETER SCHWEITZER

KATHY SCIERE

DICK SEDIA

PAUL SEDIA

THOMAS SEEM

DOUG SEFTON

PHIL SELBY

TERESA SESSOMS

GREG SHAFFIR

DAVID SHANAHAN

DENNIS SHANNON

LYNN SHERRIFFE

PATRICIA SHEVLIN

ART SHINE

JENNIFER SIEBENS

LEROY SIEVERS

PAMELA SIGNORELLA

GLENN SILBER

GABY SILON

BOB SIMON

TOMMY SIMPSON

JOHN SIMPSON

YVONNE SIMPSON

BRAD SIMPSON

MICHAEL SINGER

ROBIN SINGER

LAURIE SINGER

MICHAEL SINGLETARY

MARY FRANCES SIRIANNE

BILL SKANE

WARD SLOANE

CLARKE SMITH

JOHN SMITH

GREG SMITH

PATTY SMITH

GEORGE SMITH

NANCY SOLOMON

LEE SOLOMON

ERIK SORENSON

ANDY SOTO

FRANK SPAIN

LUCY SPIEGEL

KATIE SPIKES

MIMI SPILLANE

STEVE SPLANE

SUE ANN STAAKE

BILL STAGE

AL STECKER

NED STEINBERG

ANDY STEVENSON

TERRI STEWART

MIKE STEWART

ALVIN STINEY

ALVIN STINEY

GABE STIX

JAMIE STOLZ

TONY STREULI

HOWARD STRINGER

STEVE STROM

STEVAN STROM

CLAUS STUHLWEISSENBURG

MARK STURCHIO

GLENN SUNDEL

TOM SWEIGER

GABINO TABUNAR

CINDY TAGGART

PAUL TAYLOR

RAFAEL TERCERO

JARED THALER

EVELYN THOMAS

ANDY THOMPSON

DEB THOMSON

MARY BETH TOOLE

TERESA TOTO

LEE TOWNSEND

FRAN TRAFTON

PETE TRAYNHAM

ANDY TRIAY

DEBORAH TRUEMAN

NICK TURNER

DAN TUTMAN

BUDDY TYLER

JILL VALENSTEIN

GERALD VALVONA

DARLENE VANDERPOOL

STEVE VARDY

LANE VENARDOS

MARISA VENEGAS

TONY VESPOLI

VIC VINUELAS

CHUCK VIOLETTE

PAUL VITTOROULIS

BILL VOGAN

LARRY VOGT

KURT VOELKER

JIMMY WALL

MARY WALSH

ERIK WASHINGTON

TONY WATKINS

WILLIS WEBSTER

CHRISTINE WEICHER

RENEE WEINSTEIN

MALCOLM WEIR

ETTY WEISELTIER

ALAN WEISMAN

TODD WEISS

MOSHE WEITZ

MITCH WEITZNER

PHIL WELDON

TOBY WERTHEIM

CHARLIE WEST

BILL WHITE

JANE WHITFIELD

MIKE WHITNEY

ADAM WIENER

LAURA WIESSEN

MIKE WILLIAMS

BILL WILLSON

FRED WINTER

JERRY WOHLSTETTER

AL WOLF

RANDY WOLFE

CHARLES WOLFSON

J. W. WOMACK

TERRY WOOD

T. S. WOOL

MICHELE WORST

WAYNE WRIGHT

ALEXIS YANCEY-GEORGE

JAY YOUNG

CHARLES YOWELL

VLADIMIR YUKABOVICH

BORIS ZAKHAROV

ALLISON ZARINKO

JOSEPH ZARINKO

FRANK ZELINSKI

SUSAN ZIRINSKY

WILLIAM ZIZZA

J. ZURICH

Amnesty International, 154
anchor, as reporter, 182–183
Annecy, Lake, 181–182
Arab "street piece," 188–189
Arledge, Roone, 133, 136
Army Special Forces, U.S., 249
Arnot, Bob, 230, 231
ARVN, 282
Arvold, Frances, 155–156
Atwater, Lee, 123
Aziz, Tariq, 195, 196, 208

Ba'ath party, 202, 214
Baghdad, 190, 200–222
    Americans in, 207
    palace of, 214, 217–222
Bahrain, 191
Baker, James, 99, 206, 232
Beckwith, David, 122
Beechnut chewing tobacco, 63
Beethoven, Ludwig van, 172
Beijing, 149, 154
Belgrade, 309–315
Belli, Terri, 179
Bellinger, Paul, 239
Berger, Scott, 22
Berlin, 169, 170–175
    Rather's use of cherry picker in,
        171–172
Berlin Wall, 168, 169–170, 172–173
Berman, Al, 19, 238, 244
Bernie, Patricia, 87
Bernstein, Joel, 260, 275, 276
Bettag, Claire, 180–181
Bettag, Tom, 91–93, 111, 112, 114,
        118, 167, 180–181, 327
    in Amman, 187–189, 194–196
    in Baghdad, 200, 201, 203, 213–222
    in Berlin, 170–172, 174
    in China, 134–136, 140–154
    "Dawn of a New Era" and, 133
    instincts of, on China story, 138–139
    after Iraqi invasion of Kuwait,
        183–186
    knowledge of Japan, 131–132
    in Prague, 175
Big Cave, 66–67, 71, 72
Birnbaum, Bernie, 331
Black, Shirley Temple, 175–176
Bosnia, 231–232
Bostick, Buddy, 128
Bradley, Ed, 156, 230, 231
Branch Davidians, 125; see also
        Koresh, David

Brandenburg Gate, 172
Brandt, Willy, 170
Brezhnev, Leonid, 166
Briganti, Al, 294
Broadcast News, 21
Brokaw, Tom, 20, 138, 297
Buchanan, Pat, 115–116
Buehlmann, Norma, 302–303
Buksbaum, David, 36, 161, 167–168
Burke, David, 132–133, 135,
        136–137, 138, 144, 149, 152, 153,
        182, 186, 204
Bush, George, 20, 94, 160, 183, 187,
        195, 202
    Iran-contra scandal and, 98–99,
        100, 121, 122, 123–124
    military buildup of, 206
    1988 presidential campaign of, 97,
        113, 121
    Rather's interview of, see CBS
        Evening News interview of
        George Bush
    Rather's relationship with, 99–100
    Somalia and, 231, 232
    State visit to Japan of, 134
Buthelezi, Mangosuthu, 178

Camera Never Blinks, The (Rather),
        295, 296
Cao Bai Temple, 271
cardinal sex abuse story, 17–22
Carey, Hugh, 133
Carter, Jimmy, 45, 67–68, 116
Casablanca, 112
Casey, William, 45
Castro, Fidel, 53, 138, 177–179
    longwindedness of, 178
Catholic Church, 18–19
CBS, Inc.:
    management of, 94; see also specific
        personnel
    News Division of, see CBS News
    preemption of presidential debate
        by, 95
    Sports Division of, 90, 93–94
CBS Broadcast Group, 92, 152, 342
CBS Evening News, 17–20, 22, 24, 31,
        36, 88, 113, 186, 187, 230, 260
    Baghdad broadcast of, 204
    Christmas parties of, 156
    interview with George Bush on, see
        CBS Evening News interview of
        George Bush
    lost six minutes of, 89, 92–93

index

ABC, 133, 136
ABC News, 193–194, 208
ABC World News, 329
Abdul-Rashad, Ali, 201, 213, 214
Acting President, The (Schieffer), 123
Afghanistan, Islamic views on women
    in, 47–49, 50
Afghanistan, Soviet invasion of,
    29–61, 64–88, 162
  Afghan army in, 45
  Afghan rebels' weaponry in, 44,
    66–67
  Kabul regime in, 45, 79
  Kerala massacre in, 79
  refugees from, 37, 78
  60 Minutes coverage of, 39–40
  Soviet aircraft in, 50–51, 52–53,
    55–56, 58, 71, 74
  Soviet Kunar Valley campaign in,
    78–80
  Soviet use of gas in, 46, 88
Afghan rebels:
  cave command post of, 66–67, 71, 72
  Pakistan staging area of, 33, 35, 37,
    41
  patriotism of, 44, 67
  physical exertion and stamina of,
    55, 59, 60
  U.S. views on aid for, 67–68
  weapons of, 44, 66–67
  Western views on, 84–85
  see also Afghanistan, Soviet
    invasion of; *specific rebels*
Aidid, Mohammed Farrah, 236, 253
Ailes, Roger, 123
Amman, 186–188, 189, 191–192

telecasts from Japan of, 133
videotape from Somalia broadcast
    on, 240
CBS Evening News interview of
    George Bush:
    aftermath of, 117–124
    Bush's request for live and unedited
        response in, 101, 102
    Bush's seven-minute walkout
        comment preceding, 112
    Bush's Stahl remark after, 111
    CBS Evening News telecast after,
        120
    CBS switchboard after, 117, 120
    transcript of, 101–111
CBS Morning News, 88, 230
CBS News, 25, 87, 90, 91, 100–101,
    117, 119, 131, 160–161, 294
    Moscow bureau of, 163
    as special to Paley, 329
    staff of, listed, 348–360
CBS News/*New York Times* poll, 121
CBS Reports, 22, 260–261
CBS This Morning, 132
CBS Weekend News, 132, 152
Chandler, Robert, 34–35, 36
"Changing Face of Communism,
    The," 136, 159, 161
Cheney, Dick, 198, 210
chewing tobacco, 62–63
China, Chinese, 70, 131–154, 290,
    291–293
    Americans living in, 140–141
    corruption in, 141, 142
    glacier as metaphor of, 145
    Gorbachev's visit to, 144, 146–148
    Nixon's visit to, 160
    popular discontent in, 134–135
    Rather and Bettag's instincts about,
        138–139
    student leaders in, 140, 141
    students' grasp of political systems,
        143–144
China Air, 291
China Beach, 258, 259, 271
Christiane, Jean-Claude, 181–182,
    185
Christiane, Martine, 181
Chung, Connie, 24
CIA, 45, 67, 98, 160
cigars, 53, 66, 88, 178
Clarke, Andy, 242, 243
Cleaver, Eldridge, 177–178, 179
Clinton, Bill, 20, 116, 231, 250, 261, 290

CNN, 191, 208
Cochran, John, 78
Cohen, William, 183–185
Cohen, Stephen, 159
Collingwood, Charles, 259, 283, 328
Colson, Charles, 115
Comedy Central Network, 340
Communist Party Congress, 169
Connors, Yvonne, 132
Crawford, Bill, 114
Croatia, 232
Cronkite, Walter, 31, 36, 91, 306, 326
C-Span, 341
Cuba, 138
Cu Chi, 258, 259, 269, 271–273
    battleground of, as tourist
        attraction, 272
Currier, Frank, 21–22
Czechoslovakia, 174–176

Dallas, Tex., 129, 130
Da Nang, 258, 259, 265, 271
"Dan Rather Reporting," 22
Darra, 84, 85
"Dawn of a New Era, The," 133–134
Deaver, Ray, 128
Dees, Donna, 113–114
Defense Department, U.S., 67, 98,
    266
Democratic party, 114, 115, 116
Deng Xiaoping, 142, 145, 148–149
Desert Storm, *see* Persian Gulf War
Des Moines, Iowa, 294, 300, 302–303
Des Moines Register, 104
Dhahran, 212
Dole, Bob, 104
Donilon, Tom, 114–115, 117
Dubai, 189
Dubrovnik, 309, 315–316

Edwards, Mike, 39, 40, 55, 56, 76,
    80–81, 83
    at Jalalabad airstrip, 50–51
    in reconnaissance patrol, 57–61,
        64–65
"Egypt, Mr." (Egyptian diplomat),
    242–243, 244
Eldon, Dan, 7
Ellerbee, Linda, 78
Ethiopia, 229, 230

*Fear and Loathing on the Campaign
    Trail* (Thompson), 309
Fernandez, Giselle, 306

"Fishbowl," 18, 19, 114
Fisher, Dean, 210
Five O'Clock Follies, 266
Fonda, Jane, 273–274
Fort Bragg, N.C., 262
48 Hours, 22, 133, 161, 293–294, 300
Fountain, Mike, 19
Fox, Lucy, 233–234
Freedom of Information Act, 98
French Foreign Legion, 250
"From Murrow to Mediocrity"
    (Rather), 91

Gandhi, Mohandas K. (Mahatma),
    147
Gannon, Jim, 104
Garland, Judy, 156
Garth, David, 120
Gartner, Michael, 190
Gates, Gary Paul, 123
GATT, 291
Georgia, 253, 255
Gergen, David, 290
Germany, Democratic Republic of
    (East), 169–170
Germany, Nazi, 221
Gess, Omar, 248–249
glasnost, 158, 166, 168
Glaspie, April, 202
Goebel, Grandmother, 49
Goldwater, Barry, 68
Gorbachev, Mikhail, 135, 138,
    157–176
    China visit of, 144, 146–148
    as New Soviet Man, 158, 166
    poor understanding of
        market-based economy of,
        158–159
    on Rather, 167
    Rather's interviews of, 167–168,
        169
Graf, Steffi, 89
Great Flood of 1993, 290–303
    Rather's travel in, 293–297
Great Hall of the People, 139, 146
Gregg, Donald, 123
Grenada, 225, 250
Groer, Anne, 273
Gutting, Mark, 251

Haig, Alexander, 45, 120–121
Hamoud (Iraqi official), 201, 203,
    204–206, 208–209, 213, 216
Hangen, Wells, 7

Hanoi, 259, 261, 265, 273–278
    War Museum in, 276
Harrington, Mark, 90
Havel, Vaclav, 176
Helms, Jesse, 327
Hemingway, Ernest, 287
Hewitt, Don, 30–34, 86, 88, 193
Heyward, Andrew, 161–162
Hilgert, Christopher, 251
Hirohito, emperor of Japan, 132, 133,
    163
Hitler, Adolf, 206, 220, 221
Hoa Lo Prison, 274
Ho Chi Minh, 257, 277
Ho Chi Minh City, 259–260; *see also*
    Saigon
Ho Chi Minh Trail, 275
Hockney, David, 162
Hoeffler, Kurt, 200, 241
Hotel Mandarin, 134, 144, 151
Hotel Metropole, 277
Hotel Rossiya, 161, 163
Houston, Sam, 126
Houston, Tex., 128, 258
Howard, Michael, 224
Hue, 259, 263, 265, 271
Huntsville, Tex., 75, 128
Hurricane Carla, 291, 304–307
Hurricane Emily, 304–307
Hussein, king of Jordan, 188, 190,
    191, 193, 210, 211
    Saddam Hussein as viewed by, 192
Hussein, Saddam, 184, 190, 200–228
    Arab support for, 188
    Hitler compared with, 206, 220, 221
    King Hussein's views on, 192
    Rather's interview with, 218–222
    see also Iraq; Persian Gulf War
Hu Yaobang, 145

Independence, U.S.S., 197
India, 69–70
Iran, 67–68, 70
Iran-contra scandal, 98, 184
    George Bush and, 98–99, 100,
        101–111, 121, 122, 123–124
Iranian hostage crisis, 30, 70
Iraq, 180–228
    Americans used as human shields
        in, 202–203, 204, 206, 207–208
    F-15 fighter wings in Saudia Arabia
        and, 199
    Foreign Ministry of, 201, 203, 214,
        216, 217

information minister of, 214
Intelligence Ministry of, 214
military of, 210, 214

Jalalabad, 44, 45, 47, 50, 58
Jankowski, Gene, 90, 92
Japan, 131–134, 163, 164
    CBS Evening News telecasts from,
        133
    China and, 134
Jarrell, Tom, 78
Jayne, David, 7
Jenkins, Dan, 191
Jennings, Peter, 20, 138, 139, 297
John Paul II, pope, 89, 90, 91
Johnson, Lyndon, 68, 116, 210
Jones, Cal, 305
Julius Caesar (Shakespeare), 330
Juneau, U.S.S., 245

Kabul, 45, 79
Kaplan, David, 7
Kaufmann, Bruce, 185
Kemp, Jack, 120
Kempton, Murray, 122
Kennedy, John F., 68, 130, 156
Kennedy, Ted, 133
Kennerly, David Hume, 193
Kerala, 79
KGB, 161, 162, 163, 164
Khalis, Younas, 72–73, 74, 75
khat, 248, 249
Khe Sanh, 267
Khomeini, Ayatollah Ruhollah, 101,
    117
Kipling, Rudyard, 22, 23, 29
Kirkland, Lane, 275
Kismayu, 248, 249
Koppel, Ted, 194–195, 196
Koresh, David, 125, 126, 128, 129,
    130
Kriegel, Jay, 118–119
Kunar Valley, 56, 73, 78
Kuralt, Charles, 331
Kurds, 231
Kuwait, Iraqi invasion of,
    181–182
    Embassy closings after, 207
    refugees from, 195
Kuwait City, 206, 226

Lack, Andy, 32, 39, 40, 42, 46, 50, 57,
    71, 73, 74, 76, 77–78, 80, 82, 86,
    88

on bus to Peshawar, 83–84
"mystery meat" episode and, 53–55
nickname of, 54, 83
in Pakistan, 33, 35–36, 38
Laker, Freddie, 318
Lake Travis, Tex., 276
Lam, Mike, 140
Lasiewicz, Cathy, 294
Late Show with David Letterman, The,
    26–28
Lebanon, 222, 250
Leonard, Bill, 34, 88
Lessons of History (Howard), 224
Letterman, David, 26–28
Ligachev, Yegor, 168
Li Ruihuan, 148
Lodge, Henry Cabot, 260
Looten, Amy, 299
Lord, Bette Bao, 137, 151
Ludwig, Harold, 299–300
Lusk, Gary, 297
Luther, Martin, 142

Mabrey, Vicki, 129
McBroom, John, 198–199
McCain, John, 274
McCarthy, Joseph, 330
McNeil, Lori, 89
MacNeil/Lehrer Report, 120
Madison, Bill, 291, 297
"Mad Man Muntz," 165
Magruder, Jeb, 115
Malik (Sarajevo boy), 324–325
Malraux, André, 287
Manning, Bob, 321
Man Who Would Be King, The
    (Kipling), 23
Mao Tse-tung, 134, 139, 143
Marines, U.S., 246, 247, 248, 250,
    252, 259
    Rather's service in, 175, 283
Martin, David, 197–198, 233
Martin, Lee, 120
Martin, Mary, 123
Marx, Karl, 143
Mason, Linda, 152, 261, 275
Mead, Bob, 322
Meirowitz (Nederlander), Suzanne,
    113, 167, 168, 344–345
Mekong Delta, 267, 271
Miami, Fla., 89–95
Miami Herald, 341
Miller, Keith, 213
Miller, Thomas, 145

Mirwaz (Afghan guide), 38–42, 44, 48
  Rather's turban bought by, 77–78
  tractor episode and, 80–82, 84
  in trek to Big Cave, 55, 58, 64–66,
    73
Mississippi River, 294, 298, 300–301
Mogadishu, 234–250, 251, 252
  airport in, 235–238, 250–251
Moore, Kathy, 19, 20–22
Morgan, Jan, 40, 86
Moscow, 162, 163–164, 169
Mozambique, 229, 230
Mubarak, Hosni, 191, 192
  Rather's interview with, 209–211
Mujahadee (Afghan leader), 85
Murder, She Wrote, 327
Murrow, Edward R., 23, 84, 284, 286,
  288, 329, 330–331, 340, 341, 343
Museum of American War Crimes,
  262
Mutschler, Richie, 92, 93, 167, 168
My Lai, 79
My Thanh, 279

Naby, Eden, 57, 71, 73, 74–75, 86
  language ability of, 40
  Muslim women and, 47–49, 50
  shoes of, 39–40, 55
Naby, Mr., 39, 40, 86
Nairobi, 232, 233, 234, 235, 240
Nancy (doughnut dolly), 269–270
National Weather Service, 291, 306
Navy SEALS, U.S., 246, 247
NBC News, 190, 191, 194, 213
Nederlander, Bob, 344
Nelson, Wayne, 297–298
Nethaway, Rowland, 128
Newsday, 122, 310
Newsweek, 122, 123
  poll of, 121
New York *Daily News,* 120
New York *Post,* 120
New York Times, 91, 94, 104, 114,
  117, 213
Nguyen Van Thieu, 261
Nicaragua, 98
Nielsen Company, 91
Nightline, 120, 194, 196
Nixon, Richard M., 68, 97, 156, 160,
  184, 309–310, 314
Noriega, Manuel, 137
Normand, Jürgen, 200
North Vietnamese Army, 259, 268
Not So Wild a Dream (Sevareid), 286

Ober, Eric, 290, 293
O'Connor, Peter, 40, 57, 76, 84
"Ode to Joy" (Beethoven), 172
Operation Restore Hope, 233,
  247–249, 252
Orlando Sentinel, 273
Orr, Bob, 140
Ortiz, Al, 179
Osterkamp, George, 253, 290,
  291–292, 297
Oswald, Lee Harvey, 130
Overseas Press Club, awards dinner
  of, 139

Paine, Thomas, 141–142
Pakistan, 33, 35, 41, 70, 78, 83
Pakistani troops, in Somalia, 236,
  237, 238, 247
Paley, William S., 327–329
Panama, 137, 138, 139, 225, 250
PBS, 340
Pears, Tom, 128
Pearson, Keith, 251
perestroika, 158, 168
Persian Gulf War, 223–228, 250
  censorship in, 223–224
  changing nature of news coverage
    since, 225–228
  F-15 fighter wing story in, 197–199
Peshawar, 37, 72, 75, 77, 78
  Afghan rebels' base camp in, 33, 35,
    37, 41
Petersen, Barry, 152
Peyronnin, Joe, 340
PFM crew, 239, 240, 242, 243
Pierpoint, Bob, 322
Pilson, Neal, 90
Pizzey, Allen, 234, 238, 242
Polk, George, 7
Prague, 175–176
Presley, Elvis, 19, 27–28
Proust, Marcel, 257
Purple Bamboo Park, 134–135, 136

Quayle, Dan, 122

Rabel, Ed, 191
Radio and Television News Directors
  Association, 329, 341
  Rather's speech to, 331–340
Rapier, Tom, 292
Rather, Danjack (son), 36, 53, 73, 76,
  236, 265
Rather, Don (brother), 24, 76

Rather, Jean Grace Goebel (wife), 23–24, 36, 39, 53, 73, 76, 86, 87–88, 97, 114, 118, 149, 162, 236, 257, 265, 283, 342, 345
    Rather's civil rights coverage and, 296
Rather, Patricia (sister), 24, 76
Rather, Robin (daughter), 36, 53, 73, 76, 236
Rather's Rules of War Coverage, 226
Reagan, Nancy, 19, 98, 99
Reagan, Ronald, 19, 45, 67, 68–69, 98–99, 160–161, 163, 184, 185, 222
Red Guards, 148
Red Man chewing tobacco, 53, 63
Remembrance of Things Past (Proust), 257
Republican party, 114, 115, 116
Rex Hotel, 266–267
Richerson, Ronald N., 251
Robertson, Pat, 306
Roth, Richard, 154
RTNDA, see Radio and Television News Directors Association
Russo-Japanese War, 224, 225

Sabah, Sheik Jaber al-Ahmed al-, 182
Safer, Morley, 35, 235
Saigon, 258, 259–260, 262–263, 265, 266
    fall of, 260
St. Louis, Mo., 294, 295, 297, 300, 301
St. Pierre, Suzanne, 287
Salant, Richard S., 34, 322
Sanders, Jonathan, 159
Sando, Steve, 242
Sarajevo, 324, 325
"Satellite City," 129
Saudi Arabia, 187, 196
    F-15 arrivals in, 197–199
Schieffer, Bob, 78, 123, 239
Schoenbrun, David, 328
Schram, Marty, 310–311
Schultz, Frau, 312–313, 316–317, 318
Schwarzkopf, H. Norman, 24, 251–257, 258, 260, 266, 270, 272, 273, 288
    in Hanoi, 276
    military-press rift as viewed by, 280–282

    request to serve in Vietnam made by, 262–263
    Vietnam guide story of, 278–279
Sciere, Kathy, 19, 212
scorpions, 65
Sedia, Paul, 292
Senate, U.S., Intelligence Committee of, 184
Sevareid, Eric, 18, 156, 254, 259, 264, 282–284, 285–288, 328, 342
Seven Days in May, 161–162
sexuality, television and, 18–19
Shackman, Susan, 36, 88
Shakespeare, William, 330
Shanghai, 151, 290, 291, 292
Sheehan, James J., 223
Sheehy, Robert, Sr., 130
Shevardnadze, Eduard, 253
Shultz, George, 102
Simon, Bob, 133, 245, 250
60 Minutes, 112, 186, 193, 230, 260, 327
    Afghanistan story and, 30–36, 88
    budgets for, 34, 35
    Rather as correspondent for, 31
Smith, Harry, 306
Smith, John, 200, 215–216
Smith, Perry, 129
Smithville, Tex., 295–296
snakes, as food, 275–276, 277–278
Snow, Edgar, 145
Somalia, 229–250
    French troops in, 249, 250
    PFM crew in, 239, 240, 242, 243
    Rather's arrival in, 234–237
    Rather's radio report from, 245–246
    Rather's videotaped report from, 239–240
    U.S. forces in, 245–250
Sorenson, Erik, 17–19, 340
Soviet Union:
    aircraft of, 50–51, 52–53, 55–56, 58, 71, 74
    collapse of communism in, 157–176
    dissatisfaction of Muslims in, 69
    economic problems of, 158–159, 162–163
    gas used in Afghanistan by, 46, 88
    hospitals in, 164, 165
    shortages in, 164, 166
    U.S. overestimation of military of, 45, 51
Spencer, Susan, 133, 239
Squier, Robert, 121

Stalin, Joseph, 166
State Department, U.S., 45, 67, 175–176, 232
Stout, Bill, 282
Stringer, Howard, 90, 91, 92, 117, 152, 293, 342
Sudan, 229
Sullivan, Ed, 19
Syvertsen, George, 7

Tam Ky, 258–259
TASS, 164
Taubkina, Mila, 163
Teeter, Virgil, 128
television ratings, 91
television sets, in Soviet Union, 164–165
Territories, 41–44, 77, 78, 79, 80
Tet Offensive, 269, 272, 273, 281
Texas, 73; *see also specific sites*
Thieu, Nguyen Van, 261
Thompson, Hunter, 309
Tiananmen Square, 131, 139–140, 144, 146, 148, 149, 150–151
    death toll of crackdown in, 154
    goddess of democracy statue in, 154
Tiger Lady (Iraqi television chief), 202
Time, 122–123, 147, 210
Tisch, Laurence, 94, 118, 136, 144, 329, 341
Tito, Marshal, 308–309, 317
Today Show, The, 138
Townsend, Lee, 113
"tractor vultures," 80–81
Turner, Ted, 327

United Nations, 236, 238, 247

Vavrosek, Tomas, 175
Venardos, Lane, 152, 161, 294
Vesco, Robert, 179
Vietcong, 259, 268, 282
Vietnam, 47, 68, 71–72, 79
    American war veterans' return to, 267–271
    low-wage work force of, 274–275
    U.S. embargo of, 261, 273
Vietnam veterans:
    memories of, 268, 270–271

mourning of, 269–270
    survivor guilt of, 269
Vietnam Veterans Against the War, 269
Vietnam War, 221–222, 225, 226, 227, 256–284
    Rather's memories of, 259, 263–265
    Schwarzkopf's memories of, 262–263

Waco, Tex., 125–130
    "Dan Rather Day" in, 130
    Rather's radio piece on, 127–128
    Washington Post article on, 126, 130
Waco Herald-Tribune, 127, 128
Wallace, Mike, 31, 35, 36, 88, 156
Walsh, Lawrence, 102, 123–124
Walters, Vernon, 173–174
Walters, Vinnie, 173
Wang Weilin, 149
Washington Post, 126, 130, 213
Watergate, 97, 184
Weaver, Lisa, 140
Weinberger, Caspar, 45
Wharton, Tex., 128
White, Theodore, 145
White House, 98, 266
Williams, Pete, 198
Wilson, Joe, III, 202, 203, 208
Wimberger, Karin, 7
Winchester, Tex., 49
Woodruff, Fred, 253, 255
World War I, 224, 225

Yassini (Afghan leader), 44, 48, 52
    fort recaptured by, 45–46
    Jalalabad airstrip and, 50–51
    in trek to Big Cave, 55–56, 64–66, 73
    on U.S. aid to rebels, 69–70
Yates, Ted, 7
Yeltsin, Boris, 159, 162, 166, 167, 168
"Young British Soldier, The" (Kipling), 29
Yugoslavia, 308–323, 324

Zhao Ziyang, 148
Zirinsky, Susan, 134, 152